Threshold Delivery

Fred –
with gratitude –
Patty

poems by

Patty Seyburn *8-19*

Finishing Line Press
Georgetown, Kentucky

Threshold Delivery

ACKNOWLEDGMENTS

"Mah Jongg: An Homage." *The Seattle Review,* 2017.
"Apologia to Shirley and Coleridge." *Poetica* magazine, spring/summer 2014.
"Lightning, 1882-1890." *Blue Lyra Review*, 2013.
"Long Distance (ii)." *Askew*, 2012.
"Pith." *Arroyo Literary Review*, 2012.
"Shinus Molle." *Minnesota Review*, Issue 79, Fall 2012.
"Sigh in Silence," "A Request." *Image*, September 2012, Issue #74.
"My Mother Left Standing at Loser's Bingo." *Little Balkans Review*, 2011.
"So when she looks at her reflection." *Green Mountains Review*, 2011.
"November." www.corridorsmagazine.org, 2011.
"Knock, Knock." *Cerise Press*. Fall-Winter 2010-11.
"Location, Location" "Embarked." *Beside the City of Angels*. Ed., Paul Tayyar. 2010.
"Persona Non Sequitor Grata." *The Journal*, #10, Spring 2010.
"Five & Dime." *Dirtcakes*, 2010.
"I Have Written the Last Elegy." *Hotel Amerika* 2009.
"Location, Location," "On Cooking a Symbol at 400 degrees." *Poetry* magazine, December 2009.
"2nd of Tammuz." *Arbutus.com*, May 2007.
"Hoopla" and "Long Distance." *Women in Judaism*, 2007, Vol. 5, No. 1.
"Aubergine" and "The Train." *Verdad* magazine, Fall 2007.
"Long Distance." *Chance of a Ghost* (Helicon Nine Editions, 2005).
"On Her Deathbed, Bessie Beckoned My Mother Close." *5 AM*, Spring 2006.
"Davenport." DIAGRAM, 9-6.
"June at Hudson's Barbershop." *Mudfish* 8, 1995.

Publisher: Leah Maines
Editor: Christen Kincaid
Cover Art and Design: Cover Illustration by Mario M. Muller, *Hedy Lamarr*, 2016, India Ink on Paper, www.mariomuller.com
Author Photo: Accent Portraits by Diana

Printed in the USA on acid-free paper.
Order online: www.finishinglinepress.com
also available on amazon.com
Author inquiries and mail orders:
Finishing Line Press
P. O. Box 1626
Georgetown, Kentucky 40324
U. S. A.

Table of Contents

Watchman, what of the night?

Isaiah, 21:11

i.

November

In heaven, there are two
of everything,, in case
one breaks. Always a back-
up plan: two Zambonis
for the firmamental
ice rink, because the dead
like to glide around a lot,
cutting cunning figures
of sideways eight. Two large
needles with generous
eyes and two spools of thick
navy thread to backstitch
wayward stars into their
constellatory fabric—
some rogue cluster always
loose up there, barely tacked,
and archangels are poor
seamstresses which leaves
the task to us—flaw, husk,
raw edge in an ombre sky—
as once dead it is
not easy to fix things.

Cognomania

One story says they named the mountain after William Jennings Bryan; another claims Bryan a local geologist, the area a headland of the Markagunt Plateau— either way, I watch minute skiers from my window while my son wheezes and I wait for the antibiotic to perform its maneuvers. My spouse and I debated Spencer, Whitmer and Oscar, evaluating various degrees of cruelty when our own parents had been fairly kind. I just read a book on Jennies—mine were Karens, the ones you hated and wanted to be. And most of them had no idea who, how or what they inspired. My mother nearly chose Nola but our rabbi dissuaded her, promoting an Israeli name. She opted for a Protestant staple I could hide behind in case history did one of its back-flips and I could pass with a good flat-iron. Otto (a palindrome) the Undertaker, told me: when people of my mother's generation had two Hebrew names, *Shana Sara*, often they were very sick as children, so were given an extra to confound the Angel of Death. Genesis says God confounded language at Babel so no tower would reach to the heavens. Instead, we are scattered. Our mountain's base elevation: 9,600 feet; 10,910 at the peak. My son's middle name belongs to my husband, my husband's to his father, and so on. If the Angel rapped at our door, whom would he seek? Being cooped up with a very sick kid forces the mind into disturbing places, more hazardous than any Black Diamond run. We chose William: a great-grandfather—my practice, his tribe. One skier slips from the chair-lift. It stops. Franz Rosenzweig said: *One should be named after somebody, or something. Or else a name is really only empty breath.* I can't make out jacket colors, it's too distant.

Black-Sand Beach

i.
What propelled us down
the rough-hewn mountain road I'll never
know, though we never reconsidered, practicing

pinball syllables—*Ha'aha'a*—humbleness—
ha'awina—lesson—five vowels, seven
consonants plus the *hokina*, the glottal stop

that looks like a comma. Seizing
quadriceps, our bodies' angles acute
as we leaned back into our descent,

but like all tourists, we had a goal, edenic.

ii.
In the valley, we veered through
canopies of trees, we're told, exist here
alone—volcanic rock, minerals inflamed,

makes soil fecund, original.
The *Waipi'o*'s curved water baiting us,
we reached the vaunted beach, grains

sultry, velvet, enveloping.

iii.
The children lunged into waves and waves
lunged back, swept them out,
returned them, flanked and doused them

in white spume while I
shouted into wind that made me mute
and useless. *Ke'olu'olu*—please.

I don't want to worry you.

iv.
Wind berated us with hard-edged grains,
stole our clothes, coated
our legs with souvenir particles. We trudged

back through the green, game-faced,
kids tracing hearts and initials
in mud with crooked walking sticks—

the strongest said he couldn't—we insisted—
until we found the incline
we'd descended and saw the pastoral

path for what it was: broken macadam
with no shoulders, steep
as a story problem.

Praying for irony: a stranger in a van.

v.
Have you figured out where
we went wrong? I sicken of my own
stupidity, sweat-soaked in what

some call luck; others, grace.
The trust placed in us, too,
we placed, in what I am not sure.

We cannot risk looking back, *makai*—
toward the ocean—and cannot resist.
My chit used up, I will not ask again,

though this is likely a lie.

Embarked

We turned the boat back
to the heart of the bay,
the buoy's staccato light
bobbing as night invited
a drama of wind that ruched
the water with millions of pins.

My daughter said, *look,*
we are running away
from the darkness. She spoke
to a duck, watched a fish jump
arcs in the air by a schooner called
Dragonfly beached on a sandbar,

out of gas, smarts or luck,
scuttled, the locals might say
and as all the facades turned
to stark silhouettes—mythical
palms, crafts with ropes taut
that bind them to unyielding

docks, parked in overpriced slips—
she said, *look, it's following,*
not just behind us—I find myself
thinking of places I've never
been to. *Look, mama*, she said again,
we are running into the darkness.

Shinus molle

The pepper tree looked like a child drew it
        with a compass—wheel-round and green,
not moss or hunter, jade or forest, teal
        or camouflage—a green describing nothing
else, defining more state of mind than hue.
        The man atop the hill concerned about
his view came down the hill, as rich
        people sometimes do. This was his due,
he pointed out, according to the rules
        the neighborhood association (shades
of something sinister) prescribes for how
        to keep the peace when interests compete.
I like the peace. I like competing, too.
        I like my pepper tree, the shape it carved
out of the blue. Admittedly, it rose above
        the meeting of our lot-lines, intruding on
his vision of a slice of somewhere he
        has never gone, but only slightly. In lieu
of all horizon—as if anyone
        can take it in, in its entirety—
he'd see a swath of bright, bright green,
        white flowers in the summer, rosy berries
in the fall—*pardes*, I think, alongside
        sky, the empty infinite, the end-
lessness his property entitles him to.
        As for my lot, I'd like some privacy.
I want the pepper tree—not him—to watch
        me rattle off my spells, concoct my brew
and I'll admit to an old-school affection
        (beauty). Would he know it if he saw it?
(Said Justice Stewart of obscenity.)
        The branches crash upon my ivy and
a stump remains, pale revenant, a few
        anemic limbs. I know the hired men
don't mean to give offense—I don't shake
        my fist at them but at the ornamental
iron now revealed—if it were post or

picket would I mind as much? I am
fenced in, fenced out, pissed off and still
        the chain-saw serenades me with its roars
and pauses, the hummingbirds displaced,
        distressed, their feverish flights to find
another home. I will not move, though my
        impermanence is not in doubt. I read
the fragile branches give their water to
        the leaves, allow themselves to hollow out,
be snapped by coastal winds. Such sacrifice—
        would altruism move him? I want the man
atop the hill to see the view he craves
        is best when glimpsed—a happy accident—
instead of present, on display, and so
        there must be leaves and branches to see through.
Frost's protean voice murmurs in my ear:
        "He moves in darkness as it seems to me."
But all he knows is what he's bought.
        Tonight the darkness comes a little closer
and he has bought the absence of a tree.

Tricks

The killdeer we heard near Gourdneck Lake displayed a broken wing, limping along in a distressed fashion and so distanced me from its camouflaged eggs that resembled pebbles I tried to skip unsuccessfully, their descent into the water the hollow plunk of disappointment. *Kil-dee, Kil-dee*, jeered the bird, stay away from my progeny. I watch three children in the pool. When I see two heads I count one Mississippi and the third pops up. *Nota bene*, says my conscience. Had I lived in England in the 1500s, who would have tied a string on the wrist of my corpse, fed the string up through the ground and attached a bell? Who would have listened in case I were buried alive (bloodletting gone wrong, my hedge witch out of town) awoke, and rang it? My daughter pointed to a squirrel carrying a piece of crusty bread one-fifth the size of its head up a slim, diagonal tree trunk with just enough leaves to provide cover from crows. The squirrel gnawed its movable feast. *So cute*, said my daughter, and a few seconds later, *not cute when it bites you*. A child can read your mind. Or mimic, without intention. Or save a marriage or provide unconditional love. We heard a joke that she could not have understood, about parrying with death in a fencing match, but she laughed. Watching death play chess, when the deaf-mute girl breaks her silence, "It is finished," I am relieved. Enough symbols. Never reveal your strategy to a priest. Before I figured out what the bird was doing, the precocial babies, which hatch with their eyes open, were safely away.

Knock, Knock

The garden-variety poisonous mushroom
takes its stand overnight
      so quickly we might have witnessed
          parturition,
had we known which patch of grass to watch, were watching

how we chose to carve the dark, in lieu of quizzing
the dead on tunnels
      of white light theory. So
          the offending cap
sits on its stout stem awaiting my *kinder* in

the stage where the world requires tasting to be
understood. How I see
      Chlorophyllum molybdites:
          all agency,
the Angel Of Death's new hire. No longer do I

recognize my bucolic backyard as a place
of comfort, my borders
      breached. This should disqualify me
          from parenting
sweepstakes, though my ambitions are small, at least for now,

just larger than the danger that pops up wearing
Alice's Eat Me sign.
      And being a sensible girl
          she did as she
was told and so outgrew her domicile, then shrank

so that she almost ceased to matter. I don't care
much for mattering. I
      did before fungi demanded
          my vigilance,
my time now spent in ominous wariness, though

when I wear a seer's shawl, nobody and his big

sister listens—that is
        my curse for cavorting with gods,
            dabbling in
creation. I don't know my place and so pluck

the aggressor, which seems to sigh as dirt loosens,
surrenders its grip and
        somewhere above, below, I hear
           someone laughing
as though I had told the funniest joke ever.

Loser's Bingo

There she was, after all
the numbers had been called
and found their homes in straight
lines on players' cards:
across, down,

diagonal (voted
most likely to elude
the eye that likes a box)—
when all else took their seats,
sighing at irony,

she remained on her feet, no
more than four chips in
a row, no loud pairing
of integers and letters
declared, no respite for

the winner, success entering
through the cellar door, near
the furnace. She brought home
her prizes in a vast, cardboard box:
pink gingham, double-fitted sheet

sheathed in plastic, three placemats,
notepaper with sayings
determined to inspire, a small
appliance and more mismatched, stray
items undeniably

fit and ready for use
and we used all of it
because we knew that luck
didn't knock every day
and in a fight you need to be

the last one standing.

Long Distance

My mother calls me for the first time from the afterlife.
I am pleased to hear her voice, her tough-broad, film noir syntax, her old-world
        dubious tone.
It's not so great here, she says.
She must have run into my Aunt Toots.

The Talmud says, *Better one hour there than a lifetime here....*
I hope the Angel of Death knows: you cannot silence my mother.
Steal her breath, still her tongue, sew shut her lips, export her soul—it's no use.
The pencil-chewing, beehived operators of the cosmos will always put through
        her calls.

The Talmud says, *Better one hour here than a lifetime there....*
When she calls again, I will tell her how beautifully the cantor sang at her funeral.
The cast was DeMillean; a dozen limos.
She will know I am lying.
She raised me to be a bad liar.

We prefer doing things we're good at.
I am a fine dweller on subjects that sadden me.
The whistles and bells of remorse and mortality are my stock-in-trade.
I am a serviceable alto, though I should never be given a solo.
The Talmud says, *It would be nice if you had a point.*

This is my problem, of late: all lines, some planes, no points.
I tell my mother, *the world is full today.*
A hummingbird hovers near my voice.
I wonder if it will fly in and release my vocal chords from the burden of service.
What would I do, could I not speak?

I was raised to comb the clearance rack, fear the law and eat canned peas, excel.
It has served me well, give or take.
My mother asks, *do you have any coins in your pocketbook?*
When I was young, she forbade long distance calls.
They were for rich people. The middle class spoke locally.

Ma, don't go.
I rummage around in my pockets, wallets and change-purse, plunge my hands into
        the couch's seams.
No luck in Mudville.
My mother hums, "Mean to Me" with a little vibrato.
My mother says, *they want me to get on a bus.*

On Her Deathbed, Bessie Beckoned My Mother Close

Once, a pocket was not attached to a woman's clothing, but tied around
her waist with a string or tape.

It would contain cellar keys, a paper of pins, a packet of seeds, a baby's bib,
a hank of yarn or a Testament.

Or enough money to be buried,
so she would not burden her family.

A Request

Please give me the watches, mother.
Engraved 11-6-46.
A gold Gruen and bracelet Bulova
retired to an worn reliquary,
a remote shelf, hall closet ripe:
serial cakes of soap, tissue boxes, toothpaste on sale
in case of another depression.
I'm surprised there are no smokes in there
though dad dragged on his last too late
and you bought yours at the Edmonton px
in 1944, for the Babad family, who let you a room—poor Jews
more generous than the rich—
                    to ancient rebbe, no news.

Ma, please, the watches.
Of little value, if money is the measure.
Is time the measure? No one wants them
save me, the family excavator and architect,
digging for clues to dangle
from our scaffolding (an ancient mangle)—
occupations for which I'm poorly equipped,
me and my imbalanced sense of justice,
me and my skittish hands, the grudges I
inherited—some blessed; some dismissed.
I would have been atop someone's shoulders at Babel,
shouting higher! higher!
                    passing up impossible bricks.

And for this I am punished—shown the Old Country
but forbidden to enter—with little material,
the equivalent of straw underfoot
and mud made from dust and spit
with which to build a lineage.
You and yours wanted to strand the past
in Jersey City. The year Rose Belle was born,
101 Negro men were lynched in these United States.
The Ferris Wheel debuted at the World's Fair

and people died of fits, dropsy, delirium, cause
named for symptom. The year your brother
died of scarlet fever was the last

       Rose smiled in a picture.

So stern in sepia; *zaftig* women and wiry men
posed in conflagration with after and before.
No photographer could induce
an expression of joy—this, their first
recording of existence, determined as Descartes
to prove their presence—nothing more.
No proof preceded their likenesses: no narrative
of crossing, no village, no vision. Nothing that fit
in the palm, no talisman, and why would you
keep a battered kettle, cheap teacup?
Saving things is for big *machers* who think
themselves important, or those who didn't raise

       their children to do better.

You taught one child to be public, one private, and one
to gather up stray sheaves dropped
behind the gleaners, arms never full.
My children—what will they glean?
From their father, inherit a legion:
honor, ignominy, documented clans of the fair and redheaded:
sheriff, cantatrice, traitor.
And from me, they'll learn
to live without history.
They'll disperse the dead, stray revenants, never
glancing back to wonder who they resemble,
to seek a feature, a trait.

       How modern they'll be.

Davenport

When I asked the men to bring my couch inside, they shook their heads: *threshold delivery, ma'am* and I pictured them lovingly carrying my movable the way a bride once was hoisted. That was before me, though not before some my age, those who relish putting a nice meal on the table nightly. We trouble each other. Trouble often comes in threes and I am often found waiting for a dropped shoe or something heavier and pointy: a spike-heeled boot, part of a pair, which means there is a lone shoe, somewhere. My husband sold shoes. Four on the floor, he taught me: you should be presented with choices, and the shoe-dog should be kneeling like a prince. I invented the last part. Princes don't work in retail though it would help the aristocracy if trained to do something useful. I have a practical streak that gets dyed each six weeks—now every four. It is hard to hide. I loathe hide-and-seek, scarred from having not been found, waiting too patiently. Somewhere dark. Back then, we did not know these moments would cling, regulars at the dive-bar of your dreams. We thought they were singular, forgettable. I remember living on an edge, how blithely I averted hazard, nimble-footed. I cannot run as fast now but have much better endurance.

June at Hudson's Barbershop

Every year you get a pixie, the barbershop
near garden tools in the Bargain Basement.
Your cheeks striped with tears but
you don't say anything, you don't say
mom, I don't want to get my hair cut.
Your stick-brown hair center-parted,
almost shoulder-length, you finally look
pretty, like those girls in teen magazines.

Too hot, says your mother, and her hand lifts
your hair from your nape, *isn't that better?*
Sweat on her forehead—she is hot, always hot,
48 years old with an eight-year-old child.
Not a mistake, she's said, *just a surprise.*
She fans herself with slender hands,
long, ridged nails with white moons,
dipped in rose or mauve. Applying arcs
of lipstick, she sees you in the mirror.
Shaneh punim, she says, *pretty face.*

The plastic poncho snaps around your neck,
cool metal skims your jawline and ears,
you can hear the crisp friction. Familiar hair
spackles the linoleum checkerboard.
Pre-cheekbones, pre-breasts, you might as well
be a boy, you cry *I look like a boy* you cry
all the way home while air surrounds
your shoulders and plays with your ears.
You touch your bare neck. Coiffed in a pouf
of tall, tight waves, your mother hums
in her low soprano, some new song.

So when she looks at her reflection

If there is an anteroom
between here and an afterlife,
there paces my mother, not renowned
for her patience

so give her a break, gatekeeper,
save yourself from her exasperation
and answer when she raps
her knuckles, smartly,

two times, pause, three times—
for God's sake, let her in.
We had a foyer, but never kept
people waiting there—they were in

or out, with one exception:
the burglar who we would exclude,
had he not found his way
upstairs and scrawled a menace,

"Smile" in lipstick near my room,
having mastered irony, no ordinary felon.
I ran upstairs before my mother knew
fear, came down when I found it.

If Lethe is your transition of choice,
let her cross and begin the forgetting
and give her a life-jacket
on the way over or she will

drive you crazy: *why drown after dying?*
Lend a mirror so she can put on
her face and bring a little artifice
with her. Let the waters erase

the memory of fear, anonymous
years, indignity of the body's betrayals,

but leave the odd narrative—
shouldn't we be able to take

one story with us? Not even
a pleasant one—just to know
who you were, where you stood?
If you never had a foyer,

you'd imagine it
more grand than it was: really, it was
just a threshold, a place
to arrive, pause, abandon.

The Glass Need Not Persuade Me

This, the age my mother
started lying and I, the age
that believed her.

Now, I am tempted
by subtraction. I avoid
figures of ascent and descent,

the view from here all too scenic.
I don't like nature much,
landscape's betrayals and lessons

of perspective and am
mad at the patriarchs
who shortened our lives

with their profligate behavior—
it's true, you can
ruin it for everyone,

but even if you keep making
that face, it will not stay
that way.

Location, Location

So when you go wherever it is you will go
take the moon with you

and make it wear that democratic white shroud,
pocketless, since rich and poor,

we take nothing with us, save a small stick or dowel
in the casket, so we can all

burrow through the earth to the Holy Land
when the time is right.

Please forgive that I confessed your amusement
at Shakespeare's "mewling and puking"

in my eulogy. (No one laughed—my delivery was off—
but Otto the Undertaker smiled.)

He told me that when I shovel some dirt onto
your soft wood box,

suggestive of the trees where Eve and Adam hid
from the Lord who called—

what were they thinking?—I should press the shovel
back into the pile

before the next mourner—my husband, *not a Jew
but a fine man*, you said

once if a hundred times—picks it up because to bury
the dead is a *mitzvah*

that should not be diluted, each person who performs
the act should get the credit,

which we will need when that Miscreant Angel

comes to collect his chit.

Otto dates my step-second cousin twice-removed
and let me say: I hope

they marry. Someone who guides the bereaved through
such a smorgasbord of ritual

with Virgilian ease deserves as much happiness
as can be gainsaid

in the Detroit metropolitan area, legally. By the way,
Ma, we never recovered

your wedding ring and pearls after some *gonif*
pilfered and pawned them

but trust me, when I find him, I'll shake him
'til the rich give anonymous charity

or I'll walk away from trouble the way you taught me to—
otherwise, it follows you

home and perches near the deli tray without bringing
even a cup and saucer.

Were you ready, ma, when your soul and body
signed their final confession,

the angels acting as scribes? No *shomer* in Rochester Hills
to stave off ill-tempered

ghosts, ungrateful relatives, rodents, to watch you
until you could don

your *guf hadak*, the celestial garment being fashioned
while your soul went

back and forth between homes. I must steel myself
like the egg that hardens

when cooked, the egg I salt and bite into, half-
listening to the rabbi's

easeful voice: together we recite, offering God
consolation for His loss,

though I tell my children that you are with God,
and they repeat it so blithely

and I am so busy with mourner's occupations—
the burying, the tearing,

the endless repetitions, double-taking every mirror
I pass that offers no vision—

I start to believe what I want to believe: your absence
here is your presence there,

wherever there is, every piece of land a personal
Elysian field, the best room

at the Fontainbleau, *pied a terre* with an obstructed view
of oblivion, a corner booth

at the Rascal House and the miniature danish taste
like manna, as they always did.

ii.

MAH JONGG: AN HOMAGE

Nothing is as obnoxious as other people's luck.
F. Scott Fitzgerald

Some folk want their luck buttered.
Thomas Hardy

First Charleston, First Pass

It is nice to think that Mah Jongg was invented by Confucius.
His affection for sparrows (similar characters, the clicking of tiles
like twittering) but there's no evidence of the game before
             mid-19th century.
The Taiping Revolution was a huge peasant uprising that strove
             for a people's paradise, the Heavenly Kingdom of Great
             Peace, in lieu of Manchu rule.
So long foot-binding, opium smoking and torture, for 11 years.

It is nice to think about being ahead of one's time, though most are
             lucky to live well within the moment.
Stories of the earlier Taiping Xingguo Period (Northern Song
             Dynasty), roughly ten centuries before, include
             "The Mountain God's Daughter-in-Law," "Into the
             Porcelain Pillow" and "Love-Knot Inn."
Can a swallow know the aspirations of a swan? is a picturesque way
             of saying, *stay in your place.*

If you go to the Jewish Community Center during the weekly
             game, do not hesitate.
Choose and discard your tiles as though the hand you were dealt
             (and created) could belong to only you.
The Platters also sang "Smoke Gets in Your Eyes" and if you listen
             carefully, you will hear the cigarette residue in the ladies'
             voices, a vestige of their Betty Grable days.
The Jewish version of heaven, "Olam Haba" is a soul convention,

             but be in no hurry to get there.
The Chinese symbol for "sparrow" looks nothing like the Chinese
             symbol for "swallow" or "sorrow."

First Charleston, Second Pass

There is a prevailing wind.
The East most important; she begins each game, each round.
If playing for points or money, she earns double when she wins,
pays double when she loses.
Someone you know has a life like this. She is often called
the banker, the dealer, or the eldest.

On Noah's Ark, East was the prevailing wind.
Either the East Wind prevails over the West Wind or the West Wind prevail.
over the East Wind: Chairman Mao quoting ancient wisdom.
In the East Wind Community, nestled in the Missouri Ozarks—
an "intentional community"whose stated goal is peace,
social justice, social democracy—they have a nut-butter
business and make Utopian Rope Sandals.
They used to produce handmade drums.
The home-schooled children grew up taut and rhythmic.

The East Wind has little literary legacy, unlike its popular sibling,
destroyer and preserver, dead leaves fleeing from it, *driven like*
ghosts....
West Wind gets good press as agent of cleansing, change.
East Wind's character cold and bitter, nature's step-child.
Endured, not welcomed.
Being the more- or less-loved child sticks with you.

At the table, everyone: your friend and enemy.
The one who pretends not to care if she wins, espouses she wants
a peaceful evening away from the kids.
She will take your change, eat the expensive cheese, say something
cryptic about your husband.
Tip: do not drink much wine.
If your tile is thrown and you miss it, off in a reverie about world
peace or your dead mother, your game is shot.

Tip: it is wise to carry out the opening ceremony with careful
	attentiveness.
Deal clockwise and play counterclockwise.
Respect the revenants, who never skip a game.
They don't need a weatherman to know… never mind.

First Charleston, Third Pass

You are sending three tiles to your left.
You have puzzled over this year's card, which contains 56 hands
      you can make—some closed, which means you must come
      by the tiles naturally, which means you must draw them
      from the wall, which means your friends cannot help you,
      even unwittingly.
Luck must be guiding your elbow.

Tip: even luck wants something in return.

Perhaps you have chosen a hand of winds, one of six suits.
As you know, the East Wind—hereby called "East"—will foreclose
      on your joy.
The West Wind spoiled, a child allowed at the adult table too soon.
The fable of the North Wind and the Sun suggests that persuasion
      trumps force.
The traveler is a pawn.
Oscar Wilde's North Wind was a man *wrapped in furs, and he roared*
      all day about the garden, and blew the chimney-pots down.
He kept company with hail, frost and snow, spent seven years with
      the Cornish Ogre.
Who doesn't?
I paid his dental bills.

The Aspre is a warm, dry wind in the Pyranees, where Andorra,
      our favorite duty-free country, is lodged.
It is like the *Chinook* in the Rocky Mountains or the *Foehn* in
      those Alps.
The *Barat* is a heavy northwest squall on the North coast of
      the island of Celebes, just below the equator in Indonesia.
Cockeyed Boy is an Australian that spins across the countryside
      picking up objects, depositing them further on its journey.
You once dated him.
Diablo, Elephanta, Mistral, Nasi, Ostria, Pampero, Simoon, Tramontana.

One could write an alphabet of winds, just as one could make a list
of old boyfriends who left sorrow in their wake.

The Fremantle Doctor is a cooling sea breeze near Perth.
It happens almost every day—the most consistent wind in
the world.
There are worse things.
But no wind can be depended on.
Once you choose your hand, you must hope they are not thrown
too early, before you have a *kong* or *pung*.
When that happens, you watch the game go on without you, unless
you are the plucky type who recovers quickly.
Victorian heroines were plucky (with exceptions, like Sybil Vane
of *Dorian Gray*).
Beginning players fear winds and generally trade them away.
Be brave.
Gather them to you.

(Slip) (i)

At this juncture, you can opt out of passing three tiles from your
        hand by taking one or more of three received and—don't
        look at them—pushing them over to the neighbor on your
        left.
If only one, you will take the other two from your board, much like
        the one that keeps Scrabble tiles in place.
You would do this if you believed your tiles potentially too useful to
        surrender.
If you have the makings of two hands, and cannot decide.
One player will think, how convenient for you to remember this
        rule when you need it and not to bring it up when you
        don't.
That she forgets is not your fault.
Do not take on her burdens.

Do not underestimate convenience or the random nature of
        the game: there is little to control, and whether asserting
        control is advisable versus being open to receive what
        comes is anyone's guess.
One no longer plays because she doesn't want to think
        (direct quote).
One because she must win, and so can't risk loss.
One because her husband never comes home (direct quote).
One because so much chance offends her.

John Cage invented "Chance Music"—"Aleatoric"—from
        the Latin word, *alea*, for dice.
Elements of the composition are left to the fates—such as, what
        is playing on the radio.
Bunco uses dice.
You don't play Bunco because it's too easy.
You don't play Bridge because it's too hard.
Mahjj, like the third bowl of porridge, third chair and third bed,
        is just right.

This is not the time to bring up questions of theodicy (why bad things happen to good people).

Second Charleston, First Pass

Take a tile and turn it over in your palm. Feel the weight,
          the rectangularity.
Once made of ivory, jade, bone, bamboo, celluloid, catalin.
A Chinese set from 1920 might be cow bone with bamboo backs.
Yours made of bakelite (brainchild of Dr. Leo Baekeland).
Butter-yellow and smooth.
The game soothes, distracts, draws out complaints, desires,
          impurities like a good facial mask.
Hide your intentions.
A tile thrown: to pick up, you must be ready to reveal a complete
          aspect of your hand.
Opportunity is a fickle handmaiden.

Is desire impure?
Isn't there such thing as pure desire?
Is everything an alloy?
Bakelite, a thermosetting phenol formaldehyde resin, anything but
          singular.
You, too, are an admixture.

The tile used to be a card, in the Sung Dynasty, the game *ya pei.*
Matiao, during the Ming.
Favored among peasants.
Created by a captain to distract his sailors from seasickness.
Cards were easier to burn quickly (gambling taboo).
Though it sounds like "magic," there is no connection.
The French *magique;* the Greek *magikos.*
The latter, cited by Plutarch, typically appeared in the feminine.

There are no jokers in the Chinese version.
Eight jokers in the American, the joker an American invention,
          devised around 1870 to be top trump in *Euchre.*
The name probably comes from *juker.*
You can hear how that might happen.
Trumping is power.

Language, too.
Soon, the joker represented by a jester.
The Tarot deck has long contained a Fool.
Ma que—hemp sparrow, jute bird, black bird.
Shanghai did not require a visa after World War II.
Russia to Japan to China.
Turn the tile over in your palm.
You are holding a "soap": a white dragon: blank tile, save
        an engraved frame around its edges.
The picture you can imagine.
The weight of migration, of one culture shaping another.
As it turns out, Nazis did use human fat to make soap, but on
        a limited scale.
Somehow, my son's army men—the bad guys—are still German.

Second Charleston, Second Pass

A hand versus a handful of flowers does not exist, though there are
        eight: spring, summer, winter, fall, plum, orchid,
        chrysanthemum, bamboo.
It would be too easy.
The most you'll ever need is four to complement the other suits.
Do you remember the corsage that drew blood?
Some nights need (only) symbols.

Every mahjj tile, symbolic.
Sometime you wish they, along with everything else, could mean
        less.

The *dreidel* game played to disguise prayer.
Prayer forbidden during the reign of Antiochus.
Pull out a top and spin it.
Throw down a tile and call it: flower.
You need not identify the carved image.
This is economy of language, observation.
Your assignation should be terse.
One bam.
Two crak.
Three dot.
Names need not be flowery.

The name of the Chinese people, *hua ren*, spoken in a certain tone:
        "flower people."
Jews: "people of the book."

Chrysanthemums symbolize a strong life.
Give them to the old, but not your lover: yellow at funerals.
Orchids mean fertility: give them to a couple who yearn for a child.
Chinese 50 cent-coins display plum flowers on one side.
Its blossom represents the five *Fu,* or blessings.
Bamboo means resilience, fortitude.

Whoever chose these blooms eschewed those from the poplar tree.
They blow apart easily, unfaithful lovers.

The suits represent three extremes: dots, the Wheel of Heaven;
　　　　bamboos, the axis of the earth; craks—characters—
　　　　numbers—changes in the life of man.
We age.
The average age of the mah jongg player is 64 years old.
The duckweed has no roots.
Anything with thistles and thorns—there's no room for that at
　　　　our table.
We must be loyal, and stable, and not too prickly.
We are fragile.
We injure ourselves.

Second Charleston, Third Pass

The White Brothers introduced Mahjj to the English Clubs of
        Shanghai in the early 1920s.
Joseph Babcock, then Soochow representative of Standard Oil,
        thought the game too complex.
He simplified the rules and added the passing of tiles.
Babcock and friends wrote *The Red Book of Rules.*

The Wives Club of the Wright-Patterson Officers Club introduced
        the Charleston—a series of tile passings, to the right, left
        and over—and a set off standardized hands, now changed
        annually.
The Officers Club built where the Wright Brothers brought
        the Kitty Hawk flyer sometime after her famous runs.
"If we worked on the assumption that what is accepted as true
        is really true, then there would be little hope for advance,"
        said Orville.

The Charleston named for the famous dance.
The famous dance named for the city in South Carolina.
The rhythm popularized in a song, "The Charleston," by James P.
        Johnson, in 1923.
It is older than that.
It is difficult to pin down origins.
Not everything traceable.
Blame can be assigned, but better to take responsibility.
The famous dance came from African-Americans. Not called
        that then.

The music is ragtime jazz: quick 4/4 time with syncopated
        rhythms.
The dance uses swaying arms and fast movement of the feet.
One first moves the right foot back one step.
Then kicks backwards with the left foot while the right arm moves
        forward.

Then, both feet and arms are replaced to the start position.
The right foot kicks forwards while the right arm moves
          backwards.
A little hop between steps.
In a circle, in partners, or solo.
The acronym for remembering which way to pass the tiles is
          ROLLOR.
Right over left, left over right.
Like the dance.
The ladies must have cut rugs at their meetings, don't you think?
Thinking themselves modern, scandalous.

Try this in your living room. There's no danger.

(Slip) (ii)

When the Chinese have a complete hand, they say ho—harmony,
        peace—or *fu*—happiness, luck, blessing.
You can go out completing a pair, the only time you can pull a tile
        thrown for a pair: the final move.
Rules change at extreme moments.
When you pulled the very last tile—a joker—and won, you cast
        your gaze in the direction of the ocean (in this case, West—
        how nice your friend's home has an unobstructed view)
        representing gratitude toward higher power.
No one pulls a joker on the last tile.
Your luck, immense.

"Luck is not chance—it's Toil—".
The Japanese word *ojozu* (translated as 'skillful') means "one who
        knows how to adapt to his luck."
You cannot force luck.
You can learn to control the *likelihood* of luck, and be able
        to exploit it.
Five of the same tile (a quint) requires both, and *hubris.*
Japanese and Chinese have complex terms for that.

The Wives Club of the Patterson-Wright Officers Club (now
        the Spouses Club) plays Bunco on the first Monday of each
        month in the Thrift Shop Annex.
They still sell the Mah Jongg Rule Book in large and regular print.
Their pledge to the game is salutary.
History does not care about the present.
Those who once loved you need not come around.

Optional

Each year you buy new cards.
It is not near the Chinese or Jewish New Years.
Sometimes it benefits to speculate; others to accept.
This has nothing to do with what you cannot change.
It can be harder to accept what you can change, as you feel
      required to do so.

You may favor one section of the card but let your tiles dictate
      your hand.
On the other hand, be flexible.
And alert.
You may find yourself trying to make the same hand, over and
      over.
Set yourself the task of risk.
Losing is not the worst thing.
You do not play for honor.

Look across the table into your opponent's eyes.
How many tiles does she want?
One or two or three.
Or none.
If fewer than three, she might already have a hand.
She could be split between two.
It pays to commit early, or you will watch your tiles pass you by.

The square you build with tiles—four walls—stands in for the
      Great Wall of China.
You stuck a small piece of paper in the Western Wall, in one
      of many crevices.
In the women's section.
Davening, the low hum of reaching out to God.
Give me a hand, we say, when needing help.

The name "Hong Kong" a phonetic rendering of spoken
      Cantonese meaning "fragrant harbor."

A British colony after the first Opium War.
Opium are poppy tears—ah, the day's yields.
The tiles travel.
Language travels.
Hand it over, we say, when we want.
Here, you take what you need, but you are not always free
        to take it.
Want vs. Need: battle of the centuries.
One usually on the ropes. Draw. Discard.

Note: Many games employ this strategy:
Scat. 31. Ride the Bus. 41. Golf. Sam Sip. Paiute. Yaniv.

The goal to improve your hand toward some objective: to create
combinations that are collected, melded or discarded.

The goal is to improve your hand.

The goal is self-improvement.

iii.

Long Distance (ii)

My mother calls again from the afterlife.
I am pleased and irritated
as I have been imploring her to listen
the way Shelley begged the west wind: *O Hear!*
until, so fed up with no answer, he began
to speculate how inanimate he'd have to be

to get some attention, and finally, resorted
to that high Romantic gesture, pretending
to be injured, when all too soon, the sea
would drag his soul beyond the fathoms.
My mother pipes up: *what time is it there?*—
she has never believed in the concept of

time-zones—and I am so relieved I forget
to be angry, which is the tale of our relationship:
a tide of ire and contrition as uncontrollable
as prophecy. *Did I ever tell you that I received*
three watches from three suitors in three months?
Twenty years before my birth, I am not privy

to this memory, but know the story well,
having rolled my eyes three times at its telling.
I hear the labors of my ceiling fan, the late-
arriving jets dividing firmamental air
and wait to hear more but no Shirley—I imagine
my deeds have been counted, weighed and counted,

Mene, mene, tekel, upharsin
my character found wanting, her ghost-hand
penning the same writing on the wall
Daniel interpreted at Belshazzar's feast,
my sin the ancient disrespect. I think of how
she loved the game of gin, how subtly she slid

the cards through her stack, arranging suits
and straights with a polished nail's flick,

and wonder how she managed the battle
between soul and body—the Zohar says
when the soul departs, the spirit plunders
the body like a sailor set to sea in a wretched boat

without an oar, battered with no peace,
and asks leave of every body part,
which must give its own permission:
when true torment starts.
When did they pass that law? says my mother—
I hear her shrug in the west wind.

Kaf Ha-Kela (The Catapult)

The soul flung back and forth across
the universe, eighty-sixing
psychic moss, impurities,
mistakes, accumulated dross,

repaired for its continued sojourn.
Angels handle the machine—
a cosmic centrifuge—and while
the body casts off its concerns

(it only takes a thousand arcs
or so) the spirit abdicates
the flesh perceptions—no more feathered
hope, no unbeholden skylark's

unpremeditated strains.
Ma, must we all become
undone? While you are cleansed
of world so only pith remains

I travel back and forth along
these lines, a walking, talking flaw.
You cannot hear my modulation,
only that angelic song—

but could you try? These are the terms
I am restricted by, until
I join you, dizzy from the trip
and staring down the worms.

Pith

Fail better, wrote the man who also penned, *That's how it is on this bitch of an earth* *which makes I love you* and *Leave me alone* seem cousins versus contrary. I knew a man jailed for embezzling. *Nothing is for nothing,* he said. People are prone to saying cryptic things when on their way to the big house. I grew up in a kind of big house, one with twenty rooms: an old house in a dying city. The stairwell met the landing halfway down, then split into two destinations. Every day was choice and choice: exhausting. It made me untheoretical. *Feel better,* I did not say to my friend, on the heels of tragedy. I learned that much from the beau who said to me, earnest and quizzical, *Don't be sad.*

After Great Pain

Some can't sense it, must see blood
       or fire on hair or hand—
even then, they remain objective.
       For me, a twinge
serves better than Proust's pastry
       for a trip through
my catalog of injuries: rake punctures
       shin, rocks embed
in chin, sutures and shots and losses,
       and rejections
but those are damages the body, union shop,
       does not handle,
though it's sympathetic, misery incarnate.

Some pray it away. Or so they say. Some pay
       off: the signal stab,
tingling diagnosed in time. In labor, if your
       timing's right, the nurses
kind (poor Eve, bearing down alone),
       the stars bribed
to align, you'll be given anesthesia, and after,
       there's a child
whose pain you share, you can touch, feel, hear it—
       parental synesthesia.
Most of it, however, has no silver lining,
       save its mundane,
blessed aftermath—absence; then, amnesia.

Cicatrix

The scar's first obligation, to recall.
Later, to escort conventions of ache
and sting down the mind's entry hall.

To mar, festoon, the surface forsaken
by perfection, once unadorned.
To hold fast rented sides in the wake

of a good needle that negotiates forlorn
truce and the brain commands, stand
down and dresses the wound, torn

between badge and brand
with the balm of forgetting ferried
like those with memories banned

across Lethe. How vast and varied
our tasks: to erase, expose, review, repair
and leave the dead buried.

Lightning, 1882-1890

As witness, the amateur
hazards the first
photograph of this
phenomena, perhaps
the first phenomena—
what other tool would
the Great Cleaver wield
to separate firmament
from earth? The man
reveals the supposed
serrate closer to a straight
line or curve: ribbon
or random pattern
instead of jag, famed
zigzag, switchback—
the art of electricity
scissoring the dark—
the eye, ever-deceived.
Grievous the world
broken in two: fabric
of matter rent and
stitched by the Holy
Tailor with thread of
ether, needle of storm,
so seamlessly the seam
denies its existence:
you must have imagined me.

Gray Roof

The pathetic fallacy hard at work
this week, found you wielding a paintbrush
at firmamental trim. Today's clime:
fog and gale, reluctant dawn, *sturmendrang.*
The score a melisma of whys.

No God will be held responsible today,
each in personified paradise, big bang
cheerleaders who set the plot in motion
but won't claim consequence. And since you are
not here to question or explain,

you a man of quiet verbs
and restless adjectives
all we can do is send our selves to the weather,
all we can see: this lead veil.

In memoriam, C.J. D'Angelo, 1960-2000

Pathetic Fallacy

Pouring grounds into a pleated filter,
        I accuse plaintive daisies
                of withholding, all thirteen bracts
forcing

                petals   toward   the   center,   *capitulum,*
which sounds
        like capitulating, if you ask me
but flowers never do—

though by noon
        petals elongate, reach out, can't wait to escape
                the cooperative, and when one frees

                itself, (should you will it free will)
            it either dies or was dying. Others
(cosmos, tulips) watch, try to learn but with

no consciousness flowers can't learn—too easy to say
        so what's my excuse as though
                to be aware of existence gets one
off

                the   hook   or   crook—they are
really the same
        curved stick used to grab sheeps' hind legs.
The two major schools say

the mind is the brain or the mind
        is on its own though the guy I like most
                says we can't understand what it
means

                to be conscious, the idea can't be
        grasped by any of our tools, however
arced. Stand against that landscape, the one that mimics your mood,
        while flora and fauna gaze dully on—

                                                    and you, aware of your

                                                    awareness, vow to make
                              everything feel
  or die trying.

Five & Dime

At the Cunningham's counter the ghost of my mother orders the blue plate special circa 1967: sections for meat, starch and vegetable. Dealing with the worldwide problem of the vegetable medley she separates peas from carrots from corn, eats peas and corn, abandoning the carrots: life not always fair. I pop a balloon suspended from a laundry rope. Rewarded with a hot-fudge sundae: Sander's hot fudge, the local brand, the best brand (Pet milk, caramels, butter, milk chocolate). My children starved for descriptions of my childhood. What have I invented, to what end? I could fix it so the machine of my youth runs smoothly, so many are gone who would contradict my version, my myopic vision—I have worn glasses now for 40 years, I couldn't see the pale white addition on the blackboard but would not admit it. It took Mrs. Matthews, gentle, slim, to tell my reverent parents, *she's a fine student but I am afraid she's not seeing what she should.*

On Cooking a Symbol at 400 Degrees

I butterflied Australian rack of lamb
with shallots, garlic, parsley, butter, wine
(some in the pan, some for the palate).
Although the livestock loved in nursery rhyme
avoided clumbs of mint, it served my family
nonetheless. I am no PETA zealot
(leather jacket, handbag, wallet, shoes)
but wonder if the deeds we do pursue
us in the afterlife. Does the fleecy
creature have a tenderable claim?
My lambent mind considers our short lease
on life, the oven hot. Am I to blame?
Who gave thee such a tender voice? asked Blake.
Myself am Hell. I watch the mutton bake.

The Train

At some—and this is crucial—point
in the not-distant future, you
will hear the symbol of a train,
and trust the train to exist because
ontology has wormed its way into
our psyches—and then I begin
to lose your attention, as
the universal syllabus

tells us that whistle or bellow,
plaintive or obtrusive, freighted
with meaning, patterned
after the mating call of ancient
predators, demands you return
to some departure you never
reconciled, and you must stay there
until someone picks you up in
a paneled station-wagon with

no safety restraints, manual
windows and a sooty ashtray
holding a deuce of unfiltered butts.
Remember when you learned about
symbolism? There were those hills
and Hemingway's girl was pregnant,
Hawthorne's scarlet letter marking
Hester's and Dimmesdale's sin and
it became clear, one tedious day,

that in literature things stood in
for other things, and the downtrodden
teacher with hope in her secondary
school heart brought up, *metonymy,*
synecdoche, more specific
substitutions of one for another
but you needed no extra credit
and so ignored her desires as

so many others had, she of the

perfect cursive and knee-length
lesson-plans. Now you wonder
what a train whistle is and what
it does to your memory, what
it stands for, why it makes you wistful—
you didn't even grow up near
a train, you've never taken a ride
longer than from Manhattan's
Lower to Upper East Sides, or

the El from Chicago & State
to Evanston, you've never taken
the trip from northern California
to Washington along the coast
that everyone says is so beautiful
and you are just romantic
enough to think that beauty can
change your life though you don't tell
your friends that—that's not common

parlance even at a gallery, where
you can't find what you were raised to
think of as beauty because art
is about information and
energy and politics, these days,
as though it wasn't when painters
had wealthy patrons who told them
what to paint and the painters said,
jump how high? The Doppler Effect

makes a train whistle seem higher
in pitch as it approaches and
sound waves bunch out, and lower when
it recedes as they stretch out.

It's no tune or even a riff,
more a fragment of some 20th
century work that insists on
no story and incremental
repetition thrown in the symphony's

repertoire when conductors tire
of Wagner & Vivaldi and
you are glad this is only one
program a year—I don't blame you,
I get tired of confusion in
a stiff chair and wading in
a pool of abstraction—what is
memory without specifics?
My mother told detailed stories

of woe and grudge and rare
victory over those who wronged her—
she took three trains from Detroit to
Edmonton, Alberta, to be
with my father in the 2nd
World War and they lived where you could
be outside for minutes a day,
it was so damn cold—she hoarded
cigs for her husband while he flew

cargo to Alaska and the well-
off family that housed them was
snobby, ungenerous and if
I met one of their children today
in one of those cafes with metal
chairs I would snub him because in
that way I am like my mother,
loathe as I am to admit it,
I cannot let go of anything,

I do not forget, this is one

of my great gifts. Surely you have
a train story, surely someone
in your family has a train story.
My Austrian friend says trains will
always means death in his argot
but I cannot allow that, I
have only my own arsenal
of associations with death

and cannot afford another's,
though his is buoyed by history,
on an epic scale and mine are
local losses, meaningful to
me and blessedly, no grander.
Haven't you stumbled across some
shard of memory that will not
let you go, affiliated
with the echoing northbound caw

or beauty or your mother or
war or Canada—why haven't
you taken that vaunted trip we
discussed? What else haven't you done,
will you never do?—and you are
tempted to sit there and dwell,
to let such thoughts riddle your sleep:
this is one of your great gifts,
friends, lovers, family agree,

it makes you the best of
company, divides you from almost
everyone else everyone knows
and for that, for you, I am beyond
grateful, and if you will, I will
ignore—transform—forgive?—
the lonely note of the train—can
you?—I can, I think I can,
I think   I can.   I can.

Sigh in Silence

Ezekiel 24;17

said the Lord, this sigh indiscernible,
although the si- contained is louder than
the second fiddle, second syllable
that ebbs into its chopped-off sibilance.
The first one lasts awhile, the way we wish
that pleasure would endure, the vowel long,
it's hard to leave the bed its made, mouth wide
until the utterance has disappeared
but leave we do—what choice?—arriving late
to consonantal noise, and then its absence
(second act the same, the first a quicker
drama). Good thing there's a word good enough
to capture what we hear and don't, or else
the music might go on, or else silence would.

The Burden of Dumah

The angel of silence wants to talk,
to spill, to spew, exclaim, harangue.
The angel of silence wants to utter,
to mutter, finger-gun, to balk,

shout Bang! or Fire! into a crowd.
The angel of silence wants a voice
that soothes, that moves, persuades, entreats.
The angel wants to live aloud,

to gab and chatter cant and banter,
to allude, imply, to prattle,
colloquize and pitch, to vent, to yak,
confide, to spill the beans, enchant,

insinuate. He wants to drone,
reveal, pronounce, to trash-talk, stump
and spout, to rhapsodize, to flap
his tongue, to gossip, prate, intone,

to *parlez vous.* The angel tired
of the quiet-down, the shushing,
hushing up, the tranquilize, the still,
the calm, the lull—he wasn't hired

for this, he's wont to say but will
not say. Do not speak ill of him.
He lets the wind speak in his place.
Poor shill. His voice, invisible.

Persona Non-Sequitor Grata

I drive by the Sunset Psychic and think of the witch I consulted in Maryland, her insights accurate if predictable: you will move. Find, meet, choose, lose. Do you believe? As a child, my friend rushed Tinkerbell on stage, clapping his hands and shouting as Sandy Duncan instructed him to save the fairy's life. It worked. Peter Pan wanted stories and pockets: to keep small tokens of youth. Eliza Doolittle wanted a room with an enormous chair: privacy, comfort. Phillip Larkin wanted to listen to Sidney Bechet blow his clarinet in Storyville. I, too, wanted love's "enormous yes." What we get is TK, journalese for yet-to-be-determined, and sometimes the abbreviation finds it way into the final copy because life is sloppy. Shakespeare's father was a glover, if we believe the bard existed. My father drew car doors and windows. J.M. Barrie's father was a weaver. How many work with their hands, use them to place, to guide, to form, to fix. Though shy on commitment, I am a fan of faith, I send it letters and imploring glances. For my child, I am sure I could kill a man with an eggshell, a corn-chip and a semaphore. Dumbo was part of a pyramid of pachyderms after his mother went mad. Some cinema buffs believe that the marriage of Barbara Stanwyck and Frank Fay was the real-life inspiration for "A Star is Born." My mother said Barbara Stanwyck broke Robert Taylor's heart. Norman Maine says three times: "I just want to take another look at you." I feel the same. The witch had a dog, blacker than the Five of Cups' cape in her tarot deck (true, I was full of loss and regret), big, who may have been my old boyfriend, transformed. It ended gently and there I was moving cross-country, state by state. In order to brachiate, the siamang, a lanky rainforest monkey, needs vision, foresight, to see where the next branch is coming from. By all accounts, I lack this.

Sweater

I make my daughter put one on
        as have mothers since Victorian times—
before then, assuming mothers cared,
        have not evolved so greatly (there are
a host of infanticidal animal mamas—
        guinea hen, panda, Magellanic penguin)
assuming Shakespeare's mother,
        Charlesmagne's mother, Moses's mother,
did not want their children catching
        "their death of a cold"—a garment
with another name suited the purpose
        of thwarting the chill, according to
Thomas Sheridan's "A General Dictionary of
        the English Language" printed in London:
for J. Dodsley, Pall-Mall; C. Dilly, in the Poultry,
        and J. Wilkie, St. Paul's Church-yard,
in MDCCLXXX, which equals 1780,
        for those out of Roman numeral practice.
Life was colder then, in all those thens—
        many banked fires, many prodded embers.
I would be nostalgic for olden times
        except I can't find my ancestors, or
even the towns they claimed to be from
        (when not espousing to be American)
and so imagine that what we call
        "quality of life" was mezzo-mezzo at best
as history's documents left them out,
        we might say, in the cold. My husband's
family goes back, and back, and back—
        there are not enough backs to express
this distance with force, back a vague
        term (go back from whence you came),
rendering it useful and inadequate—
        let's just say, way before sweaters,
back to Ireland's mantles, frocks, cloaks
        cowl and celt, *brat* or *faillain*
back to Greece's chitons and himations

(they endured until the 6th century)—
yes, that clan is the stuff of legend,
        one can find them in tome's pages
with their receding chins and pale eyes,
        surviving strife, element and exile,
conquering, bearing broods and clans
        with their own plaids and coats of arms.
No secret that "sweater" shares provenance
        with "sweat" from the Middle English
"swote"—perspire, work hard—though
        in 1400 it meant "to be worried, vexed"—
one of those words that has not changed
        much, a sturdy, dependable cognomen
not unlike my ancestors, no shooting stars
        among them, their reliable villages,
professions, their limited ambitions—get out
        from under Cossack's horses's hooves,
avoid being conscripted as a child to defend
        a country that hates you. Have a family.
Stay on God's good side. By 1882,
        redefinition: "a woolen vest or jersey,
originally worn in rowing"—nice upper-class
        sport like tennis and polo. Like Thoreau,
I resist activities that require an immaculate outfit.
        About then, mine were elbowing out of
steerage at Ellis Island, yielding their
        unsayable names to workers who
did not know they were agents of change,
        their inability to translate piles of
consonants and shapely vowels—
        who could blame them? They stamped
the papers, that was enough. In 1828, the item
        used to "produce sweat and reduce weight"—
such concerns older than Jack Lalanne,
        though whether they cared more for vanity
than health will remain buried in the files
        of How Anyone Lived When Anesthesia

Meant a Hardwood Mallet. As it turns out,
          people have been knitting or crocheting
wool for 2000 years, give or take, though
          no one thought to fashion a garment
from it until the 15th century on the islands
          of Guernsey and Jersey—hence, the name.
Hence, hence, hence—so many
          explanations for how we arrive,
so difficult to maintain a linear stitch.
          In 1940, Lana Turner became the first
"Sweater girl," wearing one that hugged
          her prodigious curves in the movie,
"They Won't Forget"—based on the famous
          Leo Frank/Mary Phagan trial—"when
do we get a chance to hang a Yankee Jew?"—
          though it was easy to be forgotten, in
sweatshop and factory with a baker's dozen
          of siblings who all change their surnames,
no two alike, to sound less "ethnic,"
          making it even harder for me to find their
offspring here in the land of the free,
          no entry for them in the dictionary,
no etymology to prove their existence,
          to find their source. The appeal of having
a point of origin, someone to point at
          and say, that's where it all began,
though what a beginning proves
          and where language will take us next
eludes me, enveloped in my cardigan,
          named for James Thomas Brudenell,
the 7th Earl of Cardigan, a British military
          commander during the Crimean War.
Cardigan, Wales, home to the first *Eisteddfod*,
          a festival of poetry and music, in 1176,
and a chair at the Lord's table was awarded
          the best poet and musician, the Celtic bardic
tradition requiring the performer write

and perform, play instruments, be versed
in myth and history—what we might now call,
	"a Renaissance man" but even then, it all
could happen on a cold, clear night like this,
	a suggestive chill in the air, punctuated
by stars, with a sultry comma for a moon
	and I am slightly worried for your health,
there, dressed in shirt-sleeves, shivering
	but then again, some people like to be cold
some people need a history to feel needed,
	some people have a history they would rather
forget, and you never know who is one of them.

I Have Written the Last Elegy

I have written last elegy, the final effort.
It limboed under the bar just before the law passed.
The deadline, last night—midnight, of course.
I tried to incorporate the conventions:
        regret, sorrow, appreciation, reflection
        on one's own mortality, and the expected note
        of hope. Hope for what? I did my best.

It was not for anyone specific.
Some specialize in the occasional—
        they make their misery yours.
I focused on the overall "condition" of death
        and remembrance. Death was not the tricky part.
These used to be about love—no longer.
The meter wasn't easy, either.

I used images best unrepeated here.
I'd hate to spoil the effect. I think they stand up.
There was a nearby caw and the thin wire of a wail in the background
        that kept me grounded. After all,
        I could not sacrifice my life to this elegy.
I could not let it plunge me into some underwater cave,
        spelunking for survival.

I had to conjure up great sadness for this task.
I resorted to thinking about personal loss
        and institutional oppression.
I read the daily papers from several major cities.
This involved a trip to the library
        where I labored up a vast, marble staircase
        and admired busts of statesmen.

At first I thought, why me? and was flattered.
Then I realize that others had refused.
Still, I stepped up to the plate.
My political consciousness came of age
        in a time of well-attended rhetors.

"In this time of mourning. . ." was suggested to me
        by a popular pundit. I respectfully declined.

I tried to bring some beauty to the enterprise.
I tried to convey absence, the void.
I was counseled by those charged
        with the last eclogue, epithalamium, ode and heroic couplet.
They said, forget the weight of the world.
We gather on alternate Tuesdays.
I bring the chips and dip, being the only one with a car.

Apologia to Shirley and Coleridge

If my house, my car, my vine and fig, my lot
were all to disappear, still I'd own
regret, ma, my share and my inheritance.

At Yom Kippur we wrestle with mistakes—
we sway, we bend, atone
viduy, I have sinned, I have gone astray, transgressed

and with all my heart, my soul, my might
(the language of my childhood siddur,
parallels and *thees* and *thous* intact,

the language of the sanctuary's antiquated lure),
I believe the *rebbe* wrong who said,
the dead can hear all that is uttered in their presence

up until the day they rest, the grave's lid sealed.
Others scoffed, *until the body yields to worm,*
beyond the pall of what the mystics termed

"the hammered image" crafted by God's angel,
Samael (second string) (don't quote me)
who inflicts the final wound with gall or wormwood

poison on a sword the naked eye cannot
detect and so, cannot reject. Our sages count
nine hundred (give or take) different ways to die,

though recent architects of woe have added
to the minions. I pray you were assigned
the one called "by the kiss," reserved

for righteous sorts though not without
their flaws, a little lower than the angels
but more loved: the soul's departure

without pain, "the drawing of a hair from milk"

their analogy, mine the narrow line of light
in Barnett Newman's "Stations of the Cross"—

the 12th—the intermediary in a rectangle of night.
I hear my children cry out in their dreams, though
no sound escapes their lips, how loud they are,

their dreams are loud and Technicolor, drawn
by fears they cannot name in case a word can
will a thing to be—not since the Garden, dear.

Do you hear my *mea culpa*, ma? I have always
been the one who loved contrition, friend to guilt
and what could I have done, and so am sorry

that I could not pull your mind back to the present
though the present was a prison even with
your favorite lines from Shakespeare—

mewling, puking, you would laugh the way a kid
laughs nervily at what's forbidden. I am sorry, too,
for that awful poem you loved about the trees,

how I tried to make you run the lines in hopes
the easy scheme would trick your brain into
remembering, and sorry for the stench, for saying,

eat a little pudding, please, for sitting by your bed
amazed at time's slow stalking pace—no winged chariot
did I hear—and sorry that I was not there

to lie you down with dignity, feet pointed toward
the door, water poured around so demons
wouldn't dare cross over (they're afraid),

and was not there when Dumah would escort
your soul to the courtyard of the dead.

We're told that when the soul departs

the flesh, a cry goes forth from one end
of the world clean to the other but the voice
cannot be heard

like the serpent's sloughing off its skin. Hear, we say,
O Israel, a faith that favors ear and disbelieves
the eye. The wise man says a person

who recites the Kaddish with conviction may annul
a harsh, divine decree against him. I think
the prayer reminds the dead of how

the living sound: droning, rhythmic, repetitious,
distant from the music of the spheres. I say
Kaddish for my mother, so she'll know

I heard the cry one cannot hear, the music
absence makes, stolen from the Garden
after Eve and Adam's endless error

and all the naming fled into silence,
(not a hiss, not a whisper) and then Shirley said
enough already, talk, I will listen

—*no sound is dissonant* (she nods to a gentleman
imprisoned in a lime-tree bower)
which tells of Life.

Patty Seyburn has previously published four collections of poems: *Perfecta* (What Books Press, Glass Table Collective, 2014); *Hilarity*, which won the Green Rose Prize given by New Issues Press (Western Michigan University, 2009); *Mechanical Cluster* (Ohio State University Press, 2002); and *Diasporadic* (Helicon Nine Editions, 1998), which won the 1997 Marianne Moore Poetry Prize and the American Library Association's Notable Book Award for 2000). Her work has appeared in numerous anthologies, most recently *The Bloomsbury Anthology of Contemporary Jewish American Poetry, Poetry in Michigan/Michigan in Poetry,* and *Irresistible Sonnets.* Her poems have appeared in numerous journals including T*he Paris Review, Poetry, New England Review, Field, Slate, Crazyhorse, Cutbank, Quarterly West,* and *Boston Review.* She won a 2011 Pushcart Prize for her poem, "The Case for Free Will," published in *Arroyo Literary Review.* Seyburn grew up in Detroit. She earned a BS and an MS in Journalism from Northwestern University, an MFA in Poetry from University of California, Irvine, and a Ph.D. in Poetry and Literature from the University of Houston. She is a Professor at California State University, Long Beach. She lives in California with her husband, Eric Little, and her children, Sydney and Will.

CPSIA information can be obtained
at www.ICGtesting.com
Printed in the USA
FSHW020635250719
60370FS

The Night Travellers

The
Night Travellers

Elizabeth Spencer

University Press of Mississippi Jackson

www.upress.state.ms.us

The University Press of Mississippi is a member of the Association of American University Presses.

Copyright © 1991 by Elizabeth Spencer
University Press of Mississippi edition published 2012 by arrangement with the author
All rights reserved
Manufactured in the United States of America

First UPM printing 2012

Library of Congress Cataloging-in-Publication Data

Spencer, Elizabeth.
  The night travellers / Elizabeth Spencer.
    p. cm. — (Banner Books)
  ISBN 978-1-61703-240-0 (pbk. : alk. paper) — ISBN 978-1-61703-241-7 (ebook) 1. Vietnam War, 1961–
1975—Protest movements—Fiction. 2. Mothers and daughters—Fiction. 3. Americans—Canada—Fiction.
4. Peace movements—Fiction. 5. Married people—Fiction. I. Title.
  PS3537.P4454N54 2012
  813'.54—dc23   2011043619

British Library Cataloging-in-Publication Data available

To the great friendships of Montreal
and especially to
John Mappin

He calleth to me out of Seir, Watchman, what of the night? Watchman, what of the night? The watchman said, The morning cometh, and also the night: if ye will inquire, inquire ye: return, come.

—ISAIAH 21:11–12

Contents

Part I
The Home Scene

1

Kitten on the Roof

They had taken her kitten, whose name was Mopsy. She was white and had been last seen in the large pocket of her mother's lab coat, the one she wore for work. When Mary Kerr asked about Mopsy, they were vague. Mopsy had clawed the chairs, and that was bad.

At night Mary Kerr woke and was sure she heard the kitten, mewing on the roof. There was a way out her window, high up on the second floor, out to the roof, mysterious with its many rises and falls, its peaks and drains. Her room was in the back over the kitchen and dining room. They would catch her, surely: *Mary Kerr, what do you think you're doing?* The moon was full, very high up, and the house silent. She eased the screen out and wriggled through. Gray slate was warm under her bare feet. "Mopsy," she whispered. Maybe she had dreamed it mewed. The moon throbbed.

Mary Kerr felt wonderful out there alone. She tilted with the slant of the roof. She had good balance and never got scared to climb things. "You'll go off with the circus someday," Poppy had said. From the top she looked down everywhere, seeking a single scrap of whiteness.

Just how the kitten might have gotten on the roof she didn't ever wonder. The slate was still warm from the afternoon sun. She gained the upper ridge, the roof's spine, and straddled it like a pony. There below was the porch roof, over there the drop for the carport. She crawled over to the chimney and nestled against it, crouching down on the side toward the moon. The gutter just at the joining of the chimney and the roof made a smooth trough she could just fit into. Everything was warm. She looked for Mopsy till her eyes tired. They were sleepy eyes, outstared by the moon. She fell asleep.

"Mary Kerr! Mary Kerr!"

It was daylight. Down below, they were calling. When she remembered, she thought she would sneak back into bed. What excuse? Hiding under the bed, a joke? In the bathroom, back of the shower curtain? What would they believe? She found a window open, pulled up the loose screen, and slithered through, only to confront her mother, who came raging up the stairs. Her father was toiling behind.

"Baby, where were you?" he was asking. He was never well and his color was bad. He had to be careful.

Her mother, angry, drew back a hand for striking. Her color was bad, too, but for a different reason. She had fair skin which flamed up with her feelings. "What do you mean, scaring us like that? What were you doing up there?"

"Looking for Mopsy. I heard her."

"You know you're not to worry your father."

"I didn't mean to. Mopsy was calling."

"She couldn't."

"Why couldn't she?"

"Kate," Poppy cautioned.

So her kitten was gone for good. Mary Kerr knew it and cried.

No one was happy that day. She heard the voices of her parents, rising and falling back of the bedroom door. Then Poppy had to lie down all afternoon while she felt that something was her fault, even though he often had to pass time that way.

2

A Start in Something

She was a slight girl, not quite thin, with soft brown hair and hazel eyes. She seemed not to weigh anything, to be an essence with nothing solid about her. Since she was good at hopping around to music, jumping and whirling at one and the same time, skipping rope, and hanging by her feet from a certain low limb in the yard, they sent her to dance school early on.

Miss Ellen Thomas was the name of the white-haired little lady who taught. Miss Ellen had all the good families in Kingsbury sending their children to her. Mary Kerr was first an elf, then a wood sprite, then a snowflake. Once, dressed as a Christmas fairy, she did a number alone for a program. Her dress was pale blue, like snow at night, with sparkles sewn on. The music was from *The Nutcracker*. Everyone clapped. At age eleven she was too old for Miss Ellen's classes. Miss Ellen, having by personal admission reached fifty-five, was too old also. No more Twinkle Toes. She tearfully retired.

In school Mary Kerr was picked for stunts and dances in plays. She once did cartwheels across the stage. She and one of the boys who had been brought up in Texas learned a Mexican hat dance. He had gotten the hat out West and it swallowed him, but she could actually dance right into it and around the brim.

The football boys, once the season was over, stole a cheerleader's costume and tried to get her to dance in a local night spot where a combo played, but her mother heard about it and said she couldn't. They were from too good a family: They were Harbisons. Just as well have it understood. Those boys were high school, older; she was still in junior high. Mary Kerr had seen the short silver skirt and regretted its loss.

"You don't know how to do a dance like that," her mother said, frowning.

"I would make it up as I went along," Mary Kerr argued. She didn't know how she did this, but just did it. Her father thought it might have been fun, but what did he ever get to decide? After this quarrel, she came as usual and nestled in the crook of his arm, where it felt the best of all to be. They understood things together.

"It's Mother," she said. "She makes a fuss over every little thing."

"She doesn't think it's so little." He sighed. "You know she works too hard. She's under a strain. If anything happened to me, she'd have to sell this house. It would be too much for just you two."

"Why would it? If she works—" Her science degree from Duke, her position at the research lab, starched white coats in the closet, a fresh one three times a week. Other days, plain office clothes—trim suits, usually. Kate. Married to a Harbison, the best. She wore everything looking like a page in a fashion magazine, even the lab coats, one hand in a large pocket (except when she took the kitten), talking earnestly, precisely.

He shook his head. "It would be too much."

"There's Penney." They had had Penney as cook and maid forever, and her mother, Old Nellie, before her. Penney was named for J. C. Penney, a store.

Mary Kerr snuggled closer. She forgot disappointment, everything but being there.

"Your mother," he was going on, half to himself, "deserved better than me."

"Better than a Harbison?"

He laughed and patted her. "You'll understand sometime." He must have meant his health, but he couldn't be blamed for not being well, could he? The door in the hall opened and closed. Mother. She stood there before them, all locked together.

"I had a chance at lunch to make that call. You know, Don, this woman sounds very sensible. Where she came from with a name like that, who knows?"

"What name?" Poppy said.

"Delida. Madame Delida, at that. With her accent, I guess she has a right to it. European."

"It might be real."

"People like that," said Kate, "are like weeds grown up in the night."

"Don't have to be bad weeds."

"Her studio's over on Haley Street."

"Then the bus would be all right."

"I thought of that."

Dancing! It must be that, speaking of a studio. They were talking as if she wasn't there. (So they often did, and might as well be alone, her mother at the tall dresser mirror in their bedroom, seated on the bench in front of it, brushing out the ends of her bright, gossamer-fine hair, swirling it up, pinning it loosely at the sides for the night. The silver-backed brush, which was also good for striking with, would make a rhythm with what she said. Poppy sitting on the end of the four-poster bed, so long in the Harbison family.)

But I am here, thought Mary Kerr.

Poppy looked down at her. "Would you like that? Taking up dancing again?"

"She might even get a fellowship on the strength of it. Someday." Her mother walked off. College, she meant. So far away.

The studio was on the top floor of an old three-story concrete office building, up two flights of stairs. Madame Delida herself was a slight, dark, foreign woman with a long face—horse-faced, you could say. She had an accent, and looked you straight in the eye when she spoke.

"The dance," she said to Mary Kerr, and took her hand. "We should continue with it year by year. So do we gain the different stages."

"I studied when I was little," Mary Kerr explained. "I went to Miss Ellen Thomas's dance school. I was an elf first, then a Christmas fairy."

"*Mais oui,*" said Madame Delida, "but now you will move on."

"I graduated," said Mary Kerr.

"But from the dance," said Madame Delida, "to graduate is no such thing. To grow older, yes. Me—I am older, but still I dance."

"You don't look older," said Mary Kerr politely.

It wasn't quite true. Madame Delida's hair was dyed and her arms looked stringy. She had cords in her neck. One of her feet sat crooked, like she might have a bunion or a broken toe. But she was straight as flint, and dared to wear a boat-necked leotard and tights, though usually with a short skirt, and once with some loose slacks.

In flat shoes, that first afternoon, she held out an extra pair for

Mary Kerr. Madame Delida walked like a duck in those shoes. Following, Mary Kerr walked like Charlie Chaplin. Leading her pupil to the center of the large empty room, which breathed early summer air, Madame Delida reviewed what Miss Ellen might have taught or might have neglected.

The positions: flat, then flat again but *un relevé aussi. Le troisième, oui, puis le quatrième (ah, bon), un relevé (bonbonbon!) et en pointe un jour peut-être.* Now . . . the barre. Then came the arabesques, the pliés, the *ronds de jambe.* "The turn-out!" cried Madame Delida, in triumph. *"Parfait!"*

Madame Delida turned on the music. She took Mary Kerr by the hand once more, while the needle swayed upon the old black record, Mozart, Chopin, or something.

Madame Delida came to call.

The secluded circle off the boulevard, the big, silent, peaked-roofed houses, among them the Harbison house, with its carriage entrance. Mary Kerr was exceptionally talented, was her message to Kate Harbison, who asked her into the sitting room but offered her nothing. Mary Kerr was truly *étonnante.* Madame Delida proposed some work in ensemble, but only in the modern dance style. A mixture of modern and ballet, for as yet ensemble work in ballet was not possible. Not enough were trained to make a credit. As for modern, first groups of three, then on to twelves, it might be. A program should be their goal.

Mary Kerr practiced every afternoon in the upstairs hall.

"I'm sick of that damned music," Poppy said.

"I guess that's part of it," Kate said with a sigh.

"Can we ask her to a party?" Mary Kerr wanted to know. Her mother was giving one.

A silence at the supper table. "I don't think that would be quite the thing," said her mother.

"She's bound to have friends here," said Poppy. "She won't need ours."

"But all she has is a room," said Mary Kerr. "Over on Quinn Street. She'd like to go out somewhere, I bet."

"Over there," her mother said vaguely.

Quinn was a poor street. No more was said.

———

Mary Kerr and Madame Delida had now been joined by two girls who had previously attended Miss Ellen's school and three boys out of nowhere, who got sweaty and obviously worried about how they looked in tights. Now almost a teacher, too, with instructive feet, knowing themselves observed, Mary Kerr helped to plot out a program number, leaning together with Madame Delida over large blank sheets to map the staging and the flow of the dancers. This process had a name. Choreography.

In late August, the program.

Mary Kerr's parents not only attended, but stirred out relatives and friends by the dozens. "That pretty child of Don and Kate's. You wouldn't think to look at her she could dance to almost any sort of thing." So it was repeated.

It was a wonderful evening—everyone said so. Mary Kerr was in four numbers. She danced solo twice and once in a trio, performing "Approach of Night" with another girl and the only older boy who had lasted. He was a freshman up at Davidson College, and none of them knew him well, but he was, as Madame Delida said, very flexible. Then there was a soldier's march for twelve, girls and boys together, all stair-stepping in strict little military coats, all recruited in the last fortnight and trained to step in time. They made lines and star shapes, Vs, and ranks of different depths. They marched to "I Love a Parade," and then turned into wooden soldiers, stiff as clocks. They burst into combat and raised the flag on Iwo Jima and circled with linked arms to the red, white, and blue. Applause exploded. It was all exciting. Madame Delida, with three yellow roses pinned to the strap of her evening gown, stood in the receiving line along with the superintendent of the high school where the program was presented, his wife, and the president of the PTA with her husband. Madame Delida's eyes brimmed with tears of pride.

The Harbisons—Kate, Don, and Mary Kerr—walked home together that night. "Only a short way," Poppy had said, "and such a nice night, too," he added, refusing offers right and left to give them a lift. Mother was not so eager, but when Mary Kerr, who kept running off her euphoria and excess energy by circling them and flinging herself far forward of them, then back behind like a frolicking puppy, caught up and joined arms with them, her mother fell in step and pretended to be marching as the dancers had, while Poppy and Mary Kerr hummed.

Poppy bent to kiss his daughter's cheek. "You looked so pretty up there, honey."

"Thanks," said Mary Kerr, not missing a step or a note.

Her mother wore a long dress—they were the fashion then—and held her skirts skillfully up with her free hand. "A nice-looking boy," she remarked, referring to the tall one, Greg, who had worn a loose black shirt and played "Night." "Didn't he ever ask you out?"

"Oh, I guess," said Mary Kerr.

"She's too young for that," Poppy said, and squeezed her arm.

"High school," her mother said. "Fourteen."

They kept trooping on, this family of three, under the thick lofty trees, under the moon. To get home they had to cross a business intersection, now deserted, the lights observing their lonely task of changing from red to green and back again. They had just crossed and were passing a small shopping area, recessed in shadows, faced in dark-stained wood, locked and silent.

Some figures in what at first seemed a crowd, an onslaught, ran sudden and silent out of an alley between the buildings. There were really only four or five at the most, and young at that. Mary Kerr thought at first it was a joke, some of the dancers playing a trick and doing another dance in the street, but it wasn't that at all. What it really was, if anything, they never knew, the whole thing began and ended so quickly. They may not have been black, but Mother later always said they were. They arced in front, seemed to dart past to get away completely, but then, as if in a common undiscussed inspiration, turned and kicked a garbage can over just in front of the three of them, clutching together, with Poppy shouting "What you think you're doing there?" and pulling away to run at them. Mary Kerr and her mother clung to hold him back—he shouldn't be getting into anything, it would be a strain—but by then the runners had struck. The tin garbage lid was flying out into the moonlight like a hurled disk and the can itself was spewing contents from its mouth like a sick elephant. Rotten tomatoes, clumps of spaghetti, bits of hamburger, chicken bones, and fried potatoes came pelting out before them. Then the gang was gone.

The Harbisons stood stunned and afraid, wondering if it was over. Mother stood with her pretty skirts pulled to one side. She had gotten splashed with garbage.

"Well," said Poppy, "that was a visitation. They do go in for dancing it out." He had used a phrase of Mary Kerr's. When she talked about getting rid of anger or disappointment, she would say she needed to "dance it out."

"You can think it's funny if you want to," Mother said. Still clutching her skirt to one side, she walked rapidly ahead of the other two. It had somehow been their fault.

Cool and protected, the houses along the way stood under lofty trees in their tranquil yards, where the moonlight found whatever entry it could, pouring through the trees, splashing light between the shadows on the lawns. Then they were home.

In the hallway, just inside the door, Mother took off her long dress, with its flowered pattern of lavender and rose. She stood for a moment in her ankle-length white slip and stepped out of her shoes. Leaving the shoes on the rug, she went into the kitchen, where Mary Kerr, following for something to eat—dancing had made her hungry—saw her wad up the dress and stuff it in the garbage.

"Oh, no, you can't! It'll clean!"

Her mother's answer was to walk straight out, upstairs, and to bed.

Her father had come to the kitchen door. "Peaches," he began. It was one of his pet names for her.

"She's mad," said Mary Kerr. "I never saw them before. It wasn't my fault."

"Mine, either," Poppy said. "Just that we wanted to walk and she didn't." He turned to go upstairs, looking tired, but turned back. "You were wonderful, Baby." He put his arms out to dance position. "Here. Teach me to do that whirligig."

She caught his hands to swing him around in a simple maneuver. Then his foot went wrong. He laughed.

"Start all over," she said. "Now." Presently they both were laughing. Her bad feelings disappeared.

Upstairs a door slammed shut. They stopped and looked.

Poppy said, "Don't worry about that dress. She'll be back to get it when she simmers down."

Once again Madame Delida came to see Kate Harbison. "What a treasure do we have in her! How far she could go! Her tours! Her élévations! I speak with true feeling, Madame."

"I understand," said Kate, but this was what she said when she didn't mean it, as Mary Kerr, from the corner of the stair landing, out of sight, well knew.

It was a fact that when she danced she felt like going straight on up, never stopping. It would seem that at the height of her own power to lift, the music would come to fill in for her. It acted like wires that pull a stage puppet up; it bore her through the air like a trapeze.

She was feeling all this when, walking home one fall day from her class, she saw her father walking toward home, too, only diagonally from her own route, along another street. He had not seen her yet. It was a hot fall afternoon with sun beating fiercely through the trees.

Mary Kerr began to dance. She did piqué-arabesques up and down the Strattons' front steps and tours jetés on the sidewalk before the Van Meters'. She mimicked the Ray Bolger scarecrow dance and the Gene Kelly waltz, while Poppy laughed at her and clapped. He was standing in the sun. She swirled up to him and ended in a frog walk, clowning.

He pulled her straight. "What a show, just for me." His face was fiery. "Let's get home, Peaches, it's way too hot for all this." She moved to tuck under his arm and help him. "Splendid, Baby," he was panting to her. "My own Margot."

She sat down with him on their own front steps. It was then he said very calmly and formally that she'd better call the doctor, but by then she had guessed, she realized when she thought about it later, that they both knew already what might come next.

Waiting for the ambulance, a pale hand to a hectic face, her mother said, "What were you thinking of? Didn't you know better?"

"Better than what?"

"Why, getting him out in this sun like that. It's way too strong."

"He was out in it already, walking home. I just happened to see him."

But Mary Kerr wasn't being believed. She wasn't even being heard.

"He'll tell you! It wasn't *me*." Mary Kerr ran past her mother, toward the door where he had made it to the couch to lie down until help arrived, saying, "He'll tell you that! I know he will," but her mother had caught her arm.

"You can't disturb him now. You can't." From the corner the ambulance wail was sounding.

Twice in the hospital when she saw him after bypass surgery, she had said, snuggling as close as she dared, "Tell Mother. Tell her I didn't get you out in the sun that day."

He didn't understand. "Who thought you did?"

"I mean, it wasn't my fault."

"I will," he had whispered, and she knew that if he promised, he would do it; his splotched, patient, smiling face had never moved itself to mouth a single promise to her it would not keep. But he never said it, not actually that she knew of—that is, he never said it in front of her and her mother both. He tried once when she reminded him, but her mother, seeming to know what she had in mind, what she was trying to get at, once and for all time, had interrupted; and then, when Mary Kerr had gotten back to the subject again, the nurse walked in and behind her came the doctor, asking them to leave.

In the hall they waited too long; then in the sitting room they lingered too long there. "Is he going to die?" Mary Kerr whispered in dread. But the doctor's large step—he was tall and pale in white, white all over—whitened out her faint voice, which had been tuned only for her mother to hear. Kate was rising to see the doctor, meet him on a grown-up level, and as she rose Mary Kerr said again, "He's not going to die, is he?" But they were not listening and when she spoke louder it came out like a shout: "Listen! He's not going to—"

"For heaven's sake, Mary Kerr!" Her mother turned on her, as if she were striking off a childish hand that was pulling at her skirt.

She was sinking down then, no higher than her mother's strong firm ankle, insect-sized on the gigantic stage of the world's business. Even back in the room, grasping his hand, she could not find her voice again.

And then it was too late.

Soon after the funeral, Kate Harbison cancelled Mary Kerr's dance lessons. "I've heard too many things about your Madame Delida," she said.

"What things?"

"Oh, some man at a filling station. There's gossip. He's half her age."

"But maybe he likes her."

"Undoubtedly," said Kate. To Madame Delida she gave financial reasons. She did this by telephone.

So for a third time Madame Delida came to the house, this time frantic. Penney went to the door and said no one was at home.

"I will teach her free of charge!" Madame Delida shouted.

Mary Kerr was upstairs in her room. She overheard. She wanted to run downstairs and tell her not to worry, she would find a way to come back. But her mother had locked her door in passing.

"Don't worry!" she called out, but was not heard, she guessed, because she heard the front door close.

Kate was somewhere in the house, silent.

Mary Kerr lay on her bed, holding tight in one palm a medal Madame Delida had given her. Madame Delida had won it in Paris, she said. *Ecole de danse, rue de Corneille* was written around its rim. In the middle was a Degas dancer, one long shoe pointed, the fragile skirt flounced forward, while she leaned with arched hands descending.

That very morning Mary Kerr had started her first period and she felt a stir of mystery, with no words to explain it. It seemed a finishing off of things not finished at all. *I'll go see her,* she thought.

But when she did, she found Madame Delida packing a brass-bound steamer trunk that smelled of old perfume bottles. She was folding mysterious laces to put in the drawers. "This town will never be good to you, my treasure. You, too, will learn someday."

So Poppy was gone with his arm to snuggle under, and long ago the white kitten, and now this woman, too, was going, back into the night she had sprung up out of, as Mary Kerr's mother said, though not like a weed. She had opened doors and now was leaving. The roof where the sun and moon beat down was empty. Kate was there below it, a presence in the house.

3

Into Time: The Sixties: The Farm

Kingsbury, where Mary Kerr was born, was a North Carolina city named for royalty and built on gold. There was gold ore to the east, in the hills and streams. All during the early years, people dug for gold and found it, until 1849 brought news of more elsewhere. These people were Presbyterians largely, Scotch-Irish, they called themselves. They knew what profit was. They smelted ore to get out the gold. What was left from the process they used to pave the streets of the new town.

Kate Harbison was born a McCanless. She came from a farming family over in Jasper County. She was the first of her family to live in town.

Kate had golden hair and was always like a princess. Her family knew in their bones she would be something that wasn't ordinary. Yet she never exactly put her beauty on the block, not for anybody around there.

At school she discovered her great capacity for work. She got her highest grades in science. Things like history and literature were all right, she supposed, but you had to guess a lot. Kate preferred the answers. In the back of the book they stood in black and white. You could get them or not. She got them. She won a fellowship to Duke. At Duke she met Donald Harbison.

Kate was working through some chemistry notes before a quiz and was seated for this purpose on a stone bench built into an archway between the library and the chapel. She was wearing a brown skirt and a blue sweater with a simple strand of pearls which looked real. Her fingers, she would always recall, were stained with nitric acid. She had piled papers to one side while opening her notebook when a breeze stirred up some fall leaves, blowing them in a russet spill across the walk and going on to swirl up the papers. Kate McCanless said, "Oh!" Donald Harbison, a law student, was passing. He was already looking at her—the angle of the stone wall made a backdrop for her as good as any portrait—and was daring himself (he said later) to speak to her when here came the papers, whirling up and landing right at his feet. He doubted good fortune so long he almost missed his chance. Then he went for it.

"I don't know how to arrange them," he said as he evened up the edges.

"Oh, that's all right," said Kate. "Just as long as they're all there."

"Oh, I got them all." He was anxious to reassure her.

She scrambled through the sheets, stacking with care, until, giving up, she stuck the whole lot in her notebook. "That was a help."

He was standing there. Never mind. Lots of boys just stood there. Finally he said something. "I'm in law school."

Kate, for some time, had thought she would like to meet a lawyer. The kind she wanted to meet flourished in cities. They dressed well and knew business people. It was something in itself to say, *I'm a lawyer.* She did not often smile, but she did so now. "It's just this quiz," she said.

"When?" he inquired.

"Oh, not till this afternoon. I don't know why I'm worried."

"Have you had lunch?" Don Harbison asked.

While they ate together, she noted that he was a little shorter, a little less heavyset than exactly what she had in mind. But learning later that Harbison was a grand name to have in Kingsbury (her own nearest city!), she was inclined to overlook his minor flaws.

He was never robust and his sensitive face aged sooner than it should have. Most of his hair went early on. But in evening clothes he looked the gentleman to be proud of: kind and intelligent, he had a manner of being wellborn. He and Kate took trips in the winter and stayed in nice hotels in France and Spain. Once they took a Caribbean cruise. People would have said that Kate was a "gold-digger," playing on her family's past days of actually doing just that, now marrying a Harbison. But Don was no great shakes at business—he seemed to lose more than he could make—and his family worried over him. It was Kate who kept at it, got her graduate science degree, went on to some sort of specialized cell work at a research lab contingent on the university branch at Kingsbury. She would talk about her job if asked, but who would go up to Don Harbison's wife at club or dinner or cocktails, softly glowing in chiffon or silk, and ask about the cellular structure of the liver?

They got the Harbison house, a fine, Georgian-looking, two-story residence in an exclusive circle off Central Boulevard, where the trees grew lofty, fine, and full, looking down on other, distant trees whose names and kinship were unknown. A circular drive running up to the steps from the street was one of the very few in that area. Early in her marriage, Kate Harbison heard some mention of Scott Fitzgerald, whom she then read. What happened between her and the pages set in Long Island, New York City, Paris, and the south of France cannot be known, and she did not often mention the books, but something shone for her out of them with no sign of going out, became a guiding star, an idea of how she, when she wasn't doing her job, was going to be.

About a year after Don Harbison's death, Kate realized she had to sell the house. She expected a quarrel with the Harbisons, especially her sister-in-law Jane, who had her own ideas about what should stay in the family. For some reason Kate did not confide any decision to Mary Kerr but sent her away for the summer, back to Kate's own family in Jasper County. Though Kate's parents seldom came to Kingsbury, she had managed to "keep up" through the years; she hadn't entirely snubbed them. Her mother was a brisk housekeeper, a small woman who raised prize chickens, and her father kept cattle, though he rented out a good part of his farming property nowadays. He also had once run a country store, now rented out, too, and was deep into supporting local enterprises, everything from the 4-H Club fair to Clean Up Our North Carolina Highways.

Kate had gone out to arrange things. "Certainly you can send her," her mother said. "We're going to have so many this summer anyway, she won't even be noticed, let alone in the way."

"Do her good," her father said. "Never saw anybody this community didn't help out."

Kate sighed. "I don't know if she needs helping out." Then she considered. Don gone, and all that devotion? "Yes, I guess she does," she added. "Would you mind if she danced? Practice, I mean."

Mary Kerr was keeping on, studying with an ex-musical star who had come there with a travelling Broadway show. Al Bernstein. Maybe they had fired him there. He blithely claimed to have fallen in love with the place. Nobody had ever heard of him, so he couldn't have been such a big star. But he worked up a group of students and even found an empty building, though for a while he had had to beg the use of the high school basketball court.

"She can dance in the pasture all she wants to," Kate's father had said. "Long as she don't step in anything."

Mary Kerr packed up her suitcase and went to a place she knew very little about. Several times she had been taken there on visits but she had never stayed overnight. Yet here she was approaching a two-story country house on the side of a hill with a lot of rocks cropping out of the grass, like giants' bones, and porches tacked on the sides with steep steps going up to them. It looked as if the house were sliding off the hill. Some cows were grazing in the front yard. It wasn't really a front yard, but more like a pasture which sloped all the way down the hill to the fence and cattle gap. The cows looked up at the car, which was driven by one of Mary Kerr's uncles, her mother's brother named Pete. He had had to come into the city anyway and had offered to drive her on his way back. One of the cows ambled over and stood in the road, directly in front of the car. Uncle Pete had to honk her out of the way. "Stubborn old buzzard," he said.

In addition to Pete, there were Murray and Frank. Murray, it was whispered, had been in prison for something. Mary Kerr's father had not talked about it, and her mother said she'd never understood it, but of course it was true. Frank, unmarried, lived at home. Pete lived in the nearest little town, their post office, called Browning. But Murray had his wife and two little children living right there with his parents. It was a lot of people, as her grandmother said. Nobody seemed to mind.

Mary Kerr got a corner room upstairs in the back. She had to go around a corner passageway to get to the bathroom, which she shared with Frank, whose room was farther along the hall. Murray's family was in some rooms toward the front, and her grandparents slept downstairs. It seemed to be a house as full as a ship, but at night everything got tucked away and quiet. Then you heard the trees, a train far away, the hum of highway traffic two miles off, the buzz of a plane passing overhead, and maybe a calf running for no reason back in the barn lot. Out the window she could see the stars, all their arrangement.

At the table—it was yards long and took up most of the dining room because they had put in all the leaves—there was a lot of running back and forth to the kitchen and dishes passed every which way, over people's heads and snatched out of your hand before you could see what was there, then given back with apologies. When she didn't eat a lot they complained she'd starve to death, and they laughed at jokes about people she'd never heard of. There was business talk because Frank was starting up a Laundromat with money borrowed from the bank, his father guaranteeing the loan.

They were all so big, except Mary Kerr's grandmother, who was small and active, with hair a sort of reddish color. "They say you take after me," she told Mary Kerr. "I'm the only little one in the family."

"Mother's not big," said Mary Kerr.

"Taller'n you'll ever be," said Murray. "There's always one runt in the litter."

"Kate never even had a litter." Pete laughed with his mouth full. "Just one little runt ain't no litter."

Mary Kerr almost cried. Her father had never had any talk like this around him. Why hadn't her mother told her what to expect? Her grandfather, at the head of the table, was a tall stooped man, who seemed to be leaning forward over the whole lot of them. Maybe he was deaf and had to bend closer to hear, but she thought it was his way of making sure he had control. At least he had a softer voice than the rest.

"Going to take her uptown," he said. "Show her the sights."

"Then you can drive in the pullets," her grandmother said.

After dinner, they had to wait out in the hot sun in the pickup for the pullets. Murray brought them out in crates covered with wire, twenty-five to a crate, he said, six crates in all. They were packed in too close, Mary Kerr thought. Some were clucking and half squawking, but some were silent, panting, and all of them looked mindless but scared, with red rolling in their eyes and their heads flattened out.

"They know you're coming," said her grandmother, standing in the sun with her hand shading her eyes. "I called the plant and they know you're coming."

"Are you going to sell them?" Mary Kerr asked as her grandfather bounced along the road toward Browning.

"Sell 'em, kill 'em, eat 'em," he sang out, bumping over potholes toward the highway. "They're just good frying size."

All for slaughter, she thought. *No wonder they look scared.* When they stopped at the plant, the smell of the process came all the way out into the driveway, something like scalding water and feathers, maybe blood and insides, too, who could tell? Two black men and a white boy came out and carried the crates inside. Soon after, somebody came out with a piece of paper to be signed. The paper had blood smears on it.

They rode around town and Mary Kerr's grandfather told her a number of things about all the buildings and people there and the good projects that were going on at the school and community house, far and wide. He didn't seem to have any other thought for anywhere but right there. Kingsbury might have been on the moon.

"Kate's the only one went on to finish college," he said. "The others did a year or two and settled in for the pull. It's putting it off too long, finishing up, and farm work laying out to be done. Murray ain't killing himself, but the rest are pulling their load. You get children on the way into the world and there ain't no time to sit back and wonder what next you can learn about. Kate's never been one to loaf, though, I'll say that for her. Time you decided, young lady. I reckon she's going to put you through school, though. She thinks like that. Likely she'll marry again."

Mary Kerr felt her breath go straight out of her. "Not after Poppy. She couldn't ever find anybody else!"

The sharp glance from under the thick black and gray brows sought her out with something like curiosity for the first time. He had small dark eyes way back under there. They seemed to be hiding, coming out only when something called for them. They felt called on now.

"Anybody like Don Harbison, you mean? We can all hope not, that's for sure."

He said the last very low, the way her mother had of talking just beneath what you could hear clearly, but never quite low enough to be just to herself alone, though she still could say, *Oh, you misunderstood me, I never said that.* For the second time that day, Mary Kerr nearly cried. *You're just talking about money,* she wanted to burst out. *You don't know what he was like.* She pulled back hard within herself. She pretended not to hear. He was showing her the Presbyterian

church. It had a sign out front: FOUNDED IN 1759, ONE OF THE
THREE EARLIEST CHURCHES IN WESTERN NORTH CAROLINA. Mary
Kerr's grandfather was an elder there, was helping raise money to
repair the old brick wall at the back just before you got to the
cemetery. McCanless was a staunch name in that part of the state.

At night, these relatives all turned into other people; like a witch's
trick, the drop of sunlight seemed to give them a different rhythm.
In the daytime, for instance, they went around in striped shirts, white
and brown, white and purple, or gray, with work pants in khaki or
denim, and shirts too small, their buttons straining over hairy flesh.
It was all that food they ate. But at night, they looked washed and
slicked up. They laughed and talked to Mary Kerr. They smelled
like soap.

"They tell me you can dance," said Frank.

"I heard tell," said Murray.

"*I* can dance," put in Murray's little towheaded girl, Effie, but
nobody noticed her.

"You and me," said Frank, "let's go out and dance. Tomorrow's
the weekend. We're bound to do something."

"Where you all going?" her grandmother asked.

"Well, there's Johnson's out on the highway."

"I don't know if her mother would like it. Kate's particular."

"I'm not in favor of anybody going out there," said her grandfather.
"Lots of trouble can start in those places."

"Come on, Daddy," said Murray.

"Come on where?" her grandfather said, and laughed. "I ain't
coming on anywhere, if you don't mind."

"Martha'll go," said Frank, meaning Murray's wife.

She was stirring iced tea. "Sure, I'll go. I'll cooperate," she added,
mocking something they were always emphasizing.

"We got to show this girl off," said Frank, and put his arm around
Mary Kerr.

She knew she had to go with them, like it or not.

After that evening, Frank started waiting out in the corridor for Mary
Kerr after the others had closed their doors. The first time, after
going dancing, he was just drunk was all, but later it looked like
getting to be a habit. Mary Kerr figured out a way to use a vase to
pee in, and empty it out the window. She ran to brush her teeth

soon after supper. She locked her door, too, but still he found ways to get closer to her than she wanted, and he would grin at her and make a panting noise. He went to church, as all of them did, sat in the row with the rest, even passed the collection plate. She thought he must be two people, but then she wondered if they weren't all like that. Murray was always casting off remarks about him and Martha in bed. When Pete came by it was with his wife, who was expecting, and they made jokes about that. Part of it, Mary Kerr thought, was showing off for her, but a lot of it was just their natural way with each other. It was like they were all in a pan, scrambled up together.

One day Mary Kerr found her grandmother alone, out feeding the chickens. She hung around, not knowing how to begin.

"What's the matter, honey? You look downright peaked some days."

"It's Frank. He's started—well, at night. He tries to get hold of me."

"Get hold of you!" Her grandmother straightened up. Then she laughed. "Oh, Frank's just teasing you, child. He's always been that way. Just laugh at him. Say, 'Don't leave me be, I'll yell bloody murder.' He'll quit."

But it's not like that, Mary Kerr thought. "I don't like him," she said.

"Not like Frank! You're just choosy. Everybody loves Frank." She stuck a sack of feed in Mary Kerr's arms. "Now, come on. Help me."

Not if they knew, Mary Kerr thought. One night he had pushed it against her, she could feel it, hard through his pants. He was heaving out heavy breath. She had to squirm to get away.

She took to walking by herself toward a wood off to the north of the property, mainly in the late afternoons when the cows were grazing on toward the barns to the south. There was a line of woods there and a rise of ground, then past that a downward slope and a stream winding under a narrow plank bridge with a railing on one side. Farther upstream, nearer the house, there was a springhouse, she knew, where her grandparents had once kept milk and cream to keep them from spoiling, butter, and even watermelons to chill before they were cut. But now the springhouse wasn't used anymore; it was half falling in, but still there, mossy and quiet, with the little gurgle of water seeping out of the old spillway, between the rocks. Her grandfather had shown it to her one day. He had stood regarding it. He said he ought to tear it out, but he remembered olden times. "This is just the prettiest country," he said. "You been to the mountains?" Mary Kerr said that she had. "This country," he went on, "was made by God's own hand. I see the evi-dences of it."

Alone, Mary Kerr sat on the bridge now and watched the water. She had been on the farm about ten days. Getting off alone, she intended to sulk about a whole list of things, because she couldn't find any place in the house to be alone for a time without the others calling to her. People always seemed to be all over the place, and those two children of Martha's were probably meddling in her suitcase right this minute; but now that she was here alone she didn't want to sulk. She felt her own self again, contentedly.

Presently she got up and went beyond the bridge, through the woods to a part where she had not ventured before. Coming into the open, she saw a fence and beyond it an open space of ground with some trailers and tents set up. People were moving around them, and some of the tents were still lying on the ground waiting to be put up. A cluster of women in long skirts with some sort of odd scarf wrapped around their heads, which trailed down the back, stood talking. Two were holding children by the hand, and one had a baby strapped to her back. The baby was chewing on the tassels of the scarf. The men wore jeans and work pants, but they, too, had the strange scarf about their heads. They were picking up one of the tent poles and casting about for a place to set it up. There was a young man talking with the rest. He alone wore no scarf and it was he who looked up and noticed Mary Kerr leaning on the fence. His face seemed nearer to her than it actually was because he looked at her so long.

He crossed the pasture toward her. He was wearing tennis shoes, a pair of dirty white trousers, and a clean white T-shirt. He was blond, with hair growing long down the sides and in the back. It looked tangled. It seemed that he walked across the pasture toward her for a long time. When he got near she saw his tanned face and blue eyes.

"Come on over," he said to her. "Meet some new folks."

"I can't," said Mary Kerr, without even having to think about it. They seemed foreign to her, as foreign as gypsies or Indians.

"Why not?" he asked. He laughed. "They won't eat you."

He said *they*, she noticed, instead of *we*.

"Why don't you wear one of those scarf things?" she asked.

"Should I?" he bantered.

"They do."

"You don't have to be like everybody else, do you?"

Over his shoulder, she saw some black people. They were getting out the back of a pickup truck which had just pulled up. They were wearing them, too, the strange scarves.

"I don't know," said Mary Kerr, by way of an answer. "What's going on?"

He glanced back at the stretch of pasture, the growing assemblage of people moving about, arranging tents, discussing and pointing. The scarves the Negroes wore were bright red and orange.

"You might call it an experiment," he said.

"About what?"

"Oh, let's just say about life."

"Are you in on it?"

"No. Just curious. Sympathetic, maybe. But so far, no."

"Are you from out here?"

"No."

"Kingsbury?"

"Sort of. But really I'm from—well, off."

"Oh."

She had been very lonely, she realized. She wished he wouldn't go. When he turned around, she said it, surprising herself: "Don't go."

He turned back, looking quizzical for a moment. Then, "Come to town with me. We'll have a beer—a Coke. Something."

He had a car, though not much of a car, an old Buick convertible with ripped leather seats and junk piled in the back.

When Mary Kerr got home from town it was late afternoon. She got out of the car before they reached the farm, and walked up the drive. They asked her where she'd been and she said, "Just walking." She went upstairs without saying much, thinking things over. She was seeing for the first time why she didn't ever go out with the boys at school who asked her. If you told about yourself to someone else, even answered a question, they would change it a little, and it would never sound the same. You had to protect who you were. It was like her grandmother not quite listening, saying that everybody loved Frank. But when she answered the boy with the tangled hair, it was not like that. It was different. The difference made it seem that she had done something very important, maybe even wrong. Yet all she had done was have a Coke in the café uptown with a stranger. When the stranger had said "So what are you into?" she had replied straight out, without a pause, "I'm a dancer." And a thrill went all the way down her. It was a proud thing to say.

The house was quiet and felt odd. There was talk from somewhere downstairs, but not the usual kind. At supper she found they were all mad, stirred up.

"Uptown and buying all sorts of groceries," said Murray. "Asking for all this funny stuff. I saw Chuck Jordan shaking his head. I says, 'What did they want?' 'Whatever it was, I didn't have any,' he said. 'Some sort of fodder.' He told them to go to the feed store. They said his heart would be changed. He said he wouldn't count on it."

"Has anybody told Watson?" the grandfather asked. "He may not even know what's going on." Watson, it would seem, owned the land the people had camped on, but lived away, up in Greensboro. He had moved when he got a divorce.

"Somebody ought to drive up there and see him," Pete said. "Ron and Carson," he added, mentioning neighbors, "are coming over after dinner. We don't want to start no shooting, or nothing like that. It might get in the papers."

It was Frank who suddenly took note of Mary Kerr and laughed. "Mary Kerr don't know what's going on, I bet. Where you been, girl?"

"I was just wandering around," she said.

"It's a bunch of wild folks," Murray explained to her kindly. "They done moved in right over there." He gestured with his fork, pointing. "Nobody's quite sure what to do."

"What's so wrong with them?" Mary Kerr asked.

There was a dead silence at the table. Finally Murray's wife Martha came out with it. "Living with niggers," she said. "All together."

"Well, if they want to—" Mary Kerr began, and then stopped as the silence went dead around her. She had just said it naturally, that was all.

But at school in Kingsbury they had talked about a girl who had gotten too friendly with a black boy whose mother worked for her family, and when they grew up they kept on being friends. "If you're friends, you're friends," Mary Kerr had said to Poppy. "It wouldn't be right just all of a sudden not to be."

"I wish it worked like that," Poppy had said, because he did like openness about what people felt. "It just doesn't," he added. "Not yet."

Well, then, when? she had wondered.

Finally her grandfather said, "Nobody's standing for talk like that." He spoke quietly but firmly, not really looking at her, but staring grimly toward the wall.

Her grandmother sat up very straight. "Our people won't put up with it." But she, too, spoke in general, not really straight to Mary Kerr, showing she was still a guest—or was it that she was not really "one of them," as they recognized?

And Pete, when he spoke, looked down at his plate. "No, *ma'am.*" It sounded like *A-men.*

"I am prepared," her grandfather said, "to drive up to Greensboro and look up Watson." Then he began to slice off more ham and changed the subject. There was a new town project for a public speaking hall. He was head of the ways and means committee. They had wondered aloud how you'd keep the Negroes out.

But Frank leaned close to Mary Kerr—he was always next to her at the table, crowding—and said, "Who was that type you were with uptown?"

Nobody heard him but her. She gave him a look that said, *You tell on me, I'll tell on you.*

The telephone rang. It was Kate, to ask about her. "I'm just fine," she said.

"Gaining weight," they yelled from around the table. "Eating us out of house and home! Come on out on Sunday!"

That night, when she closed her eyes, she saw a face across a table in a booth, framed in a tangle of long, light hair, looking out of intense blue eyes. "What are you into?"

"I'm a dancer."

That was good.

4

Into Time: The Sixties: The Town

When Mary Kerr came in from the country, she found that Kate had sold the house and moved. She had found a duplex, the half of an old house on a street not far away from their old place. It was two stories and Kate had known how to fix it up, but Mary Kerr, finding her private things uprooted and placed in a new room by hands that weren't hers, was crazy mad.

"Poppy would never have done that, not without letting me know. I bet you looked at everything." This last she shouldn't have said.

Her mother's face turned chalk white and she walked out, fists clenched, back bending down. Kate was tired. She had kept her job going all during the move, and the strain had been awful. Dark blotches had spread under her eyes.

Kate had already had her sister-in-law Jane Harbison to contend with. As if that weren't enough.

"You could have let me know!" was Jane's cry, too, with reason. "Our own old family home."

"I offered it to you," Kate had said, "right after Don died. I told you I wouldn't stay on."

"But when the moment came," Jane had pointed out, "you never said a word."

"Once it was on the market," Kate had said, "you could have stepped right in."

"Raising money like that, no sufficient notice?" The true note had been struck.

Jane was shrewd. She had taken what the elder Harbisons, relocated to heavenly addresses, had left her, and gotten it to increase. She had never gotten carried away enough to risk marrying. She had provided herself with a handsome straight-up-and-down house, set high on the slope of manicured lawn, not a shaggy shrub or an untidy tree until the longitude of the front steps. Even there the shrubs were trim and rounded and the trees behaved themselves. Jane's curtains were always drawn, because of air-conditioning, and she had beautiful objects inside. Her furnishings were the best.

After the set-to over the house sale, Kate seldom went there and only when invited. She went out with people of her choice. "Get up your lessons," she would say when Mary Kerr complained of something. "Then we'll discuss it."

Lesson time went fast. Then there was a senior year to get through. Kate borrowed money for Mary Kerr to "come out" at the club, even though she said she didn't want to. "You've got to want to," said Kate. "It'll get easier once you get started." But it didn't. Mary Kerr let herself get "dated up," as they said, but no boy ever stayed around very long. Kate faced it that she wasn't a big hit. She wasn't "nice to them," was what got around. Didn't like boys? Well, some were better than others.

She worked at Al Bernstein's dance classes. She was always there in the afternoons. Three hours a day. Who could look nice in those leg warmers? She soaked and bandaged her feet when they hurt, and once got crippled with a painful spur. But the closing program of the spring, held in the Civic Center, was certainly something to talk about. A Bach number "rivalling Balanchine," the reviewer said, and there was a segment from "Giselle," with point shoes, and part of "Fall River" of Agnes de Mille—though judged "depressing"—was praised. Mary Kerr, as Lizzie Borden, got to whirl around with a cardboard axe.

Talk of college brought Mary Kerr's plea to get into a dance school. Kate stopped it cold. "You're too good in that as it is. You've got to get more things in your head. Let your feet take a vacation." The spur came back. A chiropodist advised a rest.

There was a perfectly good liberal arts college, Royal's, right in town. "I'd like to send you away," said Kate.

"Then why don't you?" asked Mary Kerr, who had dreams of Bennington, with its programs in drama and dance.

Kate twirled a drapery pull and stared out the window. "I can't afford it. There isn't the money."

"A fellowship," Mary Kerr suggested. "I could apply—"

But then Kate whirled around. "If you dare to do that without consulting—" She stopped.

They were always getting into too much anger before either of them knew it, like wading off into water where the bottom sloped suddenly and then, helpless, floundering in it but keeping on, almost drowning. At these times Mary Kerr would think *Poppy loved me,* but wouldn't say it. *You're always mad because he loved me. If you don't love me, why can't you let me go?* It was a puzzle not made for solving.

Kate, with the aid of a fellowship, could have sent Mary Kerr somewhere both for study and dancing. But she wouldn't. Was she hoping that someday everything would be smooth and good between them? Was Mary Kerr some curious experiment, like one of those Kate worked on at her research job, that she had to conduct to end results, had to supervise unceasingly? It wasn't to be solved. They were not pleased with one another.

So Mary Kerr enrolled at Royal's. One Saturday morning soon afterward, in the fall, Jane Harbison came to call. Kate, alone on her one day of freedom, when Mary Kerr was at Bernstein's studio, saw her sister-in-law's approach from the window and was confirmed in a feeling she had had for some time now, that something different was in the air.

Jane entered with the obligatory kiss, looking perfect. She sat in the living room. "Does Mary Kerr like it at Royal's?"

"She seems to."

Jane in the autumn morning, bright with sun on orange leaves. "So who is this boy she knows now?" The real question.

"She's always had boys around." With Jane, Kate took a light tone. "But she spends so much time at practice, you know."

Jane, too, was carefully casual. "You remember, of course, the time you moved, when she was out in the next county with your people. I understand she met him out there."

You understand, but from whom? Kate didn't ask. She would find out eventually; that she knew. "I remember something about that one. I never even met him. He went off somewhere to school in the fall."

"Then he must have finished," said Jane. "He's back."

"Oh?" *Well, so what? Does it matter?* Kate wondered about the angles Jane was working from.

Jane took her time. She noted, as she always did, the mouse-gray satin draperies that had always hung in the old family living room, how Kate had had them recut for this narrower space. They gave it much of its charm. The chaise longue in the corner near the bay window had been Kate and Don's own, but she had made some other good choices of things they'd inherited, old Harbison things, used now to make a setting for herself alone.

"I believe his name is Blaise." It was half a question.

"Yes, Jefferson. Jefferson Blaise, if he's the one. He comes from Louisiana. When she mentioned him, she called him Jeff."

"But what was he ever doing over in Jasper County?"

It was a fair enough question, but it let out, quite naturally, what Jane thought of the part of the world that Kate had come from.

Kate decided to be insincere. "You can't pry into children's affairs too much these days." Jane never married . . . Jane had no children . . . Jane wouldn't know. "You must wait to be told."

Jane went on stubbornly. "But this boy—perhaps you've heard this, too—Ethan Marbell told somebody he was a top student, brilliant. Blaise was the name, I'm sure of that. And at Royal's. He's there twice a week, other days at the university. And more. An ex-student of Ethan's at Hopkins."

"Ethan." Kate said just that, one word and nothing more. *That certainly does thicken it,* she thought.

Ethan Marbell (pronounced Mar-*bell*), the noted lecturer at the university branch outside Kingsbury, had been Jane's big moment back when she was Mary Kerr's age, and for years thereafter. Then they parted, surprisingly, none to say quite why, though Ethan's eccentric views were the reason usually given. Off he'd gone to lecture at Princeton after Jane said a final no. From Princeton he had moved to a post in an "important government agency," something connected with civil defense, but heavy with word of "inside knowledge." Something had happened: Ethan left the post for an appointment at Hopkins, in Baltimore. Now, since a year ago, he was back.

Gossip of former days renewed. Was Ethan back to woo his Jane? His wife, not even divorced, was somewhere, seldom at home. Among the Harbisons, all but Don had disapproved of Ethan. Don scarcely ever would come out against people who thought. "So what if I don't agree?" he would say. "They've still got a right." Nobody, the answer went, had a right to be a "pink." Ethan automatically became tainted and presumed dangerous. The step to calling him a "commie" was short and many took it. Jane had considered her own position, and reasoned herself away. Control was what she firmly prized. Community meant much.

Kate did not wish to discuss romance. "I worry about Mary Kerr for one reason only. It's this dance obsession. Of course, I wish she would meet somebody she likes—acceptable, of course. She says she's gotten beyond Bernstein. Wants to go to Winston-Salem this summer. Heaven knows, she's practically airborne now."

"Do you mean to let her?"

"I'm determined she's going to get an education first."

"But don't they have to be dancers while they're young?"

Kate felt driven into one corner after another. "She is already a dancer, no doubt about that." Having to talk to this meddlesome old maid, Kate wanted to say, *Mind your own business.*

"Such an attractive place," said Jane, getting up to go. The word *duplex* probably made her shudder. But the address was good, and there were those tall Kingsbury trees, so gallantly right.

Jane's Buick was scarcely out of the drive when here came, helter-skelter, Kate's own sister Sally, who also lived in the city now, and had for some years. An exceptional Saturday, both of them coming in on Kate. Something was really happening, though just what was vague.

Everyone, including Kate, was always glad to see Sally McCanless. She had a married name—Tomkins—seldom used, though Ed was a man of substance. Kate's older sister was her identity here, and she was older sister, too, to Frank and Murray and Pete, out there on the family farm.

Sally's old Chevrolet station wagon she was climbing out of looked scratched and dusty, and inside it was probably loaded with dress lengths, bolts of material she had found on sale, with scraps and samples stacked in a cardboard carton in the back and threads sticking liberally to her clothes or tangled in her hair. Hasty in an old cardigan and corduroy skirt, she mingled with the fine autumn light, but stopped on the walk to admire the birdbath Kate had just put up and to notice two bright cardinals who were busy enjoying it, skimming up and in, splashing.

Mary Kerr, of course, was going to be the subject. Why all this interest? It was getting Kate's back up. Sally's boys were married and gone; her husband, Ed, spent most of his time in his family home, close to two hundred years old, all but falling down, out near

Hickory Creek. Sally lived in town and did sewing in a whirlwind of goodwill, energy, and flashing needles, mouth a bristle of pins, sewing machine humming like a musical score. For programs and occasions, for work to be done hastily in time for a trip, for hems higher or lower, everybody in Kingsbury called on Sally Tomkins. The house where her work went on, shabby but homey, was not too far from the best streets. Maybe it wasn't Mary Kerr Sally had come about. Kate doubted she would be so lucky.

Sally came right through the front door, no knocking. "I won't take a minute, Kate." She wore no makeup, and her nose was always shiny. Her gray-black hair was pinned up with large combs to make a bird's-nest effect, untidy but friendly. Her horn-rimmed glasses kept sliding down her nose. She plopped down in a big armchair and sat with her knees apart; her skirt was uneven, her stockings crooked, her waistline gone. But Sally was always Somebody.

"It's Mary Kerr," she announced. "Mama came in to see me. She knows a lot from that time two years ago. She just thought he was gone."

"Who was gone? Sally, if the house were on fire, you'd still have to slow down."

"Well, it's just there was a bunch of integrated campers, extreme people, some sort of love message, I don't know what all. They upset everybody. Right next to our place. You must have heard. This boy Mary Kerr got mixed up with—now, you must remember that."

"I do. We brought her home."

"Well, now that he's back and seeing her again . . . oh, yes, you must know that—"

"She sees any number of people," Kate fended. It was hardly true: Mary Kerr had acquaintances—she knew a lot of names—but when she wasn't practicing, she "bummed around," as she put it, alone. "Why couldn't Mama come to me?" A detour, changing the subject, almost. She quarrelled with them, her country kin. She made them wary.

"Maybe you weren't at home," said Sally, not wanting to be led into all that. "Mind you, I never met this boy. When she said *radical,* want to know what I said? I'll quote it exactly: 'Radicals are often interesting,' I said. It didn't go down so well. Mama's face was so shocked it was funny."

"I'm dying laughing." Kate drew herself up. She was going to make all this useful, but her tack at the moment was not clear. "I've not seen so much of him. These boys show up for a while and then she drops them. He may be gone already." She groped. No new dress to ask advice on. "Do you want some coffee, Sally?"

"Oh, I've got to run."

But still she sat there, meditative and out of breath from all the things she'd just told, and discontented (as Kate meant her to be) with the response she'd gotten.

"Ed Tomkins, at one time," Sally went on, "was wild as a March hare."

"We all know that," said Kate, not about to give an inch.

Sally gave one last try. "I mean to say, I don't *mind* wildness."

Kate said nothing.

Next, she was thinking, *they will show up one by one about me. Men calling me. Who are they? People are saying . . . et cetera.*

Sally got up. Threads and scraps fell off her, onto Kate's carpet. Kate rose also. Sally reached out and touched Kate's cheek with bright affection. One thing she had to do: show love. Invariably. "My pretty sister," she said, and a tear sprang up and shone. Good Sally. In such a hurry she took no time to shut the front door. "Let them come to *me*," Kate was saying. But Sally may not have heard.

Now enter Mary Kerr, thought Kate later, upstairs pressing a dress. But where had she been, the great subject?

She heard the front door open, sure enough. She called. "Mary Kerr? Guess what? The Bookends were here, not one but both of them."

Mary Kerr had long ago mimed out Jane and Sally as her "Bookends," expressions of disapproval on one side, befuddled acceptance smiling from the other. But holding her together, too, was somehow in the idea of it.

"Both *together!*" Mary Kerr's head showed, coming up the stairwell. Tangled hair, needing a cut, loose white T-shirt, hardly clean.

"No, apart, but one after the other."

The footsteps stopping, wary. "Why?"

Kate made a snap decision not to tell. "Oh, just coincidence. The purest chance."

Mary Kerr passed her mother's open bedroom door, which was to her right, and went left through the landing to her own room. She went silently, but thoughts were there in her footsteps concerning things that might have been the aunts' errand. Kate drinking? It was getting known about. Kate "going out"? Jefferson Blaise? Her door closed.

Taking a cleaning label ever so carefully from a flimsy chiffon blouse, Kate pricked her finger. She rinsed off the blood drops in her pale pink bathroom.

5

Ethan Marbell

In the early March evening, winter fading, they were talking quietly, on into the darkness, the way they had been doing for some weeks now. They were Mary Harbison, Jeff Blaise, and Ethan Marbell. Jeff had wanted her there, more and more positively, until she finally went with him. "His importance to me—well, I can't exaggerate it," Jeff had said. "Except for him, I wouldn't even be here." The job was what he meant, but the relationship, she knew, went back to his earlier student days, up in Baltimore. "He's like a father," Jeff had said, capping it. She gave in.

Ethan's study was lined with books, set about with worn, over-stuffed easy chairs, one with flat wooden armrests. Through mullioned windows heavy foliage was visible as shadows, just one hour ago strongly outlined when lightning flashed behind them, noisy when the wind had blown them, leaves clacking, audible still from the dripping rain. Ethan's chair arm held one of his numerous ashtrays made from fabric pouches filled with shot. He was talking, puffing at intervals. His pipe pointed.

"Some new reports now coming out have already drawn up the statistics. The Oriental is multiplying faster than we are. If we don't kill them off now, it is suggested, they will overtake us early in the next century. My God, and this was a nation with human values once."

Mary could hear Jeff answering. The good dialogue was picking up. His timing fit with Ethan's snugly as follower and leader. Step by step.

"You're Mary Kerr, aren't you?" Ethan had smiled when she first came.

"Jeff just says Mary."

"The family had a branch of Kerrs," Ethan had observed. He had once gone out with Aunt Jane, she remembered then.

"Let's leak all these secrets to the public," Jeff suggested now.

"The shocking thought is, would they care? We're turning so indifferent it isn't real."

She stirred to leave. Others would arrive here late, bringing wine and peanuts, coffee and pizza. Long, stirring talks would begin.

"Her mother expects her for something," Jeff explained.

"You'll miss the Wyndhams, the Taylors, George Lewis. . . ."

"I know. It's too bad."

"Her Highness is waiting," Jeff said.

He was dry and superior, and Mary wondered if she liked it. How could he put himself so separate from, so above, the Harbison affairs? Yet he thought nothing of doing so. He stood beside her, not such a lot taller than she, his hair still (as it had been two summers before) a blond tangle, his shoulders strong, just missing too much muscle. Ethan regarded the pair through his smoke cloud. "Congress is by no means united," he began. Jeff sank down on a chair arm and the talk sprang up again.

Mary had never exactly wanted to be one of them. Just to be thought of as Jeff's girl was what she wanted.

Once when she was alone with him, Ethan had put his arm around her. "Look at this." Some article: OUR HIDDEN GOALS IN SOUTHEAST ASIA. "Take it home," he suggested.

"I'm too busy right now. Anyway, I just come here with Jeff." A dumb "Southern-girl" answer, she thought, made for dodging questions. Why take up with their ideas?

Jefferson Blaise had sprung up in her life again out of the campus paths at Royal's. "Mary! It is you, isn't it? I couldn't be wrong."

"Jeff!" Her heart did triple backsprings and several pulsing leaps in various directions. "Yes, it's me," she managed.

He was teaching there, twice weekly. "What happened to you that summer? No one seemed to know why you left."

"They made me. I was . . . just too young, I guess." She stammered it out. He laughed, and she remembered he had said that, about her being too young. Fifteen then; would he think the same of seventeen?

He touched her shoulder, pushing at it a little, back, then forward. A thrill tracked down her arm. "Then you're so much older now?" He was going to be the same as before. She could tell it already.

You don't know anything about him, they had said. She didn't know much more now. His mystery was part of what was drawing her. She used to think she saw him, walking away on a street at night, just passing under a streetlight, then gone into the dark again.

Ethan Marbell was mysterious as well, but anybody in Kingsbury could piece together a lot about him. He was one of them, born there.

Away in university circles, he had become a legend of brilliance, drawn to Washington on wings of numberless honors, often quoted in the press. Then something had gone wrong. What was it? Explanations, when offered at all, varied. Some of his approaches had been suspect, not what the upper echelons favored. He had married some Baltimore woman with lots of money, had a son who showed up at times, was separated though not divorced. If his house was cased in shadowy foliage, untrimmed, so was he. Sometimes he mentioned the son, though not the wife. "Wherever Phillip may be, I know he keeps a pure nature—curious, questioning, unafraid." But words like that answered no questions.

"He needs us," Mary had ventured to Jeff after an evening there.

Jeff went into one of his silences. "Never look down on him. He knows what he says. It holds up."

Mary threaded her way through the intricate ins and outs of what Ethan said. Catching the drift became a workout of mental skill. Ethan's comments about Kennedy, inside facts about the assassination, caused pond ripples of excitement, though he would always conclude frankly, saying that nobody would ever really know.

"His connections are the life stream of what he tells us," Jeff explained. "None of them are here, just that his lines lead out. Don't mention it, but he's considering setting up a paper, a flyer going out to people all over. There's a need for it. All the shit that passes for gospel truth."

"You mean nobody in Kingsbury cares?"

Out in air that day, walking. He threw an arm around her. "There's obviously all of us. But precious few besides," he added.

Mary reserved a silent right not to be any more interested in politics than time permitted. Yet she was giving time to Jeff, more than she had to anyone before.

It was true, too, that the genial untidiness, the weedy darkness of Ethan's home exuded a strange appeal. A man of no real-life ties, just thoughts and talk. His address on the side street, his flashlight through the dark to the gate, leading carefully lest they fall over something. Protective. Odd pieces of carved stone (his son Phillip had done sculpture early on and perhaps still did). The frequent insistent ring of his old-fashioned black phone, whose caller at that moment might be far away in any direction, or near as the corner grocery. The liver spots on hands that pressed her own, passed books around, poured out wine. The considerate voice asking if she meant to go into graduate studies.

"I want to stick with dancing. Find out if I'm good enough."

"She's great," said Jeff. (Twice he'd gone to classes with her, one that she even taught. He would sit on the floor and watch patiently from the corner: "Me dance? I was born with two left feet.")

"Greatness gets through," Ethan remarked.

Greatness is hard work, thought Mary. She sat listening to Jeff.

To pull him away from all this ought to be her purpose, she supposed, vaguely worried, but where would she pull him to? A life like her mother's? Or Jasper County? Ethan took no part in Kingsbury social life at all, and Jeff, it followed, wanted none, either. Jeff could have gone places with her if he wanted to. "Gotta wear a tie?" he would ask. It seemed he and Ethan, pupil and teacher, were floating above life, and only came down in it from time to time.

Even if she could change Jeff's orientation, she wondered if she wanted to. How Jeff loved the natural things around them! Not the people but the place. Paths through woods, side streets, the big park that was a bird sanctuary on the outskirts of town, where they sometimes went with sandwiches from an uptown shop. He liked side streets that went past strange poor houses, little parks and weedy waste places. He even liked the distant corners of the campus.

He would walk a little ahead of her, strong neck bent, long, light hair sagging forward, always getting his mind around something, like Ethan. She mocked his walk rhythm, the sidewise sling of one foot, toe barely pointed inward. He shook her when he caught her at it. "Stop that!" Wrestling her back against a tree or a wall, good at teasing, laughing, kissing.

But not at getting her worked up about politics. She would say she didn't understand it.

Just the stir of being with him was what she liked, even while she sat listening to how oil interests had been powerful enough to keep a crucial bill from coming before the House, and whatever related this to the pro-war hawk lobby, bypassing both the White House and the press, though the president, it was widely believed, not only knew but condoned. . . .

"Oh, hey," Jeff said now, when for the second time she rose to go.

"I'll just sneak out," she offered.

But he wouldn't let her; he wanted to go along.

6

Kate Waits

"So, going where?" Jeff asked her, driving his smelly old car. She'd told him before.

"It's just that birthday party for Mother's friend Annie Gibbs. At the club. You could have gone if you'd let me know."

"I don't go to clubs, I told you."

She jumped out at the gate, active and bouncy in air that was now even warm.

"You're not going to like it," he warned.

"I might." She did a spin around. "Change me to a princess, quick!"

"Oh, shit." He wouldn't look at her. He drove away.

Hurrying up the walk, Mary shifted back into Mary Kerr, transformed. Into the house, scrubbing at her cheek, as though his parting kiss had left a mark.

Voice from above. "Mary Kerr? You missed your fitting. I think the black and pink is what you ought to wear. Sally had to work without you, but she's good at guessing. Oh . . . Ron Bower's mother called. She says he wants to ask you to his frat party next week but he can't get up the nerve. Are you putting out the wrong messages?"

"Messages?" It was best not to think about her mother's coy phrases. "Just what 'messages' do *you* put out?"

"Nobody to put them out to, sweetie."

What a lie that was. She put them out, all right, but she would never talk as though she did. *Oh, George sent me that, he was such a friend of Don's. . . . Martin Jacob? Oh, we have to talk over some new orders at the lab. . . . He said, "Why not make it over dinner?" . . . Henry Wilson's from way up in the mountains, hardly knows anybody here but one or two classmates at Duke. . . .*

Mary Kerr often heard the late-night returns; the step in the hall as silent as Kate could make it, but not all that steady; the stealthy closing of the big front door. Once Kate fell over a chair. Mary Kerr lay debating whether to go and pick her up but didn't stir.

In addition, there were the evenings when nobody called and nobody came, and after a certain hour, the creak of the stair, the blundering toward the liquor cupboard, and the image flashed into her head of the long-fingered hand and the smartly designed label of the gin bottle, the slender glass, the crystal ice. Fashion motions in the dark.

Once Kate had described to Mary Kerr how she could see herself at times like one of the women in a Fitzgerald novel, wondered what a voice that "sounded like money" sounded like. Maybe money was all you needed to sound like that. She must have been half drunk when she opened up about that. Or did it have to do with wanting some dress-up thing for her daughter, something her daughter couldn't care less about having? Sacrifices!

Sometimes flowers came, and some few letters, masculine handwriting scrawled thick across the envelopes, but mainly there were the phone calls. On free afternoons, Kate Harbison would dress in her soft-colored silks with the sandals so neat and the stockings sheer, and in the corner on the chaise longue she would wait for somebody who just thought he might drop in for a drink, or who was out for a stroll or an after-dinner drive to visit a relative, happy to find her with the lamplight spinning its web, an aureole soft around her bright hair, put up so skillfully. She might have been on a stage, playing out this part written for her, or somebody in a book.

But I'm playing, too, Mary Kerr would think, upstairs studying, or upstairs trying to sleep in spite of the creaking and stumbling downstairs. Her breasts would swell and tingle to think of Jeff, or the actual one-time bruise he had given her at the start would wake again, not wanting to be lost. Not that she had "done anything" that summer in Jasper County when she would meet him in the dark of night, down by the creek, but just that he had pressed his hand into her there, sure and so quickly it surprised without shocking, turned her to softness and yearning without time to debate about being touched and not being touched. They had been sitting near the creek, talking, watching the flow of water, then he pushed her back and leaned closer. He taught her to open her mouth when she kissed. "Hold still," he would whisper, "you're a baby yet, I'd want you for my girl in a year or so. ... . You think you'd like that?" And then he'd say, "Put your arms up, just around my neck, and now pull down . . . oh, good . . . oh great. . . ."

And when she turned closer, he recoiling a little, she coming nearer, not knowing when she should or when she shouldn't, though of course she'd been told, *You have to wait for all that to happen when you're older and make sure you just always manage to stop.* But no one mentioned young bodies twining on the sand by the creek, or what Jeff would be like.

He had pushed her off suddenly, painfully . . . abruptly going away, returning to sit a short way off. "You're making it too easy. You know better, don't you?"

She had cried, "But it's just for you!" Why wouldn't he know that?

His short, hoarse laugh. *Now he won't like me,* she thought. But soon he pulled her up and kissed her cheek, gently, not like before.

"Come wade in the creek. There'd be snakes where I come from. Not here." They waded in the brown water. He held her hand. "The snakes here are human."

Her voice was pure distress. "You mean you don't like me?"

He laughed again, the hoarse short acknowledgment of his own feelings. "Of course I like you, baby. I like you too much."

He had led her home then, surprised to learn she'd had to slip out of the upstairs window, hadn't mentioned him to anybody. "Just always be over the fence, waiting for me." His last kiss was like the first, lingering and warm. He watched her climb the tree.

She'd never told anybody about all that. She hardly had girl friends at all. The talk they did got silly too quick, and they told on you. Would listen and then tell. So who was there to talk to? *Nobody,* she thought now, fierce and clutched up in the dark with her breast remembering his touch, tingling and swelling softly, grown bigger in the last two years, as he had noted, saying that was good. She didn't dare think how he knew so much. From Louisiana, a distant, slightly wicked land. *No way to talk about him, so I won't. I won't tell,* she thought.

What Mary Kerr didn't know was that Kate's longtime boss, Dr. Fletcher, had called her in for a fatherly chat. "Maybe the trouble is too much socializing," he had suggested. Her work, it seemed, was going slack. Just like that, Kate had dropped all the men she was seeing like rocks over the edge of a cliff, not even waiting to hear them hit. Drinking to cut down on. He hadn't said that, but she knew it. *I can't, I can't let go,* she had thought that very morning, whispering aloud, hands gripping the edge of her dresser. *Money . . . Mary Kerr . . . bills . . . job. . . .*

But Mary Kerr knew nothing of this.

Coming into the room, the girl found the black and pink organza lying spread out on the bed. "Put it on, honey, I'm dying to see how you look."

"I'm suffocating," Mary Kerr gasped, struggling with a mass of material. She emerged as though from swimming underwater, breathless. She hadn't torn anything, but everything hung crooked.

Her mother circled her, pulling and shaping. "It's supposed to hook at the waist . . . there."

Mary Kerr collapsed in a sprawl of it onto a bedroom chair. Behind her head, spirea bent from the rain was arching up once more in the twilit window. Her thin white arms were arched up, framing her head, the flushed cheeks, unpainted mouth, dark hair as careless as something in a wood, but so young and softly, uncaringly lovely, that Kate caught an honest breath and felt pride before she knew it.

"Messages," Mary Kerr was repeating. "You mean body language, all that stuff?"

Kate filed her nails. "Just try to be nicer to them. Ron's a sweet boy, and if he doesn't work out, you can meet others through him."

"You ought to know."

She said it lightly, and Kate replied, also lightly: "When it comes to social life, experience is all. You might need a little more of that, Miss Priss."

Why call me that silly name? Mary Kerr thought. *"Social life," my foot. She knows I go with Jeff, not with all those others. She's even met him, run into us uptown, sat three seats away in the movies, said hello again in the lobby. She ignores him.*

She stood to get buttoned up the back, each button covered with the same fine organza of the dress. Aunt Sally's good work. *Material sheer and wonderful, expensive even though we can't afford the best for me.*

Kate fastened the last button. Her pale arm reached up; her white hand, soft but firm, touched the deep wave in her hair that needed so little tinting to keep its fresh color. The best: L'Oréal.

"You were late. . . . Where did you go?"

"Oh, just bumming around town. I forgot."

"See anyone?"

"I can't remember. Oh . . . Nina Hawkins. Going to the movie."

"What movie?"

"I don't know. She was going, not me."

Silence. *Didn't you see me get out of Jeff's car just now?* Not said.

"Now turn around. Well, what do you think? Shall we call Sally and say it's perfect?"

"What are you going to wear?"

"Just my old blue and white. Everybody will recognize it, but it will do one more round. Nell Jenkins called. She said, 'With just a little more attention to herself, Mary Kerr could have won that beauty show last week in a walk.' I said, 'I don't want her in any beauty show.' Still, she meant well."

"Beauty queens must be the world's dullest. Tell her dance lessons every afternoon and Saturday morning is enough for anybody."

"Oh, the programs came! I forgot to tell you."

There they were, unnoticed on the dresser, enamelled cards in off-white, very good taste: *Advanced class in Ballet and Modern Dance, presented by Studies in the Dance, Inc., announces the following program: Brahms's "Variations," Ensemble . . . Solo performance, Odette, from* Swan Lake *Act II, Mary Kerr Harbison. . . .*

"I wanted to be just Mary Harbison. Couldn't they remember that?" *It's what Jeff calls me. He won't say Mary Kerr.*

"It seems not. Listen, honey, please understand. *I* didn't want you in any beauty contest. We can get that clear, can't we? Those girls who make a positive career of that sort of thing—I wouldn't have them." Cool hand beneath Mary Kerr's chin, tilting up the sometimes sullen face. "Who'd want a beauty queen in the house? I prefer my dancer."

I'm not your dancer, Mary Kerr wanted to say, but she smiled at the praise just the same. Maybe their bad days were over. *She's dying for a drink but hasn't had one. I'm dying to kiss Jeff but he isn't here. Our mother-daughter pas de deux . . . what's it all about? I can't hope for too much. The minute I think the worst is over, she changes. Quick as a flash.*

Which shoes? Which scarf? thinks Kate.

It's getting dark. . . . You couldn't afford this dress, plus the club dues. Let me go in blue jeans. I'll be a sensation. . . . Can't we turn on the lights?

7

Jeff Abandoned

Then came the time she left him; no more Jeff Blaise.

Kate had finally invited him to dinner, and that's what finished Mary Kerr with him. Though it didn't start out that way. It started out, in fact, with Mary Kerr more pleased than she'd been ever before, thinking her mother was ready to call a truce.

Jeff, too, had been amenable. "So the sacred doors will open wide. Do I bow and kiss the lady's hand?"

"You just act civilized," she said.

He came dressed as well as anybody had ever seen him, in a dark shirt with a button-down collar, a dark knit tie. And a jacket he must have borrowed, though it fit. It was a warm evening and he was urged to remove it.

Mary Kerr wore a sleeveless yellow and white dress and her mother had something on so similar they looked like sisters, as Jeff remarked. A good start. He had trimmed his hair a little, and tied it back with a narrow dark ribbon. He sat down in the living room like anyone might. He accepted a drink.

It was the night of the dance performance that he and Kate had faced off. It had happened backstage. Mary Kerr had dazzled them into acknowledging each other. Her silver headdress fitting low around her features, her eyes heavily outlined to mimic a swan's own, her tight heavy silk bodice sewn with pearls, and the white tutu sprinkled through with glistening threads—she seemed like someone else, a mythical creature, a body they could tell themselves they knew about, though not quite believing it. They stood back from her, the two most important people in her life, as though she were electric and if touched might knock them down. Then she rose on her point shoes and executed a practice turn, and they had to speak to bring their feelings level.

"I don't know that we'd know her if we didn't know her," was Jeff's way of putting it. The scarlet mouth, the fixed mask of eyes, the full circle she revolved.

"Would you like to sit by me?" Kate had asked.

So he had made it now to the living room and dinner. Jeff sat saying that Kingsbury was all right (he had been asked), not so hot here as the Louisiana country he'd come from. At LSU in the summer, studying had been close to impossible, with your brains fried during the day. Paper would stick to your arms.

"Where do you live?" Kate wanted to know.

"Over east of Royal's. I go out to the university, too, quite a lot. It's just a rooming house, but okay." He glanced at Mary Kerr.

Penney was serving them dinner. She'd come back just to help. A cold chicken curry, aspic with celery, sliced new potatoes with parsley, a dish of tomatoes, country red, with dressing. Chilled white wine.

"Tell us about your students," Kate invited.

"It's turnover time," Jeff said. "Some coming, some going, some staying put. I'm finishing up a doctoral dissertation, you know. Political science. Ethan Marbell's directing. Not much time for hanging out with the kids." He paused. "So not much to tell. What about your work? A table like this, it's hard to imagine you putting in hours somewhere."

Kate smiled. "Like you, I've not much to tell. To me, it's gotten routine. At home, I never think of it."

"I just can't imagine somebody like you into all that."

Mary Kerr barely kept herself from glancing up in alarm. ("I don't know all that much about her work." Over and over she had told him that. "No, she never talks about it at home. I think just having to do it at all makes her feel wrong about things. Poppy should have had more money, but then she—she loved doing science. But that doesn't mean it's bad. It doesn't!")

"I beg your pardon," Kate asked. Her fine eyebrows went up at him. Anybody else would have stopped right there.

"Well, just relying on animal experiments for research. Many a man would get squeamish. You must be really tough."

"What little we do is humane," Kate said. "Anyway, I'm not personally involved."

"Oh, I never meant you'd carve them up alive." He laughed rather like a bad boy discussing how he buried a cat alive, or peppered a stray dog with bird shot, only there was something abstract about his laughter.

"If you keep this up," Mary Kerr said, "we'll both have to stop eating dinner."

"Leaving everything for me." He turned the subject lightly to the food, how it was great. Then, "Sorry for thinking out loud. It's a fault."

Kate smiled weakly. "I guess that makes a good lecturer."

He could upset people without trying, Mary Kerr knew, but he actually colored, looked uncertain, and glanced at Mary Kerr as though to say he meant to be good.

One light subject followed another. The university, dancing, Royal's. Dessert. A pause.

Jeff said, "I think you probably didn't realize why I brought in the talk about animals. What's worrying us a little is the ones they are shipping in here by train at night. There's a government research contract let out here, undoubtedly. We haven't been able to locate it, let alone what they're doing exactly."

"Who is *we?*" Kate inquired.

"Oh, just nosy people like me, who like to know what's really going on in the country of their birth. Why take night for these shipments, getting them off the train when nobody is around? It's a question."

"I know nothing whatsoever about it," said Kate, who by now had poured more wine than she should have. Her tone gave away that she knew everything about it.

Mary Kerr's hands were cold. Things dating back to her kitten, other hints and words through the years. Things Poppy wouldn't converse about, though he had said she was into "noble" projects, cures for diseases that cursed the world. He had kept it general. In the car they had waited before the building on the north of town, those rare times she needed them to come for her. The concrete structure had few windows, was set down a slope reached by a walkway with graded steps, surrounded by shrubs. It was bigger than it seemed to be, for the walls extended a long way back. Mysteries.

Kate got a grip on herself. "Tell us more about Ethan. We don't see anything of him since he came back here."

"He's a terrific guy."

"Ethan was once a suitor—I guess that's an old-fashioned word, isn't it?—anyway, he was always going out with my sister-in-law, Mary Kerr's aunt."

"So I heard." Jeff laughed again. "Years and years of a kiss at the door and holding hands at the movies."

Kate was too relieved for words for a moment, and laughed with Jeff. "I never inquire into that side of things. But I strongly suspect that Ethan behaved like a gentleman."

"And Aunt Jane behaved like a lady," Mary Kerr chimed in, her giggle getting the laughter to prolong happily.

"Right down to the finish line," Jeff continued.

"They parted at the station," Kate went on, and wished she'd not mentioned the train station.

It went unnoticed, apparently. "No ground gained," said Jeff. "He went off to Princeton, with his broken heart."

They finished with their good humor regained out of Ethan's misery, and Penney took away the plates.

"Candlelight makes women look great," Jeff said. "In a room like this, you can forget about people dying . . . animals. . . ."

Another silence. Yet he did, once again, seem just to be thinking aloud.

"I have told you—" Kate began angrily. She broke off. "Let's have some coffee in the living room. It's not candlelight, but maybe we won't look too bad, Mary Kerr and I."

"You'd be great anywhere," Jeff answered gallantly. He pushed back his chair. On the way into the living room, Kate leading, he pinched Mary Kerr on the behind. "How'm I doing?"

"Awful. Stay off the animals," she whispered. "Mother can't help it."

"She doesn't want to," he whispered back.

They had their coffee, with Kate holding the floor about Mary Kerr's lessons with poor Madame Delida, who had gotten mixed up with some very ordinary boy half her age until his wife showed up out of nowhere and raised an enormous hurrah.

"I never knew that!" Mary Kerr exclaimed.

"She worshipped Mary Kerr," Kate continued. "I began to worry about that, too, as you can imagine."

"So?" Jeff inquired.

"I called a halt. Now there's this Al Bernstein. He's a slave driver, a perfectionist. Kingsbury is a catchall town. People blow into it out of nowhere."

"Like me," Jeff said idly. He obviously didn't care what Kate thought.

He did not linger.

At the door, he said to Kate, "If you should come across the lowdown on those dog shipments, pass the word along, will you?"

"Of course," said Kate, polite to a fault.

When she closed the door, she leaned against it. Tired and showing it, though she wouldn't say just how intense the strain had been. Head back against the door, she looked down wearily at her daughter.

"Attractive, of course. He's obviously that. But what a gadfly. Ethan's cloned him, I would say. What good do these people do? All they create is worry."

"But Mother—" Kate had flirted with him in that subtle mute way she had. Couldn't help it. "Mother?"

Kate was already moving up the stairs, slipping off her bracelets, drawing the skillfully hidden pins from her hair. When she turned, her hair fell shimmering, as though on cue, around her shoulders. "You were made to have the very best, darling. Nothing less will do."

"He's not less, Mother."

"I think you'll see."

Drama over, Kate exited above.

"You let them lead you around by the nose," Jeff complained. "All that polite talk, and the dinner table. Just so nicey-nice." He was seated with her on a low wall at the far corner of the Royal's campus, a spot they favored. "Now trying to fit me in, aren't you? It won't work."

Mary Kerr sat up straight and bitter with stinging eyes. The gray stone for the first time felt hard. "There is nothing wrong with eating dinner," she said. (She had heard Kate on the phone. "Oh, to me he's still very young. You know that kind of idealism. Mary Kerr thinks he's an 'older man.' I do believe she's about ready to drop him. She stays busy, of course. All that dancing.")

"You don't see that I have to be what I believe in," Jeff continued. "Not part-time, not here and there, but all the time."

"But suppose I'm not all that worked up about what you believe. Do you think I have to be anyway?"

"I think you could let yourself see what I mean."

"I told you before. I'm aesthetic."

"You learned a big word."

"I'm just as smart as you. Don't think I'm not."

Silent and hunched over for a time, he then turned to her. "Come home with me. I want you to. Now."

She meant to, she knew that. But it never seemed quite the time. It wasn't the time now, with feelings so crossed up.

"Maybe you ought to find somebody who thinks the same as you."

She'd said this before, but he'd shoved the thought aside. Now he stared at her fiercely, eyes at their bluest. "I love you," he said, so blunt it sounded cruel.

He got down from the wall and walked away.

For days she fought back every sort of wildness, including tears. She went back to her oldest phrase: *I'll dance it out.* Sometimes it even worked, or seemed to.

At other times she argued with herself. *Obviously, Mother is pleased, smooth as silk, purrs like a cat. Got her way. I can't start going to bed with anybody like him.*

But at other times she'd say to herself, accusing, *'Fraidy cat, weren't you?* And couldn't deny it was true.

8

Jeff

So she let him back into the night he'd come out of, a fish slipping into bayou-dark water, a night bird careening off into the shadows. Yet he did have his own history, like anyone else. Jefferson Blaise.

He had been born north of New Orleans, south of Baton Rouge, a little to the west of both. His mother's father had inherited an old indigo plantation, but the market for the dye had dried up long ago, and nothing else he ever raised there had much luck. Jeff's grandfather then sold the land and put the money from it in a small investment firm in Baton Rouge during the thirties, depression times, but oil coming in, the feel of really getting ahead. Alignment on the wrong side of Huey Long was what he blamed for going broke in the late thirties. Oh, the good times, suddenly gone. Jeff's uncles had left for Texas. Jeff's mother, in desperation, found his father. He was an out-of-state-born executive of a Louisiana oil company, all too soon to be broken in turn by a suit brought to contest legitimate rights to property his company had developed. Twice now Jeff's mother had had to see it happen. It seemed to take the life out of her.

His father became a seeker of small jobs in accountancy, had few friends, and found himself unable to converse with a son everyone was speaking of as brilliant, promising. When he had more to drink than usual, he would say to himself, *I'm going to call him in and explain everything*. Sometimes he did just that. But nothing was really explained.

From the early days they had lived in a large old house on the southern outskirts of town. It was white and just missed having that aspect of splendor valued in those parts. The lot was heavy with live oaks. The summers grew numb with steady heat.

When Jeff was ten he woke one night to find his room on fire. The fire started in the kitchen, they later assumed, and had spread toward Jeff's room on the ground floor. He raced out, yelling, "Fire!" His parents, upstairs, rushed down, the neighborhood sprang up to help them, and half the house was saved. A half house: They lived in that, two bedrooms above, a new, always makeshift-looking kitchen installed, one "gracious" room remaining to them, which his mother called "the library." Here, his father would draw the curtains, put out whiskey on a mahogany table left from better days, set out a crystal glass, pour a drink, and begin to "explain everything" to his son, who sat and listened quietly. In the dining room a cupboard with a glass door still held some good china and crystal and a few large pieces of silver, unused and tarnished. Upstairs, the rooms had high, shadowy ceilings. One was filled with boxes, crates of stuff salvaged from the burned half, a sewing machine, a dress model.

In the years before she died, Jeff's mother all but lived in an armchair, covered by a quilt, wearing some fragile blouse or other. "Affluence," his father would say, drawing up his chair to a table of cracked dishes, but with his napkin still waiting in a heavy silver ring. "It's affluence she misses." And she, dressed as well as she could for the ritual of dinner, would come in from the kitchen, smiling weakly, with a smoking dish in either hand. She was not at all a bad cook.

They managed to send Jeff to college, with some borrowing. During his first year there his mother died. Pneumonia with complications—she was not strong enough to start with to fight it out.

"It's a hard life, boy," his father said, sitting in the library with the curtains drawn, taking the bourbon down. He lifted an earnest hand. "It's such a hard life." Untrimmed mustache streaked with gray. Bright wet eyes. He must have been handsome once.

"You know that word *affluence?*" Jefferson Blaise asked Mary Harbison years later in North Carolina.

"I know it's what Mother likes," she said, and they both laughed.

"Being only children . . . it makes us alike," he noted.

They were walking a campus path through fine fall air. The leaves showed a wild range of orange and red.

He was older, a teaching assistant, a favored student. Why would she, only a freshman, be the one he'd settle on, except for that time out in Jasper County, or the very long-ago tie of Aunt Jane to Ethan Marbell? She found ways to ask him.

"Did you know I'd be here, when you took the teaching job?"

"I had some faint idea. I didn't ask around, though. I knew I hated letting you go. But then you did go, left. . . ." The word hung in the air, hovering, pain in its wings.

They were in a booth uptown after a movie. He coaxed her into trying some beer.

"I've never liked it."

"Try anyway. Get used to new things." Now he was teasing again.

He made reference to the two years past, had been at Michigan, then out in Berkeley. Disturbances drew him. He'd joined the student movement in Ann Arbor, not just a name on a list, but a serious worker.

She was innocent of why he would, so asked "Why."

He wanted her to know. "I think it dates back even before Ethan, back to when I first read, saw pictures and couldn't stop until I saw it all. The nuclear thing is what I mean. What we did. Take Germany. Okay, they slaughtered the Jews. A stinking horror. But when we do it to the Japanese . . . why, we're great victors, glorious winners. Read about it sometime. Eyeballs melting like wax, skin dissolving before your eyes. Not somebody else's skin . . . yours. Suppose you were dancing, a long, floating step, and wham! You'd be lucky to die."

"It was a war and it's over. Anyway, I couldn't help it."

"Well, just don't ever be proud of it. You're not drinking your beer."

"I'll try." She did try.

"You're sweet," he said, catching her eyes, then looking off. "Not one of those damned silly 'belles.' In Louisiana they even go in for hoop skirts. Crap like that."

She put down the beer.

"You're always in training, aren't you?" he went on, speculating. "Everyone's got some passion going. That's yours for now—dancing. Mine's obvious: politics. Ethan, now . . . he stumbled on this plan up in Washington. Supposed to be secret, classified, but he came across it in the files. Ethan was in a 'think tank' on civil defense. Attached to the Executive Office, the president himself, pretty high up. Later they shifted him to one of the Army Department bureaus.

He was into dreaming up what to tell people to think in case of enemy attack. Shaping the public mind. Can you beat it? The theory is, nobody knows what they think; they have to be told what it is. The media will handle it. Relax, you will be told.

"In the process of this sort of work in government offices, he had access to files and he came across it. A contingency plan. You know what that means?"

She nodded. He had a way of not looking at her when he was talking this way, of cocking one knee up and looking out across it toward the opposite wall, meeting no eyes at all.

"What it contained was what might be called 'the final solution' in Vietnam. Just start dropping the things. Why not? They've improved models since the first, and we might as well try them out. So we kill, maim, wipe out, erase several million little Orientals. We've all gone to the Colosseum for the afternoon. We're in there cheering for the lions."

Intense. They said that about Ethan.

"I can't help any of that," she said, and felt uneasily that they ought to go home.

"We all can help a little. And we're going to. We're working at it, anyway." He leaned back and smiled. "I'm scaring you. Boring you. This strange guy you met." At least he knew what she felt. Out on the street, walking to his car, he put his arm around her. "Don't worry. I may not be here too long. My draft date is just delayed till I get this dissertation done."

"Oh!" She was startled. "Then what? You've got to go out there, to the war?"

"Big decisions waiting." They had gained the car and gotten in. He leaned over and brushed her hair back to kiss her forehead. "Don't bother your pretty head." That was mocking; the kind of people who said that were those he couldn't stand. He was like that.

In the student union, they ate hamburgers for lunch, drank Cokes through a straw. "You know those people I was with out in Jasper County? The first time we met? Two of them got killed. Did you know that? Those folks you're kin to. Stir them up and blood can flow."

"You don't know that!"

"I practically do."

"You shouldn't say it unless you all the way know it."

And thinking her mother tortured live dogs to help the war along. Well, he was always worrying her. It was getting to be too much to dance away.

She let him go, back into the dark with all his darkness. Staying with him meant that dark would creep in on everybody. So why not just stop caring?

"It's not a bad loss," said Kate. "Next he'll start dropping acid and following rock bands."

She passed him on the campus from time to time.

9

The Reverend Ashley

Nearly a year later, Mary Kerr, on a spring afternoon, was working in the garden at Grace Episcopal Church. It was a student group project, but she had come much too late to join the others, because of her dance class. There was still a lot to do, and she was down on her knees with a trowel, working the soil, turning the mulch for the roses. Getting hotter. Working alone.

She straightened to look around her, and there around the corner of the church came Jeff Blaise. He was carrying a spade he must have just found leaning against the wall of the church offices, which were tacked on to the back of the main structure. Seeing her, he gave a grin he couldn't help.

How to act around him? He had been in jail once, for blocking the campus appearance of somebody high in the Department of Defense. So she just said before she thought, "Out of jail?"

"Obviously." He lifted the spade. "Thought I'd help."

Again she said the first thing she thought of. "But you're a Catholic." Later she wondered why she'd said it. She knew next to nothing about Catholics, there were so few around. It was just the differences between them that she was hitting on. The gaps there were no bridges for.

"Maybe you can convert me."

Long ago she'd told herself it was mainly just attraction she'd felt for him. Nobody else had made her feel excited the way he did. She turned away now because she was feeling like that again. Sex was making its crazy attack. Of course, he'd come there to find her.

"Mary?"

The slant of his tone told her that he was into some need that wasn't about sex at all. She listened.

"I—I finished my dissertation yesterday, turned it in. The dissertation . . . you remember. It's done."

"Then you'll be Dr. Blaise." It had a strange sound, said aloud.

"Ethan's the director, backing it, of course. I'm afraid that will be a strike against it these days."

She tried remembering what he'd told her. The subject was something about U.S. policy involving Germans after the war. Secret documents withheld, but others found. Ethan working hard at getting crucial material declassified. Walking a tightrope. Danger.

She realized something. "He told you I was here." Ethan was a sometime friend and confidant of Reverend Ashley. Ideas exchanged . . . religious biases. "No organized church will take any stand at all worth taking . . . you realize that." She'd been present when Ethan had said that, speaking of Reverend Ashley.

"I've been wanting to track you down anyway. Just to touch base, I guess. . . . I'm sorry if you mind."

"I don't guess I do." She sat down beside him on a large granite memorial stone, something with a brass plaque with an inscription on its side.

Jeff looked at what he carried. "I even found a shovel." He didn't seem to find it real.

"Well, use it," said Mary, and went back to work. "Pile the straw around. Here."

Spadeful at a time, he dutifully heaped straw where she told him to. Farther on, there were irises to be thinned, bloomed out and withered on their stalks. Flats of verbena sat waiting to be turned out and planted. It would take another day or so.

"When'd you get so religious? I never knew—"

"Being good these days, I guess. Work . . . I like it, though. Something besides dance practice."

What were they talking about? Nothing seemed to the point. Looking up at him was like stepping on quicksand, so she didn't. Then she did. His face looked strained under the sweat the sun was drawing out of him. "Mary. . . ." He touched her hair. It had turned darker brown from the hot work, the sweat. Hand on her arm. Currents running. She pulled off. "I'm not going back to you. Just not."

He spaded fiercely at some azalea roots. "I heard you got engaged."

"Don't be silly. Just dated Ron Bower for a while."

"Suit and tie type, I guess."

"I guess."

"What was wrong with him?"

"I don't know. He couldn't dance." She just said that on impulse.

"Unforgivable sin. Neither could I. Did you sleep with him?"

"No." She trampled the mixed dirt around the roses. *Why didn't I like him?* she wondered. *Maybe he wasn't strange enough.*

"Doing our gardening," Jeff said, "just like Adam and Eve."

"Natural thing to do," said Mary.

"They'll put us in a stained-glass window. Next we can grind corn and grow sweet potatoes. You can have a little papoose strapped to your back. Hiccups if you dance."

"Dig over there." She pointed, laughing in spite of herself. He was funny when he could forget all those causes.

Along the border of the flagstone walk that led from the back of the church toward the border of dark cedars some few yards away, Jeff forced the spade into ground that yielded from last year's planting. The annuals would go there. When the path reached the cedars that bordered the cemetery back of the church, it divided, spreading out into a maze, wandering every which way among the gravestones.

"If I wasn't here," said Jeff, "I'd be gnawing my nails and counting off calendar days, waiting."

"I'm sure it'll be okay. Doesn't Ethan think so?"

"Ethan's just the trouble. You know how radical they consider him."

"Then why did you—" She stopped. She couldn't probe into that relationship. Her body hummed with his presence. It wasn't fair.

At that point the back door of the church, which led to the rector's office and the Sunday school rooms, opened. The rector himself, Mr. Ashley, came out and stood on the steps. He seemed to be looking out at them but not seeing them. It was known to some but not all the congregation that in the years just past he had marched in Georgia, ridden a Freedom Riders' bus through Mississippi, gotten thrown in jail in Montgomery. But now, having settled down to pastoral work, he did not find it necessary to discuss such things. No need, either, to talk about his wife, who had recently left him, run off, the gossip went, with another woman. Mr. Ashley was "not well." His face seemed a covering for his whole life; but more than a barricade, it often became a plea for understanding in spite of it all.

Mrs. Ashley, he had explained, had not "been well," either; she needed a rest.

Mary Kerr, since the spring term began, had her own room now, out near the university. It was what all her age group were doing. Several lived in the same house, girls away from parents. Once, back in February, she had come home unannounced for some books. Her mother's car was there. When she entered, a door closed out back. Who had just left? Who was walking rapidly out past the garage, entering the next property, hurrying out a neighbor's driveway to another street where (maybe) a car stood parked? Important enough for Kate to steal an hour or so from work to meet . . . who? Did it have to matter who?

Mary Kerr could have remarked now that the roses were looking better satisfied. She mixed earth and straw while Mr. Ashley stood watching.

"What's he doing?" Jeff asked, noting the smooth cut of the shovel blade in the earth, the fall of the soil.

"I guess he's thinking," Mary Kerr said.

"If he can stand to," Jeff said, one of his puzzle remarks. Whether he knew about Mr. Ashley's problems or had church people in general in mind, she didn't know.

The rector seemed to come to himself, emerge from a private reverie. He was coming toward them.

He was thin, stooped a little, neither young nor old, just strained-looking with a hesitant, groping sort of hopefulness. Would they, in addition to doing something good, also *be* good?

"I can't tell you how much it's appreciated, this volunteer effort you're putting out for us."

The two young people—so trim, compact, their every motion a realized lyric or phrase of music—straightened to regard him. Hair long, male but long, worn as a proud badge of a singular moment. (Had not Mr. Ashley, too, gone bearded and shouting down a street toward leering men with bats and truncheons waiting? What had it come to? Some positive good, a step along the way?) He thought they had not heard him.

The young man said, "It's fucking hot work, you know, Reverend."

The girl's sidelong glance let it out that nobody talked like that to a minister.

But Mr. Ashley had often heard the like before. "I'm sure," he answered mildly. He came toward them, reaching out. "Here," he said to Jeff. "I'll just spell you for a while."

Mary was kneeling again. She separated the verbena plants by pulling them gently apart, setting them upright on the lawn by the flagstone walk to the cemetery.

Jeff, with a comical little bow, handed the spade to Mr. Ashley.

The sun bore down. A band of sweat nudged past Jeff's cheekbone, then trickled slowly down to his chin. He sat down on the stone bench and lit a cigarette. Mary knew that if he had had a joint he would have lit that—that he had thought of it, would have dared. Glitter that was more than half desire swam before her eyes, calling persistently to mind the performances that waited behind lofty velvet curtains, in halls like gleaming showcases, while jewelled women and men in dress suits searched out their seats. *Mary Harbison, a promising new recruit from, et cetera, danced a brief but enchanting solo. . . .* Her mind halted there, *pointu.*

It was then that the Reverend Mr. Ashley collapsed on the grass.

The terrified call from the parish office to the hospital, the ambulance, the arrival at the emergency room. . . . Later, Mary and Jeff waited, and at last the doctor entered. "Are you his relatives?"

"Why, no, just up there at the church garden when he fell. We were planting some flowers."

"It was nothing but a heatstroke. First hot day. He seems pretty stressed, anyway . . . something personal. You could have just taken him into the vestry. Anywhere to lie down awhile."

"I said that," Jeff said, "but she'd called you by then." He shrugged.

"I got scared," said Mary. "Because my father—he died with a stroke. A hot day like this brought it on."

"He's dressing," said the doctor. "Can you take him home?"

Jeff got up suddenly. "My car isn't fit for that. Call him a taxi." He pulled Mary to her feet. "We'll just go on."

Their route took them by her mother's house, still far from where he lived.

"Let me out," she told him. He had her hand.

He drove to the curb, stopping, but held on to her. "Come with me, Mary. I never wanted you to go, not ever. Make it just today. I need you."

She wanted to. Too much. Everything in her head was scrambling up. Everything had red in it. In one twisting pull, intensely strong, she broke his hold. She jumped like a squirrel, cleared free of the car, landed, and ran toward the house.

Poppy. She was thinking of him, and that awesome day. Poppies were red like blood, and he'd turned fiery red, not chalky pale like Mr. Ashley.

In the church office Mr. Ashley had listened when she went to talk to him one day. "I'll be a father to you, as much as you'll let me, Mary Kerr. But can't we risk talking with your mother, too? You worry that her work is 'horrible,' as you put it, but don't these findings help us all? Disease must go, don't you think? She may be saying nothing but the truth. Can't we all just talk about it?"

Later Mary Kerr ventured to ask. But Kate refused. "What does he know? Of course I'm telling the truth. I'm tired of telling you so. Go on and think a lot of lies."

Mary Kerr came slowly up the steps to the door. Looking up the street, she could see where their old house stood, the walk where she had danced up the grassy slope on the side, the steps he had stumbled to. She opened the door.

"Mary Kerr?" The voice, silvery and inquiring, floated down from the second floor. "Mary Kerr, is that you?"

"Yes, it's me. Something at the church. I was helping out in the garden and . . ."

Her mother appeared in a long, loose robe at the top of the stairs. The white banister, the fall of the stair carpet, like something royally laid down for her. A dramatic woman. Her hair loose and the silver-mounted brush in one loose-skinned white hand where the blue vein snaked upward. She had been brushing, loving her hair, seated at her mirror. "I hear the rector took a tumble." She laughed, a hoarse little chuckle. Around hospitals and labs—backstage, you might call it—injuries and alarms, chronic sufferers, carved-up dogs, crucified cats, all might just cause some little joking.

"Yes, he did." But how did Kate know about it? She couldn't be everywhere.

"Betty Mason was up at the church, working in the kitchen. She saw the ambulance. He's back now. False alarm."

"Well, I know. I got frightened about it. Took fright too soon, I guess."

Kate was turning back to her own room. Mary Kerr began to mount the stairs. Kate moved toward her own bedroom, the perfumed dressing alcove, the mirror.

"Guess you thought you'd killed another one."

Silvery, the voice floated back to Mary Kerr. Like a chill silver blade, it went straight through her, heart and all. Her feet froze heavy as ice to the floor. Had this been said? She said "What?" but only a whisper came out, and that a faint one. "What did you say?"

"I said I guess you thought it was serious."

"No . . . you said something else. I heard you."

But she believed she had heard that other thing—she knew it. *What right does she have to say that?*

Kate came out once more, no brush in hand, reaching back over her shoulder, gathering her hair in one hand, swirling it with the other. "So that boy is back, is he? Betty didn't know who it was, but when she described him, I knew it must be—"

"Jeff, you mean. I don't see him." She stood there, slight but planted, flexible legs bowed back, stubbornly set. "He came there himself. I don't see him anymore. I told you."

A toss of Kate's hair with an unbelieving hand.

"Mother! I *don't!*"

No answer. She was not believed.

Then: "I'm going out to dinner. If you want to stay here, there's some cold shrimp in the fridge. A salad, some Jell-O whip. . . . I don't know what you want." Turning back. "Your sheets are fresh."

"Mother, why—"

"Why what?"

"You'll never admit that I say anything that's true, that I tell what's so."

"How can I know, darlin'?"

"Because I say so."

No answer. *Do I plead, beg, lie on the floor until she steps over me on her way to get out her dress before she heads out to be greeted, take drinks, be complimented, settle in to discussing the real business of life with people who matter?* "Oh yes Mary Kerr is still dancing you think she's talented, well, I suppose so if they all say so. . . ." Talented, but what does she matter, except to be a credit or a worry to them? *They* matter.

"Now, you listen, Mary Kerr. . . ." The voice came floating out to her. *No nonsense out of you, Mary Kerr.*

Mary Kerr never reached her own room. She knew, standing there in the hall, that her feet would not move her forward. Her feet, so quick and accurate, leading and leaping, rising and falling, bending, pointing, flexing—now they were talking to her: They were saying what they would not do. *Don't forget before you go,* Mary Kerr thought, *I've been struck with that very silver hairbrush. I've been locked up with no shrimp or Jell-O whip or clean sheets, either, but we papered over it, but just now you tore all that paper off, you left the raw wall bare and ugly, and you're going to sit there purring like a crouched silky silvery pale blue-gray cat, waiting for the next live animal—poor little white mouse or daughter—to come squirming up out of the cage into your hands, you poised and ready, winding up for a year two years or half a lifetime just to say again what you said just now, that I was the one who killed him, when he was all I loved.*

Time to find the Reverend Mr. Ashley, right away, and say, *I know, I understand what's meant by eternity. It's what goes on forever, can't ever unhappen.* She'll go on with the same idea forever because she can't undo the what-was of Poppy and me, the way we loved each other, the way we were the same kind. But then she realized: *It's no use talking to Mr. Ashley. Not anymore.*

Her feet were already taking her on.

The feet were walking precisely, rhythmically, surely, knowing things. Left and right, heel barely to touch, weight passed to arch, then ball, the angle a barely visible spread, the rhythm passing left to right and back, out of her mother's house, taking her to the steps and porch of the house where the room she lived in was: upstairs— a quiet privacy of bed and closet, books and barre.

There was a letter in the hall, her name on it:

I waited for you to come but had to go out. I had to call your mother again about the rent. She says she can't keep the room on for you. You can stay awhile if you want to. She wants you to call her.
Sylvia Peters.
P.S. I'm sorry if you wanted to stay.

The landlady. *Oh, I know it's the second or third time I spent the rent money, but this time I needed point shoes and she just let me have this room anyway because she thought Ron Bower and I were pairing off. But now that she thinks that Jeff is back—*
I can't go back there. I cannot go back where she is.

She looked down at her feet. *Where do you want to go?* she all but asked aloud.

They knew already, and they went.

Jeff Blaise had a room high up, two flights of stairs, an old building turned graduate residence, chopped up into makeshift apartments. General shabbiness, but a good view. Jeff seldom stayed in it and might have gone to any number of places that day after she jumped out of his car.

Demonstrations. They had been springing up from one corner of the city to another, bursting out on the main streets, hampering traffic, delaying schedules on both campuses. The waiters in the cafeteria had struck, out at the university. At Royal's, the office help turned out with placards, to be photographed as against the war in Vietnam. Who was stirring up these things? "Outside agitators"? A question in Harbison circles. But, it was said now, they didn't have to come from outside—not anymore.

Jeff Blaise was usually at work. He had come home that day to be in full concourse with the chill hand now insistently closing. The committee judging his dissertation was no pushover for political protest. His work was at that moment hitting a stone wall. The boomerang from it would strike Ethan. They would mean it to do just that.

He could have taken an innocuous subject, evoking dispassionate judgment, certain approval. Then moved with a calm step toward high employment, openings abounding, straight A's and solid recommendations leading to a real "career." How much could anyone afford to scorn? His loyalty at stake for the one man who mattered to him—that very loyalty had done him in. But his own convictions, too. They were bound to surface sometime. He couldn't welsh on them.

Distracted, he hadn't closed his door. It stood ajar. He heard a running step on the stair and turned. A girl he knew from the ground floor frequently came up to his room unannounced, but never ran.

Then she was standing there. Mary.

"Why, baby!"

She looked pale, out of breath. "I can't go back to her. I can't."

Stopwatch. The game, so long going on, was done. They both knew it. He circled her quietly, not touching her. Closing the door.

"You've thought about it?"

She stepped right into his arms, pulled close, held. "About you? Thought about you? I've thought myself blind. I've done nothing but think."

She was pulling at him, urgent. They fell across the tumbled bed.

"Wait now." He soothed her, stroking her hair. The many times he'd wanted her there now seemed like echoes, long distant, even the "her" someone else. Every path seemed uncertain now, losing itself in undergrowth. "I may not pass," he said.

"Pass? Oh, that. I was just thinking of us. You told me once that's all I needed—"

"I know. Right now, it might be different."

"Why?"

"Because there's nothing sure for me ahead. You'll have to be my girl, just that. Only that. Nothing more, for now. Girls like you think about marrying. It can't be that way."

She struggled with his shirt and broke a button. "It's okay. It's good enough."

His voice seemed to come from far off. Her blouse, stained with dirt from the churchyard, was open, fallen back, and there lay the small braless breasts, biscuit flat, then tightening, vulnerable as two small woods creatures, exposed to sudden light.

She looked down, as though newly seeing herself, ribs lean as a dancer's would have to be, knowing that he knew them already from moving hands so surely when they kissed, and kissing almost the same now, but hands moving down farther than ever before, finally touching her, herself: the center of desire.

Then, in a strained whisper, he said, "You want to, don't you?"

"Yes." With deliberate care he ran a thumb across where the bruise had been, that long time ago by the creek. Did he remember? How could he not? "Oh, yes!"

He was skillful and quick. Clothes going off. Then there and near above her, with all the strangeness about him. One hand with its slight endearing tremor stroked dark hair back from her brow. Kissing her mouth in the old, wet, tender way, then her eyelids, something new.

"Just be still, relax . . . right . . . yes. You know already, sure you do, baby. Right . . . good. . . ."

The curious motion, odd pain driving slowly in, then harder, building.

Like a green leaf torn from its bough, she was clinging to what drove her, clinging and trembling, losing the trembling but not the clinging, wrapped around and holding, wanting never to drop away.

10

Marionettes

"Perhaps I did what I shouldn't have," said Ethan Marbell. He was harking back to two days earlier at the churchyard, to how Jeff had homed in there on Mary. "I had learned by coincidence that you, Mary Kerr, were up there . . . gardening, of all things. Was that right?"

She nodded.

"We're saying Mary now," said Jeff, his voice proud. "This Mary Kerr girl is gone with the wind."

"Very well—Mary." Ethan tamped his pipe and lit it with a curious, tube-shaped lighter. "George Ashley. He had called me for the first time in weeks. He had been thinking over his wife's disappearance, growing more reconciled. *Reconciled* is one of George's favorite words. He mentioned that he was even going out to help with the garden that day. He said this really fine little girl, a dancer, was out there. She had started to attend church as well. I heard *dancer* and asked her name. 'One of the Kingsbury Harbisons,' he said. 'Members on the roll, but quite unseen except for Miss Jane. Young people are the hope of the world,' said George. Jeff was here and I told him."

They sat without speaking. Ethan had drawn back the blinds. It was a dark night. The air conditioner purred.

"I was playing God, I suppose. Maybe He'll forgive me."

"Provided God gave a fart in a whirlwind," Jeff said. His manner, superior and contained, came singularly from his triumph with Mary. He knew now—ninety percent sure—that his dissertation would be rejected. Two years earlier, in a political climate less wrought up than now, he'd had difficulties getting his proposal approved. He had barely squeaked by. Ethan's prestige, laid on the line to keep the dissertation's hope of passage alive. Ethan had warned Jeff to turn back more than a year ago. He wouldn't.

Mary passed a joint back to Jeff, only one tiny puff taken. Jeff held it out to Ethan, who shook his head. "What to do now?" Ethan pondered.

He asked about Mary's latest program. *Coppelia,* she said. Little he knew about it. But he would dutifully attend. They both would. She sat on the floor in lotus position, a loose shirt, hair pushed back.

"Buddha as a little boy." Ethan smiled fondly.

Jeff, deep in a chair, was also deep in thought about his own prospects, one sockless ankle at rest on his knee. Ethan stared at his mottled windowpane as though seeing some dim shape forming outside. A war in the Orient, he once said, would cast its Oriental shadow, turn the world secretive and smiling and utterly cruel. "We're going to publish it as a book, you know. It won't be lost if I can help it."

"And get ourselves into a suit with the government." Jeff was doubtful. "All that classified stuff they wanted to take back. It would take the guts out of it."

"Maneuvering will be necessary," Ethan admitted. "I won't give up. It's brilliant work," he added. He rose to answer the door, where a rush of coming feet had stopped, along with voices, now rising again as the newcomers rang the bell and knocked.

Out of the dark they came in like a blocked stream through a spillway, the young crowd who followed Ethan's thoughts, a soft invasion. Greetings, news spilling out, laughter. Freely into the kitchen with boxes of chicken, french fries, pizza, beer, wine, and gossip. They wore their proud denim rags and talked a whirling language and belonged together. One of Mary's dance group was among them, but they hardly spoke of it. It was almost another identity here, another planet.

Trailing in a short time later, in nubby sweaters and aged skirts or unpressed corduroys, some of the older group, Ethan's age. A mingling. Word brought from distant places. Projects. Daring. Numbers. The latest escalation in the war. Berkeley. Madison. Port Huron. SDS. The Movement.

Mary hugged her knees and listened. Since the day she came to

Jeff, she gave in to feeling free. But she groped, too, for something that was gone—Kingsbury and its walls were melting down on every side. Jeff had talked to her with serious patience. If you were really to be free, there was always a price. So was there any return she wanted? She sat wondering. *I'm eighteen,* she thought, and sometimes it seemed young, sometimes old.

Then there was Ethan calling them both aside—Ethan not having to be told that things had taken a turn for them. Into his own room, privately. Sitting them down on the side of his bed, a cheap candlewick spread pulled smoothly up, books sprawled out on the bedside table. Saying, "They came earlier than I thought they would. It's the recent escalation, Johnson out to win it, Texas style. Everyone's worried. Aside from all that, I was about to tell you something. Mary, you may know it already. There's this dancer due to teach at Winston this summer. Manning. You must know about him."

"Not Art Manning!"

"That's it. I thought Bernstein might have told you. If Jeff loses out here, I could work him in there for the summer. I've a strong connection. You dancing, Jeff teaching." His frail warm face, softening at these thoughts. Still romantically thinking back to Aunt Jane, maybe.

"If only I could," Mary said, thinking, *I'll have to go through Mother. No way around that.* "And Manning's in modern, not ballet. Strictly speaking I'm an inch too short for ballet, at the very least. Unless Balanchine falls for me and doesn't care. But I want to move to modern."

How would she get an audition? She thought that if she could, Manning would be bound to see how good she was. And no threats from her mother about it being too far away.

She walked out with Jeff in the fresh air, the spring night. It had somehow gotten to be nearly three. By a corner streetlight, he turned her around, letting the soft yellow light fall on her drained face. "Are you coming back with me?"

Where to go? She'd crept into her old room late for the past two nights, knowing she had to be somewhere she could explain. Dreading a showdown.

"Where's the car?" They'd lost it, but they found it again off on a side street. Too sleepy to decide anything, they crawled inside it, gypsylike, treating it like something found, renewing identity in the smells of old upholstery stuffing and oil from the gearbox, the sagging imperfect closing of the door on the passenger's side. They fell against each other, straight into sleep.

Mary woke at daylight. The way she started talking right away let her know that she had decided a good many things in her sleep.

"We're going in there and act innocent, innocent as lambs. We're going to say we didn't mean to wake up Mother, that Ethan took us in and we stayed with him till it got so late; then we just waited out the night in the car. We just hold hands and kiss, okay? We drink a beer sometimes, we smoke one or two cigarettes a day. What's pot?"

"She wasn't born yesterday, not that woman."

"She can be awful to me, she can be just wonderful, butter wouldn't melt. But you never know. You just never know."

"Jesus." He was muggy with sleep and needed a shave. "I think you ought to walk out. Just like that."

"I can't do it even if I do it. Dying is the only leaving."

"I left. I'm not dead."

She thought about the father he mentioned sometimes. Was he dead, or simply left behind, thrown in the roadside ditch of the past?

"You may not like all these people I'm a part of, but they must be who I am, too. Anyway, there're such a lot of them."

"It's privilege," Jeff objected. "You're afraid of letting that go."

"How can they all be wrong?"

"If the bases are wrong—"

"Oh!" Ideas, at this hour of the morning. "I don't know if they're wrong or not. I'll just have to have some money from her if I'm going to get up to Winston."

"Oh, God. Money."

He let her lead him, weak in the backlash of the disappointment over his work which he knew was coming to him, thinking she might be right, it wouldn't be easy. There would be a confrontation, at least. Her small hand tugged him forward, up the walk, heading toward the sort of threshold he was dedicated to not caring for. They stood at the door.

"You should have shaved," she whispered.

"I know it, but how?" he answered.

Her key let them in.

"Mother?" Like somebody in a child's story, she called three times.

A door creaked open from above stairs and Kate appeared at the banister, wearing a long, blue flowered robe. She looked down.

"Mary Kerr? My goodness, it can't be six o'clock even. Come on in, let's make some coffee. You and Jeff," she continued, astonishingly amiable, descending. "You look like something the cat dragged in. But come on in, for heaven's sake. Come on, now."

11

The Triangle

So that, calm, cordial, and peaceful, was how it was.

Again at the table, Kate, Mary, and Jeff. Not in the dining room by candlelight but in the breakfast room, a glassed-in alcove off the kitchen, plants within and without, a long, draping tendril of wisteria, now pale green in the early light, the blooms beginning to shimmer with lavender as the light increased. Cups set out on the thick lemon-colored cotton mats on the glass-topped table. Kate's pleasure in luxury was there in every stitch, every curve of design in her blue willow ware from olden times, Harbison things, passed down. Steaming coffee poured from the Pyrex pot, silver tongs for the sugar lumps. ("Sugar Lump," Poppy had called his baby girl sometimes.)

But no questions! Kate herself gave the excuse they had made up.

"You were probably at Ethan's and didn't want to wake me up. I know how these things run on. The time goes by."

Jeff looked at Mary with questioning blue eyes. She looked back with a little shrug. Changeable.

"I've discovered my ambition," Mary announced.

"I thought you knew it already," said Kate.

"Dancing . . . oh, that, yes. But maybe different a little now. It's Arthur Manning. He's coming here for six weeks this summer. Not here, but up at Winston. Not far."

"I don't dare ask who's that," said Kate, "but I have to." She went in the kitchen to scramble eggs.

"Big name in modern dancing," Jeff filled in. "One of a kind. Works with Croom, the composer—Robert Croom. Surely that means something."

"It rings a bell somewhere." She was feeding them, hungry mouths. Coffee and orange juice, eggs, toast and jam; then starting over. "Something in *Time* recently. On Croom, I mean. He hits one note and then walks out for an hour."

Jeff laughed. "Just about."

"Well, if she—" Kate put her hand to her head in a way that meant money. It was bound to cost something. She struggled.

"I know I'm ready for it, or I can get ready. It's a chance."

"Around here she'll just go on being a swan," Jeff said. "Pretty soon she'll grow a long neck."

Kate said to Jeff, "I found some of her pictures the other day." She went off into the living room and came back with albums in her arms. Mary Kerr in elf costume, Mary Kerr as wood sprite, Mary Kerr as sylph, Mary Kerr as one of the Willis in *Giselle*.

There followed some of Kate herself, as a girl, a young woman, at her own wedding—the fair hair, the fragile dresses, the straight intense look, softly burning. Jeff bent over the pictures, puzzling.

"Where would you be?" Kate asked him. "If she goes there, would she be following you, or you be following her?"

"I wouldn't know about that." He laughed uncertainly. "No dancing for me."

But she was regarding him, softly, directly.

It should have been no surprise when a message got through to him, a day later. She wanted to see him. Would late afternoon Friday be all right, alone?

So on the late afternoon she mentioned, he came, not knowing what to expect.

They sat across the same glass-topped table and looked at one another. For a time, they did not speak. He had debated not coming at all.

"The truth is," Kate told him, "I've met someone I care for."

"I don't doubt it," Jeff said. What was this dodging around for? What they had to speak of, if anything, must be Mary. So they weren't to talk of her. All right. He said, "I loathe what you're doing. I asked you before, if you remember. You had to lie; I understand that. These new government contracts . . . you are getting them, the animal shipments are going to you, and not for cancer research, either. Word has gotten out."

"Ethan Marbell," was all she remarked.

"It's just not necessary," said Jeff, "to blame everything on Ethan. He doesn't stand alone. This whole country—"

"He does *not* represent this whole country."

"You didn't let me finish."

"We all know what a gadfly—"

"Yes, you've decided it at the club. It must be true."

Eventually, Kate offered him a drink. He accepted. They sat down with gin and tonics, having gone together to the kitchen to mix them.

"You're an attractive young man," said Kate, shoving back a little to appraise him.

Jeff said thank you.

"Brilliant, too, I don't doubt."

"So they say."

"That always goes with Ethan's favorites. *He* had a boy of his own, you know. A rather shy little man. Felt himself so put down by Ethan's expectations. Retreated to his mother, who heaven knows wasn't much of a haven. I'm saying Ethan can make mistakes. He was in love with my sister-in-law Jane. She was too smart to go along with him."

"I am not interested in Kingsbury gossip."

"I suppose not. Yet I would have thought he'd go anywhere else but here."

"What's your boyfriend like?" He was insolent.

She smiled. "I'm too old for boyfriends."

"Lover, then?"

"That's going too far."

"Really?"

"Yes, really." She offered him another drink.

Cautiously, in a silence fallen between them, he ventured, "I was sure you'd asked me here because of Mary."

"Oh, that. Well, yes, I suppose. But maybe just wanting to know you, see your way of thinking. She—you have attached her, as you know very well. And she—she has this strong devotion, never letting go. Oh—!" Her head was bent, but reflected upward from the table surface he saw what looked to be tears.

He reached across. "Look, I'm not out to hurt her."

She straightened, standing up, retreating, then dabbing at her eyes. "Come here."

He was standing by her then, before thinking about it.

"When all this is over, this feverish war thing, and all the fuss . . . you've still nowhere to go, to be anything. I never do anything without the assurance of knowing where and who and what will make the solid ground." Her white hand came up and rested on his shoulder. The ground might as well have rippled like a snake on the move. What she was saying might be one thing, but what was she meaning to do but lure—

He caught her wrist and put it away from him. "Your drink's on the table," he said. "Getting weak."

"I know." She turned, seeming about to grope for it.

"It would be one way to get rid of me for her, wouldn't it? I mean, if it was you instead of her?"

She didn't seem to have heard. Maybe one try was all she ever allowed herself, if a try had been what it was. A test, then, if not a try? But he didn't ask. Even if she asked herself, she wouldn't answer.

Her back was turned to him. Her voice shook. "Just don't be careless of her."

"Careless? I don't think I've ever—"

Two worlds were talking, that was the trouble. But one way or another she'd thrown a noose around him. *What kind of a subtle bitch did she think she was?* The impulse she aroused in him was to whirl her around, grab and shake the truth out of her, say, *Who* do *you care about? When are you* not *pretending?*

It was a step he did not take.

But for an almost fatal time she did glue him to the spot, got him wondering how a woman could be that out and out in coming on to him without admitting to herself, even, let alone to him, what she was up to.

He pulled up short, mumbled something that wasn't what he meant, and let his feet, as Mary often said she had done, decide where he had next to go. To her, of course: his girl.

Kate had loosed talk on him about young people "having fun." That must have been during the second drink. She was not sure Mary—or, for that matter, Jeff—knew what she meant by that, she said. She felt she had worked too hard as a student, getting a degree. Only after she married did she and Don take those trips. Once in France—did Jeff know Scott Fitzgerald's novels? Dimly, in courses at Baton Rouge. Then he would know there ought to be times that were just useless, dancing on a pavilion near the sea, wearing such marvelous clothes.

"You think Mary doesn't enjoy dancing?" he puzzled.

"Oh, but that's like work, not just joy. The glamour part of it— she loses every day what I was happy to enjoy."

Don't you know there's a war on? And what are you testing those helpless beagles for up in that creepy lab? But he didn't say it.

Walking home now, he said "Shit!" and startled a passing black woman, who said at once "You sho right" without even turning. He laughed, going on.

It was in her practice studio that he found Mary. She was working alone, the others all gone, the key entrusted to her, a peace offering following a tiff with Al Bernstein. She was repeating one passage over and over, a turning rise, the spin brought to a halt so quickly it was like tripping even to think of it. The door clanged shut behind him just as she did it perfectly, stopping herself in air, coming slowly to earth before him.

She was at the center of the studio room, with its muted lights and the glossy mirrors making four of her.

"I saw your mother. She sent for me."

"She would."

He put his arm around her. They sat down together on the carpeted floor. He turned her, kissing her slowly, shifting her then against his shoulder, holding. She was small, easy to hold. Kate had been his height, eyes level with his own. Too much had been suggested, too much had not happened.

"The sexiest woman I ever saw," he murmured, reflecting, drawing her closer.

"You don't think you talked to her, do you?"

"Why not?"

"She doesn't talk, not to anybody. She just makes words do what she wants them to."

He glanced at the door. "Anybody here?" His hands, fervent, pulled the leotard down from her shoulders.

"Wait." She went to latch the door, then returned.

A chance at forever. It had been made for them, like a fire laid and then lighted, a rising flame.

12

Confrontation

Kate got the call a week later.

"Get down to the lab." It was Dr. Fletcher. "I'm starting now. We'll meet there."

"But what is it? Why?"

"Some of those damn demonstrators. I'm calling the police."

Before she could ask any more, he had hung up.

She drove rapidly, noting, as she reached the lab building, a helter-skelter parking arrangement of a pickup truck and two dusty old oversized cars with gigantic fins and headlights, blocking the street. She had to stop a hundred feet away and look around for Dr. Fletcher, the police, for anybody except whoever owned these cars. There was a small gathering near the entrance, just down the steps from street level.

They called out, "Hey, lady, this ain't the place to be."

"I work here. It's no place for you, certainly."

"She works here." A laugh. "Then it fucking sure ain't no place to be."

"Tell her," someone said.

"Hey, lady, word's got out what you're doing in there."

It was late afternoon, almost evening. A low slant of sun shot past the lab. She shaded her eyes. How could they demonstrate if nobody was around to see? Just up the slope of the street behind her, there were odds and ends of off-campus buildings belonging to the university. But if this wasn't a demonstration, what were they doing? About to splash on painted slogans? Could they be breaking in?

Kate crossed the street and walked toward them, recognizing no one. "Who are you? Where are you from?" She said later they might have come off the moon. Hair a yard long and crazy writing on their shirts. One wore nothing but a pair of gym shorts; another was in a knee-length T-shirt with orange lettering: FUCK THE PIGS.

"The war's got to stop, lady."

"It's my job you're stopping! Not the war." Still no Dr. Fletcher. No police. Kate got furious. "Get out of my way this minute!"

Quite alone, mad as a harpy, she plunged at them. The line took one step forward. Arms linked, the crowd might have been one body together. She wound up on the sidewalk, purse flung wide, spilling open. Her keys! "Help me! Help!"

Her knee was bruised and beginning to bleed through her torn stocking. She was crawling nearer her keys, scrambling for them, but saw herself beaten to them by a small barefoot waif of a creature, boy or girl, with a snakelike rope coiled around its neck. It threw the bunch of keys to the giant one who had actually stopped her, blond soft beard trailing sparsely down his jaw, the one in the orange-painted shirt. *Filth,* was all she could think, grasping toward them once again. If only she'd had a gun.

There was one up the hill, in her glove compartment. Why had she forgotten about it? From the back of the lab, as she made for the car, legs numb and knee stinging awake from the fall, she heard the tinkle of breaking glass. Running steps closed on her from behind. Arms caught around her waist. She was stopped and held.

With her back to the lab, her only view was before her. She smelled the reek of young bodies holding her and heard the sounds of her own cries, cut off numbly as her breath ran out. How long?

The two battered cars streamed past her; those souped-up antiques could still run, carry a load, escape from a scene. Their license plates were covered up. The arms holding her slackened, and the two who held her ran to leap toward arms held out to them from the back of the dusty pickup.

Too late, the first wail of a siren coming off the highway toward the tangle of streets that led to her. She heard how they mistook directions, backtracked, turned, and resumed their approach. By now she was hanging on to the side mirror of her car, leaning against the door, panting as she tried to open it, climb in to collapse on the seat. No need for the gun, but fearing what might have happened to the lab. Her work. . . .

A black car stopped smoothly.

"Oh, Dr. Fletcher! They got my keys!"

13

Sally

"I've got to have the money to send her," said Kate. "Especially right now. I can't have her here with that Jeff person getting her mixed up in heaven knows what. Now it's begun to strike close to me personally. The break-in, I mean. I've just come from my third visit to the police. They're taking down everything."

"From what I read in the papers, you were the only person down there."

"The papers always are a little bit wrong, if not a lot. Dr. Fletcher called me and I got there before he did."

"Couldn't you reason with them?"

Sally had not stopped work to listen. She was sitting in her living room in a big sprung armchair surrounded by a clutter of materials. Sketches of costumes were stuck to the wall with Scotch tape; her sewing machine was pulled to the center of the rug. Threads were flying. She had a batch of orders to finish. Kate sneezed at intervals.

"Reason? I'd just like you to try. I saw more in that five minutes what this country is facing— Well, just look at my knee." She pulled back her skirt on a large white bandage.

"I wonder where they came from?" Sally asked. "I heard they weren't local."

"Somebody said Chapel Hill. They were after blood was the main object, or so we think. They raided what we had there and went straight and dumped it on the draft board files. The animals we had are either out or killed. Some of the weak ones they left for dead were wandering half crazy around the office."

"What kind of animals?" Sally measured a hem.

"Oh, you know. Mice, guinea pigs, rabbits, beagles."

"Beagles!" Sally put down her sewing for the first time. "Sometimes I don't blame them."

"Just stop right there. You know they've got campuses in such a stew nobody can go to classes. And now Mary Kerr has let them get her into some sort of stunt for a rally."

"I thought she said she wouldn't do it again. She doesn't like that kind of music. Besides, they had her up high on their shoulders and didn't know how to hold her. She told me they weren't really dancers."

"She told me that, too, but I think she'd do things he asks her."

Sally sighed. She added another to the count of finished blouses, all brightly alike, lying beside her chair.

"It's something I decided a while back. There's no use getting in their way. It has to wear itself out, like a hurricane. I don't doubt you had to go there this time. But next time Dr. Fletcher calls, can't you just say it's no place for a lone woman?"

"He was coming there to join me. He got hung up by some group or other crossing through town."

"Those beautiful children," Sally remarked. "These trouble spots are like magnets; they swarm like bees. And look ridiculous. Beards and shaggy hair. Mary Kerr isn't anywhere near that crazy."

"Well, she's not going barefoot yet, if that's what you mean. I've got to get her away, Sally. I'm frightened."

Sally picked a costume up from the floor. She held it up. "Have you seen what I'm making the children for the Fourth of July merchants' parade? 'First Graders Like to Shop Kingsbury.' There's this slogan that they're running through all the exhibits: 'Shop Kingsbury.' "

"I'm mortgaged with the bank on the duplex," said Kate. "I don't dare ask Jane for a loan."

"If Mary Kerr goes to Winston, that boy is bound to follow her. I've not got anything against him except that he worries you."

"He won't follow her if I can block it. I've got connections there as well as Ethan. Sally, you're bound to see he's up to his neck in all this trouble here. The only stronger pull Mary Kerr has is her dancing. She won't drop that, even to stay with him. Discipline. It's her strong suit. She gets that from me," Kate added.

"They do speak well of him as a boy with brains," Sally went on. "Ethan Marbell wouldn't promote anybody who was just a hothead.

You know what often crosses my mind? He's getting back at us because of Jane Harbison."

"There's no need for a local reason. These protests are all over. In New York state, I read the other day—"

"You never seem to mention that war. I don't know if I'm so much in favor of it, either. If they think they're being sent out to die for something they're against . . ." She sewed red stripes up the legs of tiny trousers. The little blue blouses were strewn with stars.

"Flags are what they love to burn," Kate noted. She would have liked to storm and rage at Sally, who was enjoying stalling around with her. She wished it had been Sally who had had to get into that lab finally, discover experiments kicked apart, dead dogs sprawled out on the floor, or crippled, limping rats running in the corridors. Plus the records missing, along with their notes on all their work.

"Just tell me this," Sally went on—cat and mouse with superior Kate, haughty Kate. Enjoying it. "What are you people doing up in that lab that's so awful?" She was cutting coarse white cotton for making little skirts, slicing through six layers with long keen scissors.

Kate got up restlessly, sneezed twice, and sat down again. She would have to let go of a little information. "It's a Department of Defense contract. They farm them out at times to university labs. It meant a sizable grant for the job. I must have mentioned it to you, but you're not to tell. They . . . don't like it to get out, what's being done. We could handle it, that's all."

"But what," Sally pursued, measuring cloth from nose to fingers, "is 'it'?"

"How would you know if I told you? Chemicals they use for certain kinds of defoliants. Then, strontium 90. It's a nuclear by-product. There's a cancer tie-in, but we can't know to what extent until it's tested."

"So you give it to the hounds. Slaughter of the innocents."

Kate picked stray threads off her skirt. "You couldn't even take an aspirin tablet if you knew what some creatures suffered to make it safe for you. You'd have to live on lettuce and radishes. Nuts and apples."

"But you did say nuclear. Are they going to start dropping those things out there?"

"Don't be absurd. Nobody has mentioned nuclear war in Vietnam."

"I doubt them confiding in you. And all those chemicals. What are they for?"

"I've told too much now. You can't explain scientific methods in two minutes. It's all too complicated."

"Not to the beagles, I imagine."

"Honestly! If we're doing bad things to those people over there, they'd do the same to us. They're into torture, all the brutality they can think of."

"They wouldn't be doing anything to us if we weren't over there for them to do it to."

Kate sneezed again, lost her temper, and slammed out of the room. She could be heard getting something out of the refrigerator, using the bathroom, and finally returned with an air of exhaustion, sitting down. "I never even heard of Vietnam before all this came up. Now I can't turn on the TV without getting a full blast of it."

Sally put down her sewing and even took off her glasses. They both sat silently, becoming sisters again.

"You know very well I never have any money," Sally finally said. "I'll ask Ed."

14

Kate on Kate

It was as Kate was leaving that Sally asked her that question: "Does he love her?"

"Love?" Kate echoed. "Oh, Sally, what an old-fashioned word. Not to me, I mean. But to them." She floundered.

"Well," said Sally, "it may be, but I just thought I'd ask."

Whenever Kate got too close to Jeff Blaise, even in speaking, she remembered that day with him alone. Just across the table. Talking. Then, touching him as they stood. A terrible attraction. *However would Mary Kerr know what to do with him? What could the child understand about the nature I know he has?*

They had both known, he and she; they had known together. It was only a moment, passing quickly. And yet—

Kate got into her car and started it. Sally would get her the money.

Kate had dreamed violently of Jeff.

One other conviction she had kept totally to herself: When the keys had fallen from her, erupting from her bag onto the concrete sidewalk before the lab, she had seen her own house keys hanging in place in the leather case that had burst open, her car keys as well— but not the lab keys. Time and time again, she remembered her sighting of them at that moment. Where were they, if not taken already? The lab door had opened before anyone could possibly have gotten there with her keys. That meant *they had them already.*

True, they had thrust them back into her hands when leaving, keys all wrenched from the clamps. There was nothing to stop her thinking that, but for Mary Kerr knowing Jeff Blaise, that lab would never have been touched. In him she knew an adversary, combatant. (But lovers, too, fight each other.) "They forced the keys from me," she had lied to the police.

So Sally would get the money and Mary Kerr would go up to Winston.

The family spoiled Kate—distrusted her, did not know what entirely to make of her, both loved and disliked her, but with her very difference as a drawing card, they kept on spoiling her.

She would get the money.

15

Ed

Ed Tomkins, who lived east of Kingsbury in an ancient house he had inherited, had a lot of money, but no one would guess it to see the way he lived. He went around in scuffed, laced-up, tan leather boots, generally muddy, and kept bird dogs, black and white setters, who ran in and out of the house at will, had burrs in their coats and fleas to spare.

Sally, though she loved him, said she couldn't live the way he did; though according to Kate her own house was a total mess, it was a mess, Sally explained, of a different kind.

After Kate's visit, Sally telephoned Ed and drove out to see him.

There were woods out that way still, though the town was advancing on them, and new subdivisions were finally going to swallow him and his old hillside, thick with scruffy, twisty oak trees. A swing still hung from one big tree limb, down near the front gate. Sally had tried to live out there, but it was too lonesome for her. After the boys left, so did she.

Today she had called ahead because, for all she knew, he might have some drinking or hunting buddy living with him, or some business prospect. He dealt in tracts of land he had either inherited or started adding way back when: worthless scrub country, it was thought, wrongly. Sally and he let the children visit whenever and wherever they chose, both living in Florida now, though in different cities. Ed would put on a suit that smelled of mothballs and show up with traces of lather back of his ears. As a rule, though, he favored checked flannel shirts in winter, cotton ones in summer, no tie. Sally thought she'd do best not to pry into things. She imagined that at intervals he found a woman willing to stay with him for a while, but whether it was always the same one, or different ones, or none at all, she didn't really know.

When Sally came up the front steps that June morning, Ed was waiting with his foot on the porch railing. He held a glass in his hand already, though it wasn't but eleven.

"If it ain't my one and only," he said. A dog marched past him and stood on the top step until Sally approached near enough to have a forepaw placed on either shoulder and doggy breath in her face.

"Get him down, Ed," she said, and came to exchange a kiss.

She sat down on the front porch to talk with him, having remarked on the dogwood.

"So Miz High-and-Mighty Harbison needs a little bit of cash. What's the girl like?"

"You remember her. Pretty little thing. She's always had this dancing craze. Now it's come to wanting it for her career."

"Dance like in clubs, shows?"

"Oh, where it may lead, who knows? But first it was ballet, and programs, now she wants something called 'modern.' I guess they give programs, too."

"Is she any good?"

"Oh, definitely, yes, she is. I've gone to see her, made her costumes, of course. It's a gift. You have to study, practice all the time like music, violin or piano."

"She can't do that in Kingsbury? What's wrong with Kingsbury?"

"Well, this is special, some special teacher, famous. I never heard of him, but that doesn't signify. I think myself that Kate wants her away from some boy she's picked up with."

"Now you're on to it. I heard something about that."

"Well, of course. He came to town with Ethan Marbell. Ethan's into the anti-war business and Kate may even think—oh, I don't know for sure—but she may think that he was behind the mess they made of her lab work. Ed, it's gotten too complicated for her. Kate thinks if Mary Kerr goes, even if the boy follows her, at least he'll be out of town."

"Does she want shut of him for a son-in-law or not?"

"Oh, Lord, ask Kate. I'd say she was hoping it would blow over."

"I got one solution to all that prancing around over this war. They want to rampage, let's us rampage back. Police dogs and a drover's whip. And if that don't work, jail."

"I guess folks have tried all that, down in Alabama over the race business. It didn't stop a thing."

"Then what would you do about it?"

"Oh," said Sally mildly, and pulled up her stockings. "I see how they feel, you know. The world's ignoring them. They've got a right not to go get themselves killed."

"Hogwash," said Ed.

Sally was quiet, not much for quarrelling.

"I heard from Patty," said Ed, mentioning their daughter-in-law.

"So did I."

"She and Jenks are going to stick it out for a while longer."

"It's what she said."

"Kate Harbison," said Ed, "is bound to have money. She's got that whole family to fall back on. What they up to? Living too high on the hog?"

"Don never had very much, you know. What little he did have he couldn't hold on to. It was that lumberyard. He borrowed to develop it, thinking those people were going to build a shopping center. Then they headed on out five miles and left him high and dry. He had to sell for a lot less, and lost—well, I don't know what he lost, but a lot. He never was well."

"He wasn't the only Harbison."

"Kate has to hold her head high. I understand that."

"You understand too much."

"Maybe."

He went back to the kitchen to pour another little half inch in his glass. He came back sock-footed and sat down again.

"The main thing, then, is to scatter them? Get them the hell out of here, is that what Kate is saying, real polite, and not putting it quite like that, but really saying?"

"I guess she is. She feels like she's a target. She said that twice. A target."

"If this school in Winston can get rid of some of all that stuff around here—that's what you're saying."

"I see it that way."

"Maybe I'm for it. . . . Tell you what. Let's you and me get all dolled up and go down to San Juan again."

"I don't know," Sally said. "You know what happened the last time. You gambled all that away, and I couldn't even find you half the time."

"This time different. I promise."

"Wait till the fall. It's too hot there now."

"Hurricanes."

"Not after October."

"Summer's cooler than here."

"Too hot to move. Or think, either."

"Wasn't asking you to think, Sal." He pinched her arm.

"I'll think anyway. I mean, I'll think about it."

Sally got the money. The check, more than adequate, was in her hand when she left.

She telephoned Kate when she returned to town, but Kate was away for the afternoon. These mysterious absences were adding up to one thing only: a man.

Why, of course, she thought, between second and third sessions of ringing Kate's number. *She wants Mary Kerr out of the way for that. She's used me.*

But then Sally put that thought out of her mind. It might have a fraction of the truth in it, but only a small fraction, she thought.

Sally was good.

16

Fred

There was in fact a man, and his name was Fred Davis.

He had come to a conference in Atlanta from Philadelphia, where he lived, to serve the interests of a small pharmaceutical firm, having inherited a controlling interest in it, along with other concerns, from his father. Certain medications and cosmetics marketed by the firm had first to undergo lab testing, and contracts were let to labs able to carry these out. Social life went on at such conferences, as well as closed-door meetings to discuss procedures, cost overheads, and reports on statistical averages and satisfactory results. Kate Harbison, lyrically lovely, with the efficiency record of an M1 rifle, was frequently sent to represent the university hospital interests at such gatherings.

She had flown to Atlanta on Sunday night and registered at the new Hyatt, having had to wade through a crowd of sit-down strikers at the airport, whose placards she did not even stop to read. She had been a little frightened. They were a mixed group—black and white, girls among them—and she was afraid of seeing someone she knew—Jeff Blaise or even Mary Kerr.

In her hotel room she revived. The spacious luxury of the room, the faintly scented, softly lighted bathroom, the curved glass outer walls broken to make a sweeping window view of a great modern city—all this filled up the empty spaces of her soul, which always went starving for the served-up beauties of the world. She undressed herself with slow pleasure, washed her pale limbs, schemed out her makeup, knew in the process her own kind of living. For the moment she could even stop worrying about money: She was on an expense account. She thought of the escalators in the hotel, the longest she'd ever seen, the slow silence of their superb soaring rise through jungle-sized plants toward spacious floors with ballrooms and corporate meeting lobbies. Going out, she made her descent on one of these, in such a coasting down from loftiness as an angel might have envied. Her golden hair was up and the light made varying designs upon it, while plants, gliding past, obliged her with nimbly changing frames. *Someone should see me,* was what she almost thought.

Someone did.

He was standing near a pool in which a pair of swimmers sculpted in curving bronze bands frolicked endlessly. Her head as she descended was almost entering the branches of a potted tree; his tailored linen jacket as he stood just escaped the spray from the fountain. His hands were folded before him and he looked like exactly what he was: a man who had just arrived, knowing no one.

He saw Kate's marvelous descent, saw her step free into the lobby and look about her, seeking someone she knew, perhaps, or someone she had promised to meet. He stepped out of the foliage and the jungly damp and took a chance. "Are you, by any chance, with the—?" She was. So was he. But here in Atlanta, for the first time, and a Yankee to boot, would she consider—?

Kate smiled.

Fred Davis had arrived.

He was dark, in his forties, though just in what part of them was hard to say. He had a quiet look, his clothes were expensive, his shoes gave no offense whatsoever. His hair was still thick, subdued to one side. He was divorced. Children? Yes, one, married, California. Residence? Out from Philadelphia, toward Bryn Mawr. Main Line? Well, they did call it that. And she one daughter, too? Another story. Another drink, then? Well, yes.

He wore curious glasses, hexagonal, outlined in steel wire. They emphasized the squareness of his chin and the straight line of his hair across his forehead. Neither of them could help but notice that blond and dark made them an attractive pair. How much did it matter? It mattered to Kate. It mattered to Scott Fitzgerald, of whom Kate had been thinking ever since she passed through those squatting people at the airport and alighted from the smelly taxi with the rasping air conditioner and entered the portals of this enchanted haven of blue glass walls and magic indoor forest, splashing fountains, gliding stairways, the soft sting of dry martinis, the crackle of a man's Yankee voice blending with her own Southern murmur.

She held her thoughts back by main force. They were hounds taking to the scent and baying to be cast, racing thoroughbreds battering at the paddock door.

"Does your kind of work make you squeamish?" he was asking.

"Oh, I'm only supervising. You understand that we go to all lengths to be humane."

"Of course you do."

17

Audition

Small was all she felt like, outside the green door, and going through it, too, when her name was called and she stepped away from the other applicants there in the corridor, who were giggling in a muted way, chatting with one another. She had not said anything. The smiling assistant, blond and thin in her leotard, let her slip through the door.

There before her he stood, coming forward, stopping, looking from a chosen distance. He was ugly. His legs, hipbones, thighs, arms, chest looked chipped patiently out of stone by someone who knew the effect sought for. But it was he, the famed Arthur himself, who had slaved and starved in New York, launched a new dance movement, traveled through the Midwest, had his big chance in Paris, and brought them stunned and wondering to his feet. "An entirely new formality has come to the dance." So said the articles. She had an idea what it meant, but now was the moment to begin to know, and her brain had gone blank. Then he smiled. The wonder was his facial planes didn't splinter and clatter to the floor, but instead warmth was all that fell out. It landed on her.

"Small," he said.

"I'm sorry," she got out, wondering if that was right. Anything might be wrong.

He came and picked her up carefully, as if she were some object in a shop he could decide to buy. His large hands were under her armpits. He turned her neatly, pushing her shoulders so that her head slanted forward. He looked down the length of her, all the way to her heels. She kept them neat, together. She remembered her uncles, checking over bird dogs they might want to get for hunting. He put her down.

"Good things come in small packages." It was better than calling her a runt.

What would she do for her classical choice? There had been a list. Debussy. Tones to interpret. He sat far in the dim back of the small auditorium, its stage plain. The assistant set the tape going, a rising tide of sound, "La Mer." Good or not? She finished on time, anyway, but how to tell? He did not speak except to ask, "Next?"

"Just sound a note," she said.

"Any note?"

She nodded. The assistant went to the piano.

It was her own idea, devising something like freehand writing of no known language, the rise and fall of distant speech lifted from sound into body motion. She circled forward, sweeping down, hair brooming the floor, then heels lifting in a graceful arc like a wheel. Fleeing, returning . . . flight and trust following one another.

Finishing after a backward hinge hard to imagine doing without a show of defiance, she came calmly to her feet at dead center, thinking with more confidence, *If he's as good as they say, he'll know it's good.* But even thinking that, it was the dance she meant, not herself.

He had risen slowly and was coming toward her. He stepped on the stage and carefully, as though improvising a new series of steps, he took her hand. He nodded to his assistant. "Strike a note," he said.

"Any note?"

He nodded.

Gravely, they began to dance together. She was hardly aware of being led, yet she must have been following.

"Mother! He's taking me! I'm in! . . . Well, no, he doesn't *say* things, you see, he just *does* in such a way that you *know*. . . . Thank Aunt Sally . . . should I call her? Can you call up Al?"

Well, thought Kate, hanging up the phone. *So that is that.*

18

More Fred

Following his wonderful encounter in Atlanta with the shimmering lady from North Carolina, Fred Davis had frequent recourse to the long-distance telephone. Finally, he visited Kingsbury.

Kate took him to the club and invited Jane to dinner along with a bachelor librarian, Jane's routine escort, and two other friends, chosen with care. Everyone said that Fred was an attractive man and they liked him very much.

The vandalism at the lab had by then taken place. Kate recounted it to Fred with despairing tears in her eyelashes, and he brimmed with sympathy and shock. She did not, however, mention her daughter in this connection, or Jefferson Blaise.

Mary Kerr was known to be dancing away at Winston. Neither by letter nor telephone did she mention Jeff. Kate assumed he had been refused a chance to teach there; she had done her best to block him. Ethan put out the word that Jeff would soon be travelling to Ann Arbor, Michigan, to work more closely with the Movement. He belonged with the student elite which Ethan envisioned as the hope of America. Someone else reported that he was to join a group invited to Washington at the request of certain senators. Kate pondered. He would no doubt leave. Twice she thought she saw him, walking away at twilight, turning up a dark street.

Mary Kerr hymned the praises of her new hero. "I never knew what a great person was before, or a really great dancer, either. I won't ever go back to ballet."

"But what's it like?" Kate asked. Mary Kerr said it had to be seen, not described. It was free, she added. It was inward-looking, too. When you watched it, you were looking in on something, an expression of feeling. Ballet faced outward, showed itself off. That was the difference. Kate was mystified. Mary Kerr sent out programs for the closing performance. The time had passed so fast. Kate shared them with Fred Davis, who was there for his second visit.

Mary Kerr was listed to appear in two numbers: "Fantasy in F" and "Hymn to Motherhood." Kate was only a little wary, being happy in the company of Fred Davis.

"Why, let's go up and see her," he suggested. "Two weeks from now, I'll come and we'll bring her back with us. If she's not ready yet, we can at least take her out to dinner, get acquainted a little."

Not even the damage to the lab could keep Kate in those days from wanting to smile. She was often hastening to the door for a box of flowers or a special-delivery letter; more than twice a week the interesting calls came through. *At my age: imagine,* she would think.

"If you still want to come for her program," she finally agreed, "I believe it's all right with her."

With one another, they talked of nothing so much as daughters. His own (Esmé, named on his ex-wife's whim out of a story by J. D. Salinger) had had a runaway early marriage, a disaster, then had met a nice solid fellow who owned a ski resort in the Sierras. Had little interest in skiing but enjoyed life there, two children, boy and girl. Only trouble seemed to be that Fred's ex-wife, frequently visiting her daughter, made something of a nuisance of herself, picking up undesirable friends. But he personally . . . bad times with the daughter? No, not really. Nothing understanding and patience would not resolve. "Persist," was his advice to Kate. "Reason." Kate said she had tried. She changed the subject. They agreed these were especially difficult times.

On the drive up to Winston, Kate said, "It's just this boy. Not even really a boy. He's older, I mean. Jeff Blaise." The subject stuck to her once she got into it. She found it hard to shake loose. She tried to tell only a little.

"But if he's here and there reforming the country, you can't be finding him so much of a nuisance, I would think."

"He's frightening. Oh, not to me personally. I mean . . . he's into all these frightening things. No control."

"What about his draft number coming up?"

"Oh, that's easy. They're all defying that. So would he."

They arrived at Winston and ate an early dinner in the ancient square of the charming old town. The oaks were gracious and still, the brick sidewalks contentedly uneven.

When they arrived at the art center, Mary Kerr herself came running out, hair flying, step fleet, ankles muffled in leg warmers, mismatched rags fluttering around her.

"Hello," said Fred Davis. "It's good to meet you."

"Oh, hi," said Mary Kerr.

"How's it going?" asked Fred.

"We're doing one more rehearsal now. It's still changing. It may change again." She spoke as though this was of great significance.

"We're taking you out later, even if it's midnight," Fred Davis vowed.

Fred had little interest, as previously confided to Kate, in seeing these children bob up and down and run around in patterns, but he was willing to sit through it all if she wanted him to. He did like music.

But when the final presentation came, he had to pay attention because anyone would feel that some tense sort of business was going on. About parents and children. The children at first obedient, precise, the parents telling them what to do and why, then gradually the roles reversing, the parents trampled down, pinned to the wall, danced over, and at the last circled and screamed at. A whirling dance of triumph. One person was left in the middle with her long blond hair streaming wildly: the mother who refused to join the others. Because all the other mothers had by now joined the children and were whirling around, chanting at the one holdout: "Mother, we're through. Mother, you bitch, we're through." There had been little music. Just a chanting of ugly lines. Killing off the parents. Fred had heard about it, how it was necessary for children to do that. *Lord,* he wondered, *have I been killed and don't know it?*

At program's end, Kate, looking shocked beyond measure, went to find the ladies' room. In the corridor, groping and dazed, she thought she saw Jeff Blaise. She knew that she saw a young man of his build with long, light hair, and now a beard to match, coming toward her, but he changed direction abruptly, swivelled aside and walked away, receding rapidly among the audience crowd, but not before his blue eyes had sent their knowledge out to her. No one else had eyes like that. She started to call but the sound dried up in her throat. Would Mary Kerr dare to bring him out with her?

No, she didn't. At the restaurant they repaired to later, Kate tried to rally, laughing off the program. There had been some funny moments, those young dancers playing at being older women, dropping off their nice little gloves and proper hats, waltzing with the young men, then finding themselves mocked once again, changing dance patterns, shedding heels, loosening hair, in some cases outdoing their daughters.

"Well." Kate sighed. "After that number things don't look too good for motherhood."

"Don't take it seriously," said Mary Kerr. "Besides, all the mothers reformed."

"Except the last one," said Kate.

"Oh," said Mary Kerr, "she was supposed to change, too, at first. I told you we weren't through. We changed it in rehearsal. First we had her burned at the stake, then flying up and getting renewed younger than anybody. She'd go spinning around over them."

"Why change it?"

"It wasn't like the poem."

"Poem?" Fred said, puzzled.

"You know. Sylvia Plath. All about her father. First he's a tyrant, then a Nazi, then the devil, then Hitler, then a vampire. It's all in there."

"Who's this Plath girl?"

"A poet. She wrote the poem."

"About her own father?" Fred pursued. "So what did she do with this awful guy?"

"She drove a stake through his heart," said Mary Kerr, and gobbled up a roll.

"I don't mean in the poem. What, really?"

"Oh. Nothing to him. She killed herself."

"Oh."

Kate was not hungry. She sipped a drink, saying little.

"Remember," Mary Kerr said to her, slicing rare steak, "how you used to tell me at the picture show, 'Don't be scared, it's just a story'?"

Kate gave a wan smile. "That must have been your father. He took you."

19

Homeward Bound

It was in the dark car driving smoothly back to Kingsbury that Kate began talking, nonstop, out of control. She had loved Mary Kerr so much when she was a baby, she recalled nothing but good dreams, everything entirely wrapped up in her, even with Don showing first signs of health problems, everything was all right because of her baby girl. But some distrust, distance, had entered long ago, maybe at a birthday party when Mary Kerr was eight—like a bad spirit in a story, or a virus you might catch without knowing it, a cell multiplying for no known reason at some secret place inside—

"Stop it," said Fred.

All right, but perhaps he should know that just back there, when she had walked to the dormitory door with her, Mary Kerr had said, "Please don't worry about that dance. We had to go by the poem."

"No matter," said Kate, "what you're talking about is hate, isn't it?"

"No, we were talking about getting rid of hate, dancing it out, shedding it. Don't you see?"

"It had to be there to shed, didn't it?"

"Oh, Mother, stop it!"

So Kate related, but she left out how she had almost slapped Mary Kerr, had had to grip her hands together to keep from it.

"She planned all that, I know it. My sister's money was what I had to beg to send her. On top of everything, I saw the Blaise boy. He didn't speak. I'm as certain as anything he broke into my lab—not personally, but he made it possible, sent them. Why would he hide?"

"Maybe it wasn't him," Fred suggested. "Why didn't you bring him along to dinner? Or you could always ask her these questions, couldn't you?"

"About him, you mean?"

"The keys, for instance. I would certainly ask about anything that serious."

"Oh, she denied it. But of course, she'd lie about it."

"Does she lie?"

"She avoids . . . escapes— how to explain her? I can't."

Fred yawned, eyes on the steady path of his headlights. He had been up since early morning, catching his flight, arriving, renting a car, making the long drive.

"It's just that in accusing her, I'd lose whatever little bit we are in touch." Kate remembered that her own grandfather had told her as a child about the "devil's touch," he an old gray man she could barely recall, but she did feel once more the chill his phrase had brought her, as though the touch he spoke of were an icy finger.

"The Blaise boy. If he loves her, wouldn't it be natural for him to be there at her program?"

"I can't see Mary Kerr holding on to him. What little I've seen him—he needs more of a woman, I would say."

Fred woke all the way up. "You like him? Is that it?"

Kate was brusque. "He's an attractive young man. Way too young for me." The moment passed.

She was grateful that it had. This compulsion for bringing him up. That day she was trying to erase. How after Mary Kerr left, Kate had found out where he lived by calling the university, had gone there unannounced to find him. She had a perfectly righteous message rehearsed on her lips, ready, but seeing him in such an untidy dump like that surprised her. Caved up in there with the reek of marijuana, almost in squalor. Sex awakened as thunderously rampant as a herd of wild horses. He was starting up from the rumpled bed he had been lying on, saying, as the shock of her appearance went fanning its wavelengths around them, "You're about to say it's her you've come about?"

"I did think if we could talk—"

"We did that once." He crossed over to his desk, looked down at a pile of mysterious papers, books open, some bristling with markers, saying almost to himself, "She's not your reason." He sat down thoughtfully.

"What, then, do you imagine—"

"Why would I have to imagine? Here you are."

He was quick with that, and she almost smiled. She searched for the words for leaving but didn't find them. What a long wait outside in her car lay just behind her, making certain he was entering alone, rehearsing words of motherly concern.

"What do you really want?" He rose suddenly and stood so close they were almost jammed together. "Trading off your own body?"

"Not a trade!" She had almost shouted. Meaning what? His grasp on her shoulder burned. She had gotten out of there some way, but at what point? In some fragment of recollection she admitted to herself that he had kissed her, but like the grasp it was riven with insolence, tainted through with defiance. And then her dreams took on where that left off, and they roiled in gigantic beds together, paths of white gravel outside the windows, curtains stirring faintly in the morning breeze, stone lions growing visible in the early light, peacocks trailing their feathers as they stepped down to a lily pool to drink. A distant glimmer of the sea, the French coast. Zelda and Scott about to arrive. . . .

Well, so she desired him. He aroused all her feeling. But it wasn't to be thought of so often as this. An ordinary case of wanting a young man her daughter found attractive. That was all, wasn't it? Yes, it was all. . . .

"I'm getting too sleepy to drive," said Fred, and turned off the road. At Centerville, halfway back to Kingsbury, a new inn had gone up recently. He seemed to know about it, for without asking her he found it, stopped the car before it, and went inside.

Coming back, he opened the door for her. "Come on. There's been too much of this."

Cold sober and sitting up straight, Kate tried to meet the present surprise. Unforeseen, this decisive gesture, looking like nothing so much as common sense. Everything she could have said would be wrong at present—that is, if she had any hope of holding on to him, there for such brief visits, carrying his practical Yankeeness in and out like a fine leather briefcase. She could ask for a separate room, insist they drive on with herself at the wheel . . . or she could follow. The gravel around the flower beds before the new softly lighted structure was fine, pale gray. She could still hear the pressure of the Chrysler New Yorker's tires as it briefly passed over the edge of the turf. Lingering in her mind's eye after she followed him into the suite with its thick carpet and glowing lamps he was now switching on was the way her own movement must have been, the slender heels of her sandals, the sway of her skirts, the gleam of her hair. She sank down in a deep chair.

"I'm sorry to be a bore," she said with quiet sincerity. "Sorry." She thought of Daisy or Nicole. One of them had said "Sorry" much like that, but in which book she couldn't think.

Sitting on the end of the bed, Fred removed his coat and flung it on a chair. He also took off his glasses. She had never seen him without them, those odd hexagons which were always making a statement. The effect of lifting them off spoke of nakedness, as loudly as a word. All he did next was rub his eyes. He never talked a great deal, Kate was just realizing. Was he interesting when he did talk? Not very. What he had, of course, was obviously money. What a relief it would be, just no longer to have to worry. Coming in here, had she risked losing him, or was she making sure of keeping him?

He reached for the phone. "I'll order a drink."

"No. Not for me."

At least she had the good sense to refuse that. Since Don had died, there had been those messy encounters, men she would just as soon forget, always with liquor getting into things. Fred was from far away, not apt to hear stories.

"Go on and cry if you want to," he advised her. He grinned at her, and surprised, almost shy, she smiled back. "In fact," he went on, "you can go all to pieces."

"Now that I'm here," Kate said graciously, "I don't feel that I need to."

Fred studied the ceiling, then the opposite wall. "Women crying," he remarked, "they're nice to hold."

20

On Her Doorstep

Kingsbury looked no different when they returned except that there was a man sitting in front of the gray duplex on the steps. He was rumpled, shaggy-haired, listing sleepily, and, even from a distance, florid. Not quite a bum, though it crossed Kate's mind that she might owe somebody an overdue bill or that Mary Kerr had gotten into some trouble.

So, still half a block from the driveway, she put her hand on Fred Davis's arm. "Stop."

"Why?" But he obeyed. The night just past had created a common motion for them, like matching steps.

"I don't know who that is."

"I'll go and ask."

"Wait. I'd rather call someone. There's a phone booth just back there and around the corner."

She called up Penney, at home on Sunday morning.

"Yes, ma'am," Penney said. "He came to the house yesterday along about three o'clock. I didn't let him in, but he say he going to wait."

"Wait for who? For what?"

"He ain't said."

"Listen, Penney. I had to stay up in Winston with Mary Kerr. It was for a program she gave."

"Yes'm. His name Mr. Blaise, he said. He got this son, that one knows Mary Kerr. I didn't tell him nothing."

Jeff. "Blaise," she repeated stupidly, clutching the phone.

"Yes'm."

She put down the receiver. She went back and sat down in the car beside Fred, then told him.

"I've got no time at all, I regret to say," Fred told her, stroking her face. "I guess you and your family will have to deal with Mr. Blaise."

People are always throwing my life off track, Kate thought. Last night was fleeing from her like water over a dam. She might never see him again.

"Just drive me by my sister's house," she said. "It's on your way: I'll show you."

I will not confront him, she positively decided. Maybe he would just go away, back to some Louisiana swamp where he belonged.

At Sally's, Kate called the police to tell them some man she'd never seen was hanging around her house and she was afraid to go there. "I don't want to bring charges . . . no. Just get him to move on."

"Kate," said Sally, "that's not a bit necessary. If he's that boy's father, maybe he thinks talking to you would help the boy in some way."

"Then he could call, or write."

When the phone rang it was from the police station. The officer in charge suggested she speak to the gentleman who was looking for her at her address. Kate's knuckles whitened on the receiver.

When the man got on the phone, a surprisingly courtly voice, syrupy with Deep South tones, spoke at some length about his concern that his son was missing, "mysteriously out of touch." He feared he might be "mixed up in something" or "been involved in some unfawchunate occurrence. You yo'sef bein' a parent, Miz Harbison, you must be able to comprehend mah own state of mind."

"Perhaps," said Kate. "But I've only just seen my daughter, and so far as I know she has nothing to do with your son any longer. The relationship is over."

"Well, now. . . ." Heavy breathing, a thinking process. "Well, now . . . Miz Harbison, I was hopin', frankly, couldn't help but hope that Jefferson might have met himself some fine little girl up this way." Another break. Tears? "There are some mighty fine characters to boast of in this old state, is how I always heard it."

Kate did not answer directly. "Someone you could see who would know better about your son than anyone else is Professor Marbell."

"I went by Jefferson's address. You know where that is?"

"No, I don't," she lied.

"He's not there anymore. They said he was gone."

"I'll give you Professor Marbell's number."

"Jefferson has spoken of him. Miz Harbison, you don't fully realize mah concern. My boy is a fine young man, very well spoken, well spoken of. Now I get reports that he's been arrested for some kind of 'protest' in New Jersey, but before I can get on the telephone he's out from that place and gone. I think there was some mistake. Jefferson is a good boy. Somebody with his name may be tryin' . . . well, tryin' whut? I just cain't say whut. Most recently here the draft board in our parish has got to have him for the armed services. Now, he was deferred for a while. But that's run out! I can't fill out a report on him. I got to find him!"

"Mr. Blaise, I repeat, I cannot help you. I scarcely know Jefferson Blaise."

She hung up the phone exhausted, having given Ethan's number out. "I'm scared to go home, Sally. That man is rabid." She considered sleeping at Sally's. She looked about her at the various dress forms, the big cutting table, the lengths of flowered silks spread out on the sofa. Ed Tomkins always said that staying at Sally's he risked being put into a hammock in the garage, to make room for her sewing.

"He didn't sound so harmful," said Sally. She cleared off a chair to think in.

"Tenacious," Kate said. "Upset, primitive . . . I'm weary to death of it, Sal. Now it's gone and lost me Fred."

"How on earth do you figure that?"

"I had little enough sense to let him come to the program. Seeing her, the way she dresses, an awful dance they did, all about mothers being dreadful people. She did it all; I know that. Accidentally on purpose. She's a past master at it."

Sally said she couldn't believe it. Kate wandered to the mirror. She wanted back to the luxury of her own nest, her usual cosmetics, her imported coffee, her *Sunday Times*. Her life would pick up as before. Fred's absence might turn permanent. She would have to start again.

She drove home, opened the house, ate crab meat with a salad, bathed slowly in rose-scented water, took the *Times* to bed. Her night with Fred: What words to use? Satisfying? Adult? Yes, both those things. But the uncertainties of romance irked and disturbed her. Was it back to lonely Kate again—husbandless, her one child against her, no lover she could respect?

She opened the *Times*. Draft cards burned in public, the card itself a symbol, fire as symbol, too—napalm, of course—Fulbright hearings, "dry tinder scattered through the country." New York marches, excrement by the bucketful dumped on records in draft board offices, barricades . . . attacks . . . marches. Would Ethan call her about the Blaise man?

If Fred cools off, I'm going to isolate myself. When and if the lab is running again, I will do my work, come home, go off on vacations alone to interesting places. Read. Get Mary Kerr into some school somewhere . . . anywhere but around here. . . .

A sleeping pill succeeded in stopping all that worry. *How not to dream about Jeff Blaise?* She saw him white and manly, stripped, his member rising up before her . . . but nothing had gone that far. She held the facts close, but the image failed to fade.

She had it intricate with her thoughts as she drifted into sleep and at first could not believe she was actually hearing storming from below, a pounding (not of her heart), and cries (not rooted in sexual delight).

She started up, grabbing up her robe, throwing it on, rushing to the head of the stairs. "Who is it? What do you want?"

Something about Mary Kerr . . . a wreck, injury? She groped downward.

"Talking to you! It's all I want! And you, why not talking to me?" It was a persistent call she heard now, and then the interspersing racket: Blam, blam, on the front door.

Oh, that man!

"I'll call the police!"

He had shifted ground. There went his face up over the sill, right in the big downstairs window. The pane bent his nose back.

"I see you! Ain't you human?"

The hall telephone was down a few steps more. It was only the sight of him to get by. But reaching it, she saw his face get bigger, livid and drunk, too, no doubt, but crying, contorted, hair shagged up across the crown. She had gained the phone when the glass shattered. Jagged fragments spewed into the very living room. He could get in! She dialed like crazy. She saw his hands reach through among the spikes of glass. He shook them at her. "Why not talk to me? It's about my boy! My only boy!"

She was giving the address to the police, but at one and the same moment a thought, completely unexpected, streaked into her mind.

Why not talk to him? She dared to glance again, out to where the streetlight, though faint, still illumined the lines of ugly anguish, of thwarted and desperate appeal. She clung to the slender ascending columns that supported the banister, as it passed near the telephone. *I can't go to him, can't. . . . Impossible,* she almost said aloud, knowing that it was. The reek of bad whiskey was so strong it came right to her. He'd cut his cheek on that glass.

"Ain't you human? Human . . . ? Mother of a child?"

From somewhere blocks away a siren wailed. "They're coming!" she screamed at him. "You'll get arrested."

More glass tinkled on the floor, but the face dropped. He must have slipped and fallen in the shrubbery. A scrambling sound came to her. Then he vanished.

Taking with him—contorted, pleading, drunk, and crazy—the face of love.

Which she could not go to.

So ran her knowledge, undeniable, below any denial her conscious thoughts might make.

21

Dancer's Return

She was standing in Sally's hallway, rolled-up jeans, leather sandals, hair in strings. Her arms looked overbrown and broken out—bitten, maybe. She was favoring one foot, like a pony that had picked up a nail.

Those poor feet, thought Sally. *So much demanded of them.* What she said was, "Why, child, come on in."

"Mother's not at home," said Mary Kerr, limping into the living room.

"But she must have told you."

"Just that she was going off with Philadelphia Fred."

"I don't know about 'going off.' She went up to visit. How did you come?"

"Hitchhiked."

"That's dangerous, isn't it?"

"It takes forever. I had to walk a lot, too. Thank you for the money, Aunt Sally." She lifted one foot and with perfect balance extracted a small rock from the toe of her sandal. "Our program was just super. I learned a lot I never knew before. We were just getting started." She dumped a swollen duffel on the floor. Something like the arm of a sweater was sticking out of it. She sank into a chair.

"It was Ed gave it to me," Sally began. "Your mother— Don't you want some lunch? Or would you say breakfast? I've got all sorts of stuff in the icebox. I think you children never eat anything."

Mary Kerr giggled and calmly announced, "What I need is more money."

When in doubt, sit down at the sewing machine, was Sally's motto.

What on earth to do with this complicated situation? "At least you're honest." But in sewing terms, it was worse than the year they all had to have hoop skirts with rosettes sewed into the panels. "You go get yourself something to eat back there, and then we're going to sit down and talk everything out."

Of course, she said no to the money. Ed had it, he just had no patience with giving it to her. Mary Kerr was burning to move on with a core number of the dance group, attached by now to this Art Manning character like a Pied Piper or a Greek god, to some other station of learning, keeping up the momentum, presenting programs in barns if need be, printing flyers in small-town newspaper offices. There was time left before cold weather when Art headed back to New York. She might even get a chance to go with him.

"I thought you'd understand." She sat down with a saucer of left-over french fries she had found in the kitchen, a poor choice.

"I do understand," Sally said. "I just can't get you any money."

Mary Kerr took the news soberly. Why ever would she think she would get it just by asking? She kicked off her sandals. Sally stared at her feet in disbelief. They were dirty. They were rubbed, blistered, cracked, and swollen. But underneath all that, their neat, muscular structure looked knowledgeable, trained. Don Harbison had once proudly remarked, "Her feet are her fortune." What would he say now?

"Honey, were you out all night?"

"Well, I started out with some others about ten o'clock. They headed west around one, and I kept on alone, hitching."

Those lonely little feet, catching gravel along the roadsides, standing back to wait for the next passing car.

"Jeff's father was here," said Mary Kerr.

"As if I didn't know."

"Jeff told me. He scared shit out of Mother. Excuse me. He scared her to death."

"So is Jeff with you?" Not alone in the night. Sally felt relief.

"Jeff's nowhere near here. He tried to teach in Winston but they were scared of him for some reason. Then they sent for him to work with the Movement. He's getting well-known."

"But you're not into all that. Or are you?" Something to tell Ed, one way or the other.

Mary Kerr laughed. "What would I do if I was? They like rock singers and guitar players, not dancers. It's true I did that pyramid act in the rally on campus, but mainly to see if I could get up that high. They almost dropped me right into the spotlights. Jeff says I'm not a political animal."

"Can't you tell his father where he is?"

"I don't even know where his father is, much less Jeff. Jeff telephones. He's always moving around. Now his father's moving around, too, I guess." She started giggling, great bubbling bursts of sound. *A little witch,* thought Sally, with affection. *All this anguish of everybody concerned, and she thinks it's funny.* Which, of course, it was. That shaggy old drunk confronting elegant Kate. Parenthood supreme.

"It wasn't a bit funny," said Sally, trying to stop laughing. "He turned up out of nowhere. Kate found him sitting on the steps. She sent him over to Ethan Marbell."

"What did he say to Ethan?"

"Lord only knows."

Mary Kerr pictured Ethan's shadowy living room, the lamp with the crooked shade, the pipe smoke, carefully chosen words, philosophy of our time. The young. ("Yes, I know, Professor, but where's my boy?")

"Afterward," Sally continued, sobering, "the Blaise man evidently went uptown. Far from soothed and convinced, which may have been what Ethan was aiming for, he just got awfully drunk. He began to rage around, or so I was told, all this down in the worst possible section, over in the southwest where they're building the new highway. Then he comes storming back into town, moaning at Kate's very door in the wee hours. Kate hollered out that she was calling the police. Then he cried, a lot like a boy himself, saying all he wanted was to talk about his boy, if only she'd listen. Then the window. Kate swears he threw something to break it, for it is just about what you might call in smithereens. I don't think he threw anything."

"Then how did it break?" Mary Kerr asked.

"I think he was really grieved. This love of children, his child . . . he was probably just determined to get some human response out of Kate and he tried and tried to look in and see her. I think he was just drunk and he fell. Whatever happened, the window broke. The police came but didn't find anybody. He knew enough to leave."

"Then?"

"Kate was nervous as a cat, scared to sleep there. There was nobody she could get to repair the window right away. All this added to the break-in at the lab. You remember that."

"Nobody could forget it," Mary Kerr allowed. "She thought I gave that key to Jeff. She blamed us both."

Sally tried to be tough. "Was she right?"

"Goodness, Aunt Sally!"

It wasn't an answer, but Sally let it go.

"What were they doing, anyway?" Mary Kerr reflected. "Just developing tortures for all those slanty-eyed little people over there."

"Aren't you getting all this politics from your boyfriend?"

"I think things ought to be fairer than the government is. He's got me believing that, at least. Fairer and more honest."

"A lot of good it does to tell that to the government."

Mary Kerr ate the last of the french fries.

Sally said, "I doubt if Kate thinks much further about those contracts than that they're just her job. I don't mean Kate isn't smart. She really is smart. But getting her work wrecked by these hotheaded people—what good does it do? There's an investigation now, you know. She and Dr. Fletcher ordered it, so as to get themselves off the hook. She's done nothing recently but write reports."

Will she mention the key in those reports? Mary Kerr wondered. "I guess then was when Fred Davis called her. Up he galloped to the rescue."

"He did ask her up there. She was grateful and she went. 'Getting away from it all,' was how she put it. However . . . have you seen your house yet? No? Well, don't be shocked. Ed Tomkins had to go there and board up the window so nobody could break in while she's away. Maybe the repairmen have been there by now, but I doubt it. Nobody's there to let them in."

Mary Kerr wondered why Aunt Sally always called her husband by his full name, but she never asked.

"Mary Kerr, don't you go calling Ed Tomkins for any money. Or anything else. I'm warning you because he's got in a raging fit about all you young people. He thinks you're making a mess of this country."

"He doesn't think it's a mess already?"

"I'm not prepared to debate about the country. I have a fresh lot of work to get through every week. I have to stay caught up. Ed Tomkins and I are going off to Puerto Rico in a week or two."

"You didn't finish about Mother."

"Well, honey, as they say, 'The rest you know.' "

"Fred called. . . ."

"Fred called. She told me that what he said was clear and to the point. (I hate to say all this, Mary Kerr, but you ought to know what's what.) He said, 'You need help with that girl, Kate. Agree that's so, if you want to keep on with me.' She said, 'Well, but do *you* want to keep on with *me?*' He said, 'I do, but not with all this revolutionary goon-talk marching through every other minute. Otherwise, she's fine with me. We can turn her around. If you care, I care.' She said, 'Do you know what that Blaise man has done? He came here. He broke my front living room window, wild drunk.' He waited a while and said, 'How much longer are you going to put up with what goes on down there?' 'I don't see what I can do,' she said, and he said, 'Well, just walk out on it.' She said, 'You mean I can come there?' He said yes, she could. She said, 'Oh God, just let it be true.' He said it was true. So she left and I don't blame her. There's an assistant at the clinic, a nice boy from the hospital, who can take on. I guess she'll come back and straighten all that up with Dr. Fletcher, but if she and Fred Davis are still getting on, I don't doubt her staying up there, marrying him."

Mary Kerr sat there for a good while without saying anything. It was past noon now. The french fries had not been all that good, and she didn't think she would eat a meal here. But she had had no money for breakfast.

"The bargain they made," Mary Kerr finally said slowly, "it's really about taking me in hand, isn't it?"

Sally looked up. How to think about that? Bitterness in young people—it was such a shame, she thought. "Kate doesn't always mean what she says. You know that."

Suppose Ed Tomkins was here; he'd pick up a buggy whip and give Mary Kerr a good licking. Did she deserve it? He'd do it, whether or not. Then he might pet her and feed her and tell her to be a good girl and there wouldn't be anything he wouldn't do for her. And if she could find a gun she'd shoot him. Sally put down her square of needlepoint.

"I'm going to get you some real food. Do you like lemon in your iced tea?"

"Please, Aunt Sally."

A few minutes later, when Sally came back from the kitchen, Mary Kerr was gone.

If she wants to starve to death, then let her, was what it occurred to Sally to think, but she didn't actually let herself think it. That was Ed thinking through her, she decided, sitting down to sew. Maybe, in some such way, the Blaise boy was thinking through Mary Kerr. But no, this curiously honest child had always come right out with what she thought. Maybe dancing let her feelings out free. Sally did not know.

22

Ethan's Turn

"Of course, I like Aunt Sally. If I died, she would sew me into the most beautiful dress for burying. She would cry on every stitch."

"But that's not enough," said Ethan.

"No, not enough."

He smiled encouragement, as to a learner in his classes, trying new ground. "You mean, basically, all these relatives of yours are alike? Good and bad, they come to the same thing in the end. Live as we live, think as we think—the same as not thinking at all. And no questions allowed."

"One question. Where is Jeff? He calls me, but he won't say where he is." She was sitting on her feet to hide them. She had taken goofballs to block the pain and keep on dancing, just as everybody did, during the last days. She had walked to get there, on gravel roadsides, wearing sandals, under the far-off dance of distant stars.

"But if he hasn't told you—"

"Doesn't want me to know. He came for the closing program. Mother got her feelings hurt over one of the numbers, all about motherhood. She had Fred with her."

"Who?"

"Latest boyfriend. Philadelphia. Rich." She laughed.

"Enough said." Ethan set the tips of his fingers together. He pondered.

"Maybe it's dangerous to talk."

"Jeff may think that."

Sitting there, she remembered all the times she was with Jeff, the only place they were both understood, so it was happy for them. She wanted to share things about Art Manning with Ethan. The quiet dynamism, the voice: "Push the idea, push it forward, nudge it to the breaking point, then break right into it. When you're there, you know it, you know. You have known, you will know . . . and know forever because you know now. . . ." It was right.

But she thought she might have a fractured toe, and her one shirt was ripped. She sat thinking of his wonderful big hands, like a dog with big paws, pushing her forward, his own step leading them all. "There are no stars here." He had said that, not to her, but to another girl, who still wore lipstick and did up her hair. "Submerge your gift," he had said. "Let it speak for you. Work honestly . . . clean."

So she sat telling Ethan, who listened. "The good things in you. They're growing," he said.

"Why didn't you marry Aunt Jane?"

"Why?" He took her question, which he couldn't have expected, as a natural one, though he almost (Mary thought) did not succeed in doing so. Something around his eyes had flinched and narrowed. "My impression was that she refused me."

"I wonder why."

His smile was weak for the first time. "I wasn't what she wanted me to be."

"I'm hungry," Mary said.

He took her back to his kitchen, a single man's supplies, refrigerator almost empty except for frozen dinners. A few cans on the shelves. "What do you like? Bacon and eggs? Soup?"

She consented to Campbell's tomato.

"Jeff is upset about the Gifford case. The immolation. You must have read about it."

"He set himself on fire, on the street corner?" *You could even make a dance of that,* she thought, *tragic, with clouds of smoke.*

The gas flame leaped up too high under the saucepan of soup. Ethan turned it down. "They were friends. I'm not sure how close recently. Perhaps he's mentioned him. They shared some strong ideals, Jeff being Catholic, too."

"Not a very good one."

"Just the same." He stirred and watched the boil form. When he turned, she had her head on the kitchen table where he habitually ate when alone. Her hair fell across her folded arms. When she raised her head again it was with effort.

She was barely able to keep her lips moving. "He writes to me. I do know about the speaking circuit, how they're financing it through the Movement. He called last night. I heard about the father's coming here. You'd told him. Here we go, maybe, he and I, me on a dancing circuit, he like a preacher making the rounds. Souls to be saved. . . ." Her head fell forward, but she jerked it up. "Poppy always said I'd go with the circus . . . the circus circuit. . . ." She started a laugh and faded out.

But she must have still been half awake, too, because she knew he had made a call. She heard his voice float murmurously back to her. "Is this Jane? . . . A voice from the past, can you believe it? Oh, you did recognize me? Yes, it's Ethan here. Jane, it's hard to believe, but I've a favor to ask. Call it for old times' sake, whatever you like. . . . I mean to say, whatever you like would please me, too. Your niece, Mary Kerr, is here. Her mother's away. She needs food, sleep, a good bath—"

"The soup!" Mary jerked awake. She thought it was boiling over, but instead it was sitting before her, steaming.

She felt herself—as if in a memory, like his voice speaking, though like his voice, it was an actual occurrence—guided to his car, his arm around her, and some minutes later a long walkway between two halves of a green lawn, dividing like the sea, and sheets of green sloping up like waves. Inside, a gentle odor of something good, rose scent, and rose shading from light falling through pale draperies and flax-colored blinds. A woman's face smiling. Aunt Jane. "She looks like Poppy. I never noticed."

"Yes, of course she does. Look after her, Jane. No questions, please. The truth is, I don't have any answers myself. Times are difficult."

The arm of a woman she had never especially liked until now closed over Mary's shoulder, and she leaned, clinging.

"I've fixed a little bouillon. Then, I think, you could use a long bath and a good sleep and some real food."

"You would have the perfect thing," was Ethan's tribute.

Mary Kerr took the mug handed to her and felt the salty fluid go down, admired the thick mug's surface with its bright flowers painted on it, how it curved into her palm, while Jane and Ethan's hands touched each other.

Then the bath, drawn and heavenly warm, with scented crystals liberally scattered in, her feet smarting from the water, the blisters stinging, the cracked skin splitting open wider with the warmth and cleansing, hurting again, all over, as she dried them with a towel, even bleeding a little. Then, staggering with sleepiness, never to sleep enough, she was sinking into the bed, dragging up a coverlet, hearing the muted click of the light switch, thinking, *I'm safe again . . . home. If only Jeff*

Ethan told her at last. She was walking again, or rather limping, on healing feet.

"We've managed by hook and by crook to raise the money for the journal. He will be going out, my roving reporter, to all these trouble spots. He will write about them. Not what gets in the national press, but what actually happens. *The Radar Screen.* Jeff's column will be 'From the Front Lines.' This is our crusade, not just talk anymore. Action." He beamed at her.

"You'll print it here?" She had some idea of a press set up in Ethan's old garage out back.

"No, not even in the South. But wherever we find to locate, it has to be a secret. There may be attacks on it. We're a country within a country, Mary!"

He handed her an envelope, Jeff's writing, a scrawled note inside just for her.

The notes kept coming. Ethan said, "He's not intending to lose you. Surely that's obvious."

"He isn't here," she said, and felt empty in spite of all.

Calls and letters were also coming from Kate. "Don't think I've left you. You must just love being at Jane's. I sent you a check. Now, don't worry . . . I'm always thinking of my darling girl."

"Yes, Mother. Aunt Jane is really nice. I smell like lilac bath salts. Say hello to Fred."

23

The Sand Runs Through

"I'm coming back, darling. We've got to sit down and talk. You've just never known what you mean to me."

"They haven't finished repairing the house yet," Mary Kerr warned her. "It's still boarded up."

"Then I'll have to come, to see about getting it done."

Phone calls had kept coming for Mary Kerr during her stay with Aunt Jane, not only from afar but from closer to home. Friends of Jeff's, seeking her out. "Come to some of our meetings . . . we're watching some movies you won't believe . . . napalm, interrogation squads, conscriptions of whores for the GIs . . . Fonda's in Hanoi . . . Baez has a new album. . . ."

None of this crowd would get the first step up Aunt Jane's walk. "I'll hire a guard with a gun if I have to" was her verdict.

But it was September now and school had started. Aunt Jane had packed Mary Kerr off to the rooming house. Ethan helped her buy books for her classes. Who would see that she "looked nice"? Sally offered services free of charge. Mary Kerr refused. Sally gave up.

Mary went to Al Bernstein and offered to help with his dance classes. "I never have enough money to get by. My aunt pays for my room."

"Where's your mother?"

"Oh, she sends me checks but they go too fast."

He gave her some of his students in modern dance. She would be taking away from his enrollment in ballet. They both knew it. He was kind to her, maybe too much.

When Kate appeared, her list of people to see was headed not by Mary Kerr but by Dr. Fletcher. She had never once mentioned that stolen key suspicion to him, but nonetheless he seemed to be laying it at her door that his lab had been raided, the government contract cancelled. Kate said she was every bit as sorry as he was.

"I've gone for interviews at Pennsylvania med school. You know how far ahead I was on enzyme research. It was the cancer cure that I had my heart set on. Surely you know I was only into the defense contract work to help out."

Dr. Fletcher drew careful doodles on his appointment pad. "You go ahead and get your marrying over with. Then I'll see what I can do."

Kate knew better than to argue. She considered tears. She settled for silence.

Dr. Fletcher said, "We got into headlines three times over that break-in. They're still out there, ready for us. Once the press—"

"Oh, I know it was an embarrassment. Haven't they caught anybody yet?"

"Had you any suspicions?"

"I? Of course not."

Yet it had also towered up in the press that rallies nightly on the campus at that time were spreading into the city. Her daughter had even danced in one, Dr. Fletcher casually recalled.

"Only once," Kate protested. "She stopped after that. It is just not her type of thing."

He took her to lunch.

"So no help from you at this point?" Kate asked. He had just looked up across the restaurant table with something like his old friendliness. He had once seemed to her fatherly, and was fatherliness all? At times she hadn't thought so. But she had someone else now, and he knew it.

"I must think it over," was all he would give her.

Kate took Mary Kerr out to dinner that night in an expensive new restaurant near the highway. "Tell me about Jeff," she said.

"Nothing to tell," said Mary Kerr. "He's not here anymore. Tell me about Fred."

Kate brightened. "He's anxious to know you better. We talk of nothing else. You're bound to like each other. I've looked into Bryn Mawr. They've got a dance program you'll love."

"It's not that good," said Mary Kerr, who was already informed.

"But in Philadelphia there might be something of interest," Kate pursued.

"Oh, I guess. I wanted to go on with Manning."

"I can't have you gypsying around the country, darling. It just wouldn't do for one of us to live that way."

People kept coming up to their table, wanting to talk to pretty Kate, interesting Kate. Old friends. What had they heard? Well, yes, she'd gone up to visit, that was all. A very interesting man. She wished they knew him. Don't be silly, just a good friend. She parried and flirted. Not much time was left to talk with Mary Kerr, after all.

When the windows of the duplex were finally repaired, Kate locked up everything and returned to Philadelphia.

When not working at the studio, Mary Kerr lay on the bed in her room with the windows up through the hot autumn afternoons. It was the same kind of weather as when Poppy had died. She recalled that golden day when she danced for him, air smelling of the crushed leaves of fall, and light tinged with gold.

Once she went around to the old house of her childhood and sat down on the front steps. A wealthy Jewish family had bought it. After Mary Kerr spent what must have been an hour of sitting there in a silent world with no one about, a plump black woman in a starched uniform came out and asked her to leave. "Just sitting out here, unless you want somebody, it's not allowed." She had a Yankee accent, unlike Penney. Mary Kerr then realized she was wearing faded jeans, ripped across the knee, and an oversized shirt stained with a purple dye they had used for costumes.

Maybe I'll go see Penney, she thought, but didn't go. She didn't know why she didn't go. She had always loved Penney.

When she got back to her rooming house, a small woman whose almost white hair was still streaked with bronze was waiting for her in a car near the driveway and followed her to the door.

"Oh, Grandmother," Mary Kerr said. "It's you."

"I just wondered about you," said Kate's mother from out in Jasper County. "I hear Kate's got this new man friend now. I guess she'll marry him any day. 'Mary Kerr might just be feeling left all alone,' is what I told your grandfather. He said, 'You go get that child and bring her on out here.' You needn't think we even remember that mixed-up summer anymore. Everybody's long forgotten it. Murray's new baby came, just the cutest thing you ever saw, and Frank's got him a girlfriend, works with him down at the coin laundry. Everything's fine. As for dancing . . . well, Pete said, 'Just tell her I'll dance with her. Anytime.' Martha said, 'Why, I'd be glad to learn. She can teach me and Effie.' Effie's their little girl, you remember her."

Mary Kerr said she would have to think about it.

Brisk and positive, that was Grandmother. "Thank you, though, Grandmother," Mary Kerr said.

"We love you," her grandmother said, marching away.

Her motor started at the first try and she drove smartly off.

Mary Kerr went upstairs. She would have cried, but crying bored her. Jeff an activist full-time, as Ethan all but said. The paper, *Dispatches,* absorbing them both. He still could have telephoned.

"So you think he's forgotten you?" Kate had asked, rubbing it in. Funny how she kept coming back to him.

"You can always go find him," Mary Kerr told her.

"I'd rather you'd like somebody more stable than that," Kate said.

"Oh, I just meant I thought you liked him."

"Liked him!" It had come out unexpectedly, but it had struck Kate off balance.

"I was teasing," Mary Kerr retreated.

"Of course, you were."

She had been cutting too many classes, had just cut another.

What to think about in golden weather, but of people going, of how going seemed to be the constant outcome of coming. Madame Delida as gone as Poppy, Mother gone, and Jeff, too, and Ethan, though only a few blocks away, had his mind leading outward in all directions; like the central office of a spread-out business, he was only a red tack on a map, with radiating lines beaming to distant points. He wasn't really there.

I won't be here long, either. Like turning a street corner and running slap into a surprise, she knew it was true the minute she thought it.

If not here, where?

The golden Carolina day was dying and night and distant stars were coming on. Out there somewhere through the blackness, there must be a landing place, some point for her feet to rest on.

Part II
Voices from Afar

1

Gerda Stewart: A Journal

From the mountain in winter, you can see the northern lights. They come pulsing up the sky from the distant pole, as alive as the sea, awesome, towering, but with something, too, like playfulness, saying some phrase, such as, "I'm coming close! Watch me!" Bright and brighter, then retreating. Gigantic waves.

(I read it over. It's not bad, for a start. This journal I am moved to keep because for one thing it is a gift and handsome. Covered with a paisley print in swirling green and gold. End papers. I used to study writing at Barnard College in New York with Professor Stephen Gaber, who once was published in *The New Yorker*. Let me go on. We will see.)

Montreal.
Do you ever think you might go there, climb up high enough on the map to touch those lights? That would be only your dream. Except from Montreal there is nowhere else to climb but to the Pole. If you don't think you'd like it so far up, this city must suffice.

Coming to Montreal, driving up from the U.S., looking ahead from the long, flat highway that leads up from the border crossing, you are taken on by a sweeping curve that rights you toward the city. First you see towers, gray, and the mountain, loaf-shaped, singular, alone. Buildings are studded along its flanks, a bell-shaped oratory to the west, the boldly lighted cross to the east. The river streams powerfully past. Soaring bridges lead you in. The city is an island, surrounded by rivers.

Montreal, my home.

"What are you, an American, doing here?"

"I'm only half American. I have to be somewhere." Plain Canadian eyes keep wondering. I go on: "I married a Canadian."

"Oh."

I follow up: "*Qui prend mari, prend pays.*"

"You're not French!"

"I can learn a little."

"You actually like them, the French here?"

Suspicion now. I change the subject.

All this at a party in a downtown club, or a dinner at someone's home. Gatherings of a social nature . . . these abound. Charming people . . . a fairly good time had by all.

Later Gordon and I drive home through darkened streets, past St. Catherine Street, a busy shoppers' artery stretching miles, east to west, on to Westmount, haven of comfort and privilege.

Perched on the mountain slope, blurred by blizzards in winter, an island within an island, at all seasons. Here we live, work, raise children, speak proper English to one another, a swirl of every language jabbering and echoing around us, unheard within our walls.

(At this point my professor would certainly tell me to get on to some narrative or other. "Where's your story line?" I'm getting to that. It's really why I started.)

"Did you know that if you try to kill yourself and fail, they try you in court as though you'd attempted murder?"

Again, we are at a party. I have had two drinks. The woman I am speaking to regards me open-mouthed. She says nothing.

"If you try and succeed," I go on, "you are still classed as a murderer. You are buried in unhallowed ground. Think of it."

"Well," she says, English Canadian to the core, "I suppose they know what they are doing." Uncomfortable, she seeks out imported cheese and smoked Nova Scotia salmon at the buffet table. Drunk, is what she thinks of me.

But drink has only released what was there already. It has let loose the strange facts that haunt me, has made them into words. In a minute I would have said, "Her name is Mary, just that. Mary."

Because that was and is her name.

————

She is more than an outsider—most of us here are that, to some degree. She is waiflike, apparently abandoned, a lost wanderer, who lives down in Seymour Street, a poor but decent part of the city. She was cut down one snowy afternoon in her rooming house, hanging from a knotted bedsheet. The sheet made too dull a surface to do the work she had wanted it for. Her face was blue, she had fainted, but was revived. Then she was hauled into court, tried, and sentenced. My husband, out of pity, paid bail. But then he let her know it. She wondered who and he told her. He owns the building where it happened. That was how he heard.

Naturally, it became a bond. Gordon's good deeds never end with being done. I invited her to dinner. She sat with folded hands among people unlike herself, wearing some sort of Indian-type robe with strings of beads, looking singularly lost and even lovely in her own way, but saying very little. Her baby girl is fine. Her husband is in the States on some sort of political work. She looks frightened. We know there is a war. We draw back from questions. We do not ask her again.

She still calls occasionally and we listen to her news. It was after the work in the dance company fell through—the place she'd been promised, working through some big name in the States—it was then she got so depressed. The blind-alley feeling. The blank wall for a future. A new decision about half the company needing to be French, this was what let her out. The latest hired had to go. No one to blame. But she was trying still. And working, though not dancing. Her joys, I gather, may be few, but life at least is now hers. She thought she actually died when she meant to. She discovered life at the moment of reviving, was that it? Or did it spring out of the unexpectedness, the outrageous unreason of being dragged off to police court to defend herself against herself for her own attempted murder? There is something ridiculous about it, unless it is happening to you. Then there is, I suppose, like shock therapy, some benefit if you survive. That's been done, at least. I would like to ask her if she doesn't think that. I note she has become hopeful and cheerful, instead of dully depressed. But we have no bond as she and Gordon do, and I think she may not like to discuss it.

Today, like me, she must feel the spring. It is only softened air— that's what passes here for spring. The landscape is still a stark etching, black, white, and dirty white. Ice is melting in the streets which yesterday streamed with brooks of water from the thaw.

Down in Seymour Street, the house Gordon bought as an investment. He keeps it, in my opinion, as a charitable institution; the stairs have to be fumigated regularly because of the old people, the old couples, who live there and who actually, I think, love dirt and stale air all containing their own smells. If they didn't have odorous reminders of themselves around, how would they know they're alive? In the air (like incense in churches, reeking of sweating stone and smoke), they can find their personal sanctities and know they are still more than dust. But for the sake of the retired hospital orderly on the first floor up, the struggling Korean mechanic in the back of the *rez-de-chaussée,* and the waif, ex-suicide, Mary, in the front, Gordon has to keep the place livable, he thinks. He will trudge over there after office hours to make sure Monsieur Marchand, his man of all work, is doing his job. Then there will have been a flaw in the heating system, a mechanic to be called, or a leak in the plumbing. I think he goes by to talk to her then; I think she is the real reason he goes there.

We never had a daughter, only boys, two, independent and knowledgeable, now gone about their business. One is a lecturer in physics at the University of Toronto, the other lives out West and is, it may be, a poet. His living comes from an art shop, posters and framing. I feel hardly close to them anymore.

Would a daughter have been different? Gordon must have asked himself that, too; I can think that now he is indulging a fantasy of the daughter he never had. But there's also the chance that down in those poor little rooms, shades drawn, he lifts her, a slight weight in his arms. I see her hair, long and silky brown, swinging loose down to his knees. He turns with her slowly, mobilelike they turn together, in my mind's eye.

She may go away, of course, at any time. Her family is in the States. Is her husband a protester, defector, something of the sort? Has he left her alone here . . . why?

"A good question," Gordon answers dryly. "She doesn't know, either, not the precise facts. Or so she says, honestly, I think."

"But why? Why doesn't she?"

"It may be dangerous for her, to know too much. Dangerous for him." So there he goes, limping away at twilight. One of Gordon's legs is shorter than the other. He wears a built-up shoe. You can hear him coming; the bob in his walk is a long-familiar rhythm in my head.

When he gets back, I inquire. "You must have seen that girl down there. She must have some news sometime."

"Matter of fact, she does. She called me, wanted me to know. A long letter from the mysterious husband."

"So she does know where he is?"

"Well, no, she doesn't. There was a postmark, of course. But she said it probably didn't indicate where he is."

"Is he coming for her?"

"Who knows? He was asking if she got the money. I think that's why she wanted me to see it, a matter of pride. Showing that he hasn't neglected her as much as it seems."

"But she hasn't gotten anything . . . nothing! Or so she says, doesn't she?"

"Something gets through. This time it did. I guess if you've a chain working, there might be a weak link."

"You mean they steal it along the way. Needing drugs, probably."

"Or help, bail, food . . . who knows?"

"What else did he say? I think he's a myth."

"Long messages to the little girl, about being good and so on. Of course, she's good. She can't even read yet."

"I suppose."

"Then . . . philosophy."

"About what?"

"His role in things." Gordon is floundering. How little we know. "About the States, national destiny at stake. He does seem intelligent, writes well, sounds as though he loves her." He ponders. "Maybe he doesn't know anything about the—well, about what she's going through here."

"He sounds very serious."

"Is being serious any excuse for leaving your wife and child?"

I risk something. "You think they really are married?"

"She says so."

I'm wanting to defend Americans, being one. But nowadays, they do seem strange. Canadians, unlike their climate, are mild by comparison, though the French keep boiling up with anger over one thing or another.

Gordon ponders on. "He did say this: that he, individually, did not matter. He said, a curious statement, 'You remember that day in the churchyard? What happened just after made me see I was to be a sacrifice.' "

"What happened in the churchyard?"

"It's just what I asked. 'Just some work he failed to get approved. It meant failing to get the degree he was working on. It meant he'd have to start working out his beliefs in other ways, ways not necessarily legal.' I think she had a lot of faith in me, even to say that much."

He's getting so attached, I think. Foolish sentiment is taking over. He can't stop talking about them.

"I'm certain he's with some underground work, not out yelling in the open. The intellectual ones. They work down deep. She did tell me once, soon after the suicide try, that he'd burned the ends of his fingers with acid to alter the prints. That means his papers must be forged. I doubt it's working, though."

"What working?"

"Burning prints doesn't change them. I read it somewhere."

He is sitting on the end of my bed, rumpling the satin coverlet. I hang things in the closet. "A new coat," he remarks.

"You saw that."

"I know." Then it's the jewel box on the dresser, left open. "You should get more insurance. Those earrings, for instance. Prices are bound to be twice what they were. Call and tell them."

"I should sell and give to the poor war defectors."

He laughs. "Sometimes I do think that."

"I've no more than what's average . . . I mean for people like us."

"Well, I know."

But trouble is in his face, insoluble. I shake my thoughts out straight. No use to be jealous, refer it all to love. A girl is watching a street for a young man who does not come. His shape is in her head. She stands by the window and holds the baby in her arms. She thinks of the form in her head.

I have to go to the eye specialist. There is a defect in my vision. One of my eyes is out of focus with the other. I wear corrective glasses which make the condition less noticeable to others, as lenses are not so easily seen into as the naked eyes. When I go without glasses, thinking that in evening dress I look better, I have seen people grow fidgety and find themselves disconcerted, as I have no gaze, really, for them to focus on in talking or listening, so they do not know where to look.

In the doctor's waiting room I recognize no one. The patients sit silently, reading magazines. A little boy, pale, in bifocals as heavy as his head, clings to his mother's knee. His sober look goes to me. I smile but he turns away. Canadians are masked people. Meeting my husband for the first time, would I know he keeps a refuge for people who need someplace to stay, would I guess anything about a stray female child soul with long brown hair and a baby to care for? No, his gaze, his talk, would not give a hint of it. Canadians do not tell a great deal.

Out into St. Catherine Street. Kaleidoscope of thrusting faces, no one race, polyglot, changing, faces pale as bits of paper blown up the street in the April wind, all different shapes, thrusting and hurrying, Oriental, Arab, Jew. French, English, bums, beggars, cheap girls, nice girls, housewives, the seeking and the sought, sucked into buses, plunging through Metro doors, dodging traffic, ignoring lights. In April there are rinds in the decaying snow, dog filth in soggy layers, a glove appears, a scarf and always the one abandoned overshoe, like a canoe. Walking, walking, the figures. Heads down, half lonely, half wise, they turn off into small old streets. Out of four blocks, two known faces ride up on the wave. You speak and part. "Hello . . . long time. . . ." "Call us soon. . . ." "Had flu. . . ." "Back from Barbados. . . ." "Take care. . . ." Remark on the tan. And some shiver in coats too thin for any season and stare at shop windows, expecting nothing. But some stride smiling, life an aerial somersault in their heads, the air parting for them like glad tall grass.

So where is she? Mary.

Turn left for a few blocks and see if she's there. Waiting in her room. The telephone is in the hall. If it rings it is hardly ever for her. If it is for her, she is afraid to go to it.

(I should invent stories. Then I could say that I know all about what happens in them. But in real life, no one can really know, can they?)

2

Gerda's Journal (continued)

Last week, they took the child away.

Previously, before the suicide attempt, someone had let her parents know where she was. They had come here, we learned later from the lawyer the court appointed. Had found her. It wasn't her real father, but a stepfather, her mother's second husband, the first having died. What resulted from this visit? Money, a little. A hundred a month, but more available, anything she could want if she'd just "give all this up, come back and straighten up." Give up her husband, too? Nobody knew what had been said except Mary herself. A hundred dollars was better than nothing, but did she even accept that? She worked somewhere, some little clerking job, but had to leave because of speaking too little French. Kept alert for something from the dance companies. Had not abandoned hope.

One morning she had called to say she could no longer afford to stay on at Seymour Street. Then, before Gordon could chase over to see about her after work, she had pinned the note to the child, left the child with a friend upstairs who baby-sat for her, and jumped from the dresser with the sheet twisted into a rope and tied around her neck. She'd knotted it overhead to the pipes that ran across her ceiling. She had gone to the library and read up on the process. Everything was supposed to be over in a few minutes.

But the baby-sitter did not cooperate. She cheated and opened the note before she was supposed to, and got the police there, double quick. They were at the door before Mary had quit coughing, though before they were actually in she had fainted.

After the trial and the psychiatric interviews, the baby was supposed to have gone back to the grandmother, Mary's mother, who lived in Philadelphia. The judge had ordered this. Mary temporized. The baby was too sick to travel, she said; and when they came to check up she hid it, lied about where it was, staved them off.

Finally she had to give in. She let them drive her to the border. Under the gaze of the woman from the city probation office, she stuck the baby into her mother's arms, then turned quickly away, all shaken up, having had to hear said to her, having said in return, who knew what? We couldn't imagine.

At any rate, she refused to go with the parents. Refused comfort, safety, soft beds, warm rooms, and the company of her own child. Did not cry on the way home. Just sat perfectly still, perfectly silent.

"Couldn't this be from drugs?" I suggested. "I mean, they're all on them, aren't they?"

"I don't think so," Gordon said. "She's too . . . stung. Even for that." He reflected on the word he had used. It was unusual.

When I go to see her, I make a point of asking, "Is Kathy happy with your mother? What's she like?"

"You mean Kate Davis?" she asks me in her wry narrow voice, giving the stepfather's name, never saying *Mother*.

"You like him, at least, don't you? You named the baby for your mother, didn't you? That must mean something."

"The little money he sends helps. But I can't stand to go there. Not with her."

"What's wrong with her?"

No answer.

"What did she do to you?"

"After my father died . . . we were just the two of us. You must have heard of the silver hairbrush treatment." She even laughs, a clean little gurgle of sound. Honest and pure, like spring water.

"You mean being spanked with one?" My turn to laugh. "But does it take a silver one?"

"Sure it does. And think how it feels across your face." The laugh gets a crazy edge to it. "And locked in closets."

"Lined in velvet," I speculate, and since she's smiling, quieter, I'm bold enough to say, "What has happened to your husband? You told the court you didn't know."

"I know but I can't say. It's why I have to stay where he left me. He'll come back. When he does, I'll be through with this probation and they won't be able to keep Kathy. We'll work. In summer we can all three go and rent a cottage somewhere, where we can swim in a lake and be together."

Scattered people.

Tag ends of life, wild upheavals in the outer world (war), in the inner world (family), and Mary the frail center of this merciless swirl. She and thousands more. *Why do I take up time with her?* I wonder, that day walking home from the eye specialist. We are both into this, Gordon and I, though hardly equally.

Now I'm doing it again, turning down the street, even after I feel the raw wind return again (in Montreal spring never quite comes), after I know I should hail a cab and head for home. Yet I turn straight into a wind that comes up from the river, almost tasting of icy floes, and here I am in Seymour Street among the tall old houses. Clotted remnants of snow remain, unmelted. Below the steps her window looks dark; she may be out for groceries. I climb up to the first floor entrance, ring the bell. I've never had the key.

No answer. I try another number, thinking the first mistaken. A buzz from the lock and the door bursts open, there's a cracked voice above the stair, hitting my ear the instant my face thrusts in. "Oh, it's you. She's gone, that girl. She left a note on the radiator. It's for your husband, though." So it is.

I see it lying on the ocher-painted old-fashioned scroll radiator under a bleached and freckled excuse for a mirror, flowers etched around the frame. "For Mr. Stewart." Not for me. I turn and close the door. And there he stands on the street below.

Not Gordon, but the one she waited for. The other.

I never saw him before, but I know him.

He is just standing there, looking in the way of just having found first the street, then the house number.

He is distinct.

Middle height, solid, firm, aware, unafraid. His face is weather-browned to the color of his hair, which is brownish, medium blond, and the duffel coat he is wearing is that color, too.

He looks from the house number to me and I falter down one step, then two, and, it must be, six or seven more. As I stop on the bottom step we are almost eye to eye, but still he says nothing. His eyes are penetrating, probing, keen. He has come out of some conflict in order to stand here. He says nothing.

"You're looking for her, I know that's who you are. Mary's husband. Mary Blaise. Aren't you? But she's gone now, left. Maybe she'll be back. We know her . . . my husband and I."

He is looking at me still, but there's no word. It finally comes. "I don't know what you mean."

I come all the way down, stand close. "You'd have to be the one! She knew you'd come! We're her friends, don't misunderstand. The only ones, so far as I know, who've really done anything for her. We—"

He turns away from me. One word: "Impossible." That's all.

He's walking off. I am clinging to the rail and in my ignorance, my state of not knowing, I think the feelings she might have had for finding him there, then seeing him turn away, walk away, have come in some measure to me. For him to leave now seems for an instant to create an emptiness so profound nothing in the world can fill it again. But I can't do anything about it. How can I?

I look up and here comes Gordon, just limping past the corner toward the rooming house. I wait.

"She's gone," I tell him. "She left a note for you. But Gordon, the most amazing thing. Her husband was here, I'm sure of it. He's just gone up the street. Only he wouldn't tell me anything. Wouldn't speak or answer me."

Gordon goes inside for the letter. He returns, and as we walk he stuffs it in his pocket. He has torn it open to read it; I can see the torn edges of the envelope. "It's no cause for alarm. She's got a dance opportunity, has to stay over in the East for a few days. But to think she missed—"

"What a strange life. When he comes and won't answer. When she's gone with no address to share."

"You don't know it was him."

"But why couldn't he say so? You'd think these people were from Mars."

The unshared note, Gordon's anxious face.

"Don't you care for her maybe too much?" I'm bold enough to ask it. "Love her," I should have said, but didn't.

"Just an old game-legged landlord. What could she see in me?"

In my mind's eye I am still seeing the blank look, the intense face. "If only you'd seen him." I see him walking off, an unwavering step, not looking back. "You'd have seen the frame she lives in, the sort of person in control of her."

3

Mary's Tape

When I was dancing, then I was happy.

When I first began studying with Madame Delida, I would hold my hands up, arms curved ("so to frame the face," she said). I lowered my eyes, but couldn't see my feet past the tutu. During practice I could see them, see how the ankles swelled forward, out of the natural line. How slow and painful to master, making this way of moving seem a part of me. I didn't take it badly that I was a little shorter than required for ballet. There was always modern dance. *It's more like nature,* I would tell myself, thinking I might like it best. But even as a departing world, ballet always sparkled, a fairyland, something to love.

In Kingsbury, after Madame Delida left and Poppy died, Mother had to work to send me to the ballet school, the one Al Bernstein had. Then she believed Jeff Blaise was gone, so she came and gathered me up one day and off we went to Philadelphia, floating on promises of how I must "go on with it," she was not against it anymore. "It" for her was just dancing; she couldn't make finer distinctions. They both said I had to finish school. They packed me straight into Bryn Mawr.

It was the end of the winter term, during the holidays and too late to register for spring, but Fred Davis had pull. He was Main Line, which meant he knew how to work things.

And there was Mother, like she always was, north or south, stipulating. "I won't agree unless we have this straight."

"All right," Fred answers. "Let's sit down and see if we understand each other."

It could make you think he was nothing but a yes man, but then

I began to see him better. He was just getting what he didn't want to think about out of the way. Fred was so sharp he could afford to look unconcerned. He had inherited everything and took care of it. He liked collections. He had put Mother among his collections. She came under the head of WOMEN . . . subdivision, WIVES.

Nobody mentioned Jeff. "Bryn Mawr," Mother said.

"All right," I answered.

"A ballet school downtown, the best," she said.

"All right."

"With permission to practice between lessons at the college."

"All right."

What else? Living in the dormitory. Out of their way, I realized. Fred hadn't collected me. Who would want this careless-looking girl straying around his panelled house with the separate library, high-backed chairs at the dining table, and glass cabinets full of old carved ivories? Imagine dusting all that. He caught me upstairs in a third floor retreat, trying actually to play with some last-century games made of carved wood with agate marbles that went spinning around in little curved troughs.

"Nobody's played with those things in forty years," he said. He readily admitted he had thought he'd heard a rat up there, so came up to check. He played with me, though, for a few minutes.

I liked him. "She's got to work, hasn't she?" he confided in me, talking about Mother. Her bid to continue cancer research at the University of Pennsylvania never materialized. They kept putting her off. She blamed it, I knew, on the bad record of the lab in Kingsbury and still suspected Jeff (I knew that, too), so was making it my fault in some silent way. I couldn't help it.

She couldn't help it that looking beautiful in Fred's beautiful house was not enough. It was too little for her energies. "Sit and knit?" she would burst out. "Never!" So Fred, who had inherited, among other things, that little pharmaceutical line that had led him to Atlanta in the first place to find Kate floating down the escalator, got her a job in one of them. Cold creams, astringents, cleansers, and such. They had to be tested. Funny, but it all came originally from tar. Tar came from coal. She got to wear her white jackets again. For all I knew, there were once again those helpless little live creatures to pick up in her capable hands, sensuous, that squirming they did in a human grasp, those frightened helpless eyes and wiggling noses. Pink, probably. Testing them. Putting them down. She likes that.

"Summers off," Fred insisted.

"All summer?" She acted like it was a sentence.

"Two months, then," he conceded.

He had a country house (inherited) up in New England. If you had it you had to enjoy it, no way out. Her turn to agree: "All right."

She had kept right on working that summer after Poppy died. She had to show the house, sell it, move. It almost resulted in a break-down. She just decided on her own that I was no help. So out to the country with me, Jasper County. And look what happened. I met Jeff. I looked across the pasture fence and there he was. Walking toward me. It seemed I knew then that for the rest of my life he would be doing that very thing, coming toward me. Forever.

We would go down to the creek. I would talk, he would talk, lying on our stomachs, pulling up grass, finding pebbles. He read me Walt Whitman out of an old tattered paperback he'd found in the back of the town's drugstore, Whitman just where he would have liked to be found, Jeff said, reading: ". . . one great star hung out of the west." We looked up and there it was.

Then we didn't talk at all.

I remember it so well, how at the same moment we both ran out of words. I remember the first time he touched me, meaning to. He had reached over me to my side, just under my arm, where the breast I didn't yet have very much of began to slope upward. But something outside, a fish jumping or some other movement, made me start, so his hand jarred hard against me, bruising. It will last forever in my flesh, I know that; like a brand on a calf it will always be there, not visible, but in my mind, the starting point of what my own flesh was waiting for. I know it wouldn't have struck me in such a strong way if the feeling hadn't been there already, waiting for the actual touch to enter and fulfill it.

His hand moved around me, around my small rib cage, tracking fire. He turned me and at first it was only his own kiss, but then mine, too—I learned it fast. My body turned to him all by itself, it did seem to me, going wide and free with the sudden nearness. But he held me back: it was something about my being too young. "Too young to hurt," he said once.

"Too young to like?" I finally ventured.

He laughed. "No, not too young to like." He reached over and picked up my hand. He turned it over in the light we'd gotten used to and could see in. Held it, small, in his palm. "Not too young to love." He kissed me again, but in a quieter way.

"What's your name?"

"I told you."

"Write it in the sand."

So I wrote *Mary Kerr* and he said, "But you say Kar, not Kur."

"It's how you say it. Kar."

He rubbed out the second name. "To me you're just Mary."

And we kissed.

I danced for him once, out on the sand. I cut my foot.

Then one night some of the new people we'd seen in the pasture came down and stayed awhile. There were some black ones, too, only nothing like Penney. I didn't feel the same way toward them. They were doing everything, smoking pot, singing, making love. There was hash, too, or so they said, but I didn't try it. The other made me dizzy. (Dizzy, you can't dance.)

On the path near the house I ran into Grandmother. She was waiting. She had a dress on, thinking she might have to go farther, I guess, but hadn't put her hair up. It was down, long and flowing. She looked like a woman coming back out of some past life.

"I won't tell the family, but I think you better stop it. A house's ears are a woman's ears. I don't care if you've got yourself some fella. Those in there—" she nodded her head toward the house, "they're mean."

"I know they are," I said. A houseful of sleeping kin, all mean.

She let me in through the door. "Meet him uptown at the drug-store," she said in a whisper. "Get him to take you to the picture show. Ask him to come meet all of us. Do regular things with him."

"But he's not regular," I said. I shouldn't have said that. It worried her.

I did meet him one more time. It was the bruised spot that kept crying for him. I would hold my hand on it at night, but still it kept insisting. It was one time they were all gone into town for a meeting on some town issue, except for the ones—Murray and Martha and the kids—who had gone fishing. Each bunch thought the others had me along.

I looked everywhere and finally ran into him out in the woods between the house and the pasture, just past the old springhouse, among the trees. I told him about Grandmother. "She thinks you ought to come up and meet everybody," I explained. "Then we could go to the picture show."

"Impossible," he said, just that one word. As if I didn't know. "But I'll see you anyway."

That night the barn caught fire, the one on the property where they all camped. They had been there for weeks and the man who owned the place, absentee, up in Winston, had promised they'd leave, but they didn't. Grandfather called him up. "You don't get them folks off this property, somebody's going to get hurt. You going to lose more than one old rickety barn." Then he said, evidently repeating something from the other end: " 'What's going on out there?' You want to know what's going on out there? Why, what you think's going on out there? Dope and sex and agitation. Colored in with white. Don't tell me you approve of it. I know you didn't say that. But evi-dently you don't disapprove—not enough, anyway."

Naturally, all the integrated bunch got blamed for the barn, though they should have been praised. It was when I was standing with Jeff, talking, down in the woods where it had gotten gradually dark on us, that we looked up and saw a pencil of red, above the trees. We ran toward it, and all the others, camping, were stirred up like an ant bed, grabbing buckets out of nowhere, making a line to the creek, dousing and beating, singeing hair, smoking up our clothes and faces, but saving most of the barn. I didn't dare tell I'd been there. It wouldn't have helped. One of the black men got burned, and one woman got her hair all frizzed from the heat. Still, they pinned it all on us, decided that a bunch of the campers had been in there, inside, smoking dope, playing guitars, and making love, when, as it happened, nobody was in the barn at all. Some said they saw a couple of strangers sneak out the back late in the afternoon. Maybe they caused it.

Back in Kingsbury, it was while I was getting over the shock of moving to another place, leaving behind the home we'd always lived in, that I told Mother about the barn. I think she believed me. We were both trying to make a fresh start.

"But what *were* you doing, out in the pasture?"

"Just talking to this guy I met. The others did a lot of things we didn't do."

"Such as?"

"Oh, you know. He wasn't really one of them. We just read poetry and stuff like that."

She didn't say anything, just looked at me.

"His name's Jeff," I said, as though that explained anything. "Do you like him?" she asked.

"I love him," I said. "We're in love."

She looked thoughtful at first, then worried. It was like she couldn't be glad about anything like that. I had just handed her one more problem. It didn't do to confide.

She decided that fall to send me to Royal's in Kingsbury instead of the university, out on the outskirts of town. "I can't stand to let her go," she warbled on the telephone to Aunt Jane, but I knew it was because Royal's was small and near enough to supervise.

But Ethan Marbell lectured there, one class a week, and Ethan knew Jeff Blaise. She met herself coming back.

Previously noted: After she married Fred Davis, she stuck me in Bryn Mawr.

Long ago, I had thought I'd never see Jeff again, not in the same way. He'd had to run north from Winston during the Art Manning summer, up to Wisconsin, meetings with those name people in the Movement. Twice he called and at first he wrote. That was all. I made up my mind to it. *No more Jeff,* I told myself; did I really believe it?

Just at dark one winter evening on the edge of the Bryn Mawr campus, there he was. I was walking home from the drugstore in the little town center and just as the path angled away from the sidewalk, there by some shrubs, I saw him standing. It was by one of the taller shrubs and it seemed when I saw him that the whole big plant jumped up and grew lighter, bright. It must have been the shock affecting my vision. I said his name.

One of the first times I saw him, when I was in the woods out at Grandfather's place, he was there at the edge of some thick trees. It was like the shadows got together and made him up. And I had had that same jump of feeling then because (or so I think) there was already an outline of him on me, on my body, weighing on my bones, just as (I know for a fact) there was a print of me on him. Maybe that sounds romantic—if so, it can't be helped. To me it's not romantic, but just the way things go. I didn't expect him; I was just wandering around Grandfather's place, the way I would do. They were all different from me anyway. He was standing off from the path down near a cool hollow. The crickets were going, and the katydids. He was closer to their racket than I was. He said "Hello," and so did I. I asked him, "What made you cross the pasture and come to me the other day? Did you think you knew me?" Because he had walked toward me that way, like he knew me. And right that minute I was a little frightened of him because even though we had driven uptown to the café that very afternoon we met and had a Coke and talked, still I remembered what I had always been told: "Make sure you know something about them, who they are, and where from." "Them" meant boys. After all, he was standing in the late afternoon on property he had no right to be on. No longer on his side of the fence.

The trees were bulking high over us, enormous at twilight, harboring the loud insects that spiralled and chanted, dwindled but flared up again; the trees were like great presences, robes black-green and drenched in dew rise—or was it dew fall?—mysterious in the way it came, and no one leaf could be seen on those trees. Yet against the sky, which held a wonderful lot of colorless light, lay a jagged print of leaf shapes just along the edges, while the trees below held themselves dense, full of insect sound and silent spirit. My breath had filled up like a spring box; now I let it out. He was larger than I, yet both of us were small, a tiny pair, by coincidence both wearing white, vulnerable to the giant sky and giant trees. We were like the first that ever were. I had asked something.

Now he answered. "I didn't know you, but I seen you before."

I said, "Oh."

Much later on, I asked him, "What made you say *seen?* 'I seen you before.' That's country Southern." But he never knew the answer.

"And me a Cajun. We don't talk so fine, either," he would say.

"You're not a Cajun, that's a put-on. And it's not the point. I think you said it because you thought *I* was country, that I talked that way, and you wanted to fit in, be okay with me."

"Maybe I did. I don't know why."

The first words people exchange are important.

Back under those trees, "Come down to the creek bank" was the next thing he said. "Wait till they've gone to bed and then come down there. I'll wait for you." So I did, did what he said.

Not to forget to mention the way I felt already, both from the first time I saw him and the first words he said, and the further words of asking me, and onward through that evening on the sand, as though a net had dropped over me, as though a segment of that net drawn about me was a fine-woven strong thread pressing against my throat, just at the spot where it hurts to press, where a man's Adam's apple is, what they call the windpipe. When I finally got around in far-off Montreal to putting the bed sheet rope around my neck, it was that spot I thought most of, how it had first responded to the net of love.

Also I had to learn more about that net: that it is woven with the history of the person who brings it, and that history descends on you along with it. They are one thing together. It is the hardest lesson.

Look at everything he caused. Because of him liking me, Grandfather's whole family personally felt they had to get rid of the colony that had settled down so close, and indirectly he was to blame, then, for the skirmish with those people that took place after I left, the insults exchanged, the shots fired, the injuries. That was my uncles, I knew well, Frank, Murray, and Pete. Some said the Brownings, the family the town was named for. It was hushed up. The colony dispersed. (Only later did I hear from Jeff that two people had gotten killed.)

Next it was Jeff who caused them to send me back to Kingsbury. Because I did go down to meet him again, though Grandmother had warned me. It was the night after the fire. When I came back up from the creek I saw the house lights burning from way across the field, and I thought, *Oh, they've gone and found out I wasn't in bed.* I got in and saw they were all up and dressed. No need to talk: I knew it. Everything was decided.

"Murray's taking you to the bus in thirty minutes," they said. "Hurry up and pack. Your Aunt Sally will meet you."

Aunt Sally, meeting the bus at dawn, said, "It was some boy, or so they said. Nobody's told Kate. She's got too much on her mind."

Weren't they just all dumb? Jeff, of course, not being one of that bunch, would certainly be back in Kingsbury sooner or later, sitting at Ethan's feet. He'd turn up and turn up, as much as he pleased. And there he was again at the corner of the Bryn Mawr campus, making the big bush he was standing by jump to life and flare up in my vision, while I jumped to life, too, and cried out, what I don't remember.

He said, "Mary? It's me . . . it's Jeff." He caught my hand the minute I got near, his touch bringing everything about him back, out of his vivid grip and straight wrist.

"I can't keep on picking out another school for you every time he shows up," my mother said.

I had told her about him, that he was there. I was counting on it that she might have improved. At times she wasn't so bad. She went to extremes, is all. After Poppy died, she'd been known to kneel down and put her arms around me. "You are the most precious thing on earth," she would say, like a chant, over and over. "I would do everything in my power for you." It crossed my mind more than once that marrying Fred was probably one more thing she called herself doing on my account. Getting me away. New environment, starting over. Pots of money. Some place Jeff's father couldn't show up and scare hell out of her. Then the lab break-in. Me able to steal her keys, so her thinking ran. Jeff being against the government contract, connecting it with the war effort.

But nobody could object to her working in a pharmaceutical lab, testing bath oil and face cream.

So I told her Jeff had come.

I was sitting between them, midway down the beautiful mahogany table: she at one end, Fred at the other. He had moved the flowers he ordered every weekend, three arrangements. He did not mention that my hair was a tangle, nor did she. Once I had showed up for a cocktail party they were having, barefoot in old torn jeans, and they never mentioned it. There had been some agreement.

"Let's have him here," Fred said, more to her than to me. "Let's meet him, get to know him."

"I doubt his coming," Mother said. She had the little frown between her brows, that special one I could put there. It was my property, that frown, and I sometimes, feeling wicked, would make it come there just to see that I could do it.

I think Fred Davis had fallen in love with her hair. He mentioned it often. When he had seen her come floating down the escalator in Atlanta, he had seen the light falling on her hair, making it shine like a web of gold. "And that lavender dress," he would say.

"Blue," she'd say, "but never mind."

"Lavender to me," he'd repeat. He'd been divorced two years before from some mysterious woman he never mentioned and had about gone crazy from being alone too much. There were no traces of her discoverable around the house. We prowled around looking without admitting it. It was one of those times we were in step. It was wonderful when she was like that, but rare.

Fred had an office downtown where he did what he called "carrying on the family business." Every day he was deciding something, whether to sell something, whether to buy something else or to "hold off awhile." He had a sister somewhere in Ohio—Cincinnati, I think—and a daughter out in California on a ski resort, married. He was on several boards of directors. Coal mining, what it started with, had led off into every direction. He had property both tangible and intangible. After his divorce he took to attending conventions to break the monotony, and in so doing he had met Mother, what he was looking for. He was a dark, thin, well-bred, detached man. You couldn't tell what he thought. You just knew that he was thinking, all the time. His office was downtown, not far from where I went to ballet school. Mother worked in the opposite direction, out near the university. Each morning they drove off in separate cars.

When she'd first told me about him, I asked her, "Do you love him?"

She thought it over. "I believe he loves me," she finally said. She was making one of her struggles to be on the level. "I think that he's an interesting man and will see that I don't want for anything. It's difficult at my age to find anyone so . . . suitable."

It was a word I wouldn't have thought of.

"What about the other Mrs. Davis?" I asked. "The first one." I was determined to give her a hard time. She was giving me enough of one, calling Jeff a hippie, never seeing he had a good side.

"I don't inquire," she said, which may or may not have been true.

"You're scared to ask, I bet."

The knife frown returned. "Why would I be scared?" Anxiety.

"How should I know? I'm just teasing."

I had always thought her fears came from Poppy's heart condition. Not so. Out in Jasper County Grandmother had said, "Kate was always jumpy. When the phone rang she'd be scared to answer it. She never knew what would come out of it, if people would say the right thing. Around Kingsbury, she's scared of being criticized. She has to be perfect, to have a perfect everything. Including you."

Well, she did always dress well, pretty, and when she talked I think Fred saw magnolias blooming in the moonlight and felt the South was rising up again, marching out to battle in ranks of gentlemanly gray. Everybody has a vision—some sort of whim, at least. Maybe it's as good a base for marriage as any.

"What about him?" Fred turned to ask me now. "Tell me what he's like."

Jeff. What was he like? "He has a destiny," I said. He wasn't prepared to handle that. I made it tougher. "I don't have a destiny like his. But he—" I suddenly saw more than I anticipated, "he is my destiny."

Fred tried not to laugh and wound up smiling. A small girl with large words.

"Their eyes are bigger than their stomachs," my mother remarked, straight from Jasper County. He liked sayings like that; they salted speech.

Mother had gotten married, I recall, quicker than anybody I ever saw. I had teased her. "Were you pregnant? Did you skip a period?"

"I'm smarter than that," she said. What did she mean? That she'd been to bed with him but took no chances, or that she hadn't? If I asked right out, she'd say, "Of course not!" But how could I believe her?

Sometimes, though, we were like two girls, females of any sort in the world, talking over the great subject: men.

"I'm just not smart enough to figure out who the woman is I saw him with two days ago."

"Where?"

"Coming out of the Barclay, downtown."

"Just ask him."

"He'll think I've been spying."

In a way Fred Davis was like a foreigner to both of us. If she'd married a Spanish count we might have felt the same. His Yankeeness was one thing, but his natural reserve was another.

"She was dark," Mother went on, "that's all I could see. I've turned this house over for pictures of her"—by *her* she meant the first one, Lorna—"but all I can see are some distance shots, group pictures, in an album. He said he packed away all the others. She was dark, and so was the one I saw. Hairstyles change."

"Maybe it was just a business date," I said.

"Then why did he kiss her on the cheek?"

"It's better than the mouth. Anyway, if you get mad enough to divorce anybody, you don't kiss them."

"Little you know," she said.

"Read *Jane Eyre*," I advised. I was studying "The English Novel" at Bryn Mawr. "Count yourself lucky she's not in the attic setting the house on fire."

But then, by gosh, *I* saw her. After my ballet lesson in town one rainy afternoon, I saw a long car pull up to a curb as I was leaving, wrapped up in a raincoat and scarf so I wouldn't catch cold after all that sweating at the barre, and carrying my tote bag of leotards and slippers for the Bryn Mawr group I had to dance with that night. I was headed for the bus stop, then hoping to get an earlier commuter train than the one jam-packed at rush hour. The car stopped, a woman got out on the farther curb, a man half stepped from the car and gave her hand a squeeze; he settled back in the car, closing the door and shifting gear to bring the car back into traffic before the light changed, but it caught him and there he was: Fred, or his double, and I recognized the car, too, a gray Lincoln. Then I saw her walking off away from me, just across the street, a dark low-slung sort of woman, eyes fixed right before her, moving on assertive strong legs that just missed being too short and too thick. Mother's legs were slender and delicate, like a nice filly.

I didn't tell Kate about seeing the woman. I quit teasing her, though. Maybe it was that Lorna, the ex–Mrs. Davis. Maybe Fred had a mistress, or a confidante, or a secret business associate. Who the hell knew about Fred? Was Mother all that helpless that she couldn't get anything out of him? He wasn't gentlemanly, like Poppy. He was ruthless in what he wanted, or so I felt. Was she scared that even if he loved her, he didn't love her enough? Was she blaming herself for those others I knew about, before she met him?

Mother's new project in the lab was testing a new wrinkle-removing cream to see if it was carcinogenic. She had a lot of little helpless rabbits to make a mess of before she knew for sure. She had always dealt in cell biology. Sometimes, it must have been, when she checked the microscope of an assistant, she would see that the cells beneath the lens were not of a clear and normal conformation, but were multiplying too fast to stop, were disordered, swollen, discolored. I wonder if she didn't maybe shrink inside when she saw what she saw, even though her face might have stayed scientific, chiselled and cool. Her own life had been hit like the cells, first Poppy dying, then me turning out not to care about anything average, meeting a subversive guy to be in love with, the craze for dancing, the attack by Jeff's father, the fear of having gotten herself snared in a marriage trap. She had worked hard all her life, she could have stopped now, but she couldn't stop now. I called her from the dormitory at Bryn Mawr, confined to campus for a week because of something I'd done or not done. (I forget what it was, perhaps never had it clear.) I said if I could wish her another daughter, why, then, I would, but she said, "Oh, my precious darling, do you think I'd exchange you for the Queen of Persia?"

Nice to hear, but I knew from the slurred voice that she and Fred had been into the martinis again. So I almost said, *I don't know, if you met her you might.* But I didn't.

It began to seem as though we might have a chance of making it.

How it all ravelled loose I don't know. Fred kept taking her on trips. She got to play at being something out of Scott Fitzgerald. She lost time from her job. She knew he had gotten it for her. She went home to Kingsbury to beg Dr. Fletcher again, about getting her into the University of Pennsylvania cancer research program, but it was no show. She was dressed in a Dior original for their lunch together and looked like a million dollars. Something else happened about some man she'd once gone out with, but I didn't ever know what it was. A Caribbean cruise didn't make her all that happy. I wanted to go up to Bennington in the summer where I had a chance at a dance group (Laura Lemming's and really cool).

I had only to mention it. She met me out on the campus and stood there before me, hair wild in the stormy spring twilight, wailing like a witch. Everything had been my fault. I made her sit on a bench. "Stop all that drinking," I advised.

"Do you know what kind of infantile stuff that Jeff of yours is writing?"

"I just know you called him to come see you and he didn't go." Nothing sat well with her. She was into furies of a personal nature. Jeff had told me, "She practices allure . . . it's her way of getting things done. I've no time for crap like that."

"Have you read this last issue?" she demanded. She got it out of her purse and shook it in my face. "Only traitors hate this country."

Ethan's paper: *The Radar Screen.* It was going out everywhere now, but only to his subscription list. Still, some newsstands dared to sell it and maybe she had come across one of those.

"Your father and I"—she insisted on calling Fred my father—"we just wonder if you could be reading these columns."

"Of course I do. I read everything." The wind tore at us. It was getting dark. She wouldn't go inside. We were out in back of the library, near the drive, alone in a streaming Pennsylvania evening. She had asked me to meet her there. Her car was sitting just before us on the drive, but we didn't make a move to get sensibly into it.

"I couldn't believe it. Just listen: 'The business community of Philadelphia is a bleeding ulcer on the body politic. It has to have the blandest diet or it curls up in pain and terror, calls out the pigs to do its dirty work. "We don't want to see it happen, but get it done," is their motto. Just don't mention that a century ago the fat cats of the Main Line stockpiled their wealth out of the black coal mines to the west, not to mention the black lungs of the workers who went to early graves digging it free of the earth. . . .' "

"They get their news from all over," I said, and took the paper away from her to look. "It's not even Jeff's column. His is over here." I pointed to "From the Front Lines," down the left side of page one. I shouldn't have.

"All right, just look," she said, grabbing it away. " 'What image of our country do you kids have? Good old Uncle Sam passing out popsicles on The Fourth of July? John Wayne in a green beret, dashing around in a gold-plated army Jeep to save the world? Or a blood-streaked giant with a friendly smile, bunch of daisies in one hand, anti-personnel grenade ready in the other? If you would choose number three for yourself, clip this as your ballot and mail it in to *The Radar Screen*. We'll send you our booklet: "Weapons of War, What The Pentagon Hides," a special section on "U.S. Preparations for Germ Warfare" . . . Read the gory truth of what we're up to every day, while this war grinds on. . . .' Mary Kerr, you know better than to give a second thought to this sort of garbage. It flies in the face of all you've been brought up to know."

"Nobody ever taught me any politics," I said. "Besides, I never write anything for them. I couldn't do it, for one thing."

"That's no answer!"

"Well," I said, "it's the best I can do. I've got two exams tomorrow." I was getting cold out there.

"Your father and I," she half screamed, "love this country!"

I never know any answer to something like that. "It's where the gravy is," I said. That was unkind. I sneezed and shivered. Up north you take chances, thinking too early that it's spring. Evidently you take chances thinking your mother loves you too much to strike you. It won't do with Kate. She hit so hard I had blood on my tongue. It was time to leave her, her mad, long, blond hair tearing out of the pins and coiling up into the wind.

The next night she called up, calm as anything, pretending nothing had happened. My tongue was cut and swelling still.

"Fred and I have talked it over. Of course, you can go up to Bennington. He only wanted to read up on the program. In dance, of course, you know so much more than we do. You're absolutely right, darling. It's the best."

Bennington. Jeff followed me there.

4

Mary's Tape (continued): Bennington

"Following, following," Jeff said. "I'm always following. My feet keep walking back to you."

That was a song. What happened, actually, was that he was not so much following as circling. What he was following was the Movement, covering teach-ins at a lot of the Eastern colleges, checking into Harvard and Columbia, Dartmouth and Burlington. He would come and go, talk to people, see them at their demonstrations, engage in teach-ins and rallies, then write his column: "From the Front Lines" by Your Roving Patriot. It was the patriot part that must have made Mother so wild.

Meantime at the Bennington dance festival we had worked up a piece of choreography that fit into the spirit of the times. It started with an enormous crown onstage, and dancers swarming up it, gradually taking it apart, piece by piece. Next a hangman's gallows, all for us to frolic on, climbing up the supports, doing a playlike hanging, a trapeze act on the noose, finally skipping rope on the stage. And third a great big painted backdrop of LBJ himself, with a real papier-mâché nose and great big ears, bombs and airplanes sketched around him. We would end by swinging on the nose, dancing down the ears, painting out the armaments, then blanketing everything out in rock dancing for peace. (I never did rock dancing, but it wasn't hard to learn. We had amplifiers set up with Dylan's and Hendrix's tapes.)

Talk about blowing in the wind. What happened was, our scenery blew down. This was important for us, but especially for me. Laura Lemming was out to recruit some new dancers for her group. I had had the biggest hand in the choreography and was hopeful. Then the auditorium had gotten too hot for some of the audiences and we'd set up for an outdoor theater in a big meadow beyond the main campus. It should have been great. All afternoon we worked on the lighting, tested the amplifiers, made the paint bolder on the back-drops. The crowd that came was big and murmuring. Our adrenaline was topping out. It could have been great.

I always blamed the collapse, as we all did with one voice when we spoke of it afterward, on the wind that sprang up out of nowhere and rushed through. It turned the whole crown around. I was on an ascending place on the ramp, just where the crown skewered over, one divider twisting like the plywood it was made of. It hemmed me and two other dancers right in place. I knew we had to get down some way, so I turned and slid down the plywood surface like on a slide in the playground and my short little skirt flew up to my neck. The others followed. Everybody clapped.

We got a poor substitute spot on the program after that and danced our second choice, something called "Dreamcatcher," pretty but not strong. I wound up with an interview on choreography, but no real audition, so I knew I didn't have a chance with Lemming. By then I knew very well what we all knew—the construction guys in our group hadn't been all that focussed. They were users who had gotten into something cheap and easy, and the set might have collapsed even without a wind.

"Bad luck," was Jeff's comment. He was due up in Burlington to do some talking to a student group at the university. I went with him, having something to tell. I waited till we got all the way there and were moved into a trailer some student couple had turned over to us.

"Well, now," he said, the first silence melting away into another, then a third (all different qualities), at last broken. "Well, now, a baby couldn't be anything but great." He stood and folded me up to him. (Men always like to pick me up; I have been forced to notice it.) "You said the wind was unexpected. How about this?" He held me like a doll that might break. "How about this?" He just kept standing, holding me off the floor, and I could feel his heart going like crazy.

"Put me down," I said. I stood on my own two feet. "You don't want actually to go on and have it? What would we do with it?"

He looked astonished. Then he laughed. "Do with it? What do people always do with babies? Raise them, of course."

"You've got to consider—"

"Consider what? I considered we were preventing it. It didn't work. That must mean—"

"Mean what? It's just that sometimes maybe we forgot. Or something."

"I didn't finish. It must mean that it wants to be. Wants to be born, be with us. I'm against dying, Mary, not against living."

"But Kate and Fred," I began. "Jeff, I can't earn anything from dancing. You're away all the time. It won't work. She would never accept me having it and no husband."

He sat down and took my hand. "We'll have to get you one."

I saw he meant himself. "You always said—"

"I said I wasn't settled enough. Ethan will help us. The system we're into has a heart. You know what I've been thinking about, even before this? I thought you might get the big dance break. Okay. It didn't come. There's a word I want you to say. Say it over and over to yourself. *Canada*."

"Canada?" It was right up above us on the map, but so was the North Pole.

"Canada. As for Kate, I've been thinking for a long time we ought to put her out of her misery."

"Do what?" I thought he meant kill her, which to tell the truth had often crossed my mind.

"Marrying," he softly crooned, and his laugh still had something to do with Kate. "She could never ignore that."

"It shouldn't have anything to do with her. Why can't you leave her out of it?"

But he was into too many emotions at once, almost falling off a little chair, collapsing on a couch, standing up, lighting a joint, pinching it out. He went bouncing around in that mobile home till it rocked like a wagon.

Finally he flung himself back on the couch, arms spread out. "I'm thinking of everybody, born and unborn." He flung himself back on the couch, grabbed my arm, and pulled me down, rocking and laughing. For him, the more curious the way things happened, the better. He never expected any ordinary way.

He flung open a drawer below a shelf in the kitchenette. He was looking for a match to light up again, and in rummaging found what he wasn't looking for. He shook the envelope twice and held it up to the light. "Well, hot fucking damn."

It was coke. He opened it a crack, pinched out a little, and sniffed it into his nose.

"That's a messy way to do it," I said, getting mad all over.

"Let's cut a line."

"It throws me off. Anyway, it's not ours."

"There're fifteen people through here every day. It was a drop for Hawkins, bet you anything."

"Not us."

"Okay." He put the envelope back into the drawer. "I've got to call Ethan. New scheme. He's bound to like it. Talks with resisters in Canada. I can come back for the convention. Chicago. It's going to take the best. But you . . . you'll be out of it, not pushed around and worried."

"I haven't said I would! I haven't said I wanted to!"

The coke was taking hold. He fell back on the bed, smiling at me in complete contentment, holding out his arms for me. I turned around and ran straight out of the trailer, out into the night.

My body is all I have . . . using it, that's what's happening . . . making use of it. . . .

Dizzy with resentment, I found myself seated on a ridge in the night air. Below, Lake Champlain glimmered in the moonlight. It was big as a county, that lake, and the elephant color of it showed gray and changeless, though the moonlight was painting itself on the surface.

If I could vanish into it . . . walk right down this slope and into the heart of that gorgeous rug of light, the gray beneath would take me in, not a moment wasted, ripples fading, no more decisions to make . . . deciding . . . and everything finished. Because everything that could be decided has something wrong with it.

"Mary?" He was roving around, calling, no idea where I'd gone. I saw his white shirt at a distance, veering closer, searching. "Mary? That short trip's over, not even a bus stop. Where are you? We've got to talk some sense. Get a notion of what you want to do. Forget about me. It's what *you* want, okay?"

Then he found me, was kneeling by me, folding me up under his arm like a puppy, raising my hair, kissing my neck, bundling me in close. "You'll catch cold out here. Let's go in and talk."

His voice was tinged with a new anxiety, the sound of a father-to-be. I heard it and knew it and the funny thing was that I liked it. I was resenting and hating every single thing that was trapping and directing me. My own body had trapped me. No dance ever devised would let me jump out of it. Liking the tone of Jeff's voice that night wouldn't be cast out of me.

But *Canada?* What did I know about it? Did I want to go there if everything about it was grand, except for all that cold in the winter? Dancing. Did anybody up there do it? Or did they just whirl around on ice skates? I would go back to Bennington and talk it over. If there were any contacts . . .

But something did begin to dawn on me. It would be away from Mother. A country she and Fred didn't, between them, think they owned.

5

Mary's Tape (continued): Montreal

At times during the winter after Kathy was born it would seem we were doing nothing so much as hurting other people. Jeff had his calling, but suppose I didn't? That was always the trouble.

Before she was born, he went down to Chicago to the convention the Democrats had. There were riots from the first day on. The police were awful to them, was their story. There were riot squads, beatings, arrests. Jeff got pulled in with the rest. "Crossing the state line with intent to riot." Next thing I knew he was out on bail. Five thousand dollars. You'd say right away the Movement would find the money to get him out. He was important to them, lots of ways.

But no, it was Fred Davis. Went out there and put up the money. How did he even find out? We couldn't figure that. My own guess was that Ethan told Aunt Jane and she told Mother. It was like the Greek legend. If you cut off one head of the monster, it just grew five more.

But was it a monster? I never was sure.

Kathy was with us now, but too little to talk things over with, and Jeff had to go back to the States. I was alone.

I thought for the longest time he was reporting for trial. But he'd no idea of doing that.

"Then Fred will lose his money," I said.

"Of course," he said, not even looking up to debate it. He'd never intended anything else. "What's five grand to him?" he asked. "A fucking leak in a back alley. Forgotten already."

But he'd left me alone, to think about it. Just with her, my baby.

How beautiful she was. Jeff's light hair and his blue eyes, at first, though changing now to gray. How helpless she was. I was helpless, too. I tried to stay on in the apartment Jeff and I had rented, but sometimes the money he sent didn't come through or wasn't enough. I'd no way to call him. I'd no way, either, to shake off the other exiles who knew the address. They thought of it as a pad they could hole up in whenever they needed to. They promised me money, more than enough, for passing on hash, coke, and acid, keeping needles, and all that stuff, but that meant when they came they wouldn't leave. I'd be stepping over them to get out the door. I'd get busted next, I told them. They cared, but not enough. There were the serious ones, who had wanted Jeff for starting a paper out West, his talents needed, and wanted him to go speak in Toronto or fly out to Edmonton. Growing, growing, was all they wound up saying, but did they have to grow all over Kathy and me? I found a place to go and slipped out in the night so nobody would know.

It was Gordon Stewart's house I came to. The room was large and airy, even if the house was run-down, but I could sit there alone with Kathy and think about it all.

Gradually it dawned on me that the only answer to the trouble I was in was myself. The one wrong was me. With me gone, she could go back to the family: Mother had been awful with me, but maybe I had caused it, being awful to her. Aunt Jane was back there, with money. Aunt Sally was always sending things: bootees, little knitted sweaters, funny embroidered romp suits. They were thinking all the time about Vietnam, how it was bound to end sometime. Mother could never be the way she was twice. The only one was me. I was wrong. Then I thought again of vanishing, the way I had thought of it on the shore above Lake Champlain the night I told Jeff we were going to have her if we didn't stop her. Whether I was glad or sorry, she was here.

I was alone a lot. All those gypsying friends we'd gotten to know along the way—in Burlington in the trailer, out from Montreal on the Lake of Two Mountains, living with a Hungarian couple who played violin music and drank gallons of red wine so dark it was almost black. Then in our first apartment waiting for Kathy, the rental woman's friendship, the other defectors, the women in the clinic waiting room, with their friendly talk, comparing symptoms. All gone. My fault? It must be. Other people had friends.

Vanishing. How did you do it?

I knew a woman upstairs in the rooming house, a retired nurse, living on a pension, alone, but not unhappy about it. She used to take care of Kathy when I went out. She didn't know when I went out one afternoon, into the snow, that I was going to the library to read up on suicide. I had to do it while Kathy couldn't know about it, wasn't old enough to feel all that trouble and loss. It would just be a blur to her.

I'd leave a note to the Stewarts, Gordon and Gerda: *Take her back to Philadelphia, this address; or Kingsbury, North Carolina, this address.* They would always do the right thing.

Could I stand the thought of Kathy with Mother and Fred? I wouldn't be there to stand it or not stand it. The one that was wrong was me. Kathy could be the one who was right. It was possible.

I had blundered into a current in a strong swift river I had never known about before. The things around me—Kathy's formula and changing, dressing, diapers, walks outside; the run to the grocery, the plants on the windowsills, food cooked on a hot plate, eaten on a card table in the corner; snow one day, no snow another—all became like dream objects and motions in a dream, moving in the current with a dreamy rhythm. I couldn't shake my head and get the current to go away. It kept pulling anyway, numbing and cold, not able to hear what I was asking it. I couldn't fight the current. *I can't go back to Kate and Fred. To me it's the land of the dead. I'd rather die.*

At Bryn Mawr I'd studied anthropology, chosen it, since I had to choose something, because of a picture I had once seen long ago. It had grown on me, become like a vision, not to be lost. It was a picture in one of Mother's science texts at home in Kingsbury. A group, a family, imagined as having lived long before any history began to be written down or even remembered. Three were in it: a mother seated by the fire, the child on her lap, the father just standing from having built up the fire, just turning from looking out into the dark to reassure their safety, just about to turn back to them. He was holding a club. They were all wearing skins. While Jeff was there, from Burlington onward, I would think, *This is the way we feel about ourselves, the three of us, the way it has been and will be.*

If only he had stayed. He thinks they are getting money to me, but sometimes it doesn't work.

Outside, on a milder day, through a crack in the window I heard singing out in the street, something like a children's song I used to hear in Kingsbury as a child, only the street was frozen stiff, snowed in, only half cleared, with one pair of twisting car tracks down the center, so I couldn't be hearing Southern children jumping rope and singing. Yet I thought, *Kathy has a right to hear that, too. Maybe Mother will take her home and she'll hear it, the way I did. Maybe Aunt Sally will get her, make her pretty little clothes. Maybe Aunt Jane will take her sometimes, and teach her how to wear them.*

As I wrote the note, the snow began to fall again, monotonously, unchangingly, as though it had never stopped. I tore the sheet up and knotted it. The night we first came across the border (we had spent so much time filling out forms to make us "landed immigrants" it had gotten dark), it was raining, and in the slant of wind the rain kept slanting into the headlights, materializing white and steady, never stopping. So I asked if it could be snowing. It was only July. They laughed, the people driving us. "No, it stops sometime. Maybe for two months." It was only rain, coming white at night on people travelling at night into a land not their own.

I carried Kathy to the nurse upstairs. On the way up I said to her little face, "I love you forever." I had put it in the note, too. She was half asleep and didn't even gurgle—just as well.

I went downstairs and tried to do what I thought was necessary, a sort of getting rid of my unwanted self, like putting something away in a drawer you'd never have to open. But I couldn't make it work. I failed.

6

Mary's Tape (continued): Return of People

Soon I found myself on trial in another way, literally. They arrest you in Canada when you try to kill yourself. It's as if you broke into a store or ran over a child.

It was Gordon Stewart who came down to help me. I think that must have been the nurse upstairs who told him, just as she got the police who cut me down.

Gordon got up and pled for me, tears in his eyes. My husband had deserted me; I had been upset and depressed and quite probably had been temporarily unbalanced. (Crazy? Why not say so?) I felt in pillory—I think they call it that—or maybe up on a scaffolding for all to look at me, wearing my scarlet letter *S* for suicide.

Giving testimony the best I could, I held my bruised throat long and straight the way I might if dancing. Gerda was there. Several strangers had wandered into the little courtroom out of curiosity; a public hanging draws crowds. Had I been in the papers? I think they were just those people who drift around watching other people's misery unfold. I hoped I didn't wander into the paper in the States: DRAFT RESISTER'S WIFE TRIES SUICIDE. But why do that when there were big things to headline from everywhere else in the world: Washington, Vietnam, and all the trouble spots in between? The trial was in the new courthouse building on rue Notre Dame.

Underneath all their silent practicality, some Canadians are romantic. Gordon Stewart was one of those. He took me home that day. The court had put me and Kathy in his custody until they could break the news to Fred and Kate. Then Kathy was to go to them for six months until I could come back and prove I was "stable." I had to report back. He had put up a thousand dollars for bail.

It was after we got back to that room that he sat and held my hand. "You're sure you're all right?" He said it over and over.

I said that I was.

"Weren't you afraid to die?" He was stroking my hair.

"Dying to me is probably not like what you mean, everything over. Nothing is like we're told about it."

"Then what is it?"

"It's something else. I was getting out of the way."

He didn't understand. To him a word he knew would just always be what he always thought it was. Kathy wasn't there. I missed her. They had ordered her into some sort of nursing care, "supervised detention" for a week, until I was "balanced." Did they think I'd try to kill Kathy next? Stranger things happen, every day.

Gordon was getting more romantic every minute. "If I had a daughter, I'd want one like you." He held my hand against his chest.

"You're supposed to act fatherly," I said. I pulled back. "You with that proper wife." I thought I'd make him defend her, but he didn't seem to hear. He stood, bent to pick me up, then walked all around the room with me.

"Poor darling," he said.

"If you think I could sleep in that jail, you're mistaken." My ankle itched. "Furthermore, I think I got fleas."

"Got what?" He set me down at once.

I sat on the bed and scratched my ankle. He sat in the one chair. "I hate to leave you."

"If you really want to help me, lend me enough money to start back with my dance lessons."

Don't think I hadn't found somebody, early on. We had met at one of the anti-war meetings. A resister who used to dance with Art Manning. He'd travelled with him for a time, the way I'd wanted to, and he even knew Croom. Graham had auditioned him, too, in New York. She had liked him; but it was Art he'd leaned to. As long as the money Jeff sent came through, I'd have enough to study. But if it didn't, I'd need extra. Dancing "balanced" me, I argued.

"That important?" Gordon puzzled. "I will, then." People who have money when you need it, it's funny what they'll give in to and what they get stalled on. God knows why he said he would. But he kept promises, I knew that.

Gordon Stewart limped away.

My neck hurt. It would hurt for a long time. I wanted Kathy; I wanted Jeff. The agony had started up again. But the quality was different. Maybe I was coming up with the current instead of going down.

The man I studied with, homosexual, haggard-looking beyond his years, but wonderful to work with, long, wiry legs and arms, great timing, had given me credit until he couldn't anymore. "I got to eat, doll baby," was what he said. I respected that. He got me what work he could, wrote to core companies in Montreal, found auditions, listed my number.

His name was Estes Drover.

Money Gordon Stewart had given me still wadded in my hand, I went at once to telephone Estes. On the telephone, though, a volley of French. Not to be deciphered. I went over there instead.

I bused through streets where ridges of hardened snow clung black along the feet of bare trees. I climbed three flights to a top floor hall, where Estes kept a small bedroom behind a flimsy partition at one end, an office at the other with a telephone and a cluttered desk. There was another bed, hardly more than a cot at the end of the room near the partition, and disorderly piles of clothing. But no one.

Behind me on the stairs, footsteps—and then a mouse-faced little Arab-looking man came in the room.

"Ess-teas? *Cherchez-vous* Ess-teas?"

No wonder I couldn't make out his French.

"*Oui. Je le cherche. Où est-il?*"

"*Il vient. Assoiyez-vous.*" He waved his hand, but the studio was bare, not a chair in sight. Scars on his arm. Cold, but he evidently wasn't feeling it. His feet were bare in those leather Indian sandals with one ring for the big toe. Everybody smoked grass, but I never wanted into needles. I took it for a sign of something about drugs that the stereo was gone, probably hocked for cash. I meant to hold on to Gordon Stewart's money.

"*Le stereo?*" I asked. "*Qu'est-ce qui se passe?*"

He looked around, registering comic astonishment.

"*Disparu. C'est évident.*"

I waited a time, but no Estes.

"Tell him to call me," I managed in French. "Say I'll soon have enough to pay. *Peut-être.*"

He woke up then, coming closer. "Maybe now? I . . . give to him."

"No, not now. Later. *Plus tard.*" I was quick leaving.

No stereo, not even any tape deck in sight. Maybe he'd locked them up. I had come in leotards under my jeans, shirt, and coat; dance shoes were stuffed in my bag. Hurrying for the bus.

Keep running, yourself will catch up with you. Yourself will catch up with you. She will dance right into your bones. If you don't keep running you'll find yourself doing something crazy and they'll take Kathy for good.

So moving . . . moving . . . there I went. What I was good at.

Then . . . Gerda Stewart.

There she stood, either that day or the next, back on Seymour Street.

Gerda and Gordon, paired off by alliteration, you'd have to guess, for want of knowing a better reason. She was from Connecticut Eastern schools, educated in the best way. Canadian father, but brought up American. She couldn't cope with me, quite, because to me none of her "background" made a particle of difference. From the first she meant to be kind, though. I kept thinking of her eye going up at an angle and of his built-up shoe. If I'd let him be a lover, I would have seen the short leg. Maybe for dancers that's worse than for other people.

Gerda wasn't as kind as before. "I was happy to befriend you, but now you've all but managed to annex Gordon. I do find that a bit much."

"It was unintentional," I said, and added, "I appreciate everything, Mrs. Stewart." Those being my Southern manners which Mother had brought me up to have.

All I had done, the way I saw it, was let Gordon help me out.

I gave Mrs. Stewart some instant coffee and we fell to talking about Canada, two ladies at tea. "I find friends here," she said, "but it is hard to relate them to anything except comfortable living. There is no center to their thinking. I find in this regard that the French Canadians are better. They do relate to something, their own past, their families, their language. This is all to the good. Yet in America we always relate to our public life. Isn't that true? We are always concerned."

"It's a Quaker trait," I said, suddenly remembering Bryn Mawr. They always seemed serious about everything.

"I'm not a Quaker," said Mrs. Stewart. "Why ever did you think that? My family was of German extraction, some French—from France, that is, not Canada. Gordon, of course, is a Scot."

"With all that means," I said.

She challenged me again. "What exactly does that mean?"

"They're romantic, aren't they?"

"You, I take it, are not."

"I was studying anthropology," I said, "but I wanted to be a dancer. I was going on to write a thesis for a degree, though, in case the dancing didn't lead anywhere."

"Gordon and I have a pattern of life," she said, about to leave, but getting back to it anyway, what she came for. "It is what we have developed, especially after the boys went their separate ways. I find this has been—well, I hate to say it—but you are disturbing to our pattern. We were safe, we were steadily going through life. I'm glad for him to help you, but I do think he is getting neurotic about you. He worries continually."

"Why don't you tell him all this?" I asked her. I suddenly felt reasoning come back, like a steady ground beneath me. "I never did anything on purpose. I just rented the room."

"I know it seems that way."

"It is that way." I hadn't spent my life sparring with Kate for nothing. "Can't you get him to stop it? He belongs to you, doesn't he?"

She could have brought up something right away about Jeff, but then she wasn't very quick, and she was way too nice.

I pushed ahead. "I tried to get rid of myself. Sorry it didn't work, so you wouldn't have to worry."

Her mouth fell open. "Oh, my dear, I'm certainly not advising you to try anything of the sort a second time. Why, you don't think for a moment that I—"

I said no, I didn't think for a moment.

She left soon after.

People were at least present to me again, not shadows, not just a whisper of moving feet. But were they real people, or just copies of people who had come before and made them what they were, neg-ative exposures? There must be real ones somewhere. I waited for Estes to call. Estes was real.

When Kathy gets returned to me, I will know I'm real, and so will everything else be. I want her back. I want to carry her like a kangaroo mother carries her baby, in a pouch, while leaping yards at a jump, through the snow. Or like a papoose she can live on my back while I skim and slide over ice.

It's breaking up now, melting and getting filthy dirty, trying to hold on, but fading. It's going. Dying is going. It didn't work.

7

Mary and the
Lady Psychiatrist

DR. SKOLETSKY (after a number of repetitious questions): Where
were you married?

MARY: In New York state, not far from here. A little town called
Champlain. There was a justice of the peace, only it seems he was
a retired minister, too. He lived in a barn. Or rather, he had some
rooms built on the side of an old barn. He was reclaiming the barn,
he said, for some reason I forget, maybe a store he would rent, or
a pottery place. We went out in the big empty hall of what had been
a barn. He brought out a sort of pulpit. He put out some chairs. He
even had a song for a wedding on a record player, an old record.
Jeff thought it was all sort of funny, like a play wedding.

DR. SKOLETSKY: Were you alone?

MARY: No, a Hungarian couple was with us. We had known them
down in Bennington. They had come down to watch the dance pro-
grams and met Jeff. I think they started him on Canada, saying we
could live with them. They came down to see us over the border,
and getting us married and all was a better way to be landed immi-
grants. Also, I was pregnant.

DR. SKOLETSKY: What happened to them?

MARY: They quarrelled a lot. I think they're living apart now. They
were nice but they always were mad at each other.

DR. SKOLETSKY: How did you feel at your wedding?

MARY: It was sort of like make-believe. Like Jeff said. Marvin had
bought me a veil.

DR. SKOLETSKY: Who?

MARY: Marvin Hawkins. A black man. He's into the anti-war move-
ment. A friend of Jeff's but with different ideas. He couldn't stay

for it, but he said I ought to have a veil. It was Sunday, and all he could find open was a sporting goods place. They had some mosquito nets in the camping equipment, so he bought one of those and they draped it all around me, and that's how I got married.

DR. SKOLETSKY: How did you feel about it?

MARY: How would you feel about it?

DR. SKOLETSKY: Does the machine help you talk?

MARY: Let me keep it. It helps me.

8

Mary's Tape (continued)

Yesterday I ran into Madeleine Spivak.

She and her husband, George, had property just around the corner from Seymour Street. Jeff and I had an apartment there when we stopped living with the Hungarians. By then I was six months along with Kathy and big as a cow.

Madeleine worked in her husband's rental office on McKay Street and so found the property for us, a listing of theirs. She used to come over to see us from time to time. It started honestly, I suppose, with some idea of helping us, seeing after us. But I had to go to the hospital twice before Kathy actually came and I was sick a lot. Jeff confided in her, I had to guess. She was around more often than not. The first thing any of us knew, she had fallen for him. Jeff never had to put out much energy to get himself fallen for.

Madeleine Spivak was married to a Hungarian real estate dealer. Hungarians were all over the place. They came out to Canada in 1956, at the time of the revolt. She herself was brought up French Catholic, Quebec variety, though she spoke English without any accent, from birth, we supposed.

She thought we were pilgrim wanderers. She was right. To ourselves, as well, we were pilgrim wanderers, holy and superb, homeless, trusting, lost and innocent in a strange land. We were also, it was obvious, far better than the public image of mindless hippies, lice in their beards, acid in their veins. Madeleine Spivak at least had the sense to see us as we were: Jeff an intellectual, I a talented dancer.

And she—dark, sexy, approaching forty, covering the coarse gray strands that were intruding like weeds in her heavy hair.

It was Madeleine Spivak who got us to the hospital when Kathy declared herself unmistakably on the way. She called to find we had waited thirty minutes for a taxi after the ambulance people said it would take them an hour or two, and we had no real prospect but having to struggle with it right there at two in the morning on a night of blinding snow. "I'm coming now," said Madeleine. And she came. Jeff wrapped me in blankets up to my head, held me on the backseat of the big Spivak car. She had thrown a mink coat over her nightgown, not bothering to dress.

Out of the night at every turning, down every street we drove, all I could see was snow, materializing white out of the infinite dark, dark deeper than any pit could be but at some point in itself giving birth to snow, whirling whiteness out of the black depths.

Then Kathy.

It was a troubled winter. She cried a lot. I had to go to the doctor over and over. The last thing I felt like was sex. For a while I hated the thought of it. Sex was a robber in disguise, was what I said. (Aloud? Maybe.) Sex had taken my freedom, I said. (To him? With tears, or anger, or both? I think maybe I did.)

I found myself getting robbed again, losing Jeff to this chic French item, who had pledged herself to look after us, but who now was out of her head with love.

As they say in books, tension mounted.

That bitter winter could hardly be called any picnic, and just as it ended Jeff left us both. Me and Madeleine Spivak, both out in the cold.

He'd done little or nothing since he returned from the Chicago orgy but interviews with the tribe of resisters who had come up to Canada, sore from their bruising experiences at home.

But all of a sudden things waked up for him. I found him one afternoon, in from a walk with Kathy, with lots of small bottles and wads of cotton spread out on the table, a smell of acid swirling around, sulphuric and something else. Jeff had recipes for everything. He got them out of government pamphlets and kids' magazines. He claimed he could even make napalm. I didn't know why anybody would want to, but he said it was useful for burning up records in draft offices. It had gotten warm enough to run up a window and let the smell out. What he was doing was altering his fingerprints. Something was up.

"You're a private self-torturer instead of the public kind," I said. I was thinking of the Buddhist convert who was one of the recent ones to dump gasoline on himself and strike a match. "I can't stand it," I went on. "I love your hands."

"They'll heal," he answered, not looking up.

"It doesn't do a particle of good," I went on, "if you're trying to conceal who you are. They'd know you any number of ways. Of course, you could always cut them off," I suggested, thinking of Madeleine Spivak.

He kept grinning and hurting. Spring came before he left. Full force, summer seemed to arrive, just the next day. Full leafy green.

I held his hand in the night, running my fingers over his. "What did you do it for?"

"It's the mark of my mission." He was joking, but meant it, too. "What mission?"

All I learned was he had to go down to New England, then out to California. He had been into heavy telephone talks with Ethan lately. Wanted for everything from rioting in Chicago to wrecking draft board offices in four or five cities, he was also a fugitive from his own draft board in Louisiana, and if that wasn't enough he owed five thousand dollars on skipped bond from my stepfather. The group there in Canada treated him like something holy.

Letters would come, he promised. Through courier, mainly. He had grown wary of using the telephone. He was rising on the lists. The FBI was deep into laying traps, was said to be working with the RCMP. Also, if you could dodge them, there were the Justice Department, State, Immigration, and the CIA. So it was said.

"Nothing changed when Nixon got in," Jeff said. "The war's gotten bigger. They're hating us more every day. I'm better off being active there than just sitting around here."

The war was a running sore. The more you picked at it, the worse it got. Also, the peasants were winning it.

"Why don't they just call it off and get out?" I wondered aloud.

"What do you think this is all about?" said Jeff.

Then he was gone.

When men go, what's left but worried women? There was Kate on the phone, wanting to come up and just see. . . . If I told her Jeff was gone, if she saw he was, she'd have dogs to sic on him. "No, Mother, please understand. Just no. . . ."

There was Madeleine Spivak, recovering from love, if that is possible.

There was Gerda Stewart, fretting while her husband made limping tracks through summer green down to Seymour Street to the room I moved to after leaving Madeleine Spivak's apartment, her charity being no longer digestible.

And there was me. With Kathy standing in line for her turn, though she didn't know much yet except that Daddy was gone.

Gerda: "Why did you name her Kathy if you can't abide your mother?"

Me: "I never thought of that . . . honestly. At the hospital when she was coming, I heard somebody repeating, 'Athy or Pathy, or Kathy, or something like it, over and over, so it got in my head. It is her name."

Summer . . . winter . . . snow and suicide . . . court and Kathy gone to Kate . . . but life again now, and spring coming, though snow and wind are holding on, trying not to leave.

Estes Drover calls the minute that Ahmed, his friend, decides to give him my message, having weighed out all the advantages and disadvantages to himself and probably decided that I have more cash available than I'm letting on about. I go like a shot, even knowing that if I give Estes the money to get the stereo back, Ahmed may go and hock it as soon as our backs are turned, then it's all to do over. But I say on the phone I have to have lessons till he pays me back the loan for the stereo, and we settle on that because he wants to see me back, too. And I'm out before I can put down the phone, catching the Metro, shooting through dark tunnels, past bright stations, climbing out to fresh wind, climbing the stairs, snow melted from my boots before I get to the top, practice shoes stuffed in my old red duffel.

"Can you give me two hours today, Estes? You know I've been in trouble all this week."

"What trouble?" We are going out to free the stereo, me with the money ready, Gordon's loan. "I tried to kill myself. See?" Pointing to my neck. "It didn't work."

"For Jesus' sake," he says, turning, arms around me, right on the street. Trembling. "For Jesus' sake, baby. Little lamb. Child."

For a minute I cling; then I stiffen up. "Oh, shit, Estes. Let's get that thing out of hock and go to work. Hurry."

I used to be a nice girl.

9

Minutes of a
Distant Meeting

PLACE: Old empty warehouse, its basement a meeting place serving as clearinghouse and headquarters for important and existentially active segment of anti–Vietnam War movement in the United States.

Bulletin board notice causing comment: *Blazing Boy Jeff's wife M. left behind in Monte-Can with infant pink bootees because (1) not well enough to hitch and (2) not totally committed—we suspect. Has attempted self-Xing but failed.*

FIRST SPEAKER: A neurotic weakness in her character, inherited from her mother, an incompletely liberated hence schizo as hell Southern female. M. not admitted to full confidence for this reason.

SECOND SPEAKER, A WOMAN: But it's the worst thing of all for Mary's mentality not to be trusted. Take it from me, being in the dark is the pits . . . darkest pits. If trusted, she might find the strength to stand up to anything.

THIRD SPEAKER: Might. Might not.

FIRST SPEAKER: We have to have pretested character. We can't be a testing ground.

SECOND SPEAKER: Where is Jeff? Where is Jeff Blaise?

FIRST SPEAKER: Going out of his mind about her. He's fit for a lobotomy. He'd have his brain out if he could get her off his mind. She hung herself from a hook by a bed sheet.

THIRD SPEAKER: Yeah, but what's he really doing?

FIRST SPEAKER: Talking to Hayden on the phone. Writing out speeches for 'Frisco. They need us there again. Things are going slack.

FOURTH SPEAKER: Then stay on track, you guys. Never mind

who's overdosing, or whatever the fuck she did. Hayden wouldn't be interested in any old picnic.

SECOND SPEAKER, A WOMAN: What about Baez?

FIRST SPEAKER: Definite interest. Definite. And we're talkin' Rubin, we're talkin' Ginsberg . . .

FOURTH SPEAKER: Jesus.

FIRST SPEAKER: Father Tomlinson's on the guest list.

(Pause.)

THIRD SPEAKER: I thought Spellman had sent him off to Bolivia. They're exiling Christians these days.

FIRST SPEAKER: If so, he hasn't gone yet.

FOURTH SPEAKER: Say ten Hail Marys for mentioning that napalm hurts.

General laughter.

An opening door.

THIRD SPEAKER: Hush, I think it's Blaise.

FIRST SPEAKER: Why hush?

THIRD SPEAKER: I mean about his wife. He's going up the fucking wall.

FIRST SPEAKER: Why is that? I mean, precisely.

SECOND SPEAKER, A WOMAN: You stupid prick. He loves her.

FIRST: Why doesn't he just go there? A short hop and he's seen her.

FOURTH: Why doesn't he just go there? A long hop east, a short hop north and he's seen her.

SECOND: He did go. She wouldn't see him, or missed him. Border crossing dangerous. Calls difficult. Also . . . trouble with her over something he did.

FIRST: Did what?

SECOND: Three guesses.

FIRST: Three fucking guesses?

SECOND: Right.

Silence as Jeff enters.

10

Conversation at a Main Line Dinner Table

PLACE: Dark but beautifully appointed dining room at Fred and Kate Davis's home. Four couples to dine, all carefully arranged in advance by place cards, all looking much alike.

Comments on the present state of affairs in Southeast Asia, on Daniel Ellsberg, the Chicago trials, secrecy in wartime, drugs, how to deal with younger generation.

WIFE OF ONE COUPLE: I suppose, Kate, you might prefer us not to talk about it.

FRED: No, she doesn't think that. She's very open. It's a test of courage to be that way, I grant you, but I do think it's best.

HUSBAND OF ANOTHER COUPLE: And very much to her credit.

KATE: Oh, thank you. I do appreciate your understanding. It helps keep me going.

DIVORCED OLD FRIEND (MALE): I guess it might be hard for your girl, too. Not to have her baby with her.

FRED: It's a little bit of a shock to me, to find myself changing diapers again. Of course, we got a nurse right away.

KATE: Oh, I don't mind a bit. It's just a real joy, a baby in the house again. A sweet little thing.

FRED: Looks like Kate. Very pretty. (Tops up his wineglass.) Cries.

KATE: Oh, no more than normal.

DIVORCED OLD FRIEND (FEMALE): But what about your daughter?

KATE (confused): We hardly know how to begin.

DIVORCED OLD FRIEND (FEMALE): Sorry, I shouldn't have asked.

WIFE OF ANOTHER COUPLE: I know what I'd do if one of mine got mixed up in—

HER HUSBAND: Now, Rosemary . . .

WIFE OF ANOTHER COUPLE: They'd never cross my doorstep again.

FRED (covering quickly with a glance at Kate): We haven't taken that attitude. In fact, Mary Kerr can come home whenever she likes. We've made it clear.

KATE: Certainly we have.

An awkward pause. Maid appears, passing dishes of sliced roast, browned potato balls, french beans. . . .

Far away, from upstairs, a door opens, a baby wails. A door closes. Silence.

I sat by her crib watching with the greatest affection even a mother could know, but when I reached in to ease her head into a more comfortable position on the white hand-embroidered pillowcase, she turned her head herself and struck at me. It reminded me that Mary Kerr once had bitten me on the side of my hand between the wrist bone and the little finger, and I felt . . . But Fred said, "You're being silly, all babies do nonsense things." Was she striking at me? Why does she coo at the nurse but not at me?

11

With Dr. Skoletsky

MARY: If I have to see Mother, I'll get some arsenic some way and do a better job. Mother has her breaking points even lower down the scale than mine. If I had to stay around her, she'd be screaming mad inside a week, no matter how sweet and calm she starts out.

DR. SKOLETSKY: In spite of all your negative feelings toward her, she is financially able, she is willing, her husband is willing. She will keep your child until you are able to establish yourself in a job that will help support both of you. At present, you are unable, without risking severe depression, to stay at home with the child. You are unable to pay anyone to keep the child until you have a job. You are unable to prove yourself stable enough to keep a job until you get a job and keep it. Is all this true?

MARY: Yes.

DR. SKOLETSKY: There is also the risk of malnutrition.

MARY: If you say so.

DR. SKOLETSKY: You are legally able to work here; your landed immigrant's visa is valid. Your husband's absence is unfortunate, but no one is able to locate him. We assume that he lives elsewhere through choice, perhaps under another name. We have to suspect that he may not return. You are to go for interviews tomorrow at these addresses. We have set up the appointments for you.

12

Mary's Tape (continued)

Dr. Skoletsky's march of logic is like spiked boots trampling over my spread-out feelings, which now seem mangled beyond recognition. I didn't tell her much.

The truth was I was getting some money from Jeff, though no one knew it. Some was filtering through. I knew he was sending me much more than I got; some was leaking out along the way. Maybe it was needed at different checkpoints more than I needed it. Maybe somebody just had to have a fix, a hit, a square meal—and the chain would break there.

One contact I knew about was the wife of a retired dean at McGill. In her proper Westmount home she used to answer the doorbell, drying her hands on her apron, hear the right password, take the package. She hid it in the oven—not the one she cooked on, I suppose—but well out of sight until another messenger passed, saying the key words, and then and only then did she take it out of the oven for handing on to me. "I could go get it myself," was what I suggested, "if I knew the address." But no one would ever tell me; we were all in danger of a trap.

So finally I said to Dr. Skoletsky, "Okay, so I'll take the job"— the second one they'd offered—"and work and get her back."

The doctor looked exactly the way I knew she would, like somebody closing a file and thinking of the next appointment as she showed me out the door.

That terrible day when he took so sick, Poppy was walking home, knowing something bad was happening or about to happen, but just the same when he saw me he put his arms out, just in the most natural automatic way. Later when I saw the picture of the napalmed girl running down the road out of a village, on fire and screaming but running (if you're running, then you are running toward as well as away from), I would think of her running to me. I would have caught her, fire and all. Would Kathy run away from Mother, and if she did would she run to me? I sat in the McGill University anthropology library and worked at the filing job they gave me (training for being a full-time assistant during the upcoming slack summer season), and thought of all this. If Kathy ran to me, flaming or not, we would dance together out of sight.

Fred!

I sat down twice to try to write to him. *I have the job, I am making it, send her back.*

Because Mother is busy planning. I knew she was, even before she wrote me about it.

I know they say it's better for you not to have me come there, so I am sticking to that. But I thought you should know I've never been so happy, I am having a second chance, raising my little girl. I've bought little dresses for her, but if only you could see the ones your Aunt Sally sends. Just darling. She's walking now, if you can imagine. I know for some reason I never made much of a success at being a mother to my only baby girl, but now I think some kind fate has seen that I need to try again. As you know, Fred stopped me working for a time. I couldn't bear the thought of you alone and possibly not well up there, and then, when you felt driven to do this awful thing to yourself, I was in such despair I could not force myself even to do the simplest task at the lab. Summer will be here soon and we will be at the house in Vermont. We are hoping you'll let us extend the time we can keep her, why not indefinitely is my dream, with you with us too, because you must see the advantages she could have, that darling little thing. . . .

Maybe it's true, I thought, *but why didn't she ever mention Jeff?*

A whisper started, and I had to listen; plain common sense and past experience demanded it. It said: *She is out to win.* She was always determined, planning and scheming—at what? Why, at defeating me. Whatever I had was hers first. It had to be. I had nothing. I could not be permitted to have anything. At the farthest back of my mind

I always knew something else, which was that she had either seduced Jeff or she had tried to. "Did she?" I used to ask him.

He would laugh. For a long time he would back off like a smart handsome dog not wanting to give up a ball he was carrying. Bringing it close, then frolicking off with it. Daring you to run for it again. "Did she what?"

"Did she try to make you, get you to bed?"

"Well," he would say, "lots of women try. Doesn't mean they succeed." But then, dead serious, he whirled me around, backed me against the wall, and said, "No. Just no. Stop thinking about it."

I was left with what I knew: that she would not have been able to help trying. She would have noticed right off that trim jaw, that back and shoulder, pelvis flat, and full even mouth. More than that, I had claim to him. What I had, had to be hers. She understood everything so much better than I did. Including Jeff.

As long as I just knew this it remained painful inside me. But when I speak it out on the tape, it gets out of me. I feel better. I play it back. I feel better still.

I want to live, not die. I want my daughter. She belongs with me.

Finally in that summer still upcoming, I conspired with Leonard Abel and we stole her, stole Kathy away and brought her home. To Montreal: home.

13

Mary's Tape (continued): The Heist

Try it, sometime, a heist of your own child. From Vermont, go and get her back across the border into Quebec. At least it wasn't so far away as Pennsylvania.

Fred's summer house there had been bought the way his family bought everything, as an investment. He shared it regularly with his brother, who had used it when the children were young. Now it was standing empty. He had decided to take Mother and Kathy there and make like a family. He was bent on soothing her, that was clear.

Her nerves were apt to fly apart at any given moment, I could tell that from her letters and calls, sometimes on, sometimes off.

On the telephone: "You never told me that!"

"Oh, yes, I did, you've forgotten."

"I never forget anything."

Why, when I left the womb, didn't I keep right on crawling? No, she couldn't visit; it was against professional advice. I was getting my footing back (not the best phrase to use to a dancer, but try telling it to a woman psychiatrist who stared down at her notepad as if terrified of making human eye contact). Everything had to wait. But during the wait the ends of my nerves were screaming out their hurt pride: *What right does anyone but me have to Kathy?*

I worked at my job at the library five days a week. One day I looked up and encountered Leonard Abel. He was medium height, with tousled dark hair, curly and worn fairly long. A first I took his hair for black, but then saw it was laced with gold, a mixture, but natural, no dye. He had a strong measured way of walking, wore a loose striped shirt, three buttons open, chains, and strange Eastern–

looking rings on his brown hands. A belt with a silver buckle. And then the eyes as he leaned toward me—they were startling, dark but flecked with gold like his hair. In a certain light the gold flecks would shine; you would think Midas had been at work on him. He was looking for books on the tribal nomad life of the Middle East, prehistoric, perhaps, back before Bible days, 9,000 B.C. would be a good start.

The truth was I knew very little in an academic sense about anthropology. I had written it down because I needed to say I was interested in something besides dancing. A few names like Margaret Mead and Ralph Linton, Clark Wissler in American Indian studies, were about the extent of it. But I was the only help in evidence at the moment, so I said, "Let's look over here."

He followed me, but even before we had gotten there or started a search, he began to ask me about myself, staring at me as I answered, searching my face, repeating my answers carefully to make sure he had things right. He wasn't used to the way Southerners talked. He said he liked to hear it. Then he asked me, copying down call numbers, "Can you come to my house tonight? I'll pick you up. Will you come? My wife, Hilda, is there. She would like you to come. No, you must come. All right? I'll be by at seven. Tell me where."

So that night was the first of many at Leonard and Hilda Abel's.

It was the first contact I ever had with them, and it seemed to me to have something to do with their Jewishness, European Jewishness, sufferings under Hitler and all that, that they could so completely, right away, open up their hearts to me.

Hilda was the more inclined of the two to go all out. That was clear to me in the way she talked about parents like mine—materialistic WASPs—as bound to be wrong. How could they ever understand a sweet vulnerable girl like me? Even I knew better than to be one hundred percent committed to that point of view. Of the two, Leonard had more sense.

But I basked in Hilda's sympathy and ate all the food she cooked. (She went in for recipes from various countries, lamb Iranian style, Pakistani curries, Greek shish kebab, and homemade Mexican tamales.) Since Madeleine Spivak and I had quarrelled over Jeff and poor Gordon Stewart was heavily suspected by his Gerda of favoring me charitably because of his desire, a nice faithful married couple was what I needed for company.

I'd only snips of time for dancing, and Estes Drover, whom I missed, had that Arab boyfriend capable of slipping me the wrong kind of pill. I still would go to lessons, though.

"All these dinner parties," Estes complained. "You'll be making the social columns next."

Don't think we didn't have an April blizzard. I caught a cold, which cut down on my timing when I danced. It seemed to muffle the rhythm I was going by, so that I missed by a second or two. But in time, my cold dried up; the weather warmed into June.

At the dinner table, others present, Hilda hymned away. "You think they care about you? Of course, they don't give a shit. They're keeping you from him"—she meant Jeff—"because they don't like the way he thinks. He don't think like them. You sit there not seeing the way they are. They live a hundred times better than you. You think they care?"

I had to stop all this.

"It isn't true," I said, "that everybody is doing the wrong thing. They think they're doing everything they can. They have to reason things out from their standpoint. It's just that nobody knows how much I want my baby."

At this I started to cry.

"I want to hold her and carry her," I bubbled into a glass of red Bulgarian wine. "I want to talk to her and change her diapers and put her to bed and wake her up and feed her. This is my *right*. I've got to do it. I'm going to if I have to sneak down there and steal her."

I began to shout, "They're right down there in Vermont. near as they can get to me. For them it's a rest. For me it's torture."

All this with two other couples present, strangers to me, not saying very much by way of answer or encouragement, so that I'd not the ghost of an idea what they thought. Then we just kept on eating. Afterward, we finished the meal and the wine and went out in their living room. Leonard played the guitar and sang some of his own poetry. (He had published a volume or two and was always composing more.) Hilda sang as well. They had no children, though Hilda was always going to the doctor to check up on why at age thirty she couldn't. Even before Leonard finished a round of songs and put his guitar aside and looked at me, I knew something about their child-lessness was in the air and working toward some end.

"I'll go with you, Mary," he said.

"Where?" I asked, thinking he meant it was time, after my hysteria, to get me home.

"We'll go and get her," he said. "You're right. You ought to have your child."

" 'Ray, 'ray!" cried all the guests, laughing in a way I thought must be Jewish, recently out of Europe, being warm and bitter at once. To me they were foreign and new.

"We'll try at one of the little crossings," Leonard proposed. "They hardly wake up to check your name, much less go to see if you're on a list."

"Do you really want to?" I asked doubtfully at the door after he had driven me home. He nodded, but his face in the scant light looked long and dogged. In this way I glimpsed the effort he was making for me. There were circles like stains under his eyes. The eyes themselves looked into mine, with their strange glints of gold. It had all happened suddenly, like getting afloat in a swift current. I couldn't help but connect this daring offer with what I knew about his past in Europe, how the family had made it out through the Iron Curtain after World War II, coming one by one across a dangerous border. Night crossings. Regroupings. Did he want to live that again, maybe, in some secret part of him, tempting another fate?

Until we got across the Vermont border, Leonard was so tense we hardly said a word. The crossing was done at a little U.S. customs station along a wooded highway southeast of Montreal, a small white cottage of an official outpost that looked both lonely and homelike, the way isolated places often do. Leonard whisked his Canadian I.D. under the officer's glance and mumbled something about my being his cousin. Then he declared he was not taking in any liquor or cigarettes and no gifts: we were on a pleasure trip. He all but winked. They didn't ask me anything, though I was ready with Hilda's I.D., my head tied in a scarf. As a backup I had brought my immigrant's visa, but that might betray me on some list as Jeff's wife.

We started the car, turned with the road, and were through it, relieved. Leonard's tension returned, to my surprise, this time as anger: "I'm doing this for you. Do you know how much I'm doing?"

For the first time in the weeks I had known him he spoke with such a thick accent it made his words hard, unfriendly, tougher than would be possible for a person brought up in English to make them sound. I remembered that some of his relatives here had been refugees who had gotten out before the Anschluss, and I saw with humility how much he was risking for me of his present status in Canada, and how probably, too, he was unique among the persons I had met in knowing that it was important to take that risk. He knew that ties strengthen under separation and that frustrated passions grow stronger. He had pity on me, I saw that.

The soreness along my throat seemed to go completely for the first time since I had jumped off the chair with the twisted sheet around my neck. That very spot grew soft, filled up with tears.

"Oh, Leonard, I'll never forget you for this, I'll love you three times over always, but you shouldn't risk anything for me. Kathy is safe; nobody will kill her. Mother is strange, but she never actually poisoned me. Leonard, you've got to go back."

But now he was laughing, rollicking with unexpected fun. "You're a bigger child than your little girl," he said. "Of course, I've not come this far to turn back. What would happen? Hilda would throw me out. 'You fucking coward,' she would say. 'Out of this house. Me, a barren woman, and no wonder.'" He was mocking her to a turn.

I started laughing with him, laughing and crying both, sun and rain together. I'm good at that. Some sort of magic I started feeling might rub off on this baby rescue journey. I was grateful for his sense of humor. When the crossing was well behind us, I began to feel this was an adventure, and fun.

Suppose we succeeded. Was Kathy to sit in Hilda's lap and learn her little Yiddish songs, and then, with Hilda's heart so warm with love, was conception itself supposed to follow? But I had to stop this cynicism. Leonard was not scheming ahead to that extent. Kindness doesn't have to have a motive, does it?

Still, with his Middle Eastern chain, the chink of the old coins strung on it, his glinting rings in beaten silver, sexy was the word that came to mind; and at that moment I felt his hand on my knee, moving upward, and his softened voice beginning to put his message out, though not without hesitancy or consideration for how I might feel. He was just trying to lift my spirits.

He said we had some spare time.

"Hilda told me when I left: 'Help her, just as much as you can.'"

I sat imagining her rich dark-brown eyes filled up like two pools—those twin lily pools of the daughter of Zion—and her voice quivering. She was so sincere it half wiped me out to think of it.

Leonard's hand had proceeded halfway up my thigh and was aiming higher. I was not especially ready to object, but driving these back roads was not getting all the attention it needed, and the car suddenly struck a huge pothole over which a limb had fallen. If a car could be said to trip, that one did. In leaping over the limb, the right wheel forced the limb to swing forward in front of the left wheel, so the car's momentum wedged it between the two. What happened next, though caused from below, felt as if something had reached down from above and twirled us around, up, down, and to one side, just for fun. When we caught our breath and looked around, we saw the fallen limb had twisted sideways when we struck it, and was now wedged between the wheels. One front wheel was perched on top of the limb, the other was down in a pothole.

Leonard and I crawled out and between us dragged the limb clear. We pushed the car up straight from where it was tilted over. At this exertion my blood raced healthily, and when I got back into the car I was struck as unexpectedly as the car had been by such a wave of longing for Jeff Blaise that I almost threw up.

Leonard, starting up the motor, had fallen into one of his laughing spells. "See the effect you have on me? I couldn't have made myself seem more sincere. No, I don't see how I could have."

Driving, he grasped my hand and squeezed it. I now burst all the way into sobs; I was practically squalling. I was not any daughter of Zion, and retreat into the veiled mysteries was not for me. I was back with that picture in the book that had inspired me to study anthropology, but those three in their skins before the rude dwelling had names and faces now: they were Jeff and Mary and Kathy.

"I just want Jeff," I wailed. "And Kathy. That's all I want."

I watched the picture in my head: movement. The young man had satisfied himself no threat lay out there in the woods: he knelt to start a fire, bringing straw and kindling, stirring ashes back from live coals, blowing through his hands till a flame leaped up.

But to Leonard Abel I said, "You have to understand, I'm one of those Airedale types: one dog, one master."

14

Mary's Tape:
The Heist (continued)

"Have you thought out what to do when we get there?" Leonard Abel asked.

"No, but then, if we didn't know how to go I might just have found it anyway."

"Is your emotional radar as good as that?"

Over winding roads through the Green Mountain foothills, we had seen farmhouses painted red or pale yellow in large meadowlands, rolling peacefully, sunlit. It was a fair day with large free-floating white clouds, none coming near the sun. We circled among the houses in town, like the clouds ourselves, checking names on the mailboxes, but never found the right one. Leonard said he'd have to ask, make up a story, while I sat in the car on a side street with my dark glasses on and my head in the scarf, huddled down under a corduroy duffel coat I had brought from Montreal. He came back looking cheerful. It seemed the road to Fred's house was a branch-off, a bit hard to find at first. It paralleled a state highway on the other side of a beaver marsh.

I could tell Leonard had enjoyed his contact with the people in the little store. But I was afraid he wasn't careful enough. What story had he told? In little towns people take note of everything. If we really succeeded in making off with Kathy, somebody would come up with a complete description of us, car and all.

The truth was, Leonard loved America. He was of a mind to find Fred Davis to be a reasonable man. Such energy as Americans had! Such a great country as they'd built!

I told him his enthusiasm might be getting the better of him.

"Why, I thought I should have told them the truth in there—everything," he expanded. "They'd probably help us."

"One out of forty would," I said, "and we don't know that one."

"You really mean that? One out of forty? You're a cynical woman, Mary." He was growing more euphoric than ever.

On the edge of the house property, which we saw and then backed away from, we hid the car in an unused and overgrown driveway leading to a house that had burned long ago. We crept into the shelter of pines and birches and sumac, over a brittle, glittering, micalike substance that seemed to have come up out of the soil of that area. It was hard on the knees and entered the skin like glass splinters. I scraped my leg on an exposed pine root, the blood prickling out along a band of flesh. But I hardly noticed once I heard a sound from below, from Fred's house. It was a closing door.

On the side of the house nearest us, there was a paved terrace with some garden furniture around a glass-topped table, a pool with varicolored paving stones, and a small cast-iron fountain, water spurting from the mouth of a curved fish which was leaping upward. It was here the door had closed, and here the three of them appeared together: Mother, Fred, and Kathy.

I grabbed the binoculars, literally forced them out of Leonard's hands. They were coming out. First it was Fred leading Kathy, then Kate lifting her down some steps and setting her down. And for the first time I saw my daughter walk, holding Kate by one hand only.

Kate was walking, too. In beautiful white slacks, her bright hair put up so short for summer you'd think she'd had it cut back to the twenties fashion. (But she wouldn't do that, not to that hair, Fred's pride.) She had on some kind of brilliant scarf—lavender and vermilion mixed—and a navy blue top. The effect was what she wanted—the best. Still she couldn't help touching it, worrying over it, fingers to her hair, an adjustment to her glasses, the fluttering brush of her hand at the scarf's knot near her throat.

I wound the knob between the two fine German lenses until I had her fixed in them—it was her I knew that I had to see now, studying everything, finding for reassurance what I knew would be there: the prettiness, the nervousness, the restless glance, the impatient line between the eyes. Only then did I lead the focus of the glasses downward to where the slender hand with the long, lacquered nails was holding Kathy's. And I saw in that little hand my own's likeness, stubby, mosquito-bitten in the hot summer of a North Carolina street

when walking along beside Mother. I swept the lenses to the side
and a little distance higher, and there, jammed into my face near
enough to kiss, was Kathy's talking mouth and reaching eyes. (But
what to talk to, what to reach to? To going home from a visit to a
neighboring house, saying, "What did I do wrong? Why don't you
tell me?" hearing, "You know very well what you did," saying, "Then
tell me," hearing, "I don't care to talk about it." At home before a
closed door, "Please, Mother, please tell me." Then silence.) *God,
don't let her have to get treatment like that.*

Leaning to follow closer, I lost balance, almost fell out of ambush,
but Leonard caught me. He was quiet and watchful, and later, re-
membering, I liked him for that. He knew why I had to kneel so
long watching the three of them as they sat, while Mother positioned
herself half in the shade on the chaise longue to open up a magazine
and Fred took Kathy by the hand to walk her near the pool. She
had on a pink sunsuit with crossed straps at the back—cute. Mother
always could find the right things, or maybe Aunt Sally sent it. And
little white sandals with two buckles each. She leaned toward the
water, and Fred bent down as faithful as a kind servant, unlatched
her shoes, and carefully shook each one free of her foot. Then he
lifted her as she faced him, his two hands brown against the pink
sunsuit, and set her into the shallow pool, but not without first a
swing upward, so that I, avidly following her face, saw her laugh
break out on the upswing, bursting into louder delight as her feet
struck the water. She looked down, still laughing as she plunged
foot-, ankle-, and nearly knee-deep into the water. Right away she
began to splash him.

Fred had on a blue sport shirt with tan slacks. They must have
come from some fancy Philadelphia men's shop and probably were
ten times more expensive than they were designed to look, but he
let her splash him anyway and would have, I thought, if he'd been
wearing his best business suit.

It was when Kathy got tired of all that and came bobbing over to
Mother (Fred with his finger out, barely holding her little waltzy
steps upright) and caught her by the leg and tried to climb up that
I saw it—the upward glance, the swerve aside, the sharp frown and
recoil and hand lifted in a kind of reflex I knew so well, a striking
hand. It was Kate all over, roused once more out of her eternal
dream. Which was: herself—the lovely, impeccable, talented, effi-
cient, desirable woman—waiting for the one true touch of the ador-

ing, unchanging, passionate lover. For her there had never been a child. How could there be? Here one was again, one she said once more that she wanted there—but did she? Lover into father: What right did they have to change like that? Children take what lovers have, they take it right away.

But she didn't strike. She pushed the little wet hand from her leg and opened her magazine. Kathy's shadow, drawing back from Kate, was longer than her tiny body, but I could see the beginning of what would shape into a larger pattern, and I almost cried aloud. I gave the glasses back into Abel's hand.

"It's Fred we have to see," I told him firmly. "Fred alone, if we can manage it. It's the only way."

"Don't you exaggerate?" Abel asked me, as kindly as if kin. "She might listen to you, decide you're right."

I shook my head. No time to explain Kate to a good man.

The thing to understand now is that though I said I was going to get Kathy and take her back, I didn't really think we could succeed in doing that. I think that Leonard really had no more faith in it than I. It was just that he was active and affectionate, and believed in doing something, believed, too, that by doing something I could relieve the pain of being static.

For we had no scheme for kidnapping, no ladder or accomplice like a maid to hire and place inside the house. We had brought no guns to march in on Fred and Mother, and as a getaway car, Abel's red VW beetle was no good at all. It could be sighted a mile off and was inclined to stall. So what was intended, I feel, was basically that I would get to see Kathy—just see her. That having seen her, I might find the courage to call Fred, and having called him might be given a chance to see him, talk to him, not just binocular-type seeing. From there to push further, somehow, some way.

Mother was still reading in the chair. Fred had taken Kathy inside; maybe he was even into diaper-changing now, or bathroom trips, or drinks of water. I rolled over on my face to think. Leonard had gone off somewhere alone, perhaps to let me ponder. Lying there, I heard a breeze stir, and sitting up, I heard it more plainly, the rustle made not by a wind but by a stream nearby. I moved up through the trees until I saw it down a slope, clear and reedy, with a slanting willow above. I knelt on the marshy bank and put my face in the water. I did not try to hold my hair back but let it float and swim around me, like another sort of reed. It was cool and wonderful and I felt my face growing pale, healing back out of the strain of recent hours. I pulled up for air and heard a movement behind me—Leonard. He might have been a shepherd, taking a break from a dry hillside. He caught a handful of wet hair and drew me gently up. I got up and walked to a grassy place below a gray boulder, the grass fringing up at the boulder's base—gray and green like Canada—and sat down there, leaning back, one hand cupped in my lap. Leonard knelt by me, then over me. I saw his face, which was near, as though it were one with a frame of leaves, not so much framed by but made out of the darker leaf shadow, which changed slightly, undulant, as the muscles moved. His lips at first were like the dense, smooth, dark surface of summer leaves. I put my arms up around his shoulders, or rather they seemed to go up there by themselves, and then I thought of Jeff and forgave him for Madeleine Spivak because touching and holding is such a good thing.

In the midafternoon I called Fred from a highway phone box.

He answered right away. It was almost as though he was expecting me.

15

Mary's Tape:
The Heist (conclusion)

Fred and I agreed to meet at a place near town down at a lake where people came to swim and picnic in the summer. There was a pavilion there with a screened area above, where they sold sandwiches and steaks. The downstairs was a boat dock, a place to change for swimming, and perhaps a dry dock in winter. But Fred and I met outside and sat at a picnic table. He was wearing the blue shirt, the tan slacks, same as earlier, but had added a foulard, something for going out.

Fred Davis had a lean, rather blank face except that his eyes back of those odd-shaped glasses were intelligent, and he observed everything without asking questions. He seemed receptive to whatever was going on. I hadn't seen him since I left Philadelphia, and I now felt, seeing him again, that he had brought his house—that atmosphere—with him, and that even here it was forbidding. It had seemed not only rich but mysteriously so; there was a darkness about the wealthy that had gone into it; the money, which had originally come from coal, might after that have also sprung from railroads or the stock market or real estate—there were stories about all three. If I'd asked the right questions I might have found out more. I would ask Mother, but she'd only smile faintly, distantly, and say "Business interests," which means nothing.

"You can bet it was business interests, all right," Jeff had said. "Now the guy's got nothing to do but swap good investments for better and sit on boards of directors and enjoy a sexy new wife."

Yet I wanted to tell Fred things. I wanted to then, and I wanted to now.

For instance: "I know I made good grades at Bryn Mawr at first, but I'm not interested in being educated. I know I fell behind. I'm just always practicing. But I thought I might follow up on that other thing, anthropology. I couldn't act interested in a lot of other things. I can't pretend. Also I wanted to be with Jeff. Maybe I would have been happy in your house except for things I couldn't help feeling."

"All that," he said, and looked out at the lake, where a small sailboat was tacking uselessly, for there was no wind that day. Some children were going hand in hand out into the roped-off swimming area, making small uncertain steps forward where the bottom sloped un-evenly. "But you could have talked to me." He coughed.

He went up to the pavilion and came back with a drink in his hand; it looked like bourbon. He took a sip and sat back down. "The day you ran away from Bennington I had just made an appointment to go out to Bryn Mawr and see your faculty counselor. I had a feeling things were difficult for you. There were other schools. There might have been a way of talking things over with Jeff, too, if you'd have asked me. As for your mother, I know she demands things of you—'measuring up,' she calls it. Don't you understand her ambition for you?"

I thought it over. "What does she want me to be?"

He turned his gaze slowly toward the restaurant pavilion above and then to the dock below. Near the gas pump some fuel had spilled a multicolored film in the water. It rocked when waves from a speed-boat finally reached shore. "What does she want me to be?" I re-peated, wondering if the pendulum swing of his gaze, as though he watched the world's slowest tennis game, was going to pass me again.

"She wants me to be a credit to her," I said bitterly.

His eyes turned back to mine. "Surely there's more to her than that."

"If you don't know, I don't," I said. And added, "And if I don't know, you don't."

He laughed. The laugh began with a smile but couldn't stop there. He suddenly found it worthwhile to have seen me. The laughter which crinkled up the tight skin of his face stopped as suddenly as shutting off an outboard motor.

"You could have passed any course you wanted to. I think you were defeating us, defeating your mother in some way. Perhaps you were unhappy."

His gaze was wandering again. He shifted once or twice and moved his hands nervously, like a smoker who had no cigarettes. He left his drink alone.

"I just wanted love," I said suddenly.

He did not register surprise. Life to him was to be played like a hand of poker. But at least he did not disturb the force of what I had confessed.

"You're no different, I imagine, from most of humanity on that. No different from your mother." He had gained safe ground for saying something about her.

"But she gets what she wants from you." Being certain about what he'd said had left him open for a moment.

Now he looked at me with more than interest because just for that moment I was the tortoise and he the hare; he had gotten behind and he knew it.

"Nothing left over for you, you mean?"

"Not from you."

"Was there just this Jeff guy and no one else? No other ones you ever liked?"

"Things either click or they don't." I recalled two or three heavy-breathing students from Haverford, a boys' school near Bryn Mawr. They have to be from top families or they wouldn't be there. One had hid in my closet one night when my roommate was out of town.

"That's true," he agreed.

"Are things really working with Kathy? I mean, does Mother really want Kathy with her?"

Now he got to thinking hard, because he knew we had reached the nub of things, to where we were heading all along.

Fred's not answering made me know I'd gained some ground.

I pushed a little. "I've got a right to ask, if anybody has. Haven't I?"

He finally came out with it flat. "No, I wouldn't say that it is working. Not altogether."

I waited.

"At first she was so eager, she thought she was having a second chance to bring up a child and this time would be . . . well, a correction. She feels she wasn't such a great success with you. But now something has started—a real impatience, I think, a longing to shake out of it. I thought we might get through the six months, though. I'd no great wish to baby-sit, waiting for the 'reevaluation.' Don't they call it that?"

"You'd have ways of extending it; you know that. But if the risk grows that she—"

"Risk? What risk?"

I stopped. How could he not think I was just being the neurotic one if I started remembering out loud, all about the silver hairbrush, myself locked up in closets, one nasty surprise after another?

"On your side of the fence," he said, "it can't be too healthy for a baby girl to walk in and find her mother has killed herself."

Right out with it. He was testing to see if I could take that. Not so dumb, Fred. I could. "I'd never do that now. She's old enough to know me."

He was astounded. It took a while to digest. "You mean you were working it in before she could register what happened? Would never know?"

"You can be told things, but unless you experience what they are . . . It would have been just a fact, a shadow."

"I'll be damned." He sat frowning. "There is definitely a strange thing with Kate. She sees herself in a role, being a certain way. But let her get what she wants, and she's trying to get out of it. There's a gap in there somewhere. A puzzle." I waited. " 'Risk,' you said. Are you actually afraid she would be negligent, let something happen that—" He broke off.

Now of course, he wasn't the one who wanted Kathy anyway. Who would want his wife's grandbaby wished on him this early in his second marriage? I was remembering the woman we'd both seen him with in Philadelphia. Fred moved to his own inner music. He was at his own command. He scratched his brow where something had bitten him. He broke out in a foolish smile. "The truth is, I'm getting very fond of her. I'm trying not to, but she's a capital little girl."

"Parting hurts," I said, and he caught the irony, and gave it back with a smile. He thought of his bourbon and drank some.

I wondered about telling him something: about that time after Poppy's death when Mother and I went on a trip together to visit some cousins in Mississippi and stopped off at Lookout Mountain, Chattanooga, over in Tennessee. She was holding me up to see the view through binoculars fixed to a stand. When you put a coin in and your face close to the circular lens and turned a small wheel for adjusting your vision, you could see battlefields and a river, seven states, a city. She was holding me up to see, and suddenly, as though to tease me, she gave me a little push, first swinging backward to make it stronger still, and then farther out toward the railing, with its long drop below. I cried out; I nearly screamed. People looked up and at her, and she said, all but dropping me on the gravel walk, "Don't carry on that way—everybody's looking." I had thought she meant me to fall. I ran away from her and got lost among little scenic paths, boulders, signs, water fountains, flower beds, was stared at by statues of dwarves, was called after, caught by a guard. Back at the car, I crawled into the backseat and lay down still like a travelling dog.

Then we drove to Bessemer, Alabama, and spent the night. She tried to make up for what had happened, never admitting anything. We went out to a restaurant and ate some chicken. There was a tower over Bessemer that rose above a foundry, I guess, because they mine iron there. It was belching out smoke-colored red against the night clouds. We saw it and went in and ate peacefully. When we came out we were, for no reason, happy. Maybe, I sometimes think, the tower of flame was the male image we didn't have just then, or maybe it was the Pillar of Fire we'd heard about in Sunday school: we were watched by One Who Cared.

But if that were so, then Fred Davis should have been the appointed one to create nothing but goodwill and happiness. Except maybe he wasn't all hers. Maybe he had collected her like a pretty Southern mockingbird for his photographic birdwatching collection. . . .

"So since, as I said, it isn't altogether working, God knows why. I'm inclined—" he began, and set down an empty glass.

"Inclined to what?"

"To let her go back with you."

I stared in blank astonishment. I'd never hoped for that.

"Think you could manage it?" he asked, jibing at me a little, daring me.

"I'd die to," I said, and meant it.

He pointed out that the important thing was to stay alive. I agreed to.

"You're going to have problems. You're going to have to dodge the probation people, not trust just anybody to know you have her. Perhaps in a large city it will work, but if it doesn't I will have to say that in an unguarded hour you spirited her away, something vague like that. If it does work, I'll fill your documents out when the time comes—how much longer is it—three months?"

"I've friends now," I cried, triumphing. "Oh, I know it's going to work!" I felt like leaping up and waltzing around, doing a Ginger Rogers act over tables and benches, ecstatic.

Fred sat observing. Maybe he was wondering if he wanted another drink. "What friend brought you here? You didn't come alone."

"He thought we should talk alone, I guess. He must just be in town for a while." I wondered if I hadn't come there with a spirit— an angel, sort of.

Fred was tired of sitting on the hard bench, I could tell. Now that his decision was made he was ready to act on it. Men in business act this way: they think, decide, move; that's that. But I sat still for a moment.

I remembered how after Mother met him she had come in so light and happy, taking matching bracelets off, summer bracelets set in blue and white, something plastic and glossy, saying, "There's this man asking me out occasionally now, the one I met in Atlanta. He just came down today from where he lives in Philadelphia."

"Do you want to get married again?"

"Married? Oh, don't be silly, I hardly know him."

"But do you?"

"Any woman, I suppose, prefers to be married, any real woman. . . ."

I remembered Jeff, one particular memory buried off in the Jasper County woods, reading while I lay curled half on my side—"like a cat," he said—and read by twilight and firelight and flashlight, Whitman being the best, he said. Nobody but him till you got to Crane and Frost. Poetry had something to say that life was saying, too. Then he would read again, stopping now and then to gather me up under his arm. He'd make me close my eyes and shine the flashlight on my face. "Your face is poetry," he would say. And we would kiss. I had to make myself numb when I remembered all this, so as not to feel too much.

"Why did you marry Mother?" I asked Fred timidly, the smallest possible question.

He had passed off somewhere beyond our conversation, but finally decided to answer anyway. "We have," he said, almost negligent now, "what most people look for and never find."

"Would you call it love?" I pursued humbly, because I wanted him to see that it all related to Mother, that I'd spent at least half my life trying to understand, and that if he and I could agree that love was what she felt for him, and he for her, then that might be a base for understanding her in a new way. But he just kept looking down at the table and shifting the little bits of ice that hadn't melted in the bottom of his glass.

Finally, he said, "I hesitate to use that word, about anything."

"But why—" I stopped, thinking of the woman Mother and I both knew existed, wondering if it was she he cared more about. "Is it somebody else that you—"

He looked up and was really displeased now, about to get mad. "Who's giving you the right to ask? No one has, or will."

That reaction was cold, a bucket of freezing water. He put out his hand, already regretting. "Come on, now, let's stick to you, not me."

But, dashed, I had already left the table. They were they; he was not about to let me in. I found the ladies' room on the basement floor and went inside. I leaned my forehead on the rough cement wall. I might as well have beat it on the wall. Eventually I heard Fred outside talking to some woman: "I can't find her. She's not well. Did you—"

"I'm coming," I called. "Coming."

Fred was standing in the middle of a wide area with a few bare tables for snacking pushed back against the wall, useful I guess for summer dances or maybe in winter for dry-docking, a cement floor painted gray under this man who was used to Oriental rugs and green lawns mowed and rolled, and marble entrance halls. He looked like he owned it, though. He seemed to have decided to sell it and was wondering how much to ask. He came to me.

"Come here." He actually took my arm, to draw it under his own. "It's all right," he told the woman. "She's been upset." He led me out then toward his car.

"What did I do?" I said.

"I thought you'd never come out."

"Mentioning love is the wrong thing," I finally said.

For once he made no answer. He handed me a comb for my hair, not unkindly.

We moved in step together over the gravel toward his car. "She's not really a mother," I said, "wasn't meant to be."

He opened the door for me. "Kate, you mean?"

"She can't help not being."

Again he said nothing. He closed the door.

"You're in no state to take this step," he remarked, starting the motor. "They are probably right about your testing period."

"I shouldn't have showed anything," I said, half to myself. "I've hurt my chances."

He backed and began to drive out of the parking area. "I think you have to take her now. Stopping you now . . . you couldn't take that." The car was wandering back home. Before we turned into the drive, he drew up by the side of the road and spoke to me. "If pushed, I'm going to say you stole Kathy, took her away. I'll have no part in it. You understand?"

I was a waif in rags and tatters; he wore slacks and sport shirts with labels that sent a message to the world.

"This country is in a war," he said.

I was stubbornly silent.

"Don't you think you should use that comb?" he asked. "And where is this 'friend'?"

"He'll come," I said. I should have said *I guess he'll come,* because how can you know about anything, anybody? Maybe Leonard had taken me here just for holding me as he had in the woods; now, things getting difficult, he might have retreated home. Good faith may be a never-never land we hope to die and go to. But letters from Jeff and checks: my secret hold on the world were those.

"Money, of course," Fred was saying, "can be arranged."

"Money," I repeated, having just been thinking of it. It was more to me than he knew, more than just eating and paying for things. It was proof that Jeff was still alive and free. Also, Jeff caring, Jeff getting word through a living network.

Fred began slowly driving again. Now I had combed my hair and smoothed down my eyebrows, even smeared on a little lipstick.

"Outrageous, what's happened in Washington." I wasn't up-to-date on what he meant. The Pentagon march was way back. Maybe something new had happened. Maybe what he said was a bid for what I knew.

"You helped Jeff about Chicago," I said. The bail he paid, five thousand. "It was such a mix-up as to who did what."

"It was no mix-up that violent elements took over, or tried to. You do realize that?"

"It was the police that got violent." I did know that much. "All Jeff's crowd was trying to do was get into the convention. To get a hearing."

"Nobody wanted them," Fred said dryly.

"A lot of people wanted them. They just wanted to be heard. Why did you help Jeff, if you think they're all so wrong?"

He stopped the car again to speak to me. He used his words slowly, deliberately, as if talking to someone not sure of the language. "I do not know this Jeff of yours. I went solely because of your mother's interest. Her daughter's husband was in jail. Her distress was evident. Understand?"

The car moved again.

The wheels pressed the fine gravel, the house loomed close for the first time, yellow with white scrollwork trim, even a little lightning rod sticking up like a candle on a child's birthday cake. We approached flat on, so that the house seemed dimensionless, like the backdrop for a ballet which rolls down on a weight, and if anyone came out of it they were coming out of nothing like an interior because it was all make-believe. The drive led the car in a small circle. We stopped before the door as though we were guests. I thought, *I can't do it, I just can't,* but I was getting out just the same, with legs numb, and he said, "Wait, she had no idea when I went out that you—"

But the door opened and out she came, onto the stage of my life once more.

So I stood waiting, holding on to the side of the car. She came on and on with crisp, beautifully fitted slacks creasing and uncreasing with the forward motion of legs everybody, including herself, so admired. Going up the steps to her, I stumbled, and this threw us together because her arms were out and we were half shaking and half crying together like the one body we once literally were.

It was a real upheaval.

They led me—she and Fred between them—into the house.

"Kathy's here," said Mother.

"I know."

"Of course, you know. I must be crazy. To think you wouldn't, I mean."

"We're causing so much trouble," I said.

"You're back to stay with us, aren't you? In the States, I mean."

"No, not back."

Causing so much trouble was just a Southern phrase that fell out of my mouth without my meaning it to. It meant that life would have gone on in a smooth way if I hadn't come into it, at this time, at other times, at any time at all. It meant, *Excuse me for existing, for breathing the same air you do, for occupying the same planet, for being anything but what you think I ought to be. Excuse me for trying to kill myself. I was only trying to get out of the way.*

We all went inside.

I was always amazed at Mother. She sat so quietly in this new turn of events, so correctly and beautifully, as though she were about to get a present from somebody and would know just what to say by way of thanks. Fred also was filling his role, sitting like a leading Philadelphia businessman.

I wanted to yell at them, *Are you thinking it's just ordinary, like I came for dinner?* But what I said was: "I just came for Kathy. I know it's a little early, but I'm okay now. I can manage."

Mother broke the silence. "You can't mean to take her back out of the country?"

"Just to Montreal," I said. "Not an hour up the road." It was more, but that sounded good.

Another silence. "How did you get here?" she asked. "Did your husband bring you?"

"A friend."

"Oh." *Where is Jeff?* was hanging in the air, unsaid. She would never say his name.

When she was working in cell structures she had this idea of getting cells enlarged into poster-sized colored pictures, which she mounted by buying some department store reproductions of paintings, throwing out the pictures, and using the frames. She hung them in a small sitting room we had in that duplex we moved into. They looked smart, like a series of modern paintings. I wondered if they were healthy cells or sick ones, and which, for that matter, were prettier to look at.

"Where is she?" I asked. I looked up the steps. Could they just hold me there?

"Asleep," said Fred.

"As a matter of fact," Mother said, "she had a little cold this morning. I don't think we ought to get her up."

I was on the edge of my chair.

"Have you kept up with your dancing?" Mother asked.

I thought, *This is where Jeff Blaise would get so mad he would pick up a vase and break it.*

"Tell me about Montreal," she continued. "You've met some nice people there. The Stewarts, wasn't it?"

This is where Leonard Abel would smile and answer courteously because, he would explain, they are just acting out dreams of themselves. But what power those dreams have! Kathy was asleep upstairs and I couldn't go up to her.

"I'm taking Kathy back with me," I came right out and said.

"We'll talk about it," Mother said. "First we'll have some lunch. You must be hungry."

"I've eaten already," I said.

Mother said, "It's been like having my own little girl again." She had real tears in her eyes. *Somebody to slam the door on, is that what you're missing? Will she get sent to the attic for a whole day, no food?* Kate had on that beautiful scarf dyed by some New York or French designer to a natural freshness of light and dark, sat hiding all her anxious demands. Like, *Where is he? What's he mixed up in? What's he not mixed up in? New Jersey break-ins? Berkeley riots? In prison? Do you have a job? What is it?*

She's trying to think of something, anything, to stop me, I knew.

I glanced at Fred and saw his tension, too.

"I think she's right in wanting to take her, Kate."

She whipped around to him, cords in her neck, eyes flashing. But what could she do with him? Fred, however he had had to get it, enjoyed his control. Seeing them locked in conflicting stares, I didn't waste a second. By the time they turned back to me I was halfway up the stairs and vanishing fast. "No!" sounded behind me, but he must have caught her. I didn't dare turn back to look, nor want to, either, with my child almost at a breath's distance from me.

Nothing stopped me. I rushed first through a door, but it was wrong, the wrong room. It was their room, and something on the dresser caught my eye, only momentarily, but I was to remember it later. It was a full page torn from a magazine, a cigarette ad or some such. It showed a girl in a fluffy pure white dress standing with a boy in duck trousers and a yachting coat. They were leaning together, elbows touching, over the rail of a white-painted gazebo—all carved woodwork and graceful posts and peaked roof—so beautiful, both of them. So charming, social, entirely right. *It is what she'd dreamed I would be,* I thought, passing by it on thudding feet, crossing the hall to another door. Now she was dreaming for Kathy. I opened the door.

The room was gotten up like a nursery, everything new and expensive. My baby was there, quiet and awake, lying in a little high-railed white bed. I leaned over it. "Mommy?" she said at once, like there was no doubt I'd be there, ever.

I picked her up and we left together.

16

Mary's Message

Fred Davis had driven them both into the town and let them out beside Leonard Abel's little red car, which was waiting as faithfully before the one restaurant as a tethered pony cart. Now he was back and found Kate still sitting much as she had been, in the same chair, her legs crossed, her face still strained.

"Thinking what?" he asked, straight into that look. She would not entirely rebel, not openly.

"That they've gone."

"What's that mean to you?"

"Well, just that they shouldn't, of course. Neither one of them belongs—" She stopped.

"Go on."

"Belongs to be out—well, in outer space like that. It amounts to . . . chaos."

"You mean we've no control. They've got to regulate themselves some way."

"If these were ordinary times—" She put her long fine fingers with the painted nails to her brow, pressing the skin outward. "She did take the toys?"

"Yes, some. I helped her."

"The driver?"

"Just a man. I didn't really get introduced, come to think of it. I can't say I wanted to be."

"What did he look like?"

"Shirt but no tie. Older. Some subversive beatnik type, I imagine. A lover, maybe. Is she really married?"

They sat silently in the spacious room, so full of outer summer light during this rare warm New England month, and both had before them as a vividly remaining image in all detail the girl so recently there, her still face with eyes fixed on them, how the long hair which framed it had flowed trembling when she moved.

"Your daughter has beautiful hair," Fred remarked casually. "Darker than yours, but yours just the same. The texture."

She nodded. "Kathy will have it, too."

"A line of three women." He had said this before. It seemed to please him to think of it.

He sat down near his wife, not touching her as yet. She was as tight as a reined mare, headstrong thoroughbred, barely under control. He lit a thin cigarette with a marble lighter and drew a matching marble ashtray closer to him. Articles like this, which pleased him, he had brought here from the Philadelphia house.

"Why did you let them go?" She put the blame for it squarely on him.

"If it ever 'came out' in public ways that I was harboring connections of this kind—"

"I know that! We discussed it all before. You took a chance for me. I know. But once decided—"

"Perhaps neither of us knows exactly what we're talking about. What's out there?" He gestured toward the whole outer world. "A bunch of crazed children, mad at everybody and high on drugs. The 'big chance' I took might be understandable in every circle that knows me. I haven't asked." He got up and prowled the room. "It's just that one thing leads to another. We've not heard the last of the Blaise boy yet. My impression is that he charges through things like a bullet."

"To be a cause to you, and indirectly through me—"

"A cause for what? Trouble?" He pulled her to her feet. "I'm ready to stop fretting over it." He kissed her slowly, deliberately, quietly, his hands exploring the rich curves of breast and thigh. "At least we're on our own, alone again." He turned attention to her neck and shoulder.

"I wish you could root him out," she said.

He was startled. "Who? Blaise?"

"You could find him. Listen. He's showed not the slightest gratitude to us. He's leaving her to God knows what sort of life. If he were gone—"

"But prison was the very place you didn't want him— Oh, dead, you mean?" He was half amused, engaged at the moment in giving pleasure, in ways long since approved.

"Blotted out some way. I didn't say dead, exactly, but I—"

He took it all as part of lovemaking, its sometime extravagance. "If I get him here, you can shoot him full of poisoned darts. Use him for target practice."

"You think you're joking, don't you?"

He drew her toward the sofa. "I think I'm not thinking about him. Hell, Kate, drop it." But she stiffened again, this time suddenly, looking past his shoulder.

"What is it now?"

"There's something out there."

She was pointing. Out where the white-painted gate stood open, fastened on either side by a chain that ran to a hook fixed in cement, something had been placed that had not been there before, tied to one of the chains and floating skyward, almost gaily, with an air of festive detachment from all events except whatever it had in mind to celebrate. It was large and blue. Breeze-tossed but stable. A balloon. Mary must have gotten her mystery driver to come back and tie it there.

Kate ran out the door to meet it as though it were a person. She ran toward it. On the gravel her sandal twisted and she fell, hands out, recovered, got to her feet before Fred could help her, ran again.

She stretched out her hands to the wavering balloon. It was a strange conical shape, blown up into an amusing pseudo-animal form, rather like something in a comic strip, which might have had arms but didn't, had a waistline and a belly, but seemed happy to have nothing that could really be called a head. Written in large, wavering, uneven letters in chalky white paint across the sky-blue surface:

Dear Mother, I love you, Mary.

The delicate white hands with lacquered nails, the palms hurt by the fall in the gravel, pieces of which had been driven into the flesh and would have to be brushed or plucked off, bringing up blood, were reaching toward the balloon and its message.

Fred, not outdistancing her, carefully untied this object to bring it inside. But not before he had helped up his wife, straightened her, seen that she was all right. Anyone watching through the hours would have thought them more than a little odd, he supposed, going in and out in threes, the balloon now a surrogate for the child they had let go.

He brought it through the door with her, but then debated what to do. He tied it to a wall bracket near the stairwell. Its sweetly disturbing message filled the house like a perfume not clearly likable. He thought of sticking a pin in it. Kate went upstairs to change. *Humanoid,* Fred said to himself, wondering if finding a name for it was a step ahead or backward. Kate came down in a graceful cassock. They decided on steak for dinner.

Coming in from drinks on the terrace, they saw that the balloon had slipped its mooring and was floating around the house. It drifted off into an alcove of the living room. Kate did not mention it.

Early the next morning, Fred got up before Kate. Purposely, he went searching for the balloon, and concluded it had disappeared. Then there it was again, half deflated, huddled midway between floor and ceiling just at the edge of the stairwell, in the shadows. The white paint had flaked and crumbled as the surface had shrunk, but nonetheless the message was legible still. If it had ever looked human at all, it now looked less so, almost but not quite returned to simple balloonness.

Surprising himself, Fred struck at it with his fist. He missed. Then, deliberately, he took hold of it, brought it close, untied the knot at the mouth, and let out the air. There was nothing whatever now to compare it to, he thought, ironically, but maybe a used condom. It went into the garbage before he put on coffee and got out the eggs.

If Kate suspected what he'd done, she never said so. Before lunch, the telephone rang. Some friends from Doylestown gave them an invitation to their summer home on the Cape. Fred said they would think about it. Their routine ran on as if of itself. They did not make love.

At drinks that evening, sitting out in the improbably mellow summer daylight, the lingering of a prizeworthy day, their silence continued. The following morning, without discussion, they packed, closed the house, and went away.

17

The Northway

Encased in the small red car like something put up in a tin, Mary held Kathy, who slept nearly all the way in her lap. Mary's own arms went to sleep and grew numb, dead-feeling, but she did not want to wake her.

"Did you ever nearly die?" she asked Leonard. She thought of the flat road before and behind as she visualized it on a map, climbing northward, out of the below they had descended to for bringing up Kathy. THE NORTHWAY, said the signs, the white letters for a moment in sunlight seeming to blaze as they passed, becoming a heavenly message spelled out boldly on a green background.

"I once dreamed I died," said Leonard. "The night my brother was killed in a car accident, skidded and went over a cliff, off on a trip in Italy, the mountains. I woke in the night and dreamed the fall, lay mangled in the wreckage trying to cry for help." He reached to touch her hand. "What do you think of that?"

"That you're always reaching out." She shifted her shoulder where the child's mouth had wet it. "Because of you I've half of everything I want."

"If I can get you both over the border."

"You will."

"I won't take the same road. Put your scarf on, we're near the crossing. Get yourself on the backseat. Take her with you. Cover her."

Precautions all taken, they moved forward to another obscure crossing where no one gave her a second glance. They mounted then, skyward into Canada, safe and dreamy in summer, green and wide, where the tree branches, starved for light during the snow-dim winters, grew high up on straight trunks, like fronds stuck in tall vases, then bent kindly earthward, like hands in a dream.

"What's the other half?" he asked, when they could begin to breathe again.

"Jeff, of course. You can't get him for me."

"He'll come for you."

"Of course he will. I know."

They were crossing a little river at a town called St. Henry. After that would come Sabrevoix. Leonard moved his hand. "I'll be happy for you," he said faithfully.

She smiled at his gentle tone, glanced at his dark gypsy profile. His cry of love she had heard that day was now like smoke on a far horizon, or the distant call of a bird in a deep wood.

That night at Leonard's house, Hilda held Kathy on her generous lap. She had cooked a supper of blintzes, cucumbers in yogurt, and generous slices of pot roast in warm spices, smelling like a narrow street in some Middle Eastern city.

Back on Seymour Street, Mary found the letter. Gerda Stewart writing to say,

Dear little friend,

I scolded you when it was Gordon I should scold. I should only have shown you my sympathy. It's what I deeply feel. Where are you? Let me hear. We must stick to being fellow Americans here. Let's discuss anthropology again sometime soon.

The telephone rang. It was Estes Drover, saying he had organized a group for a modern dance program and even booked a small theater. A grant had come in. Could she join?

At the buzz of the intercom she ran into the hall. A muffled question through the outer door, answered in the nonsense phrase she had learned—"Ten for a penny and sixteen for a dime"—then the hand reaching through. The envelope with fresh bills folded snugly together inside. Jeff's promise kept again. The passing-through of many nameless hands. A new beginning.

Mary sat cross-legged on the floor and wrote a postcard.

Dear Mother, Don't worry. Where people care you are never alone.

Sitting up to her ears in the warm tides of that same caring, she forgot the card and she wondered at it all. She thought of the strong forces that had come into play around her. She had drawn them without meaning to, without even knowing why. They had come to flash and circle her being—northern lights—and in doing that, they had created a self within, unified, tender and able. What was this warmth in a land that seemed for nothing but ice and snow? She dropped the card unfinished and went to lean over Kathy, asleep in her little basket of a crib Jeff had made out of coat hangers. *It's she I should tell it to, the magic she needs to know.* Her hands hovered above the small face, contentedly profiled in its nest of hair. Even the tips of her fingers might send the message of what gifts were there to be given by hearts that cared. Both of them, she and Kathy, were children of the dark. Other children of the dark had leaned in to help them.

It was out there in the light you heard the harsh voices: *Unfit mother . . . Who's giving you the right to ask? . . . That's another one you've killed. . . .*

But we don't have to live in the light, do we?

"Travelling at night," Jeff had said once. "It's the only way."

18

An Afternoon Message

It came at four—Mary was on her way home from seeing Estes Drover, having left Kathy with a friend of Hilda Abel. A voice called and a young man in a blue windbreaker, the only soul in sight on Seymour Street, jogged past without stopping or turning his head. But she knew.

Casually, as though she all along intended to, she slanted across the street, stopped as though checking her bag for something, and turned to go in the direction he had vanished in, eventually turning a corner, where she saw, up ahead, a flash of blue entering a small corner grocery. She entered, too.

The face that turned to her was not the one she longed for, but of such a type that suggested the other, haircut jagged, thoughtful mouth, waiting eyes. She all but caught his arm. He reached for instant coffee. She knelt for sugar. "Around the corner," he murmured. "The park. By that statue in the middle. Feed pigeons."

She bought a box of bread crumbs.

19

The Torch Song of Madeleine Spivak
(Love Does Not Grow Old.)

When alone there, coming there alone, I sometimes stop and rub my hand across the wood on the outside banister. I lean down and smell the wood. The banister is painted gray, weatherworn, uneven. Near the door, I note, with a proprietor's eye, the bushes are growing up taller, are hanging over onto the steps, also lifting up against the windows. Canadian summer green, another summer.

It was I who rented the downstairs to them. My husband was out when they came, I did it myself. I befriended them. Then, between Jeff Blaise and me, I could no longer call it friendship. What did he call it? "A need," he said, and another time, "An understanding." Again, gratefully, "I reached the end of my rope and there you were."

"Waiting for you," I replied.

He couldn't accept romantic ideas, shook his head: "Fortunate accident, after so much fucking bad luck." Bitter.

She couldn't manage; she wasn't coming through. New country, no family, no friends to speak up, hard birth, new baby, recurrent illness, ice and snow. What was he asking for? A good wife, singing and happy? Tasty meals served up smiling? Whatever, both in and out of bed, he wasn't getting. That was clear. I have to say *was,* because he isn't here. It cannot happen again. Each day I teach myself this lesson. It cannot be again.

Through the window, I note that the present tenants have kept the off-white bleached denim draperies I selected for them. I can see beyond the fold of one to the empty fireplace. If I mount two steps more I will be pressing my face to the pane as I have done many times since they left. I will be seeing into the narrow hall past the stairwell, seeing ghost images in motion.

There I go as I went back then—I'm not much changed since. Jeff Blaise is following, height only slightly more than mine, moving in neat sand-colored chino trousers, and I, swaying now and then out of line with his more direct motion, in dark cotton, the piping of the sleeveless shoulder cutting into deeply tanned flesh. His two steps make an easy three of mine. Young America follows at my sandal heel. Young America is here on a Montreal street because of principles about a little Asian country nobody knew anything about ten years ago. High principles. Very high.

He pulls the blinds. His wife is still in the hospital with the baby, coming home in a day or so, the third time they have both been sick since that hard birth back in the dark, snow-streaked winter.

"I'll do what I can for you." I've said that, not meaning this.

"What's between us is different," he had told me, "something completely apart."

My clothes are dropping on a chair. His fingers touch my arm, press into my bare back. As their warmth spreads out, my nerve ends leap to life, wild and strong.

"I don't like to do this here," I murmur.

"Why not?"

"You know why not."

"Anywhere's the same." We're kissing, pressing close, and the words float out toward nothing.

At the memory, my spine shudders, I spin off as though from a physical blow, lean against the warm wood, facedown.

I have to ring the bell now. Somebody will notice I'm just standing there like a woman in a dream, or drunk, or fainting from the sun. The street is a narrow old one where some people stay on for years and some of those, secluded penny-counters, barely getting by on their pension checks, see life from windows only, a patch of pavement, two façades, a changing tree. I mount to the landing, ring. The face that appears in the left of two oblong windowpanes which flank the door is not that of Jeff or Mary Blaise. It is a woman, gaunt and ugly, with an Indian's large bone structure at the eye sockets. Mary Blaise was gentle, with long, dark hair; at a time when good little American faces might be found with a joint stuck between their lips, she never smoked, sipped milk, had to be coaxed to eat enough. She had a musical voice, pleasant and low, and kept a barre in the bedroom for practicing what she loved most, her dancing.

Once I tried to hang my dress across it.

"Don't," he said.

The large woman back of the door recognizes me, her landlady. She yanks the door open, lets out a squawk like an old phonograph record.

"Oah! It's yew!"

"Excuse me, Mrs. Welford." I go into my lie. "I had a call from a tenant on my answering machine—I couldn't make out the name. As I had to come this way, I thought I'd ask. Was it you?"

"No, we ain't called I know of. You remember about them storm windows, eh?"

"That's being taken care of. You'll get them back before fall."

"It wasn't us."

"Sorry to bother you."

"Why don't your husband never come?"

"I told you before. He's tied up in the center, or out in Westmount, too. These below St. Catherine are mine, my job."

Shall I say, I never dreamed of managing rental property, low rent, high rent, or what have you, before the Blaises came. Then I begged to. "I can take some of that off your hands. You think I enjoy life these days? You think I like lunching with other women, shopping for clothes, giving dinner parties? It gets pretty boring, always the same. I've had enough. Fire me if I'm not good."

Even after the Blaises left, I held on; to keep those houses tended gave life to my memories. "But what, Mrs. Welford, are you doing in this very house, making a discord of the past? Yet Mary Blaise herself had made the first of the discords, as she'd had a perfect right to do. I can hear her still in that living room I glimpsed just now through the window, and again, from the hall, through the open door:

"Our good angel, weren't you? Thanks a lot, what a joke! If I could throw all your good deeds out with the trash I'd be happy to. It was bad enough here already. Being called a quitter in the war, walked away from at parties, shunned on the street. Oh, yes, Canadians are really against that war, but when they meet somebody who's done the honest thing and refused to fight it, they act like you've got leprosy. But it was you who 'understood' us, wasn't it? You were our only friend. Wonderful to us. Just great!"

I wish I could get angry in return, but I can't. I hate seeing her smooth features distort, hate the tears that keep smearing off into her long hair, gluing the locks together.

"Aren't you angry with Jeff, too?" I ask, and almost smile, for there's a wry humor in it all. Jeff and I had landed in a thicket of desire without meaning to. The pregnancy was precarious; a time or two at least, it almost ended. "Their only friend" had to be there if needed. And when it sprang to life what there was between us, had she rather Jeff and I would sit about lusting? Plucking out the thorns of desire? Watching the salt blood flow? Avoiding eyes and touch? I, who had found them the place to stay, did not press them for the rent, even found them friends.

"I thought you knew all along," I tell her, quietly honest. Montreal is a lax city. What people here won't tolerate has not been named.

"How long did it go on?" She's calmer now. As a child she must have exploded often, been ready to burst with rage when the world wouldn't hear her out, found there was no way to win, then calmed down into plain humanity again, having changed nothing. She was not something Americans seem to prize: a "winner." But she had something else, a kind of lastingness. She did not go away.

"I can't remember," I answer, evasive. I could if I tried. But reality like mine and Jeff's is not boarded up into time; does she think that? "Not so long."

Then I get a little angry, too. She could be fairer with me. Their marriage was never at stake. A younger man, just my need at the time: a young lover. "It's Jeff you ought to talk to; not me."

She does not say anything because there is nothing to say. He's gone, vanished from us both. I ask myself a question then: *What's sadder than two waifs together?* Answer: *Two waifs apart.* Q.: *What must I do?* A.: *You must get out, let go.*

She is speaking softly now, soft rain after the cloudburst. "I can't go away so long as he needs me to stay here. Where would I go? Mother would turn on me. The little life I had, I trusted you to come into it. And you did, and you damaged it. It won't ever, ever be the same. It's all messed up."

So it's me you're telling about it, I think harshly. These Americans! I sit in the living room with her most of that September day. She had telephoned in the morning, having to see me. The baby's asleep when I come, the room is chilling down toward evening. We will have an early fall, October snow. She needs me. Hates, resents me, but has to see me. Has found a passionate note from me to Jeff, stuck away in a drawer and forgotten or saved to treasure, read again, who knows?

The street outside, its leaves turning, it narrow modest French Canadian look, is no part of her. Gray stone façades, green leaves in summer, leaves turning orange, gray stone in the snow—that's Canada. Dormer windows above in the mansard's drop, painted to match the doorways—white or yellow or blue or red—and always the steep steps in shining gray paint—that's Montreal. French Montreal, and no part of her. Nor am I part of her world, though brought up by a mother from the West, speaking English equally with French. Shall I say, everything I have and am, have had, have been, always gets "messed up," as you put it, one way or another. I take it for granted. It happens to everybody. It's just life.

Then it is out of thinking these things that I discover something. Americans want, somewhere, somehow, a purity, an inviolability. So why did Jeff Blaise, young husband and father, want to "mess up" his marriage by an affair with me? I think I know. His purity was his stand against the war, a stand that Mary, for all he treasured her, was not very much involved in taking. If she had been dedicated like him, then some kind of affair would have cost her no more than a gnat in her eye. But she wasn't like that. She came from somewhere. She knew somewhere else. Her mystery was in that.

"I loved him," I told her. Out with it. I thought she ought to know.

What did she answer on that September afternoon? I can't remember. The voice, slight and distant, whirls away in time.

"I need to go back to the bedroom," I say to the ugly Mrs. Welford. "I have to see the size of the windows. We wouldn't want the wrong size."

"Don't look at the mess."

I walk there, hear the sun's heat alive on the tin roof, even through the floor and ceiling of the apartment above, but I know that ahead, in the back bedroom across from the kitchen, it is cool, sheltered by the shrubs grown up at the windows, darkened by the dusty Venetian blinds he always closed. His heels sound in my memory behind my step in the hallway, two steps to my three, repeated four times over.

I gain the room.

The barre is gone, the bed a tumble, as predicted. As though marked with chalk, I can see the very spot where he habitually turned.

We always spoke to each other equally. "You know what I think about that war?" I asked him. "I don't think anything about it, nothing at all. It's funny, eh?"

"I'm dying laughing, it's so funny."

"Don't you think I should?"

"It's not your country, why care?"

"I want to be honest."

"So?"

"I doubt if I would care if I was there."

"Selfish bitch." He laughed.

Another time, he said, "I go alone. Alone, and I don't mind."

Speaking so honestly, man to woman, woman to man, it seemed to me at times that Mary and her baby were both our children. That was the heart of what we reached to, or so I felt it to be.

I had first seen their faces before me one day when in the downtown area shopping. I had stopped by my husband's office and, finding him and his secretary both gone to lunch—together, for all I knew—I had sat down at the front desk. So the young couple, entering for the first time, took me for the secretary, able to answer something about an apartment. "Have you got something for us? Something we can afford?"

He was straight, strong, with fair hair flowing almost to his shoulder; she younger, darker, dependent, and pregnant; and the snow outside was melting away. They stood there hand in hand. Out of the talk between them as they'd entered I had caught the name "Mary." Mary with skin palely luminous, with hazel eyes steadily serious, her mouth innocent of makeup.

A room at the inn, perhaps? I almost said, the first I'd thought of convent days in many a year. But with that phrase popping up in my head, I could recall the rustle of nuns' skirts along polished corridors, see the flat arrangement of furniture, the harsh colors of cheap religious pictures. I thought I had hated it, but a secret meaning hidden beneath its plain surfaces broke open for me at that moment. In the living presence of the two before me, I found tears rising to my eyes. I was theirs from that moment. . . .

"Sorry to have to trouble you, Mrs. Welford."

I leave the room, the little house in the poor street, maybe for the last time. But going, I think of one further thing.

To reenter the country he came from, Jeff Blaise had to get a false identity, through channels tricky to deal with, methods he never discussed. He went so far as to alter his fingerprints by scarring them with acid. Necessary or not, I never knew. He got directions from somewhere, and bent studiously to this punishing task. Politics are powerful, reaching in to change the imprint of a lover's touch.

Mary, were you hurt by this, too? Did it hurt you as much as it hurt me, to see his fingers burnt and changed?

Part III
Scatterings

1

A Box of Crumbs

"Priorities?" He gave her an envelope and held out his hand for some crumbs.

On the park bench, shivering only partly from cold, she tilted the box into his hand and watched him cast them. The pigeons were making pigeon talk.

"Is he well?"

"Fine. Except for the strain. Anybody would feel the strain. Then not hearing anything from you."

"Not hearing!"

"Not enough. What you think you're doing to him? Have you split and never told him?"

"Split with Jeff? Listen. It's me never hearing. I had to call to Ethan—this guy he writes for, those articles. I ought not to call him. He's suspected of Lord knows what. Then there's no money. . . . Does Jeff know that? I think the machinery broke down. The wiring's bad."

"But that was Jay-Bo."

"You can be dead sure I haven't seen that Jay-Bo bastard in a month, and before that—"

An old man with a walking stick, poorly dressed, went by. She stopped talking, then resumed.

"A year before that. Even when Jay-Bo showed, he was on the run. Couldn't stop to say a word."

"You're kidding."

"Honest A."

"What the fuck happened? Jeff don't know. He thinks you just turned brown over something named Spivak. Is that a code?"

"I wish it was. It's a two-legged code that's starved for men."

"So that was it."

"I thought he dumped her before he left."

"If he said so, sure."

"Waiting's no great game. I've had a few breaks."

"Got any now?" Men. He thought she meant men. No need to mention the friendly natives, Len and Hilda, Gordon and Gerda. Nor Estes Drover.

"I meant work." Who could she tell all about it? Maybe Jeff someday, reunited with him on some smiling shore, island in the sun, with happy Calypso singers frying bananas and dancing the limbo flat as pancakes, while the drumbeat pulsed. But maybe forgetting was best. *Guess what, Jeff, I tried to kill myself. Isn't that silly? Hohoho. Hardly any news . . . I thought you left me, after that Madeleine bitch.* And he: *Kill yourself . . . ? Why, baby . . .*

"Just plain money is the crying need," she went on. "I can't think how to get any. Sucking up to a lot of these kind friends. They're a help but they wonder about Jeff. What can I say? I don't know myself."

"You really don't know, do you? What he's pulled off, I mean."

"He's not supposed to 'pull off' anything. Just write about it. It's gotten him into trouble, I guess. Somebody blew his cover. Does he live in a basement somewhere, eating peanuts and sending out for pizza? Has he gone down a copper mine to hide?"

"He took on one of the big ones, that's for sure. Wasn't supposed to, but he did. That was out West. Listen, if he knows Jay-Bo didn't get through and didn't tell him, he's going to kill Jay-Bo."

"Then don't tell him. Maybe Jay wasn't to blame."

"He could have said. Come on, let's go for a joint. There's a guy near here, one street over—"

"I'm off all that. With Kathy, you see— Look, what's the message you have? Why can't you spell it out?"

"I'm just now seeing it all. Why they sent me. I got no green. I'll have to dig."

"Dig where?"

"Places. Places. I'll find out. Back of the fuse box at the Salvation Army, good ole Sally Ann. A suite at the Ritz. Some judge's pissed-off wife. All I do is drift by."

"When?"

"When I get the word. What I came to tell you, you've got to move."

"Move? Where? Not out of town? And why?"

"That guy Jeff worked for—still does, I guess—the one that has the paper."

"Ethan."

"Right. He's scared to send Jeff to Montreal. It's gotten too tight here. Writing is one thing, but the kind of job he was on—they want him, see? Coming up to you is what it's all about. They've found a safe place. You'll go up there; he'll come. Then, later, when things cool down, you'll both resurface."

"But go where? My dancing—it's going again. Don't you see I'll lose my edge."

"Your what?"

"Skip it."

"Should I?"

"Who cares?"

He had gotten up and begun to stroll away, still talking. He seemed to be going nowhere, moving toward the slope of Atwater Street. She followed at a little distance, as though a stranger.

His words came floating back. "Above Ottawa. Say it's for health reasons. Just for a short while. Jeff has to build up insulation. Test waters."

"But how long? What does a short while mean?"

"Hard to tell. It was a big job, remember."

He certainly looked in need, frayed jeans, an oversized windbreaker with some stuffing coming out. When he turned they stood apart, like he was asking directions. She was slipping into constant subterfuge without noticing it. She kept pointing when it didn't mean anything. Passersby were no longer innocent. She was sliding underground.

In one last normal petulance, she stamped her foot. "Maybe I won't. Maybe I don't want to."

"Don't want to! We got the whole fucking deal set up, and you don't want to!"

"But you don't tell me anything!"

"Believe me, if I have to pass it on that you stalled on him, he'll about die on the spot. It's you keeping him levelled off. You going to split, you better say so. You going to stick, you fucking well better mean it." He looked up, searched meaninglessly around building roofs, the clouds.

They're making me choose how to die, she thought. *It isn't fair.*

"That's not the choice, if he's going to always be—" *Gone,* was what she meant to say. *Gone, and I have to figure my own life out.* A wind was pulling at her hair. His hand closed cruelly on her arm, demanding.

"It's the choice, all right."

She clenched her teeth and spoke through them. "I just can't do this anymore. No. I won't."

His grip tightened. "Listen, bitch. He not only wrote you but he had to think you didn't answer. He not only wanted to see you, he came here."

"*Came* here?"

"Yes, came. I know it. I drove. We were scared about crossing. He couldn't find you. Some woman in magnifying glasses kept blabbing at him. He thought she was one of the pigs. He couldn't find you, Mary. We had to get out. You weren't to be found."

"Turn loose." Her knees were too weak to stand. *Came here, and I— But I was probably just over with Estes. That must have been Gerda Stewart who—* She could hardly speak. "All right, I will. Just this once more."

The hand dropped down. "Tonight. Somebody else. Cash if I can get it. Directions: You got them there in your hand. What I gave you. A word to remember: Gatineau."

She nodded. "I'm not a bitch," she said.

He grinned. Instantly farther off, he was already moving down the hill, leaving like a dirty sheet of newspaper picked up by the wind. He vanished into the dark uprush of Atwater traffic as the light changed. On the park bench, he had slipped a thick envelope into her bag. That must have been just when he said: "He's done the big one, brought it off. You ought to be proud."

Proud of what? They didn't want to tell. But that was as close as she came to knowing.

"Sorry to be late," she told the sitter, Hilda's friend, a dark-haired girl with eyes like smoky lamps. "I had to stop at the shoe repair but they weren't ready."

If she could ever stop lying she'd probably continue anyway, just out of habit. Lies had gotten easier to invent than the truth was to tell. For telling the truth, you had to work to remember. The truth was a witness box. She searched for the few bills she owed.

Kathy, walking everywhere now, toddled in from the kitchen nook. "She was making cookies," the sitter said.

"Not really."

"Oh, she was, weren't you, Kathy? We put them in the pan and then we put them in the oven and then when we pulled them out they were done."

"And we ate them all, I guess," said Mary, and picked Kathy up, cookie crumbs on her mouth. A crumby kiss. "See you tomorrow," she called as the girl left. But would she?

Only after Kathy was fed and tucked in bed did she sit down to open the letter. It said where she was to go. It was all there, directions, names, arrangements. Above Ottawa. To be met by, etc. Train ticket. Up the Gatineau, a river.

And there at the bottom of the other, thicker, more closely typed pages, a thin folded sliver of a note—oh, merciful!—from Jeff.

I'm having to love every minute of my thoughts about you because that's about all there is for me to love. In the middle of everyone that's around I turn ice cold to think, *But she's not there anymore, she split the way she ought to, she's gone forever.* I slide down to the bottom of the bottomless pit and before the snakes and rats get me, I think of you again, and I cheat them one more time. I'm floating on the clouds, I'm walking in a straight-up world on a sunny day. I'm sitting with Kathy and watching you dance from the fourth row center aisle of Lincoln Center. I'm loving you forever. From the front lines. &$%%.

Out of nowhere, she heard her mother's voice: *If he means all that, which I doubt, where is he? Putting you through all this. You're a fool, do you hear me? You're a fool.*

One more try, she promised herself. *I'll just give it this, and then, on my own, I'll—*

"Kathy, did you know there's a river called the Gatineau?"

2

Up the Gatineau

"They are coming soon," said Madame Pelletier. "*On vient bientôt. Il faut changer la chambre.* You must move. Downstairs."

Mary had just come in with Kathy. They had been walking, up to the ferry and back. It was going to snow.

"Who are they?" She spoke each word slowly, fully, repeating in French, "*Qui sont-ils?*"

Anyone who came might be carrying some message from Jeff stuffed in a back pocket or buried in a gun case. A hurried telephone call was all she'd had to go on, back in Montreal, plus that scrap of a letter folded in with the tickets.

"Hunters," said Madame Pelletier. "My brother take them tomorrow. He does his living this way."

"American?"

"*Je suppose.*"

Madame Pelletier, who had called her from the house as she passed with Kathy, pulled on a coat and hastened down the front steps, hustling before them along the road to the little lodge next door. "*On cherche des moose,*" she could be heard to say.

Then they were moving, changing rooms. Mary had had the corner room upstairs in the lodge since she had come in late September. The few couples who had arrived to fish had taken the small room downstairs. Now there would be three men, one sleeping on the sofa bed in the large downstairs room and two above, in Mary and Kathy's room. Mary and Kathy would move into a little downstairs room with upper and lower bunks.

Madame Pelletier was in a hurry. She had dinner to cook for the lot of them. Mary barely managed to squeeze past her on the wooden stairs to the floor above. Once in her room she seized the framed picture of Jeff, and a handful of letters, thrusting them in her carry sack. Her heart beat loudly. In what she admired daily, others might see a wanted man.

Madame Pelletier, entering behind her, flung open her closet door. She glanced back at Mary. She was a quick, square-built woman, once pretty, whose brown hair was laced with gray. Some locks curled free from pins, along the back of her neck. "*Je vous aide.*" She smiled. There was nothing insensitive, Mary knew, about Madame Pelletier's intrusion. She had probably never given a thought to privacy. And now she probably had to drive three miles and back to shop for groceries before they came.

"We go back to Montreal, Mommy?"

That was Kathy, hopeful, swinging on the bedpost. She had gotten tired of daily trudges either up the river or down, back into the woods or out to the pier. It was only a few times a week that Madame Pelletier thought to ask them in to watch TV. On Saturday mornings Kathy often missed Captain Nemo.

"No, precious, we're just changing for downstairs. Just for tonight."

"Tomorrow, too. Maybe. I don't know." Madame Pelletier laid a sheaf of clothes across her arm.

"Maybe tomorrow night, too," Mary filled in. She was gathering up boots and shoes. It was all quickly done, in two trips. Kathy helped, carrying small armloads. In the new room, she looked doubtfully at the bunk above. "You can sleep with me," Mary promised. Otherwise she'd stay awake, with visions of a small body tumbling past her face.

"Oh, Madame Pelletier?"

Madame Pelletier turned back from the door.

"The bathroom—" Mary began.

First there was puzzlement, then comprehension. There was a downstairs bathroom but it was across the whole width of the big open lounge where the fireplace was, and the dining table. It was partially a junk room, with a corner containing a rusty shower that had no curtain. The toilet sat out in the room, like a chair.

Madame Pelletier considered. "Okay. You walk out the back. You come to the house." She pulled on her coat, a man's duffel, fleece lined. As she left the lodge the first flakes began to fall.

———

"Not bad atall," said the heaviest of the three hunters, his back to the fire. They had been eating silently, with Madame Pelletier running back and forth from the kitchen to offer more helpings, and her brother Gérard Belliveau rising often to replenish the wineglasses from half-gallon bottles. The pork roast had been cooked in Madame Pelletier's big black range up in the main house, but she had brought it down to the smaller kitchen in the lodge, where she had roasted potatoes and cooked the little tart Quebec apples, quartered, in the roaster with its rich drippings. She had heated the beans in an iron pot.

"You eat like this all the time?" the heavyset man said to Mary, who sat across from him.

"It's very good here," she said.

His gaze lingered on her. "American?"

She nodded. "It's been good for me here." A theme of health. It was best to let them think that.

The lean brown-faced man sitting next to her spoke across to Gérard Belliveau. "Will the roads be open far up the river?"

"Maybe to St. Ange, fifteen, twenty miles. Far enough. *Pas probléme*. But inland, if it snows all night . . . impossible. Still, we can try."

Mary had seen them arrive. They had gotten out of a rented car that was smaller, she guessed, than the Cadillacs and Oldsmobiles they were accustomed to driving. They alighted with a cramped look, especially the heavy man, and all three shook themselves like big dogs. They wore things bought in American stores, most of which looked new. L. L. Bean. Their vinyl zip bags bulged with extra clothes and the clear outlines of whiskey bottles. The guns, in fine tan leather cases now, leaned in ranks against the wall beyond the two sofas and the coffee tables, where the highball glasses and the whiskey, reduced downward, had been left. Mary helped Madame Pelletier while the men drank. Kathy was frightened and stayed in the room, reading one of her large bright books. When the meal was ready, her mother led her into the room.

The lean man was saying something about the other time, the one the others had missed, and how the moose had turned and looked at him gravely, steadily, without the slightest fear, just before he shot him. "The damned thing looked like a U.S. senator," he remarked.

The heavyset man laughed. "That's a sketch," he said.

The hunters would put the dead moose on the top of their car, like ski equipment, going back.

It was not a noisy group. Mary thought they were subdued on account of the snow and maybe because of her. They probably hadn't expected to find anyone staying there.

Madame Pelletier had explained: "She stay in the back room there. Okay?"

"We have to get up early," the heavyset man said.

"She don't hear nothing," said Madame Pelletier. Next to Mary, the lean man stirred coffee in his thick mug with a long, brown hand. He had never once turned to look at her.

"Can I go?" Kathy asked, squirming down from her chair.

"Come here, sweetheart," said the third hunter, just down the table. He had thinning red hair and a round agreeable face. Red hairs fleeced the forearms below his rolled-up sleeves. He had taken a handkerchief from his pocket and was twisting and tying it deftly.

"Go on," said Mary. Kathy moved distrustfully toward him.

"Look ahere." The red-haired man held up a very solid rabbit shape, long ears, round nose. The forepaws were his own fingers. The nose sniffed, the ears waggled. Kathy gave a gurgle of laughter and reached out her hand. "Pet him. Pet his ears. Watch out. Don't let him bite." A sudden grab. A little shriek, a sharp withdrawal. Everyone watched.

When Gérard and his sister spoke in French, laughing, Mary laughed with them, but of the hunters only the lean man understood.

"He says we eat it," explained Madame Pelletier. "Tomorrow night. For dinner." That was the closest they came to being merry.

After she put Kathy back in their room, Mary helped Madame Pelletier clear the table and wash up in the lodge kitchen. When she came out, the men had gathered around the table and were drinking beer. Several chilled six-packs had been brought from somewhere.

To go to the bathroom, Mary had to waken Kathy. She dressed herself and Kathy warmly, then went quietly, unobserved. The snow was so thick they could hardly see the house, though a few steps along the path took them to its side door.

The inside was stove-heated, deliciously warm. On her cheeks, snowflakes turned warm as rain. Odd objects, carved from wood and polished, sat about on the tables. On the walls there were pictures of lakes and woods with deer stepping down to drink. Madame Pelletier, who was watching TV, turned her head.

"The dinner was so good," said Mary.

"Not bad," said Madame Pelletier.

In the bathroom, Mary lifted Kathy up to set her on the tall toilet. "I don't like the man," said Kathy.

"Which one?" Mary asked. "Not the rabbit man."

"That other one," said Kathy.

"Which?" her mother asked.

Kathy did not reply. She was sleepy.

Outside, Madame Pelletier was waiting. She held out a large china chamber pot, painted in pink roses. Both of them smiled at it. "Marie Antoinette," said Madame Pelletier.

Reentering the lodge, Mary did not look into the room with the fire and the cleared table where the three men sat and drank. She felt rather than saw that Gérard Belliveau had gone up to the Pelletier house to sleep. Perhaps she had heard him come into the house while she was there.

As she closed the door, she heard a fragment of talk.

"—make of it?"

"Her? Oh, Vietnam, probably."

"I thought that, too."

"Pretty brown hair . . ." Then, later, a laugh. They went on talking, sometimes with the cadence of argument, though she couldn't make out the words. Later in the night she heard the sound of feet in thick socks, going up the stairs.

In the morning, I'll go out early, she thought. *At least I can keep out of sight.*

At an early hour, they saw her from the lodge entrance, walking up-river to the left, the opposite direction from the Pelletier house. She had the child by the hand and both of them were bundled. As the heavyset man watched them, taking his gun from the case for loading, he thought how early she must have gotten up and gone to eat—at the Pelletier house, he supposed, if at all. Something in her going off at this hour reminded him of flight or, at the least, avoidance.

Behind him, the red-haired hunter turned back into the lodge for something he had forgotten and the lean one said "Here we are," looking up to the house where Gérard Belliveau's jeep was just pulling out. They all heaved up into the jeep, knowing already who would ride where—the heavyset man in front. The doors slammed.

Gérard burst into an unexpected grin that simply split his face in two, cracking the weathered skin in all directions.

"*Allons!*" The jeep started forward.

"Yaaa-hoo!" said the red-haired man. All of them laughed, at one in the hunt.

The heavyset man, however, was leaning forward a little, and so noted that human tracks had crossed the road, one pair very small. No one was in sight.

The snow had stopped in the night. The air was clear, but uniformly hazy; there was a great vacant stillness now being torn by the jeep motor and the bump of the high-set four-wheel drive. If he had not been so attentive, would he have heard the cry? It was thin and high, and at first he thought it to be some strange arctic bird, or some small animal in a trap. He caught Gérard's arm. "I thought I heard something."

They halted and sat for a moment.

"I didn't hear anything," the red-haired man said from behind.

Gérard was about to start again, but now they all heard it; a cry for help. He switched off the motor and vaulted down.

"Shit," said the lean hunter. The heavyset man clambered out and the red-haired one soon followed. The lean hunter sat still, holding his gun upright, looking straight ahead. The other three went down into the woods to the right of the road. On the downward slope their boots sank heavily into the snow.

"Eh, Marie!" called Gérard. "Eh, Kathy? *Où vous êtes?*"

"Here . . . *ici*. I can't—"

The heavyset man began to run, followed by Gérard and the red-haired hunter. The thin hunter remained behind, stamping his foot where his sock rubbed. He bit his inner cheek and looked ahead.

Now they were climbing back up into sight. The red-haired hunter was carrying the little girl, who was crying, though seeming only to be frightened, while Gérard and the heavyset hunter were supporting the girl between them. Her leg was extended oddly to one side, as though she were holding it out from her. Just back of the French Canadian's shoulder, one arm dangled loosely. Her head was hanging forward. Her cap had fallen off, and the long, brown hair was every which way. The thin hunter watched as they walked her slowly past, going toward the house. Cursing to himself, he put his gun aside and walked back also.

Madame Pelletier was out on the porch, wearing only a sweater over her shirt and slacks. *"Qu'est-ce qui se passe? Oh, mon dieu . . . !"*

Turning off before he reached the house, the lean hunter banged into the lodge. When the red-haired man entered, a few minutes later, he did not look up from a magazine.

"Not even TV," he said.

"The poor kid," said the red-haired man. "They're taking her across the river. Doctor is over there." The lean man went on reading.

"Ted wanted to go, too. She slipped into some kind of gulch, iced over, and what with the snow, almost couldn't stop falling. Some type of dancer. Scared about her leg."

"Ruined our start." The thin hunter turned a page. "This fucking *Time* is two months old. Don't even know Nixon won."

"It must not mean a whole lot up here, the U.S. news."

"It must not." He threw the magazine at the nearest couch. "Else they wouldn't let her stay."

"You can't be sure of anything, Cass."

"I can be reasonably sure. They've run to this country like roaches."

"Elle danse. A dancer," Madame Pelletier was explaining to the heavy-set hunter, whose name was Ted Melford. "She scared about dat."

She and Ted Melford stood on the front porch of Madame Pelletier's house, looking out across the river from top of the broad flight of steps that led up to the narrow gallery. A motorboat had just swirled out from the small dock below. Stretched out in the prow on blankets they had arranged for her, Mary could be made out for a long distance, though she began to seem like an item of cargo, a tent or some bundled-up game that had been shot. In the boat, hand at the steerage, Gérard sat up straight as an Indian. At his feet, wrapped in a blanket like a miniature squaw, Kathy huddled. Stubbornness was visible in her small back: they had wanted her to stay behind.

The boat swung free of the thin rime of ice near the shore and met the central current. With the buckle and rise of the boat as it angled into the flow, the bundle in the prow convulsed with what must have been pain or fear, maybe both.

Ted Melford tensed his fist. He had seen her face when they were bringing her in, flung back, white, drained, famished as though hungry and tired for too long, for months, even longer. Letting go into pain and fear. A dancer. Way up here. It made no sense at all.

Madame Pelletier put her hand to her forehead, shielding her eyes. Across at the opposite landing, a car was drawing off a snow-covered road, approaching the river, stopping. Gérard raised his hand. He shouted something. He was answered.

"They come now," said Madame Pelletier. Over there, from some unpronounceable town, she had telephoned a cousin who would meet the boat and drive them to a doctor.

Somewhere in the car on the way to the doctor Mary must have passed out. "Mommy, Mommy," Kathy was saying, and she opened her mouth to answer, but nothing came out. Then she was sitting in a room while a man in a white coat was saying, "Right over here, take it easy, that's right. Good."

She felt him gently pulling back her heavy wrappings, then examining her leg. *The leg, the knee, the ankle . . . oh, no,* she thought. *Oh, no! Dancing. If it should ever end.*

"Gérard," she said, but he had gone back in the boat. To kill a moose that looked like a senator. It was his job. "Broken," she was saying. "I heard it when I fell. Something cracked like a stick. I grabbed for Kathy. She was sliding in. Lord knows how deep it was. I just kept grabbing."

"There we are." The doctor's fingers hit a pain point.

"Oh," was all she let herself say. It was high on the ankle. "Just a sprain, I think. We'll x-ray. But I'd say it's minor."

"Not broken!" A clang of relief all but sounded like a struck bell. Mary rose straight up. Her weight trying to land on her elbow sent a rocket of pain from her shoulder down her whole length. She must have cried aloud, but had not even heard herself.

The doctor eased her back. "Hey, wait a minute, now, let's just see." He was gray-haired—*un Anglais*—with a friendly professional voice, but serious eyes into which she tried to gaze and keep down the pain he was now discovering as he moved her arm from one point to another.

"Yes, there it is. Well, determined to break something, weren't you?" He laid the arm down across her like an object. "Probably a clean break, but we'll have to see."

She closed her eyes. "Kathy?" Where was she?

"Right outside. The guy who brought you. His wife's there with her. Easy, now."

She looked outside through a window set close to the ground.

There was nothing there—this must be the outskirts of a village. Nothing but a long flat stretch of white—clean, plain, unbroken.

Once again the three hunters tramped down the steps to where the jeep sat patiently waiting. The sun was breaking through the haze, and though Gérard had taken less than an hour for the whole crossing and return, the dim hours when the woods might yield up a sleepy nighttime prey blundering about in search of water were lost.

The lean hunter was still angry, not less but more so. He had stiffened, in fact, into a kind of sustained, silent fury. It might have been because of the delay over the girl—it was certainly partly that; but it might also have been because of the French Canadians, not reckoning how much time they were squandering (and did they still expect to be paid as much as ever?). And his fury might also have included Canada for not hurling war resisters over the border. The two other hunters thought of all this but did not want anything specified. The red-haired hunter felt the need for tactful silence, hoping things would simmer down; Ted Melford wondered after the girl. Once more the jeep started. The red-haired hunter gave a mild imitation of his former college cheer, and they tried to laugh together, and to lean their spirits forward again, into the hunt.

"It's over now. You can rest," the nurse said.

The little hospital, one floor only, was quiet and neat, though down the hall a baby was persistently wailing. Kathy had climbed up on Mary's bed and was playing with something she had brought with her, a tiny car. She had found it in the pocket of her blue kapok windbreaker, along with a message she had forgotten all about. It was for her mother.

Scribbled on the back of a leaflet advertising camping equipment, Mary read:

> I'm sure you're going to be okay, but maybe you ought to know that one of these guys is into government stuff, connects to Washington, I mean. He noses things out. Maybe you don't need to know this. Maybe you do. Take care.
> Ted Melford (the fat one).

There were two hundred-dollar bills folded into the paper. She stuffed them under the pillow.

The nurse touched the cast on her arm. "Does it still hurt?"

"No." The plaster felt new and cool.

Moving on again and again. Would this go on forever?

She wanted to stay on with Madame Pelletier, who cooked and cleaned and never bothered her. Who did not care.

She crumpled the letter tightly in her hand. Tears kept welling up. "It's goodness makes me cry," she explained to Kathy, smiling. For goodness, she had to judge, was what it was—what had appeared once more like something green and alive pushing up through the snow.

But where was Jeff?

3

King of the North

A day or so later Mary and Kathy crossed the river with Gérard. By now she could hobble around on a crutch the nurse had pulled out of a closet. Her broken arm was in a sling.

It was Madame Pelletier who took Kathy for her walks, sat with her nestled by her at night to watch TV until both of them fell asleep. Hunters came and went. They did not always want dinner or to rent the lodge. What they wanted was Gérard. He earned his way.

Mary had run out of books. Kathy's storybooks were worn to tatters. Mary was hungry for a meal in a restaurant. To see a city street seemed an odd wish, but she wished it anyway.

Madame Pelletier's husband arrived. He lived farther north in a mining camp, where he was foreman. No one said what he mined for. He spoke no English at all. His beard was so heavy you'd think it was for keeping him warm. He was tall, rough, with arms that hung far down toward his knees. He hunched forward, walking with a bent back, and seemed continually about to lunge at something. He said *bon jour* to Mary and stared in silence at Kathy, who got scared enough to cling to her mother's leg.

"*Contentez-vous?*" he asked, and when Mary did not understand, he shouted "*Heureuse?*" so loudly she jumped and shouted back, "*Oui, oui!*"

"*Oui, oui!*" Kathy echoed.

"*Bon,*" he said, turning away. He smelled like wet tree bark.

Mary had come to ask about books, but slunk back to the lodge with nothing said. From her window later on she heard them quarrelling.

The river had frozen over in the past few days and plumes of smoke from the sun's warmth were rising as though from fires set and abandoned. Monsieur Pelletier's voice was a steady roar, which seemed not to be in any human language. Above it Madame Pelletier's cries rose in counterpoint, *"Je n' peux pas! . . . peux pas!"* Mary thought fearfully they might well be quarrelling about her. Had the money for her lodging not been enough, had she been already reported as suspicious, located as someone married to a wanted man? Wanted for what? She could only say, if questioned, that she didn't know. But perhaps they knew and were deciding to turn her out. Would they only do what was better for them?

Gérard, she recalled, had cared for her. His strong arms had carried her up the bank. He had taken care of Kathy in the boat. Kathy adored him. But these people were doing such things every day, probably had been for the last three hundred years. Maybe they thought nothing of it. What is it if you don't call it that? Would they help you one minute, throw you out the next?

"Peux pas!" screamed Madame Pelletier. Mary thought she might never quit.

Right in the middle of the uproar next door, she heard Gérard enter below in the lodge. He would be after traps or snowshoes or shotgun shells. She crept to the head of the stairs.

"What's wrong?" she asked.

He stopped and stood in the middle of the large room, unshaven as usual, with his plaid wool cap flaps hanging loose, yellow teeth like an animal's showing as he answered. *"Ah, Marie? Quoi?"*

Kathy slipped past. *"Monsieur Gérard."* She went bumping in a small bundle of her thick red snowsuit down the stairs. "Did you shoot me some *animaux?"*

"Mais oui, ma fille. Mais certainement."

"Où sont-ils?"

He caught her up and flung her toward the ceiling. She yelped out her delight.

My God, thought Mary, *she's making a life in this place. She'll be some sort of animal next.* Already she was wanting to *aller au* jeep.

"Non! Chalice! Peux pas!" cried Madame Pelletier.

"Qu'est-ce qui se passe?" Mary asked Gérard.

"Oh." Gérard laughed. "He want the money you bring for room and food. She spent some for what she need. But he want, *quand même."*

A roar without beginning or end, with no change or modulation whatsoever, now was swelling up from the house. An envelopment of sound like a vast cloud rose around them all. *We'll be swallowed in it,* Mary thought. Kathy got scared and squirmed out of Gérard's arms. Footsteps came sounding, and a slamming door.

"What will he do? Will he kill her?" Mary cried.

Gérard laughed his oddly genuine laugh, the one he gave whenever people talked of danger or killing or death. "No, jus' a fight. He come home, he fight."

Through the windows near the door, Mary could see Madame Pelletier running, being overtaken, caught, thrown to the ground, rolling in the snow. There was a quiet as sudden as switching off the radio. Monsieur Pelletier had her by the arm and hair. He was pulling her like a carcass back through the snow. There was a bumping up the steps, doors closing. Silence.

Gérard laughed again. "Once I try stop." He raked a finger down his cheek. "Still got scar."

"You mean it's just a love fight? Nothing really wrong?"

"Oh, wrong, *mais bien sûr,* wrong. He want money he think she got." He moved across the room toward the storage closet, after what he came for.

"Will he get it?" Mary asked, and got no answer. She sat down on the steps, holding Kathy in her lap.

"What they do, Mommy?" Kathy asked.

"They're playing a game," she said. "It's all right. It's just a game."

When Gérard came out again he was carrying a black, valise-shaped metal box that looked to contain fishing tackle. Ice fishing, she imagined. She had heard them talk about it.

"Gérard, when you go to Ottawa next, or just to where I can get a bus, I want to go with you. I need to buy some books for me and Kathy. We've worn out what we have. And some clothes for her, too. She's outgrown her boots."

"You got money?" asked Gerard.

She knew she'd better not mention the two hundred dollars. "I could call some friends in Montreal. They'd let me charge a few small things."

"Maybe I go next week." He continued toward the door.

"But you're always going to the village, and the bus goes from there."

He said something she didn't understand. The door banged shut on his words. Mary sat down on the frozen steps to think.

That evening she went to the back door and called Madame Pel-
letier. She said Kathy had a cold and she would just take some food
back for them both. She held out a plate. Madame Pelletier had a
black eye and a large, swollen, egg-shaped bump above her temple.
She seemed glad to give the food in that way. Mary took the filled
plate and returned.

If she reached a telephone in Ottawa, who would come for her?
Gordon Stewart? He had put up money for her bail and she'd not
only gone and got Kathy before probation was up but had left town.
Hilda and Leonard? Leonard would come. She would go over to the
eastern part of Montreal and stay near Estes Drover, who had just
gotten a Canada Council grant from Ottawa to keep his dance group
going. She could make enough to eat. But then the creepy hand of
the law reached in. She'd be questioned, delicate lines would fray
and break. *A fugitive,* she thought, *and I've not done one damn thing
but try to commit suicide.*

Jeff counts on me. But where is he?

Slings and crutches. That night she loosened the sling and let the
arm hang. In a week they would take off the plaster. *During that
week Monsieur Pelletier will be in residence. He is the potentate.* The
quiet next door proclaimed it. He had arrived like a King of the
North out of the northern lights, the ice and snow.

At every window she looked out of she saw nothing but snow.
Long after dark that came down in what seemed midafternoon, the
snow gave off a visible glimmer; a blue perpetual twilight rose from
white surfaces, stretched out in every direction, obscuring the shape
of the river and the turns of the road that ran by it. Over the scene,
in every direction she looked, she could imagine the mammoth loom-
ing shape, now coming with a club in hand, now loaded down with
a carcass slung across his back, antlers nodding. Snow surfaces crack-
led and broke to his step; he sank to his knees but marched on. How
are myths born, but out of fear?

We will go tomorrow, she thought, holding Kathy to her as though
the winds from the four corners of the earth were trying to snatch
her away.

4

Flight

Every morning since she had come, she took a walk with Kathy. The morning after Monsieur Pelletier's arrival from the north, she took Kathy by the hand as usual and could be seen descending the lodge steps and heading off up the road. Hunters had come in the early morning hours. The snow, heavy during the night, had stopped. Her boots squeaked on the packed snow of tire tracks. There was a tiny answering squeak from Kathy's steps, like an imitator, even down to the slight limp remaining from Mary's sprain.

Kathy was a silent little girl, who seemed to think she was born to be trudging in one direction or another, following, her way of earning time to sit and be read to by her mother or cuddle against Madame Pelletier's warm thigh, watching TV. She was a clinger. She passed from skirt to trousered leg, clutched happily to Gérard's greasy fleece-lined coat, reached to lowered hand or extended arms.

"Shadow," she kept saying from behind, sticking loyally to every footstep.

Mary looked back.

"Shadow," said Kathy. It was their own shadows she meant, marching faithfully behind them.

The road curved and the shadows fell behind. So did the house and lodge. Of all they had there, Mary had taken only Jeff's picture, removed from its frame and stuck beneath her shirt in the back. At the last minute she had not been able to leave Kathy's teddy bear, frayed and chewed. She stuffed it under her coat, beneath the sleeve. The town was two or three miles away. The bus to Ottawa passed about twelve. In her duffel she had a letter for mailing to Madame Pelletier, telling her to keep the money already paid up, and someday to send the things she had left if she didn't come back. She said her arm was hurting and she wanted to see a doctor in Ottawa or maybe Montreal. She would send an address, she said. Mother and child went on through the white silence.

Twice they stopped to rest. The second time they were in sight of the village, a few scattered roofs as yet, sticking up like the tops of the snowbound bushes, just there against the near horizon before them. The river had swung away from the road but now was returning to run near it. It would run on to skirt the village. Out near the center of the river, water showed through in patches. There was smoke above the village. She had only to get there. One hour till the bus.

They were passing a sign beside the road which read ST.-VINCENT-EN-CAMPAGNE, the name of the town being bigger than the town itself, when she heard the heavy snort, a roar, of something like a truck on the road behind them, and before she could even think that a truck did not normally go so fast, she knew it was Monsieur Pelletier. Gérard had gone out with the hunters in the jeep. Why would he need a truck, unless Madame Pelletier had fled from him in the car?

By this time Mary was hiding with Kathy off the road, behind a six-foot pile of snow scraped up by the road-clearance crew. Maybe it wasn't him. But there the truck roared by, a medium-sized truck with an empty bed behind and a high seat occupied by Monsieur Pelletier, driving like a fiend. After what? Whiskey, in St. Vincent? Madame Pelletier? Mary and Kathy? Or just anything he could find?

The truck vanished into the village, behind a cloud of white exhaust. Mary crept out, trembling. She carried Kathy over the snow lumps. She considered return. Nobody in the village would be able to stop the King of the North. She walked on.

Even the sound of the truck had vanished. A dip in the road, and the village seemed to vanish, too. They passed along slowly, two small figures in a world of white, encompassing, steady, eternal. He could smear them down and out of life itself, like rabbits frantically zigzagging over a stark frozen field, finding no refuge. But why would he want to? Above them a large bird wheeled silently on great wings. They went on.

Surrounded by the village, she began to see people once more and to ask herself if he would dare hurt her and Kathy with witnesses. The truck was not to be heard, but he must be somewhere. The tavern, maybe. She asked a woman who was shovelling snow before her house where to find the bus stop. She was pointed on. There were the few business houses ahead, an excuse for a main street: filling stations, a post office, a *taverne*. Signs: PATATES FRITTES, CHIENS CHAUDS. Even a little store with recessed windows, a few coats and dresses set out. Here she stepped inside with Kathy, meaning to ask again for the bus stop, when a car passed going back along the way she had come.

The driver was Ethan Marbell.

She thought she must be mad, hallucinating, but leaving Kathy near the window, she dashed out into the street crying his name.

It took over a block to bring him to a halt. People were watching, and the dreadful truck was creeping out of a side street. By then she was inside the car beside him, clutching his arm, crying, "Quick, go back there. It's Kathy."

He reversed, and she ran out to snatch up the child. The truck was stopping by the curb. Monsieur Pelletier was getting out.

"Marie, Marie. Viens, ma fille. Ici. Viens à moi."

"Don't stop to reason," Mary said, and held to Ethan the same way Kathy was holding to her.

"Which way?" asked Ethan.

"Back the way you came. Just get us out of here."

5

A Patch of Blue

"They probably weren't after you at all," said Ethan. "I think you had been alone too long. That and the accident, those hunters. You began imagining things."

"I think he was after whatever money I had. I think he thought I was a walking gold mine from the U.S. He meant to dig out what he could."

"It's hard to know," said Ethan, and lit his pipe. "These are foreign people."

He had signed them into the first decent motel he had come to, near Ottawa, in a town called Hull.

"I don't understand their French," said Ethan. But he had spent some student years in Paris and now had whatever he wished, a large order of dinner from a restaurant, even a bottle of French wine from the ample menu. "Beautiful burgundy," he observed, gloating over the label. On the bed Kathy was snuggling with the teddy bear and watching TV.

Mary had gotten her crying done. She had been so sure that Ethan was here with Jeff. It seemed too much even to think Ethan would come alone. "Not here! Not with you!"

"My dear, please listen—"

"I don't want to listen. Weeks in this dead end of a place, and now I have to listen!"

She had flung herself on the bed, all but hearing her broken arm scream beneath the plaster, and let go into sobs she must have been saving up for months.

"Mommy cry," said Kathy.

Ethan had soothed her like a father. "There, now. I've news. The next best thing. And letters. Come on, there, you've been too brave for anything. It's over, this time here. It's done."

Reduced to sniffles, she had finally dried her eyes. Ethan had left to find some food for them. Kathy located the knobs on the TV.

Now from beneath the white covering over a loaded tray the smell of wine and garlic were at work, magical.

"But if you couldn't bring Jeff, why are you here at all?"

"I had begun to feel such a load of guilt. I had sent you here, hoping you could meet up with him, stay out of Montreal—meddling on your behalf. I couldn't rest at night. I tried to telephone. Imagine what I felt when I heard nothing but '*hôpital.*' The hospital! I couldn't rest for a moment until I took the next plane out."

"But why leave Montreal? It's a paradise compared to this. I went flying out of it blind, trusting. I'm a fool." She bitterly massaged a bare foot, hoping it was still able.

"I sent you here because of what Jeff got into. You don't even know what it was. I'm sure that little oddball of a courier didn't tell you. He stays scared of telling too much.

"Jeff was supposed to be doing the usual job for us. Reporting, covering a 'happening.' We'll say, just off the record, that yes, it was subversive, and yes, it was dangerous. We needed him out there for the activities this particular underground group had gotten into. Further, I can't say. We needed the word out, we needed the eyewitness touch; we needed, furthermore, Jeff's skill at writing it, his special way of reporting with a guiltless, detached slanting of style, so that a reader wouldn't guess— Well, you know his gift. We sent him out.

"Now, picture it. A dark hillside outside San Francisco north of the city. A hillside, an installation. What sort, not even you should know. But of intense importance in the field of, let's say, for example, weaponry. There's a war. More and better demons are at work, making even more horrendous tortures for the innocents who are in their way just by being where they've always been. You know the latest phrase for what they call them, once they're blasted dead, skin burnt from head to toe, not even recognizably human any longer. It comes out of a corn flakes box: Crispy Critters. Don't dwell on it. The war gods are dancing for joy.

"Anyway: The group Jeff went along with got over the fence and inside. All plans go. They zapped out the night watchman. Gates opened from within. Everything set up in minutes, but Jeff saw they were doing it wrong. If you are to blow up something with any degree of success, put it out of commission, you have to hit the central mechanism. Else in one afternoon, the minor damage repaired, the wheels start to move again. It's not for me to say how it all works. I know what the end product was, and believe me, that's enough.

"He'd no time to explain. Went in himself. Came back out. They ferried the night watchman a mile away, revived and dumped him at a shopping center near an all-night diner. But on the way to the car Jeff himself hit the detonator, remote control. Up goes the plant, a perfect hit.

"One fault. Somebody along wasn't to be trusted, an infiltrator. It's done quite a lot these days. They know who it was, who turned; in the best of bunches there's a Judas."

"So nothing's wrong with Jeff. Just that he's a real criminal now. Great," said Mary.

"I'd call him heroic, but then, points of view in this country haven't been farther apart since the Civil War. I knew I had to get you out of Montreal. Reports are coming in. They've got the RCMP cooperating with wiretaps. Mail could be opened. Even your nice friends I've heard about could find themselves on lists. . . ."

"Up here alone, and not a word to go on." Mary wasn't about to say it was all right. "Some hunters came and they suspected—oh, I don't know what they suspected. I should have just stayed in the city. I know how to hide there. Out in the eastern part. I'd just be any old fish in an ocean, bouncing around from one snowdrift to the other. Who cares?"

Ethan put his forehead in his frail scholarly hands. "I had a troubled mind for you. Let me remind you, my dear. I *am* here."

But I should never have been here at all, was what she thought, but didn't load him with.

Now Ethan sacramentally uncovered the plates he had brought from the restaurant. He set the telephone book and telephone on the floor, dragged that table to the end of the bed, and set the one straight chair to one side of it. Mary sat opposite him, on the foot of the bed. She rubbed at her ankle, where it still ached.

From under the metal covers, steaming beef bourguignonne appeared, crusty French bread, a crisp salad. Ethan set out knives and forks. Tenderly he drew the wine cork. The restaurant had even sent cloth napkins. "To come so far for this *bon repas*," he murmured. "Better than Kingsbury."

"You brought some letters?"

"One thing at the time," Ethan said. He sipped some wine and buttered a morsel of bread. "The letters are another story in themselves. You know we had to move the press. *The Radar Screen* is now printing out of New Jersey, a point just over from Manhattan. Lots of details of no interest, except that we learned they had located our whereabouts. They were in the process of condemning the building. Next we'd find our operation smashed. Moving out, one of the typesetter-editors-proofreaders and general boys-of-all-trades came across two letters addressed to 'Kerr & Co.'—wasn't that the address he'd taken for writing you? Supposed to go to you care of that Jay-Bo character Jeff counted on. I never thought him worthy of trust and evidently I was right. I was frightened for you. If Jeff's letters could go astray that way, fallen by the wayside, were you even getting any money to live on? I suppose your people—after all, that stepfather of yours had gotten Jeff bailed out in Chicago. Perhaps he helps you.

"I sent out the word: 'Search everywhere. There may be some more letters missing.' They started finding others. Some buried in with committee material from one of the meetings back in Madison. All sorts of odd circumstances."

She saw with surprise that though he was eating with such gusto, he wasn't well. His color was bad, his collar looked too large. When he moved he seemed stooped in a way that did not seem correctable.

"Ethan," said Mary. "I want to thank you. Jeff always said you were a father to him. Now to me."

His smile was from the heart. "Trying."

"Do you talk to him?"

"At times. Even that is chancy. But he's well. Not even unhappy except for you. He thinks that you are not answering him. That because—oh, how can I meddle in these things? Some woman in Montreal got him—well, involved, would you say?"

"Laid," said Mary.

"He says it didn't mean anything. He's told me a dozen times. Truthfully, Mary, I cannot imagine— He loves you. You must be convinced of it."

"Where are the letters?"

"You'll have them all. Just now . . . Do you know, three of them were found shoved in a duffel at a drop point in Saratoga, New York. The owner of the duffel had disappeared. An ex-student of mine, working out of Cornell, happened to see the name on the tag in the baggage room. He was out of jail and looking for something halfway decent to wear for making a speech at Yale. He lied about the claim check and got the duffel. The letters were there. My heart sank when I heard this. It seems my heart was always sinking, but I did nothing about it for too long. Were they so unkind to you?"

"Madame Pelletier was okay, but the men—they're like animals. Maybe not Gérard."

"*Où est Gérard?*" Kathy asked at once, without looking up from Tweetie Pie and Sylvester the Cat.

"Turn it off, honey," Mary said. "Come on, now, and eat some really good food."

"*Je veux un* hot dog," said Kathy.

"Don't be crazy, this is grand. Come on."

"Just a minute," said Kathy. Tweetie Pie flew off a cliff; Sylvester walked out on air, paused, looked down, and fell shrieking. Kathy gurgled.

"A patriotic child," Ethan remarked. "TV and a hot dog." He refilled their plates, portioning out helpings to Kathy. "The thing to understand is that Nixon is frantic to find some Red connection to the anti-war movement. If only he could, it would be the best Christmas present he could wish. He must get down on his knees every night to pray for it. Come on, now, Kathy. Try a little."

"Where are the letters?" Mary asked again.

"Out in the car," said Ethan, sopping up wine sauce.

Persuaded away from the TV, Kathy sat by Mary and ate. She got a little wine the way Madame Pelletier had fixed it for her, mixed in with water.

Ethan went out for the letters.

Safe. For the first time in months she breathed in secure air. Maybe someday the Spivak wound would heal. She held the letters in her lap. "Do you see Aunt Jane?" she asked.

"What a coincidence. I was just about to say, I see your Aunt Jane from time to time. How strange life is."

"You started that day I came home and Mother had flown off to Philadelphia Fred."

"We found . . . well, that old feelings did come back, oddly enough."

"Why odd?"

"I don't know. Her rejection before, Kingsbury gossip. Me such a radical. She such a Harbison. Even now she doesn't say she should have married me. We see each other in a quiet way. At my age, an 'affair' would be a silly thing to embark on. Still—" He paused and sighed. "Still—" Such softness as he felt.

Aunt Jane, of all people. Something of his feeling now was passing through the letters under her hand, conducting lines leading to her, passing through her, circuiting. Jeff had been sending such feeling out all along. He had come to see her. But she never knew it. And didn't know where to write him. Or how to call. It was all this that had led her to the twisted sheet.

"When are they taking off that cast?"

"Soon, now. It's getting dirty. It itches."

"Scratch," Kathy advised.

They finished up the *tarte aux pommes*.

Mary and Ethan drank the last of the wine. Kathy fell asleep in air that had grown peaceful with the good food and the thought of love. They might have decked it with jasmine white as the outside snow.

6

Explosions

Like everyone else his age, Jeff Blaise knew how to blow things up.

"Where do these children learn what they know?" Ethan Marbell had once exclaimed. "How to break locks, jimmy windows, set off plastic explosives. It seems a nation of subversives were trained and graduated out of family basements meant for Ping-Pong and gin rummy."

Jeff seldom went into the details about his own education. All he said was, "Any popular science mag has directives on that plastic explosive—C-4, it's called. Even government pamphlets can tell you how to use it. Ironic, wouldn't you say?"

But with him it really went back farther still, to Louisiana and the swamps when, as a boy in high school, he had gone with a friend of his, already a sophomore at LSU, up the river to farming property the boy's family owned but seldom saw. There they discovered flooding out of control, the row tops in one field barely visible above the water. The beavers had built dams along a bayou. The overseer had wanted to use dynamite, one reason he had called. Jeff's friend had volunteered to "attend to it," but Jeff's idea of that was to do it themselves.

"Dynamite's old-fashioned stuff. There's a plastic they've got now. All you do is mold it, sink your fuse in, play out a line, and hit the current."

Before the week was out the dams were blown sky-high, the beaver population reduced, and the water draining back into place. The boys left, thinking themselves heroes, while the beavers were already at work on major repairs.

The year he finished college, Jeff (still with the memory of that bright flash against the scraggly line of bayou trees) was in possession of a fellowship grant for graduate work at Hopkins in Baltimore. He would be assistant to a professor there, possibly even to Dr. Ethan Marbell. Money, extra money, was his need, for clothes, travel, room rent. This was why he found himself working through the summer for a small oil company with four rigs out in the Gulf south of Grand Isle.

Every day in the company launches he went out with the two other supervisors to monitor one or another of the pumping stations, to check on the flow, regulate the gauges. They ferried out alternate crews to replace the ones already stationed. He shared quarters with the two supervisors and the crew ashore in two mobile homes near the marina. He burned nearly black in the sun, a curious sight with blond hair burning paler every day and a stubble of light beard. On weekends, showered, shaved, and fresh, they headed up to New Orleans for a night of drinking, sometimes a pickup, came back late Sunday with slowly fading hangovers.

If a fire started on any of the rigs, or if a hurricane struck, they were commissioned to set a charge that would blow shut the oil flow. They also had to evacuate the crews.

In late August, after a week of oppressive weather, the warning came: a hurricane was off Jamaica, moving toward New Orleans.

There were long phone calls to the head office in Mobile. But Jeff, as he was later to recall, made none of them, had no conversations with the powers there at all.

It was toward noon when they went out into a choppy sea, turned charcoal gray, a mottled gray sky vertical before them like a standing presence. The nervous swollen day sensed its own troubles. One of the supervisors kept throwing up over the side, making the other two lean toward the opposite gunwales, trying not to hear or look.

At the first rig they mounted to the platform. Jeff carried up the C-4 explosive, marked HIGHLY DANGEROUS—but even at the onset, looking behind him, he saw Frank, the other nonvomiting supervisor, climbing behind, hauling with him a second canvas sack.

"Hey, that's too much," Jeff said. "Careful of that stuff. You know what it—"

Frank, with his black Mexican mustache, his sidelong look, never said a lot. He didn't now. He walked to the other side of the platform, where the ladder dropped down into choppy water. "I'm going down to set it up."

"Why?" Jeff had been hired because of some experience—the beavers had earned it for him.

"Save you trouble," said Frank, and entered the cabin carrying the sack as though up to something private.

The rig bobbed in the uncertain sea. Jeff helped the crew members transfer their gear to the boat.

Frank came out of the cabin. He was stripped to his shorts and wearing a diving helmet, carrying the sack, though he had changed the canvas for a length of tarp, waterproof. The sidelong glance. "Save you trouble." He vanished over the side.

In this way they went on through half the afternoon, till the last rig was vacated. "You ought to have let me," Jeff told Frank.

"I done it a lot," Frank said. He suddenly grinned. "I'll tell the boss it was you. You gettin' credit, okay? And you can blow it, too. That's credit, ain't it?"

Jeff said he guessed so. But he had noticed something.

Two packages of the plastic had gone out with them. A few ounces would have been enough for the four rigs. But now when he looked only one package was left. Not half of it there, from the way the bag bent.

"What happened?" he asked. "It's gone."

"Maybe I dropped some," said Frank. "Maybe I had to come back. Maybe we didn't have so much to start with." He turned suddenly to Jeff, who was holding the detonator in his hand. "Go on. Blow it."

Jeff refused. "The radio phone," he said. "Call Haskell."

They refused. It wasn't working, they said. Still, he wouldn't comply. He went back to the shore and called his boss, who said, "Hell, yes, I want the oil shut off. What's stopping you? Seal it."

"I'm only saying it looks like there might not even be a hurricane. Then you've got all the trouble of getting them opened up again. I'd say wait an hour at least, maybe two. Keep checking. It can't—"

"Can't what? What you think I hired you for? You got the charges set?"

"Not exactly. I didn't—"

"What the hell, 'not exactly'? Lemme talk to Frank."

Frank took the phone. He said that yes, Jeff had set the charges, he just wouldn't blow it. He turned to Jeff. "He says he's hired a powder man, why for chrissake can't he act like one?" He spoke further, then said, "He says no work, no pay."

Jeff pressed the detonator.

Over the stretch of gray water before them, choppy with uncertain brooding, they saw the four rigs, barely visible, like the crests of undersea cliffs breaking surface, suddenly rise up with one accord like breaching whales, an instant later flying every which way with planks broken apart, into the close cloud cover, equipment spraying out its wires like seaweed lifted free of water, one boot, one coffee pot, falling. The platforms spun like a drunk quartet, made an effort to stand, failed, and dropped foundering and useless into the gray water.

A hundred miles out to sea, the hurricane, whose name was Bertha, stalled and seemed to think things over. An hour later, slow as an elephant, Bertha turned on ponderous feet and headed toward Texas. No one, it now seemed, had talked to Ed Haskell, the boss over in Mobile, except Jeff Blaise. So Haskell said. So Frank said. So the rest, by their silence, said.

Pickens, the second supervisor, the one who had been seasick, had a drunken talk with Jeff. He evidently had some finer feelings. "It's not gonna do you no permanent damage, son. We all knew what was happening. You didn't. That's all there is. He was losing money. You were the way out. Now he's insured and all, and you're fired— well, that's tough. You could sure touch me for a loan, but I got none to spare. This ain't your work, no way. You're a real smart boy, innerletchal, and you're going on to a real fine life, I'm promising it to ya."

"I intend to sue that bastard," said Jeff.

"I wouldn't do that," Pickens advised.

"It's a clear-cut case," said Jeff. "You know it is. Why, you could—" He stopped.

There was silence. The silence said that Pickens would not do anything to help him. It said he would probably lie. It said that everything had been decided already.

"You look like a nice boy," said Pickens, and lit a cigarette. He was drinking a lot of beer. "I always did say that. Ask anybody if I didn't."

Back in New Orleans, Jeff tried to shake at least his back pay out of Haskell, but Haskell refused. Haskell threatened Jeff by letter with prosecution for blowing up his rigs. Jeff replied that he was suing Haskell. Nobody did anything.

Nightly, Jeff saw now, not the worthy muck of the beaver dams shooting skyward out of the heart of the bright flash, but oil rigs going up in splintered lumber, catching fire, a black smudge rising above the flame. *Ten times the charge we needed, he must have sneaked it aboard. All planned. . . .*

He returned to Baton Rouge. Decent clothes for Hopkins, hopes of looking like a grad student: all dreams turned to dust. He would have to ask his father even for bus fare.

"I hear you flubbed the dub," the old man crowed, sitting beside his crystal decanter in the twilight he could bring on a bit earlier than could nature, by drawing blinds and pulling curtains. "Yes, sir, you sure flubbed the dub."

How had the old man heard? Jeff turned on his neat heel and left the room.

In his own old room upstairs, he found that his mother's familiar rocking chair and footstool had been moved from his father's room to his, also a large oval straw basket where she once kept quilt scraps, socks for darning, diplomas, family photographs, newspaper clippings, and other such things. The old man must have cleaned up in there. Maybe he'd gotten a woman, and she did it for him.

Jeff lay awake in the dark, trying to clear his head. The one thing to think about was how to get to Baltimore. To hitchhike with a suitcase full of books and a few clothes seemed a poor option, but he was afraid he'd have to take it. Kind professors who thought him such a prize might certainly have helped, but he could foresee the time when the insurance company, debating Haskell's claims, would be tracking him down as a witness. He would need professors then. He had few friends. Though not unfriendly, still he was a loner.

The moon was bright on the lawn outside. Bushes that his mother had planted had flourished. The spirea, long past blooming, something he couldn't name with an icing of small white flowerets, and the crepe myrtle, pink, white, and red. She'd done the best she could. His father's car was missing, but soon it returned. *Out for more liquor,* Jeff thought, and turned over to sleep.

But this was not true. The steps that soon mounted the stairs did not waver. They came straight to his room, where, mistaking the direction of the bed, he stumbled over the large work basket and fell into it. The son pulled him out of scraps and torn shirts for mending, the house dresses never to be hemmed, the packs of letters (mainly from Jeff) bound in rubber bands that broke, spilling them out on the floor. But the smell of liquor was missing and the old man came up easily, saying, "Damn to hell. Couldn't see in the dark." The moon had clouded over.

They both sat down on the bed.

"You don't understand about the oil rigs, Dad. You see, I—well, I was only following orders. It wasn't even me who set the plastic— the explosives. I was supposed to, but then they—" He stopped, wondering what was the use. His father would believe whatever he'd heard rather than any report Jeff could give. How had his father heard about it anyway? Were they tracking him down already? Laughter at this college boy, bright in his books, but who hadn't got the sense not to blow up the whole company, equipment and all.

"Here's some money," his father said, and passed him over a check, through the darkness. "It's made out to you. Ol' Wight Hébert agreed to lend it. Won't ever believe I hadn't just run out of whiskey. You ought to go on up there in good shape. Just a thousand, but enough for a new suit of clothes, a ticket, books. Take a plane. Arrive in style. I'm proud of you, son. Those oil folks down there are crooked as snakes."

All Jeff could say was, "Dad. Oh, Dad." He sat holding the check in disbelief.

His father patted him on the knee. They didn't know what to do next. There were so many things left unsaid through the years, and these things were like night moths, swarming softly through the room with nowhere to light. The dark made it easier.

"I get these love spells," his father confessed. "Your mother, son. I think of her and I could just break in two. Your baby sister that didn't live a week. Night of that fire. You won't believe me, will you?"

"I believe you." Jeff was gladder than ever of the dark when warm tears started down his cheeks. "You're so different when you drink, Daddy."

"I know. I know that, son."

It was hot and still, late August heat in Louisiana, the worst there is. Jeff drew a breath that contained a sob, and then the storm rolled in, lightning crashing into thunder just outside, rain sluicing in even across the bed, onto father and son. "Feels good," they agreed.

Then Jeff said, "It wasn't just losing the pay. It's being made use

of, being set up. I think everything in this country runs that way. I
think that's how it works. It's happened to you, I bet."

"I reckon it has, son."

The storm faded. Jeff must have fallen asleep sitting up because
when he woke sprawled half across the bed, a coverlet had been
spread over him. It was broad daylight and his father had gone to
work. He held a minor job in an accountancy firm in downtown
Baton Rouge, twenty miles away.

They did not speak again about the strange night talk and except
for the check it would have seemed to Jeff only a vision of something
hoped for, unreal.

Years later he told Mary Harbison about it. That was out from
Burlington, the summer of decision. He had just come back from
Cornell, an energy-burning foray like all the rest. Marches, the chant-
ing, thunderbolts of rebellion crammed into auditoriums too small
for the crowds. Students hung from the windowsills, the balcony
railings, crouched in the aisles. Dow executives and Pentagon offi-
cials; speakers from the Department of Defense brought their body-
guards and wished they'd stayed at home.

"So how's yours?" he asked her, in the dark. "Your mother,
I mean."

"Don't ask. Terrible quarrel. She tracked me out to the campus,
wild as a banshee."

" 'Tracked,' " he repeated, flat. "You track wild animals, don't you?
To them that's what we are."

He lit a joint. They sat in the dark, cross-legged on a lumpy bed
in a borrowed trailer, inhaling, feeling the welcome lightness begin,
grow, the sure turn-on of mounting desire, holding back.

"Then she called up and said I could go to Bennington."

"Hard to figure."

"She's mad."

They turned and moved together, certain as a tide.

He had more still to tell her. Day followed day. Decisions that she
couldn't make. The worst was up in Burlington, when she told him
about the baby. She thought she was giving up her life for him. He
strung out his story, like an incantation willingly chanted as long as
she would forget leaving him, forget she didn't especially want a
child, forget the price she was paying. He was usually shut-mouthed
about his past. Now he evoked it, vivid as talk could make it.

Like arriving in Baltimore, the search for a room near Hopkins, the wait in the corridors of the political science department for Professor Marbell to come to an interview. Thinking he'd be rejected, passed on to someone not so great. The man himself appearing in the hall, hand outstretched, opening his office door. The invitation to dinner that evening: "If we should work together we should talk . . ." a smile, "man to man."

On then to the comfortable brick home with its odd peaked gable dominating the façade. "We thought it would be nice for my study, a second floor of one large room only. Rather magisterial."

And there, too, was a wife, Sybil. She stood before the still-cold fireplace of early September. The deep sofas, her silver bracelets, the brilliant woven rugs and shawls mounted on the white walls. The soft burred sound of the woman's Boston speech. "Mexico, yes, I adore it. My life grew mystical there. I shall never either forget it or completely understand it. I only know that it happened."

Jeff confessed to not knowing what it was to have your life grow mystical, but he knew better than to ask. Instead, "Do you go back?"

"Of course. For months, sometimes for half the year. As often as I can. My son is there."

Her son? Jeff's confusion was apparent to Ethan, he felt, who met his gaze over the head of dark, loosely brushed hair, laced with gray, the peasant blouse stitched in parrot colors, the chink of silver as the glass rose to her lips. *I need a son,* Ethan seemed to be saying wordlessly. *She's taken this one.*

Jeff had heard that mothers did that. He wondered, *Do I need a father?* His own father was encased in that dark Louisiana night when the black cloud threw down lightning, lashed them with rain. There seemed to be no way to get the old man out of it; what letters he wrote were scrawls of ironic comments, broken by black wavering dashes: *Out of work again— Time wounds all heels— Can't say I really cared when they axed me— Yrs. Fr.* What few times Jeff went to see him, he found his father telephoning to some woman he was crazy about. She worked in an investment office. "Just a wonderful woman, son," he said over and over. They used to meet twice a week in a downtown bar and drink together.

Ethan Marbell had only come to Hopkins recently, asked to resign from his Washington appointment to the Bureau of Civil Defense. Fired. (Something that happened to fathers?)

"I knew too much?" he said to Jeff. "No, not that. Everybody in Washington bureaucracy knows too much, or thinks he does. No, it was the sense to discern direction, to see the drift, to try to change it. It's too late now. We're on the road, following wherever it leads us. Where? Destination hell."

So Ethan Marbell, the celebrated scholar, his many titles on the spines of books behind his head, began to sit up late hours before the fireplace with this wonderfully bright boy from the Deep South. They delved the rich and varied opinions of experts on international law, war reparations, chains of command, directives to State Department emissaries around the world. Jeff found himself more drawn in than ever before as he sat in the study under the slant roof of the strange pointed gable, the walls here, too, book-lined. Some days he could no longer recall the night his house caught fire, or the afternoon when he sat in the churning boat while sky and sea grew to one leaden gloom and said, "No, I won't do it." But he never lost the night with his father, though it was locked away in the time and space that had always contained it. It was just that it could never get out.

"That's a glorious town, Washington," he told Mary, walking in Vermont woods. "The good parts, I mean. And the layout. Fantastic planning. A real sweep."

He was often out in it with Ethan. They visited the National Gallery and spent a whole week exploring the Smithsonian. "Ballet? No. If I'd foreseen you, I'd have gone every night." They stopped at a pasture fence, two horses grazing not a stone's throw away. "Art, though. Painting." He had discovered art as personal for the first time sitting on an upholstered bench for what must have been one long entranced hour before a Renoir so alive he thought he could have walked right in among the crowd on that Sunday afternoon as they picnicked along the river.

"I want to go to Paris," he said to Ethan Marbell out of the trance.

Ethan's wife Sybil had long been gone back to Mexico to be with their son, who was a sculptor. Jeff never met him. Ethan said he was quite accomplished. Sybil said he was a genius.

"Oh, I don't know if I believe it or not," Ethan confided. "The stuff looked pretty way out to me."

Vermont pasture land lay before them. Mary was still trying to think what to do.

One of the horses was approaching them like an old friend who had recognized them after a long absence. He came to the fence and put his head over it. Jeff stroked his ears. His leathery, tender mouth nibbled gently at Mary's hand.

Jeff took the other in both his. "Let's have what's ours."

It was the child he meant. She saw that he was scared.

7

Letters

"In my mind," Ethan said to Mary, at last extending to her the russet file envelope he had brought her, "I see you as lost children. Wandering apart, or wandering together. I have had a hand in this."

Her hands closed on the packet, but first she looked up at him. For a while, as though the packet contained a living presence, she simply held it, breathed differently with it in her lap. With the significant object, blessing or curse, a dancer would whirl for long savoring turns before putting it to use.

"Are you okay?" she asked Ethan suddenly. "Not sick or anything?"

Ethan hesitated. "Well . . . perhaps Jane or Kate let you know. . . ."

"No. Nothing."

"I haven't been too well, to tell the truth. It's enough to prompt this trip, isn't it, thinking I may not have too long a time left to me. Jeff is my own creation. He seemed a boy without ties, homeless in a sense, but loaded with sheer, tough intelligence. *Sui generis* . . . that is to say, his own person. A teacher's dream."

"But what about you?"

Control and the wry smile, fading. "I told you, my dear. I may not have too long. Enough for now, though." He watched her open the packet, unwinding the ribbon that bound it.

As though a find of treasure had been dredged up and was finally piled in one hoard for sorting, she spread the white oblong envelopes out on the bed, first moving Kathy, who had fallen asleep from the wine. All the runaway panic of the morning seemed a week ago to her. Mary spread the letters around her like the sea around a shoreline. She sat straight, with her strong nimble legs folded neatly under her. She began to open the envelopes and spread out the sheets, noticing datelines.

"These begin in San Francisco. That was long after I lost touch. He would call sometimes and say I should be hearing, but I rarely got anything. It was so depressing that I thought, *Well, he's gone for good.* I tried to work, I found friends, I played little games of good cheer. But finally, last winter, I just wanted out of it, everything. Out of the world."

"Jeff heard something of that. He was nearly wild until they told us you were well again. But surely you got something? Your mother—"

"Mother!"

"Your aunt passed some letters along to her because we heard you were moving, old address no go. It seemed to me logical. Surely you got them . . . something. . . ."

"Nothing. Ethan, if you gave Jeff's letters to her—"

"I simply cannot imagine—" He could not imagine Kate.

She sat with closed eyes, trying to smooth an inner image that had formed already, leaped to life by itself. *If she got them, she read them.* It would not do to think about it. Those long, firm, white hands, tearing the white paper. And she had wanted him, too; the original of Madeleine Spivak. *I've got to stop this. Thinking what she must have done.*

"A misunderstanding," Ethan pled. "I'm sure your own mother would never—"

Drive me to suicide? "No, of course not." There was a burned-out cinder lodged black in her heart. It would remain.

Before she shrank to nothing, Mary straightened, like a limp plant given water. She surveyed the spread of papers. "I have these."

Ethan responded to her mood, smiling encouragement. "Read them, then. While I, well-fed and weary—" He approached the second of the twin beds and began to arrange the pillows. "I'll just rest awhile. It comes on all of a sudden these days. Go on, my dear. Read."

8

Letters Opened

Somewhere near SF, thinking of you on this 9th day of October
Why, that was the day I took the train to Ottawa, Mary thought.
The very day.

Mary: Always Mary:

It's no better for you than thinking you're married to some guy
in jail to think of me, I know, but you know how we've talked
and that I'm just one of thousands. Concentrate on it and know
that I can't, cannot surface for a while. Not after what we just
managed, though I wasn't supposed to be involved personally,
only to write about it, I saw they were doing it wrong and had
to grab hold. So now—great job of sawing off the limb I was
sitting on—I'm known about, listed.

Believe that it's another civil war, the one we were still talking
about down South when I was in college in La., maybe in NC
too. Only now we can't secede. We're too scattered out. There's
actually been some talk of making a separate country, taking
over some unwanted land in the Southwest, if only they'd allow
it, but all that's unreal. They'd just know where to find us. And
treat us like Indians to boot. But when I think how strong the
underground is, and those thousands still above ground, too, I
come around to Ethan's line of thought. We're holding them
back. Yes, praise God

<u>We are holding them back</u>

They're itching for more destruction, and though I can't quite buy
into Ethan's pet theory that they want more than anything to drop
a dozen more little Hiroshimas (what's 20,000 more casualties to
worry about?), we've got them where they wouldn't dare. Even

though they'll say they never meant to anyway. A-bombs) what's that?

"I guess what he means he's done is that blowing something up you were telling me about." She spoke over her shoulder. Kathy, sleeping, flung out an arm. Ethan snored. She read on:

I can't describe these guys I'm with or tell you exactly where I am. I hardly know myself, but I check the compass every so often. It's because we got spied on during the Big Job. I had to take more part than I was supposed to. Some people have better intentions than know-how. So for the moment I can't put my head up. Well, this is to send you word. There's a wild scheme of Ethan's to send you up the Gatineau when I can shake free enough to move. He thinks Montreal is too set out with traps. That would be way above Ottawa. But I'm asking you not to leave Montreal, Mary. It can't be such great territory, very iso-lated, especially in the dead of winter, and you with Kathy. What if she should get sick or something? Well, then your danc-ing, too.
Mary, Mary, why don't you write me? Hundreds of words, pages filled to the corners I've sent you, since I left. I don't blame you getting mad as hell, any woman would, but letting me go this long . . . Have a heart and call me what names you want to. But let me, let me, hear them. Something. Anything.
Later.
I think these guys here go out and steal everything we eat. They talk a lot of shit. No class. Not the sort I got used to in Wisconsin and all the other locales. Not Ethan's type, brainy and fast. Really I think it would be worse to have them in charge of everything than to have the ones we've got now, is my judgment. I have to stay though till we get word it's safe to move. If we get raided and I can slip out of it I might be able to make it down the coast. (They're risking getting raided so often, I think they want it to happen.) There's a town. San Cristobal. I saw it once, passing by bus up the coast from when I was running off Ethan's column down below Carmel. It's not in the mountains, just part of a break, a valley right near the sea. I got a glimpse only, but I thought, I'd like to be there. If the world ever turns sane again (was it ever?) we'll follow our whims and explore our glimpses

of paradise, take those leafy little side roads that might lead there. Maybe not all our dreams are just fantasy, not if we want them to be real.

Send some shots of Kathy so I'll recognize her when I see her. . . . When I think of you I just about die.

J.

November

San Cristobal

Well, Mary, they sure hit us, I think it was a week ago last Wednesday, but I can't be sure. I wasn't listed with them, neither before nor after, thank God. There was a lot of tear gas around and I think some of it must have got the pigs as well as us because I started walking not running down toward a street and nobody seemed to see me clear enough to stop me. The guys I was stopping with looked like Panthers—black leather, haircuts wild, the works—so they got in the net, though what they'll be charged with I don't know. Maybe they'll think of something or make it up. Several were in Chicago at the Convention and may be still on the lists from there for something they did in the riots. I'm on a dozen lists I would think about the Big One, but not on this one I guess since they weren't pushing for anybody that looked like me, same as ever. I got a bus over to Sausalito where there hasn't been much of a crunch, and stayed with a kid from Wisconsin at his pad. I knew him back in Madison and just happened to run into him down by the wharf. We had some interesting talks.

I kept thinking of San Cristobal. It ran in my head. I could sing it almost. Met a guy in a hamburger place who was going down as far as Carmel, then I hitchhiked, a slow business. People have gotten scared to stop. I should cut off my hair, shave maybe. But didn't. Finally made it.

Tired and passed out with some hash which I never get into but it seemed a good idea at the time.

Slept. Woke. Guess what? I've been elected mayor of the whole damn town!

I didn't know about it.

The guys here I was with and some others scattered around were mad as hell at the mayor (former) because he had invested a lot in building a fish factory and paid to have a line of houses along the beach condemned so he could put it up. What with all the Chicanos and others he had scared to put up their hands and be counted—a lot I guess were aliens, no work permits, etc.— there wasn't enough of a count to stop him. But his election was due—supposed to be a shoo-in. The bunch here ganged up and started getting out the vote. They've got pads up and down the seafront, old rambly three-story houses, lots of steps and balconies. But midway through, they thought they didn't have anybody to run, nobody wanted to be on the ticket. So they said <u>There's that guy passed out up at Johnny Poag's pad</u>, so they put my name down—I had told them it was Jeff Blaylock— and I won. I didn't know about it. They came in spewing champagne everywhere, telling me the news. I turned over and went back to sleep. Seems like I been tired since too long a time.

Finally woke up. Mayor Blaylock. I'm appointing Johnny Poag. I can't be a mayor, I said. That would be advertising myself. You think I want a picture in anybody's paper? Nobody asked me why. They got bug-eyed.

So Johnny will run the town okay. Father Tomlinson is here. A priest, friend of the Berrigans. How <u>he</u> got there is another story, long as a crocodile's tail. He's got them praying and singing. Got them trimmed down out of the heavy stuff. Nobody's shooting up. Just grass is all, not even hash. Out with LSD and acid. Grass may go too but he's playing that one easy. It's a real uprising here. What this country could be! It's not for thinking about. Thrilling.

The old mayor's not for taking all our shit. He's over drumming up support from the county seat, wanting to make out we did it illegally. They'll find a way. But meantime the new ways might turn out such an improvement nobody will want the old times back. It's just singing and chanting with them, sunrise worship, sunset communion, all together, day after day. They're mostly fishermen and truck farmers—artichokes, dried flowers, one or two small vineyards. This is such fun, not like Chicago. Ginsberg and the others in C. made it out this was the real life-style of our times, one perpetual war. I know there were readings and songs and poems, but it was too high-key. Emotion too hyped up. Now I've gotten the chance to know Father Tomlinson, I've come down to calmer waters. I'm getting hopes up to see the Berrigans again. Daniel's books stick in my head.

Meantime, with Father T.'s blessing, I'm putting out. Being sworn in as mayor I'd have to present documents. Even if they're fake, they might wind up on somebody's list. Word gets around. Pictures are spotted. Besides, who wants to be mayor? I know this pad in Monterey where I can stop. I can work there. Ethan's dispatches are not going out as regularly as before, not from me. I know he's worried. I'm trying to get through to you. I'll have to go through SF at some time and that's where the danger for me lies. Don't worry. If I can get elected mayor anything can happen.

SF area, inexact on purpose.
Mary, Mary, Mary:
I walk along the beach and think of you and want you here, with Kathy, too, walking right by me. I think of you when I get up, when I sleep, when I don't sleep, when I want to explain something, when I want to eat something, and as for the other whens don't even mention it. Hit don' get no better. I'd tell you exactly where it hurts but I'm always scared of somebody wrong finding these letters. I'm just a clean-minded upstanding young American male. Just happens to be outraged at his country, but otherwise he's o.k. It's Father Tomlinson who got me here, safe again. I should be ashamed. Two safe places now. Or at least partly. No mobility as yet. Here I'm sure of protection. Elsewhere, too many question marks. Here I know the turf. Scared to move but (irony) I was even king for day in San Cristobal, or, if you prefer, His Honor the Mayor. Wasn't there a character in a Victor Hugo novel who was a convict, got to be mayor, too? But always on the run. I know how he felt. Father T. wrote me about coming here when I was in Monterey. A college where Berrigan taught for a while. Father T. himself is being shunted off to South America. It's where they send them when they get out of hand, won't listen to the going policy, try to act like Christians. I said it the other day, to one of the faculty: The church goes up in holy horror if you act like a Christian. He said, <u>That's always been true of anything operating in society, hasn't it? Not just the church.</u> Why argue? I'm taking courses in child psychology to pass the time, thinking of how Kathy would react to this or that. Only to see her. Do you get anything I write? Can you write. . . . Why don't you call Ethan? He'll

find a way to say what you need to know, get something from you that I need to know. I'm afraid you may have given up, gone back . . . oh God, the nightmares will start. If only you could come here. J.

Later, same afternoon.

They're turning up the heat. I think somebody's blabbed. Along the line you meet the kind you like, think you can trust, but those punks I landed with after the Big Job, I can't say I took to them, nor them to me. A poor boy from Georgia was there, had wandered in thinking to find his own kind, played a guitar. He wouldn't go out and set just anybody's car on fire with gasoline bombs. They were hitting up on anybody happened to be parked near this installation, an induction center. I said to leave him alone, it wasn't body count we were after, it was protest effect. You couldn't burn down the whole country. There was a sign they fancied:

WE ARE THE INCUBATION OF YOUR MOTHER'S NIGHTMARE.

I don't think they knew what those words meant. The Georgia boy certainly didn't. He'd be distressed if his mother had nightmares. Maybe he couldn't even read. I know he couldn't read music. He could just play, nice and low, sort of comforting. Dylan songs and Baez, Peter, Paul, and Mary, and some of his own stuff. But he either couldn't read or didn't want to credit anything he read because when they got him down one night and told him to stop any kind of good thinking about his family— you have to imagine what they said—he said he wouldn't, they ought just to meet his grandmother, she was that good. They started threatening him with live cigarettes and one guy was farting in his face while the others held him down. So I said Stop it, you're acting like pigs yourselves and then they started trying stuff on me and we all got knocked around some. But all that is going back before San Cristobal. I'm having to get out of here, the college, because the FBI has given notice twice they want to talk to some faculty I'm working with. They always arrange to be at prayers or "in retreat." But we know when the handwriting is appearing on the wall.

One of the fathers, Fr. Widget, studied with Ethan at Hopkins, has a wealthy friend up the coast who is part of the Movement and has been from the first. He's sending me up there tomorrow.

I may make it, maybe not. All that trouble I went to altering my prints, burning the damn fingertips with acid. They say it didn't go deep enough to work. Those fool lines will show up anyway. Like your soul showing through, every one different from the next. Every little snowflake that falls, every bloom on the honeysuckle vine, etc. Maybe next I'll be writing from jail.
Next day
One of the fathers went out and bought me some vegetable hair dye from the drugstore, dark, the kind you can wash out. All the clerks did double takes at him, just what they always thought of these priests, a bunch of oddballs. God, I wish I could say to myself and believe it that Fred Davis is on the up and up. I know he came and paid bail for me in Chicago back in '68. Maybe now he thinks he's lost five grand, enough said about me. Of course, we mean to pay it back one day when the nightmare's over. Tell him, if you're in touch. No, strike that. Don't tell him anything. He's either at work against us or he's not. (By "us" I mean you and me.) I've come to one simple conclusion: You either know or you don't know. Know what or don't know what? If you know you don't have to ask: if you don't nobody can explain.
Mary, you always know, don't you? I couldn't be that wrong. Even if you don't write, maybe it's just that the letters aren't getting through or you've taken the wrong route for yours. I still have faith that YOU KNOW. It never mattered a bit that you turned out to be the niece of Ethan's old True Love, like something in a corny plot. It doesn't have one thing to do with it. I love you because you <u>know.</u> I think of you and wonder, though, if you've ever known enough about yourself. For instance, you are funny. I like you when you dance funny, like a little jack-in-the-box hopping up on a spring. My aunt down in St. Francisville had one. It scared me when I was a kid and everybody laughed at me. I know you do all that other stuff— "Pavane for a Dead Princess"—running backward in your little short black chiffon skirt fluttering around your knees, the black shoes and all and the turns you said were Balanchine's, not ending but keeping on like a chain of explosions. But what I like best is when you romp. You could bounce like a circus character, tango to rock, do Russian kicks to the "Star-Spangled

Banner" . . . oh, I love to think of it. I'd laugh right now but
want to cry instead and I can't.

Got to go. I live on hope. &$%%

"Maybe I could," said Mary.

"Could what?" asked Ethan, starting to awaken. The room was
overheated. Kathy was back at the TV. Mary climbed over the thick-
ening pile of pages to flex her legs and stretch. For a moment, from
there near the Ottawa River, she went floating off in her imagination
to join Jeff on the West Coast.

"Do comic dances. Some we do already," she told Ethan. She meant
herself and Estes Drover. "Never mind," she added.

"How is Jeff?"

"So far, so good. California. Back to San Francisco. Is he still? Can
I go there?"

"It would be dangerous. Mainly for him, but you, too. What money
is there?"

"It's always money."

"Mine's gone into the paper. That and now doctors. A drain."

"Kate and Fred. If I'd go back for a while. Pretend."

"Then leave again, deceiving them?"

"Well, they're always saying, 'Come back to us. Everything will be
forgiven, forgotten, wiped out.' They don't mean it. The next step
would be getting me a divorce. Out with Jeff."

"Afraid you're right," he agreed.

"I just want to be with him."

"I know."

She bent her head to read again.

9

A Castle by the Sea

December, rain and cool or cooler

Try being on the run and there's bound to be a stop like this one if you get lucky at all. I'm elected to be in it anyway, even if I don't deserve it. It must be that somebody has the right connections as they say in that other world, the one we left.

The woman up here in this fantastic house has turned out to be a beauty, a real old beauty, it's true, but if you could just see her and her place here. It's three-story, big stories, sort of Gothic design, built out over a drive-in garage, lion faces carved into the stone arches, windows open on the sea on every floor. "Charmed magic casements" . . . something I had to memorize once. She's the widow of a guy who used to be in the Orient, China, in foreign service, got every kind of rug and scroll, carved screens, bunches of jade ornaments, figurines and all that, put out in glass cabinets. (Fred Davis would have a fit. He'd hire two more servants just to dust.)

This woman's for real though. She doesn't notice all that. She's got nearly white hair, short and brushed back, and goes around in wool skirts or pants and silk blouses with a shawl or some great-looking sweater. She calls me her "brave boy" (can't say I dig that) and gives me everything: breakfast downstairs, use of her library, lunch alone (she's usually out), and then in the evening we have drinks and dinner, just the two of us usually, but sometimes—here's the touchy part—she asks in other people, but it would be hard to know just who they are. I gather they're important. Art gallery people, making their kind of talk.

People into charities. She doesn't exactly tell them who I am. They don't ask her. They don't ask me. They know how to talk around things. Sometimes she doesn't ask me to meet whoever comes. She's making these judgments, choices. She writes a lot of letters. She has this servant who does everything, goes for the mail, has a fire lighted at night, serves the dinners. He's a Korean man, silent. I don't know if he speaks anything I could understand. Then there's a woman comes and cleans the house. There must be a cook, too. But it's too big for me to find her. I see the cleaning woman, she looks Mexican or something, but she doesn't say anything, either. It's like living in a beautiful palace where the people all walked out of it years ago, and now she's in it, and whoever built it is long forgotten. But this is just imagination. I know it was her husband built it for the two of them, a very wealthy guy. He got killed, drowned in a ferry accident up in Canada one summer, and their daughter with him. She decided on giving her life to what might be worth her life. So she says. First it was art museums, then it was work for women's prisons, libraries and better conditions. Then she took on better treatment for animals, and then she went to an anti-war rally and gave up the art and the animals to put more time on that. She's got Father T. into getting together an evening for me, flying Hayden out or some of the Madison bunch. She's even mentioned Berrigan, but I don't think it's going to work. Fr. T. will come, but the others don't think she's quite for real. If you have to tell stories about it, it's not for real. She went over to Alcatraz once before they shut it down as a prison. She inspected the library and set up some art classes. But if you tell about it it isn't real.

Right now for instance I think she likes talking to me but how could it not cross her mind that here she is alone with a young man not so bad-looking and what if somebody made a move? (She must be seventy if she's a day, but when do women stop?) I have a feeling that some night she's going to pour one glass of wine too many. But so far she's holding a patrician edge, and I think she's not going to let that go because no matter if she favors the classless and the helpless with all her heart, as she explains, it still matters to her more than anything else, that edge, or so I read it. Then I think, <u>One night I'm going to have one glass of wine too many.</u>

You know what I do? I talk about you. I tell her what a wonder
of a dancer you are, always interpreting. Even a walk down the
street is different with you because you've got this way of playing
a girl walking down the street and that's different from just
walking down the street. She understands. Right away she's got
you cast in the SF ballet company, doing dance choruses with
the opera—she could arrange it. I wash my jeans, I wash my
shirt, I iron in the basement, I wear my old duffel coat out in
the chill and my sweater. I walk on the beach in the late after-
noons and get in in time for dinner in my one clean shirt. I hear
about China and the threads that led up to the Red takeover,
the Long March and so on and the dispatcher her husband sent
back. Her name is Bethany Burlingham. How's that for a Nob
Hill ring?

Later, later, always later

I'm reading her husband's books. They were published after he
came back, had to get out, late '40s. He was "recalled." Maybe
he was leaning toward the wrong side. Ethan was "relieved of
his position," or maybe they said they would "accept his resig-
nation." It's what happens when your policy line is not in sync
with theirs, and you've gotten to know too much about them.
In the mornings after breakfast, guess what? I study Chinese
art. I never knew much about it, how it went on through the
various dynasties, changing from one form and emphasis to an-
other. Mixed up with philosophy. After that, I guess I'll read
their history, a ten-volume set, and after that there's always more
to learnlearnlearn, until one day on the inside I will be like one
of those big trees they turn into little trees, a spooky miniature
of whatever was meant to be. Else they'll find a little mound of
fine gray powder at the top of the third floor stairs—that will
be me. The last sound I will have heard will be Long Li, setting
the bronze fire tongs in their rack by the fireplace, closing the
screen for the night. How many years from now? How long a
sentence do I have?

At the college, temporary. . . .

Oh, Mary, what a skunk I am. I got up after breakfast and said
to Bethany Burlingham, Mrs. Burlingham, I can't stand it any
longer. She turned a little pale, but then she composed herself
like a thoroughbred knocking down the rails on one jump but
right away in stride for the next. She sat very straight and put

down her coffee cup. She must have known her toast was cold. She said, <u>What will you do?</u> I said, <u>Maybe they'll find me, maybe not. I'm going back to the college and see what's needed next.</u> So I'm here and writing on my knees in the mess hall. They'll find room for me, though I'm risky property to have around. I know their charity, and their fears. I was advised to lie low for a whole year, but I can't make it.

This morning I went down to find the bunch I was with before San Cristobal. The Panther bunch that had gotten run out, you remember. But where would they go? I was worried about Leon Reed, that boy from Georgia they were always giving grief. I don't know even why he had to stick it out there, he was supposed to report for induction and then didn't report back to his draft board and didn't, but they couldn't track down everybody who didn't do that, and I thought at the time we weren't doing enough to help him, they were all the time telling him he had to get his attitudes in shape, he didn't know what to hate or how much. But he kept holding out and saying he didn't hate anybody. Then too he was dumb, because he thought that it was his duty to work on them, change them for the better. He had some religion mixed up with all that. He played hymns some of the time. Their argument had gotten pretty daily up till the time of the tear gas raid.

I thought to myself I bet they'd gone to Haight-Ashbury, not being exactly flower children, but they could fake it and the grass was easy to come by, cheaper there. I went to a street for some secondhand clothes and got some sort of stuff with the few dollars Fr. T. could spare. I thought I'd never be caught dead in rags like these, some black flared pants with silver buttons down the side and a vest with tassels. I drifted around Central Ave. in H-A till I ran into Monk, one of the bunch from the raid, and asked about Leon. He said "Oh, chrissake, what do you care? He'd never be cool." But then there was Hairy Moment too coming along and I said, "What about Leon?" He laughed and said, "Last time I saw him he was still in the dark." I got a feeling they'd killed him. I met this girl in a beer place (don't get worried) and talked her into going to the precinct station up in SF and acting like she was a relative, asking for any word on him. She went and learned sure enough he'd been found dead in a parking lot back of The Cove, a night spot everybody goes to and sings. It made me plain sick.

I hear they've found some who were involved in the Big Job and so things will be easier for me if nobody tries to say I was major to it. Some lines do hold. They might not even say a word about me. Anyway

I HAVE TO SEE YOU

I'm coming up there if I have to walk.

I read in the paper that Mrs. Bethany Burlingham's house got burgled. They took a lot of her rugs and jade and had gotten into a whole batch of her jewelry when something scared them and they got out with the job half over. I bet myself it was Long Li, but it could have been most anybody who got in there on one sort of invitation or another and kept their eyes open. She let people from all these different groups in there for their meetings and causes, and somebody might have gotten real bug-eyed. I guess they might even suspect me now. One more thing. Father Tomlinson must have robbed a collection plate. He's shelled out a little bit more and I can make it there by bus and train if I'm careful. I've kept up with my "Front Lines" column for Ethan, though I can't keep up with his contacts without putting my head up to be shot at. Still, I've earned my back pay. Being in touch is a danger to all concerned.

Think of me as coming to where I think you are. J.

10

Gerda Stewart's Journal

I'm convinced the phone is tapped but Gordon says we aren't to inquire about it. He thinks that Mary is back; he thought he saw her over on St. Laurent when he got out, absentminded, at the wrong Metro stop. He usually takes a cab home when the weather's like it's been recently, pouring out snow without any end to it, but cabs are hard to find some days, so he took the Metro and went the wrong way. The station was so packed he decided to go up the street, St. Laurent, what they call "the Main," and try for a cab there. We never go over there unless we've heard of some restaurant that's good: it's all French there, or immigrant Italian, Greek, and so on. But there is where he saw her, walking away with Kathy, down a side street. He started to run but a fleet of snowplows came across the road between them. Then he lost sight of them. In that weather, so wrapped up, how could he be sure? He said, "Never mind, I was."

Then I said, "In a way I'm glad you didn't find her, because we said when asked that we don't know where she is. You've lost your thousand dollars in the bail you put up for her; just her being out of touch has kept her case on their active list, I can well imagine. You'll have to go down there one day and swear to things you know aren't true."

I never thought she'd do what she did, but it only goes to show, these kids are not thinking at all in terms of money—it's preservation, surviving.

"They think we're the haves," I said.

"Occasionally," said Gordon, "I do feel obliged to think in personal terms. There's more than money at stake."

I used to feel I was such a "liberal"; I guess I do still, but when I think how Gordon fretted over her, tried to do good deeds for her and that little child of hers, and how he lost that bit of money without so much as an explanation, I feel my soul must have been nothing but conservative all along. Our money is ours, our property belongs to us. We can share, but when we do, it ought to be appreciated. It ought not to be simply ignored.

I think I have a right to say all I just said. I think I have a right to feel that way. Just ignoring certain facts for the moment—but no, I can't ever for a moment ignore the facts. That would really be lying.

All right.

Gordon loved her. Poor Gordon with his limp, a wound to pride never to heal, and poor Gerda with her funny eye, always to be that way. No amount of success in business, no multiplying number of jewels and mink coats and Westmount houses and trips can ever erase a basic wound. Added to that, she is young, and vital and talented as a dancer, or so I would suppose, and—and what? His love was not returned. He was used and ignored. That is all.

Only it isn't. There is something that remains. Our decency. We can't tell on her, or stop protecting her. Inquiries have been made. I think he is in some trouble—the husband, so absent, but so present, too.

"I helped her some time back," Gordon says on the telephone. "She was obviously alone, in difficulties. I think, however, that she went back to the States. No, I don't know where. She had family there, but I never met them. You'll have to check further. No, I've no names to suggest. No, I know nothing else. Nothing. No."

11

A Return to Montreal

"It was all such a bad idea," she told Ethan on the road back. "I never wanted to do it. That boy that brought my orders made it sound like I was murdering Jeff if I didn't take them."

"I thought of Montreal as a baited trap. I lay awake and saw both of you falling into it."

"Every place may be a trap. I know how to hide in Montreal. Not even a rabbit can hide in a field of snow."

Ethan had made her go back to the Pelletiers for her things. "They might report you," he argued.

"She's married to a wild man," Mary pleaded. "Let's just leave."

"Gérard!" wailed Kathy. *"Je veux le voir."*

"Even wild men pass out from drinking too much," said Ethan, and firmly put the car on the road.

Frail and scholarly, Ethan could get as active as anyone if he chose. Mary marvelled that he never seemed to be afraid for himself, and saw how he was driving, skidding at times, not used to icy roads, but getting there.

Madame Pelletier came out. She clutched Kathy to her and lamented. Back from his hunt, Gérard gave a calloused handshake all around and grinned with yellow teeth. Monsieur Pelletier's truck was there, but no sign of him. Gérard laughed when Mary asked. *"Il dort."*

Madame Pelletier's bruises were powdered over. *"On prend mon enfant. On prend ma p'tite Kathee."*

"Il faut les rend visite," Ethan advised Mary. Mary said Ethan was her uncle.

Groping over snowy highways, Ethan drove on to Montreal. He

spoke of matters in the Movement. He feared for its unity. The violent ones were getting a stronger hold; the brilliant ones, like Jeff, Hayden, Rubin, what had they in common with Panthers and Weathermen? Yet so much progress. College faculties who sympathized en masse, judges who would not convict, legal groups joining together to protest. All the while, the younger ones burst into conflict, arguing like Russians. If Nixon wanted a Red connection, that was it: too much argument. "But," Ethan said with a sigh, "I can still boast of that one thing. No nuclear strikes. None so far means maybe never." Out of his frailty, when he spoke, his exultant head seemed to rise up, vaunting over all.

They had passed Ottawa. A thin slant of snow had started falling. "*Gérard vient me voir,*" Kathy said from the backseat. She was shaking a doll he had given her. It was made of sticks, screwed together, and was wearing a green snowsuit.

"If Jeff had kept out of that bombing business, we could live up here."

"Decide that between you. Perhaps it still is possible. Attention has shifted to Toronto. The drug scene is thought to be worse there. More drugs, more protest, is the common cry."

Mary was going straight to Estes, to start work again.

"Jeff may be on the way," Ethan encouraged her. "Right now. Remember he's Geoffrey Blaylock. We've got papers for him."

Mary wondered how to believe anything. *At least,* she thought, *I know more French. So does Kathy. Thank you, Madame Pelletier. Thank you, Gérard. The damned cast comes off next week. I broke an arm but not a leg. I'll chop the plaster off myself. We'll get by.*

But Ethan's hands are shaking on the wheel. His voice fades into a weaker register when he talks. It isn't just the snow driving against us.

Why are things so hard? For us especially, why is everything so especially hard?

12

Letters Missing Forever
(A Former Mystery Explored)

The letters Jeff Blaise had written to Mary after he left Montreal
were for some time hidden in a carved wooden box in Kate Davis's
room in the house near Philadelphia. She sometimes sat alone near
a window overlooking the clipped lawn, watching the progressive
march of shadows from the handsome trees. She would hold the box
on her lap. Don Harbison had bought it for her, hand-carved and
casket-shaped, on a stop they had made at a Mexican port while on
a Caribbean cruise. She could not remember the name of the port.
The box was beautiful. An Aztec god danced across the lid. It locked.

Jane Harbison had given Kate the letters, passed to her by Ethan
Marbell for sending on to Mary Kerr. Things were uncertain, where-
abouts mysterious. Mary Kerr was leaving one Montreal address for
another. Kate would know where. Kate looked at the sheaf of four
or five thick white envelopes. He liked to write, she recalled: those
awful articles were at least well phrased.

For a long time she did not open them. "Do you hear from Jeff?"
she asked Mary Kerr by telephone.

"Sure I do. He calls and writes." But the voice was too bright. It
lied. (Just as she lied in even asking.)

After a month, she told herself she had a right to read them. What
was he doing? What plans should she not know about? She had to
protect those innocents, daughter and grandbaby. Fred's paying bail
for Jeff after the Chicago upheavals had been only that, an act of
protection. For Kate. He had come home disgusted. Had not even
seen Jeff, who was in another detention center, they called it. Who

knew? It was chaos. *Jail* was more correct a term. But his name was clearly listed.

Fred inveighed, "We can't even hold a decent political convention anymore. Those goddamned freaks have about trashed that city. They had squads of police running for their lives. Don't talk to me about peace."

"You did it for me," said Kate, "and I'm grateful." What he'd done was more than the decent thing he called it. Five thousand. She was afraid Jeff would never show up for trial, if she knew him as she felt she did.

More letters came. She found them in a manila envelope along with the other mail, as the winter of '70 came on. A letter from Jane was enclosed. She went upstairs to place them in the carved box with the others. Or to take them from the box, give up, and send them all on together. But first—she sat down, opened the letters one at a time, and read them.

Something stirred up from them. His words—words of love, intimate, nothing she'd ever heard from him. Yet in her head she could hear him. The peculiar offbeat drop in his voice at times, leaving, returning. It was odd, but true. How well she heard. With the words came a persistent sexual murmur, the rise and fall of that, his own drive and tough sustained rhythm, bursting, tender. The thoughts she never thought she had of him, or if she knew she did, she'd never let anyone know about them. *I should read these in Cap d'Antibes,* she thought with a laugh at her own folly. But *he,* she had to admit knowing, *he* had known what thoughts she had.

Kate came on hints of an underlying mystery. Mary Kerr was admonished not to worry about someone. It hadn't meant anything. Did she know how hassled he had been that past winter, and this older type—well, what to call her? "Call her a bitch if you want to, it might help how you feel. But it wasn't like that. And she'll never hold a candle to you anyway. I knew it all along, every breath, I swear it. . . ." *Older woman,* thought Kate, confirming what she knew: Mary Kerr was too young.

But what of the pleas?

You wouldn't let me come there because of this letter you found, the one she wrote. But you can't stay mad forever. Can you meet me down in Burlington? I could get there for a day or so, or however long you want to stay. We can go to all the old places. Maybe the same horse in the pasture will come and say hello. Mary, please, consider.

And then, in the next letter, complaining of no answer, and she wasn't there when he called, and winter will set in on him, along with despair. But he really couldn't believe . . .

Kate thought that she should do something but didn't know what it should be. She returned the letters to the box.

Weeks later she chanced to see an activist paper on a newsstand in the city, and bought it. There she read an announcement that Jefferson Blaise and others would be speaking at a Vermont college called Barnwell, and she was shaken by a feeling of something inevitable about to occur. Not that she was ever going to decide in advance what to say or do. But she would be able to make contact, establish—well, what? She didn't know. She only felt she had to go.

She telephoned a college friend in the Barnwell area. "Don't mention a word about this call. I don't want Fred to know. But write and invite me. Say it's important, a crisis."

"Katie, love, what are you up to? It sounds like a hot love affair."

"Anything but. It child-worry, of course. Not Fred's and mine, but before that. Don died, you know. My daughter's the problem."

"I'm beginning to get it," said the friend, whose name was Rose Hellinberg, and who was fortunately good-natured. "When should I ask you for?"

They plotted it well. Kate would fly up to Albany, rent a car, drive as far as need be.

Rose Hellinberg had married a man wealthy enough to afford a handsome country estate plus a New York City address for the winter season. Kate woke up to breakfast on a tray. She mused out the bedroom window over green fields laced with stone fences. Jasper County was not so much like this, though she often spoke to strangers as though it were. In her talk the fences were of cross-railed wood, painted white.

With Duke University far in their past but not forgotten, Rose and Kate chattered away a whole morning.

"Now, what's this about your girl—Mary-something?"

"Mary Kerr. One of Don's family names. Listen, it's not her. She's a joy, a perfect delight to me. Her dancing . . . well, I think she might even have gone to New York with it. I saw no obstacle whatsoever. But then, as usual—"

"The wrong guy came along."

"Understatement of the century. The worst possible guy. Antiwar activist, speaker, writer . . . oh, my God, my prayers for her got in the wrong box."

"That's awful. I was scared about one of mine for a while Jody—that's the younger one. But he's got interested in pre-med. High grades, too, so somehow managed not to be drafted, though I guess he might even have thought he ought to go."

"The rally up at Barnwell. I'm going there, Rose. He's going to speak there. I saw it in one of those papers they spread around everywhere."

"So she'll be there, too?"

"Oh, no, I would very much doubt that. It's a big risk, maybe, but worth chancing. But even if she's not, I want a chance to see him, talk to him a little. We've never been on any terms with him, Rose! He's like a foreigner, came in and just carried her off. Like a bandit."

"A robber bridegroom." Rose smiled. She had been an English major.

Kate, vaguely aware of a quotation in the air, nodded. "Exactly."

The two women sat over coffee in a sun-flooded room, the house to themselves. Mr. Hellinberg, with far-flung commutes for a national brand of frozen foods, was off somewhere in midair. Rose's hair in her college days had been black, short, smooth, and glossy, and so it remained. Kate's, pale blond and long, was its old self also. They sat in robes de chambre of identical make, Rose's orange, Kate's mauve.

"But in Canada," Rose pursued. "It certainly sounds like an antiwar move."

"For him, yes. Or so I assume. He's never acknowledged us to the extent of telling us anything. But she's been able to adjust, or so she says. She's with a leading dance group now. Fantastic talent. I want to go up and see her. And the little girl is just lovely. Between them, they can charm you into thinking anything about him. The perfect family man. I know that's a charade, of course."

"I have a right," said Kate, "to speak to him, be recognized by him, at least to say that I am more than just a bystander, a distant relative, somebody who reads the papers. . . . Don't I?"

"Why, certainly you do," said Rose. "Have you met the Ellisons yet? They're Main Line . . . coal money."

By evening, Rose had worked up to wanting to go with Kate to this rally. What little she knew about the Movement was that in Albany once she had gotten stalled in the middle of some sort of march, and came out finally with lots of anti-war slogans they had cheerfully painted on her car. One had even written: JUST MARRIED. She thought that was pretty funny. The car wash took it all away. Now she wanted to venture out with Kate.

"How will you get home?"

"Drive."

"Alone?"

"Listen," Kate said, "I'm striving to make a real contact with him. If that occurs, no outsider should be there; it would—well, weaken things, don't you think?"

Rose was a little miffed. "I'll look for you when I see you. That's what you used to say at school, wasn't it?"

So Kate went alone.

She had dressed herself with care. A pearl-gray fall suit, ice-blue satin blouse; the gold shell-shaped earrings made a discreet gleam beneath the curved line of her hair. Dressing well meant holding on to herself; she knew that.

The meeting hall was an auditorium set off to itself on the far northern edge of a spread-out campus.

Inside Kate groped and edged her way. She kept asking, "Do you know Jefferson Blaise? Where is he? Do you know if Jefferson Blaise is here?"

The crowd hummed like a gigantic bee swarm.

"Attention! Attention!" A man in a correct suit and tie was at the podium.

"Quiet! Quiet!" A hushing hiss. A big yell: "Shet-up, you stoopid acid heads! Freak out, you fucking freaks!" Something like attention finally resulted.

"As president of Barnwell College—" A vast squawk from the microphone. Roars from the crowd. Above, legs in blue jeans began to dangle from the cross beams. "As president of Barnwell College, I have been persuaded to allow this meeting, in the name of a democratic society which allows all sides of public issues to be presented publicly. However, let me emphasize that our agreement with your representatives has carried with it the solemn pledge that decency and the laws of orderly behavior will be maintained throughout. If this agreement is not kept, I will have no recourse but to notify the authorities. I am counting on your sense of honor and decency to abide by your word."

The president left the microphone vacant. Kate had gotten no answer to her questions. The students shied away from her, as though she came from another planet and was not quite visible, certainly had no means of using words. Probably they thought she was a reporter or a spy. She took a seat far to the side, near the front. Someone piled a huge duffel on the floor beside her, crowding her legs. She began to look through the mass of flyers and tabloid-sized papers that had been thrust at her when she came inside. Sure enough, there was *The Radar Screen*. Its headlines: THE TRUTH BEHIND PEOPLE'S PARK, WHAT THE PAPERS DIDN'T TELL and COOKED FIGURES FOR FAKE VICTORIES— and there at the left-hand side a column as usual, "From the Front Lines" by Jefferson Blaise, with a subhead: THE KISSINGER CONSPIRACY: THE BERRIGANS SPEAK.

So no longer just a "roving patriot" . . . he was out in the open. It seemed ominous to her. She turned to a girl sitting next to her with hair like three dust mops. "Is Jefferson Blaise here?" The girl stared at her and burst into laughter. She whispered to the boy next to her. He leaned over to look at her, like a specimen just arrived from a zoo.

"Who's that?" he asked.

"Never heard of him," said the girl. They laughed to one another. No one asked her anything.

There was a sudden great roar, filling the entire audience, mounting to the rafters. Two musicians had appeared, one with guitar. Would the building stand? The crowd was wild.

They just stood there, adjusting the microphones, grinning at the applause they drew. Their clothes were stark black leather vests, no shirts, black boots studded liberally with silver, the belts great disks of silver strung with leather, dropping far down the hips, and silver chains.

"Ain't stopped tripping since Woodstock," said the guitarist, his words so amplified they might have been thundered from a cloud. His fingers touched the strings of his guitar, as big as himself. A roar.

"Let's go! Let's travel! Let's hit 'em in their fuckin' hearts. 'Scuse

me. Bad language is a no-no. Bad! It's okay to torture . . . kill out
a race . . . napalm children . . . rip up pregnant women . . . lie to a
whole nation. . . . But no *bad* LANGUAGE! You understand?" He
touched the strings again. The roar. "You gonna be good?" "No!"
Whispering: "Hush, children, what's that soun' . . . ?" Laughter.

Then, the music.

Kate could not either stand it or understand it. It hit like a furious
wave. It told them to walk right in and sit right down, to let their
minds roll on. It mentioned Uncle Sam and Vietnam. It cried, Hell
no they wouldn't go, and asked Joe DiMaggio where he had gone.
It spoke of darkness as an old friend. It declaimed that answers were
blowing in the wind, and the stanzas for that went on and on while
everybody shouted the words.

Kate clamped her hands to her ears. Her head throbbed as if cleft
with an axe. This could go on for hours, sweeping over, around, and
above them, while they willingly let it drown them. Living inside the
words and beat was what they were doing. The beat came from
everywhere, thundering and wild. The lights blazed at sunlike in-
tensity. The lights blared sound; the sound flamed with light. She
could not have heard herself scream, as the masters of war were
indicted for crime after crime.

Defying gravity, daredevils up on the rafters were riding them like
bronco busters on bucking ponies, locking their legs close, clapping
and shouting. Arms linked, human chains had formed at the foot of
the stage, swaying and leaping to the music.

The silence was a shock. It ended the uproar as neatly as though
it had gone off a cliff. There was nothing, just nothing. The musicians
were moving back, unplugging cords, shoving the amplifiers aside.
A single microphone was left.

Announcements by some bony tramp in rags. More rallies to come.
Surrounding news. The front. "We know he's always on the move,
and that's why he can't stay here long, but everywhere he goes he
lets us hear about it. You know who I mean. It's the guy who's always
at the front lines. . . ." Cheering had begun, almost drowning the
name: Jefferson Blaise.

He walked out. He was just there, standing there, serious and all
together, just as she remembered him. The cause of all her trouble,
was what she thought about him. But he did have presence, she had
to grant him that; he was solid with authority, conviction. Kate's gaze

on him was so fixed she had to draw back from her very self, turn her eyes away.

He spoke quietly. Statistics on the war were unofficially much worse than published. Villages wantonly destroyed were in numbers now rising. Repatriation really meant forced living in detention. Interrogation squads were torture centers. Defoliation. Anti-personnel bombs. The home front: He had talked with the Berrigans. In prison, they were calm, cordial, full of good spirits. Personal messages of cheer were extended. The president walks around among a tribe of bodyguards, afraid in his own country. Is this imperial Rome or the land of the free? A word about *The Radar Screen*. Readers displeased when the column on the rock/sex/drug experience was dropped, due to too much news and not enough room. Reinstatement in the next issue. More funds needed. A box at the exit.

The applause had hardly burst out before Kate was squirming out of her seat and into the aisle. He would be leaving, leaving, according to what they said at the first. She stepped over bodies. Somebody tickled her legs. . . . "Slumming, Lady Astor?" A voice cried: "Hey, the message is love." Half suffocating, she burst into the narrow lobby, its long table before the doors lined with pamphlets, stacks of logos, T-shirts, and, invariably, *The Radar Screen*.

"Jeff." She said it aloud in spite of herself. He wasn't there.

Through a narrow door at the side, she found a corridor leading perhaps backstage. Hastening, she followed it.

Another door at the end of her run, and there he stood. Back to her on a narrow stairway leading up, she guessed, to the wings. He was talking to someone. She had noticed, in contrast to the wild regalia of nearly everyone she had seen, onstage and off, that he was quietly dressed in trousers and dark shirt. Not even jeans.

She reached up a hand toward his arm, but before she could actually touch him, he had turned, a wary suddenness in the move. She was facing him now, and he came the one step down to put them on a level. Vaguely, she was aware that the person he had been speaking with had gone up the steps and away.

"Well," he finally said. "It's you."

"Is Mary Kerr—" she faltered.

"Not here." Then, "Why?"

"*Why!* My daughter, and you ask me why!"

For a moment she thought he was actually about to turn and walk away, as though she had never existed. "I need so much to talk with you," she said quickly. "I made this effort. Surely you owe me a few moments."

His eyes were an intense blue she thought she had forgotten. "What exactly did you have in mind? Describe your best scenario." There was a thread of mockery, and she remembered that, too, but it might be only a habit with him, a habit intellectuals often had.

"I only thought we might go somewhere and talk. Have dinner, even. My son-in-law, after all. Speak about her. We both love her."

It was after consideration that he said "Come here" and walked before her through the doorway he had come out of. She climbed the steps and followed. Backstage, he turned into a room, empty of people, but with deep shelves for microphones, music racks, podiums, a long, central table scattered with leaflets and flyers, *The Radar Screen* among them, and some cartoon drawings she scarcely dared let herself look at. A drifting smoke cloud reeked. He dumped an old sweater off a chair and pulled it forward for her. He sat on the table. She felt him waiting, and the annoying impression she had was that she was expected to speak to him as his inferior, that he held his rights above hers.

"Have you left her, then, for doing all these things?"

"Of course I haven't left, except for what I have to do. What is it you have in mind for her? What's the scheme?"

"*Scheme* isn't the word. I just worry, of course. Thinking of the best thing for her. For you both, I mean. I worry about both of you, and I think—"

"What do you think?"

"I think, If only—" She hesitated.

"Go on."

"If only we could all be in contact, a group, a family. No matter what differences there are, a family has to know about each other, bear things together, work problems out with each other's interests in mind. Don't they?"

He laughed. "That's the candy-coated come-on. That's the sugar tit. You're all dressed up and playing lady, aren't you?"

He said such things in a very good-humored way. She remembered the day she'd gone to find him, way back there in Kingsbury, the strong flash-on current of sex. His words in those letters he didn't know she had, words to her daughter, but words she had, in some way mysterious to her hungry self, claimed as her own. But hungry for what? Her husband was satisfying. What did she want? Why, as he had demanded to know, was she really here? She had every right to be. She could always, with conviction, assert that. He couldn't deny it.

"I've every right to be here," she said, and rose. "My whole concern—"

He interrupted. "Is what?"

He was crowding her out of herself. Well, these people were trying to confront a whole country, so why not her, a good example of it, she supposed? She saw his room again so vividly she might even have counted the creases on the rumpled spread.

"Back down there in Kingsbury," he asked her, "did you want me out of the way, or what? You and Mary never got along anyway. She thinks all that caring is a fake."

"Oh, no, it isn't that. Not a *fake*." For a moment she felt such an awful division of herself it was like a physical wound. "I always wanted her to be . . . well, something it didn't seem so hard for any girl to be—"

"And when she wasn't, you hated her for it."

"Hated her? Oh, does she—" She broke off. She had wanted a talk, an agreement, some sort of touch, maybe more intimate than she could admit, a joining of forces. But confrontation of the kind he was forcing on her, that was something she couldn't stand. She felt he was driving her into a fire.

"You always seemed to be wanting something from me," he went on. "But what the fuck it was, you left me to guess at. I didn't like seeing you because of this Southernness in women. I don't care for it. She didn't get that from you. Thank God."

Kate felt like a hurt child. A cousin of hers had once slammed a door on her hand. She had thought he liked her, and she knew he had done it half on purpose, so her tears were for her feelings as well as her fingers.

"You think I owe you some respect," he said. His face, framed in the hair that was longer than ever and kept hanging forward around his cheeks, had remained unchanged throughout. Only his voice seemed capable of saying what the range of his feeling was, how he meant to be understood. "Well, all right, maybe I do. If you think I don't love her, you're wrong. We speak our own language to each other, that's all. Nobody is out to chase *you* down, do anything to change *your* life."

"You owe me nothing, I suppose, for the fact that Fred—my husband—paid your bail for you?" Money. She would hold on to that. A fact.

"I owe him five thousand dollars."

"And no thanks."

"Thanks . . . oh, yes, someday. When, if ever, I find what his motive really was. Up till now, I've thought he did it for you."

"If he did? If that's right?"

"Well," said Jeff, and for the first time he smiled. "Well, thanks."

She smiled back at him, edging toward triumph. Every room she entered, there was never any doubt that Kate Harbison was the most attractive woman who could be there. *Mirror, mirror on the wall. . . .* Had she come, in part, to prove that?

The intermittent cheers and clapping from the auditorium beyond them now burst out into singing. The music had started once more. The door swung open. A tall black man was standing in it. He saw her and said, "Jesus."

"Hi, Kink." Jeff Blaise broke out laughing. "It's my mother-in-law." He couldn't stop laughing.

The black man said "*Mother*-in-law!" and began to laugh as well. "There ain't no such thing," was all she could make out that he was saying.

Jeff sobered, but her interview in this strong presence was, he might as well have come right out and said, concluded. He might have been a top executive of some thirty-fourth floor office, showing her to the door. His curious parting left her with nothing to say: "If you had me, what would you do with me?" he asked.

He had caught her arm, latching it, in the movement of her going through the door, tightly into his, like a catch and pass movement in a children's game. Drawn, she gripped it to her. "Jeff," was all she said, an intimate word, as the shock of his touch went racing into her senses, while the puzzling insolence of his words stopped her thoughts. Then he let her go and shut the door, and she stood trembling for a time, hearing the massed tumult from the other side of the corridor wall, the stamping, the yells, the enveloping thunder. And then one steady roar, like a country creek in full tide, roaring.

Before her, a linked line of what appeared to be naked boys and girls, painted all over, was dancing in the corridor, and from over their heads she saw, just appearing, like celestial bodies rising above the horizon, the blue coats of police. She edged along the wall, trying to dodge the waving arms. One of the policemen grinned as she passed him. "Time you was getting out of here, lady."

Driving home, Kate felt her conflict deepen. Desire awakened did not fade. Phrases from his letters to her daughter kept wakening in her head, pulsing and warm. When had anyone ever written her like that, praising the velvet brown of her nipples, the soft spun hair below, the spring of milk and honey there beneath, the arch of her foot, the small of her back? Young love. And not her own.

But then he had checked her, dismissed her, acted as her superior. *What right did he have?* She and Fred were central to this country; people like them had worked to make and preserve its values, created its greatness, while he and all his unwashed crew of shrieking dissent . . . *What right did they have?*

Without deciding to, she pulled up on the gravel before a wayside restaurant, righted herself in the restroom, stopped in the lounge to steady herself on one drink only, but wound up taking two at least and asking the barman, "What right does he have?"

"You got me, lady," the barman said.

"I've only one daughter," she explained.

On the road home, she missed an intersection, groped through a freeway turn to find the road again, almost ran down an embankment. She had been driving with the window wide open and had loosened her hair so that it streamed in the wind, wild and wonderful. She reached the Hellinberg house long after midnight.

"No," she explained to Rose Hellinberg at a late breakfast, "I saw him, but it was far from satisfactory. Not that he was especially rude or anything. He's really from a very nice background, I'm convinced, a Louisiana family, and highly educated.

"It's just that they take themselves so seriously. You know what they remind me of? Old-timey ministers or political speakers running for governor—in the South we see that sort of thing. Always with the converts or the constituency. Always on the road. Now, don't ever give me away to Fred. I'm going to say you had gotten lonesome up here and just valued a visit at this particular time, for reasons of some personal problem all but resolved by the time I arrived. At any rate, Jeff did reassure me that Mary Kerr is all right. I felt she was telling me the truth, but sometimes they don't want their parents to worry."

"Go see her," Rose advised.

"Yes, I plan to."

The two women embraced at the point where the front steps led down to the curving gravel drive, and Kate, with a backward wave, drove away.

In the winter that followed, the authorities in Montreal advised her that Mary Kerr had tried to kill herself. She threw the box of letters into the Schuylkill River, unable to bear the sight of it.

13

Train Heading East

Picture a land half again as wide as the United States. A massive land like something in a trick mirror, broad at the base, its head narrowing, snow coming in to blind its distant northern brow. Snow blowing southward, shifting and slanting out of the jetty, dark beyond the windows of the Trans-Canada Express. Jeff Blaise sits close to the windows, hearing the muffled passage of the wheels, glimpsing at times the red-and-black striped engine curving inward, miles ahead. He turns his face toward the windows, or thrusts a pillow against them to sleep a little. He keeps the end of the pillow twisted across the lower half of a face somebody passing might see and call out to. "Hey, Jeff!" He might awake, answering before thinking.

Darkness and the car lights on. Now he sometimes sees his own face reflected in the glass, framed in hair darkened with dye. But, half dozing, he sometimes starts to consciousness thinking that there in the glass is the face of Leon Reed. The face is seeking him. And that's not fair. "Not fair," he says once, quietly.

But it comes back. Its eyes are engaging him, the lips are moving: "My daddy got burnt up in this tank. It was over in Af'ica. I been told about it. They throwed this bomb. His tank done cooked him like a live turkey in a red-hot oven. Oughtn't do that to nobody. I usta dream about it, that I was him. I wasn't even born yet. This here war they got now's too far away. If somebody was trying to run us off where we are, down in Georgia, or somewhere else in this country, then we'd all join up and have us a war, I reckon, but the way they talk about this one, it's worse'n Af'ica in someplace I ain't never heard about—so I jes' don' know. If they said it was right, maybe I ought to abin there."

He vanishes. The puzzled eyes, seeking Jeff's, and what did he answer? Lots. Encouraging, too. They could talk. The only two in that misbegotten bombed-out crew who could find anything really to say. A brother feeling. A brother Jeff never had. A sister longed for, who died as a baby, appearing just over the pasture fence at twilight. Open gaze, "What y'all doing?" Trust.

He remembers in those days coming back from a walk in the dark, the only exercise he could get. "Where's Leon?"

"Leon? Who's that?"

"Leon the lion?" says Hairy Moment. "Panthers shit on lions."

A sad little bundle in the corner, and Jeff going over, whispering, "Yeah, I know they think all that stuff, but you don't have to."

A bruised cheek. "If they ast me I'm sho going to tell 'em. I don't hate no fam'ly. My mama's this real sweet lady."

"I know, Leon, I just know she is. Mine was, too."

"What happened to her?"

"She died."

"I'm real sorry to hear that, Jeff."

"Leon, go on out of here. It's not for you. Go join up. I'll tell you where. They're easy out here, easier than most. You don't have to tell them anything. Say the mail was just now catching up to you. Say you don't know any of us. Say you lost your draft card, didn't burn it at all. They'll write your board back home. If they ask about that plant blowing up, say you never heard of it. They won't believe you, but they won't bother to doubt you."

"Then I'd have to go on over there to the war?"

"This might be worse for you than the war."

"I just don't hold with fighting if I don't know nothing about it."

"Leon, listen. They'll explain it to you. And if you still don't hold with it, then you just have to tell them that. You'll fill out some papers. You might have to go somewhere they say. But you won't have to fight."

"Aw, naw. It don't work that way. Once they got you, they got you."

"I'd go with you, but now they're after me."

"Maybe these guys here will calm down," Leon concluded.

They all were freaked out with grass by then, sprawling around gummy-eyed. The place was full of smoke. It went on like that. For a couple of days more, they took turns nagging Leon. He was getting like a crazy. He was scared to just walk out on them. Somebody had gotten him to go along on the Big Job against the munitions plant; they needed somebody to help with the gear, that's how he had gotten listed. A coward. Well, you have to call him that. But mainly it was because he didn't understand what was going on. If he had once understood he might have been braver than anybody else. Who can honestly say they're not scared sometimes?

"Scared once, then the consequences of that just follow on, Leon," Jeff said in thought to the image that came and melted away into the ever-changing slant of snow, white lines coursing across the jet surface of the infinite dark—the prairies. A few flights flicked past, a glimpse of storage tanks, a water tower, some lonely spangle of a distant outpost, far away, and Leon, back again. Can't he ever stop?

Listen, Jeff. The night you left me. The night you deserted me. They knocked me half blind, man.

I didn't mean to leave you, Leon. I came back as soon as I could.

I heard you were looped on hash, snugged up down the coast.

I had to hide, Leon. They were after me.

Those two black guys, they wanted me to draw a picture of my granddaddy's face and shit on it. I said, "My granddaddy was just a real fine man." They said, "Yo' granddaddy lynched niggers, boy, he just didn't bother to tell you." I said, "He didn't tell you, either, ga'damn it." And we had us another fight.

Leon, it wasn't any of it my fault. I told you to walk out. Join up, I said.

Jeff, that fight was—

Shut up, Leon.

The snow stopped. He slept.

He woke in the thin dawn light, a long stretch of gray over white fields, still and infinite. Pale streaks of light in the windows and, from down the corridor when the door to the cars up front opened, a whiff of coffee. He got himself together, stood in line for the washroom, went to eat, came back forgetful of those long, unnatural hours of night, as if spent in some myth country never before heard of. The country was so vast, so empty, a dream in one place would take a century to reach another. Still, in late afternoon, he thought of it, and knew that night would come again, inescapable night, and then once more, sure as clockwork, Leon Reed would be back at that window, when the snow started falling again, saying,

That fight was the last one, Jeff, the last one. You wasn't there with me, Jeff.

Oh, shut up.

He thought it in advance and hoped to make it stick enough to get some sleep, as they passed over the Manitoba border and the shadows got longer than any he could remember ever having seen.

Because I'm going to Mary, he thought. *I'm gliding, surf-riding, flying, coasting, skimming, soaring, straight as I can. To her.*

Part IV
Reunion

1

The Purple Window

In those days everybody went to the Purple Window. It was where they came to be together and sing. Mary went, too, because she knew that if Jeff came back he would come there. She did not like the music, but she sang along like the rest and clung to strange hands extended out of the dusk. The mellow vocalists, the throbbing guitar strings. They all sounded about to cry. Hands reached out over troubled waters, the answer blew in the wind, my friend. Other winds, four strong ones, blew lonely way out in Alberta. Mr. Tambourine Man was there to beg for a song. It was March and the winter, grown stale with old snow, was snow-drenched still at times, thin snows raining down in the night, thick flakes flying in the twilight hours.

Leonard and Hilda Abel came to the Purple Window at times and sat with Mary. Hilda was three months pregnant and contentment radiated from her as if she were a small stove. She willingly sat near Mary as if knowing that Mary and Kathy had to do in some psychic hidden way with her conceiving at all. She squeezed Mary's hand in the dark.

"Word from Jeff?" she leaned to whisper.

Mary shook her head, not wanting to say. Yet Hilda was afraid, too. Now that she had this child within, she was afraid of losing it. She dreaded slippery surfaces, gripped banisters on stairways, thought that a bad dream might cause her to fall out of bed. Beside her, Leonard held her hand. When he sat near Mary, he would take her hand as well. Mary thought he had such a large friendliness that if they both lived with him, he would think nothing was the matter with their arrangement.

She heard her own little voice back in Kingsbury Sunday school: "What's a concubine?"

"Well, it seems to be another lady in the house, doesn't it?"

"What's wrong with that?"

"Ask your mother."

But Hilda would mind her being there. That must have been in the lesson, too. Never mind, she'd found where she wanted to be. With Estes, who was home with Kathy.

The guitar player achingly sang about Suzanne and her place by the river. It went like a chant, weaving garbage with flowers, heroes and children and seaweed. The man who wrote it was from there, and it must have been the St. Lawrence he had in mind. They said he sometimes came and sang there. She hadn't seen him, but knew that Jamie Manchester came, a Southerner like herself, a singer blown here by the same strong wind. Her mind drifted, braiding in slow motion through the plaintive triumphs of the song, and in its fading sound she looked up and saw Jeff sliding through the smoky entrance of the large inner room where they had gathered. In one smooth dancer's motion, she had shot to her feet and was beside him. Their hair flung together, draping their faces. It was instant welding, but she kept shaking in spite or because of it, like struck metal in a sudden shift of place and temperature, bleeding out tears.

"Kathy?" he was saying or asking, shooting glances out through her hair's thick curtain.

"Home with Estes . . . a friend. I wrote you. But maybe . . ."

He was pulling back to look at her, her face, stroking it, pushing back the hair.

A murmur was going around the room, swelling. Jeff was known about. One of the resisters who had made a big leap, done a Big Job. But there was uncertainty. Momentarily, like someone taking the briefest possible bow for an instant of bravery so daring as to be all but private, Jeff nodded his head and held on to Mary. A splatter of applause. In discretion and understanding, the heads turned away.

Arms clinging together, Mary and Jeff moved through the dark at the back of the room. They came to Leonard and Hilda, and Mary introduced them all.

"I thought you had blond hair," said Hilda. "She said you had blond hair."

"I do," said Jeff. He gave her the winning grin. "This is temporary."

"We ought to have champagne," said Leonard. But he looked

personally set back, knowing he had to adjust to this turn in things. His lease on Mary was terminating without notice. Mary had seen him seldom in recent months; she could not think of herself as so important to him. Maybe she thought, she might be an outsider which his tribal soul hankered for—stranger in the midst. She remembered his touch, his mouth cavernous and wet.

"We have to pass up tonight on celebrating," Jeff said. "I've been travelling."

"Where from?" Hilda asked.

Jeff took Mary then and bowed out, among a hiss of whispers, another spattering of applause, hands reaching up out of shadows into the semi-light, looking white and seeking, these hands, like the last outreach of spirits to those leaving. Some he grasped.

2

Estes in Moonlight

Sometimes when he is there alone in the house he is buying now (with the loan his ex-lover Ahmed coaxed out of an uncle), Estes Drover gets to stay with Kathy and she gets to stay with him. He reads to her and laughs with her and talks to her and teaches her little miniature dance steps, around and around his room. She falls asleep there, holding on to his hand, tucked up on the couch. Mary, returned, will pick her up and carry her upstairs to their room.

The house is three stories with a basement apartment. Looked at from the street, with a certain lack of faith, it does seem to tilt slightly. But there is another house close to the left, and an alley to the right, and both have remained in the same proportion for the last year. It is better not to consider such things. The ground floor and basement apartment are rented. The second floor houses Estes and two extra rooms (one rented, the other vacant). These rooms are better let to the slightly deaf, as Estes and Mary's dance classes take place in a large room on the top floor. In a room off this one, Mary and Kathy live. They cook on a small hot plate. Their bed is under the window overlooking the alley, shoved against the wall.

But Kathy feels peaceful enough to sleep in Estes's room. When she falls asleep, Estes strips naked sometimes and stands before the window in the dark, watching the moon on a clear night, pouring out over the snow-silenced city. He enjoys his lean dancer's body, his sinewy rhythmic legs. Sometimes, with practiced silence on the rug, he will spin with folded arms or execute a whirling jeté over the sleeping little girl. Then he will kneel, touch her cheek, with his finger push back threads of her hair. He has always longed for this warm protectiveness he is now able to give. As a child, he had pet dogs and cats for the best of reasons. A sickly child, he had over-anxious parents afraid of animal germs, or fate decreed that they be run over in the street, or other parents lured them off to delight other homes. One way or another, he lost them. And then there were the younger children he wanted to escort home from school, who soon got wary around him because he had all the symptoms early on of the way he would grow up to be, and their mothers warned them. But to himself Estes never grew up to be anything: he simply was.

He loved Mary. She didn't go around making the sort of distinctions that others had. Mary knew he would never hurt Kathy. He would, in fact, die for her. Mary trusted him. It was for Mary he had given up the fiery pleasures of Ahmed, who still called him to rendezvous but who couldn't stomach to live there, or so he said. (Nobody had invited him.)

It was Ahmed nobody could trust. Nobody knew for sure what state of mind he would be in next, what he would do. The uncle who had backed their mortgage had no faith in Ahmed, either and was very conscious that money was desirable. Mary thought that Estes would make good, even to the uncle's satisfaction. Mary saw Estes as a nice Indiana boy, conscientious, whose family had rejected him over his sexual preferences long before anybody had ever heard of Vietnam. He probably would have been in Canada anyway, or some other retreat.

Estes's talents were strong. In New York, he had auditioned with Graham, had danced one summer with Lemming. As for permanence with any company, something always went wrong at the last minute.

"We could work together," he ventured on Mary's return to Montreal. He sounded casual; like a timid man proposing, he held his breath and almost shook. But weren't they working together already?

"Okay with me," she said at once. He went joyously straight to apply for a grant from Ottawa. There was money for such combinations. He gave her the small room upstairs for nothing, while waiting to be answered.

Mary wrote to Gordon and Gerda Stewart:

Don't worry. I know you must have lost the bail money you put up for me, but I'm back in touch with the probation lady. I quit the psychiatrist. Thank you for getting me permission to keep

Kathy. I'm working and I'll pay you back. It's all I have in mind.
Mary.

Mary may even have thought that this last was true, except it couldn't
happen yet. There was food to buy out of Fred Davis's monthly
check, and money from Ethan and Jeff was for needed extras—when
it came.

Jeff and Mary walked home together from the Purple Window. It
was a route narrowed at times by banks of snow, heavy with chunks
of ice, dimly lit. Dimmer still as the business and university areas
dropped behind and the eastern city opened up its devious streets
before them. Small crooked corner shops appeared and passed—
dépanneurs, they were called—wearing faintly legible signs.

"Ethan was here," said Mary.

"He told me. He brought a stack of letters."

"All the San Francisco ones. Some earlier I never got."

"Lost somewhere. In some old locker in a bus station in the middle
of Texas."

"Are you still on the run?"

"I guess I always will be. The Big Job, you know. The damned
thing backfired. Still . . . it's done."

"What good did it do?"

"It was one more thing, don't you see? They've got to stop some-
time. Or so we tell ourselves."

He sounded tired of his own voice.

"Ethan's publication is folding," he told her. "No more 'From the
Front Lines' by your roving patriot, Jefferson Blaise."

"Ethan's too sick," she guessed. She walked close as if to warm
him, the cold being a new thing for him. "So what will you do now?"

"Work here if they'll let me alone. We've still got those immigrant
papers."

"Let you alone?" she repeated.

"I must be on the books for something in every state I've lived in
for more than a week. Jesus, you're the only warm thing in the world,
aren't you?"

"I've gotten used to it, is all. We're right up the next street. Just
a block. Let's run."

Estes, waiting, heard footsteps on the stairs below, more than one pair of them. He grabbed up his robe, reached for his trousers, stood waiting and dreading Ahmed, those quarrels he brought with him like the coat on his back, repulsive companions apt to be stoned, all that riffraff Ahmed could pick up. Kathy waking. Then the steps quieted down to one pair and he recognized Mary's.

She came in quietly, with her own mouselike peering around the barely cracked-open door, her eyes seeking out first Kathy's little mound, now thrashing around in wakefulness, then turning to Estes. She closed the door and crossed the room to him, with the floating motion of not seeming to move, the way he admired. He had barely fastened his trousers. She laid a gentle hand on his wrist. "It's Jeff," she said. "He's come back."

"Oh," was all he said—nothing more, just the one word. When he spoke again he seemed to be distant, his voice muffled. "Kathy?" he said at last. "Do you want to take her?"

"Could she stay here? If we wake her up . . . and she'll want—"

"Sure. Let her stay."

"Estes. . . ." She tiptoed and put her arms gently around him. Then, like someone with a gift of becoming invisible, she was soundlessly gone. The pairs of footsteps resumed, going upward.

That night Estes wept. Dimly, Mary seemed to hear the sound of it floating up from below. Exhausted from travel and love, Jeff slept like a stone. But Estes must have awakened Kathy, who crept upstairs by herself. A knower, though small. She hadn't had to be told that her mother was behind the door she struck her fists against, pushing, thumping, but waiting confidently, all the same, to be let in.

It was the one night Estes could never bear to remember, the night in his life he felt a testing that must be a lot like being in a war. His soul seemed straining to tell him something; his heart was trying to jump out of his chest. Once again, what was his was being taken from him. It wasn't fair. Even when he slept, Mary came right into his dreams. His fantasy arms had folded her to him, time and again. They did so now.

In troubled half sleep he saw Jeff Blaise, hairy as a bear unnaturally walking upright, fallen ferocious and avid across her small body. And she, with a witch's smile, welcomed a monster.

Of course, he didn't rationally think that. He woke and went to the window. The inner of the double panes was cold but clear, the outer piled halfway up with snow. He leaned his head against the pane, looking out through a frame of snow. Picture postcard.

The gods were looking in. They saw Estes's face framed there. They laughed. He thumbed his nose at them. He would go on.

3

A Sigh from Madeleine Spivak
(Whose Heart Does Not Grow Old)

She thought she saw Jeff Blaise.

She did not think it, she knew it. She saw a sturdily built young man walking away from her down a length of street, St. Catherine, just where it takes a slant down from the center to join the streets in the east that run up from the river. There was an outline, a cutout like a child's cardboard image, in her heart, and he (and only he) can fit into it, exact.

Her heart gave a jump as if to prove it true. *(But his hair was blond, now it's dark. Never mind, it's him.)* Her heart felt as if voltage had gone into it, direct. She felt the shock travel outward, head to toe to fingertips. Her eyes blurred. She hastened, only to see, just to see. To speak, maybe. If he's here, then she must be here, too. *I'll only speak,* she thought. *I gave you up in that other way. As we both understood so well. I gave you up forever.*

But he veered suddenly, did not ever once look back, though seemed to know he had to hurry. Turned into a tiny street nearby between two rows of tall old houses, red brick, a snowy alley. When she got there it was empty except for garbage pails and a fence with a gate in it, no footprints and the snow piled high, a long drop of steps down from a second floor fire escape, no footprints. Piled high with snow. *Les neiges blanches et eternelles.*

So will my quieted heart be, a still gate in a fence, piled high with snow, thought Madeleine Spivak.

4

Gerda Stewart's Journal

It was sometime after the boys left us, married, and on to better things ("Montreal's a dead city," they said. "The French are out to ruin it."), that I had a serious talk with Gordon. "If we don't watch out," I said, "we will start choosing the best retirement home, where we can go mark time till the grave. We have got to save our lives." "How?" he asked. "We will do it," I said, "by our enthusiasms."

Sure enough, it worked. Not by taking to cross-country skiing, but by trips, each year a different island. We started with Bermuda and worked downward. By the time we had reached the British Virgin Islands in the Caribbean, having gone through Nassau, Jamaica, Puerto Rico, St. Croix, and St. Thomas, that was about when the anti-war movement arrived and with it those children, Mary and Jeff. We shelved the islands for a time. Gordon said they would remain right where they were.

It's clear to me now that Gordon was long overdue—as much as ten years, according to one authority—for his midlife crisis. In other words, he was due to fall in love. I'm only a little resentful, now that it's over, not of him, but of her. How could she have turned him down? I might have wound up divorced, it's true, but I doubt it. I doubt her ever fitting into Gordon's life style. Yet they did each have, I decided, something important in common. An odd thing: decorum.

Her poor little one room and kitchenette she settled in in Gordon's house might have been a cave, a mud hut, a tepee. But how quietly she made it her own. Bright with cheap little ornaments, cushions, spreads, and plants.

She said she was "tribal," something drawn out of the anthropology study she meant to major in, but I think it may have been a discipline, the sort a dancer cultivates day by day, keeping the steps neat, graceful, precise. She said the suicide she tried was only to get out of the way. Whose way? I asked her that. "Everybody's," she said, and threaded a needle to mend something, squinting at the process. Mending was so domestic it couldn't be done by a desperate girl. Seeing it astonished me; it wrenched at my heart.

Then she was gone, and Gordon fell to his real depths. Even when she ran out on the bail he'd put up—is every young person in an entire American generation out on bail for something or other done in defiance of a society they've no use for except to get them to write checks?—even then Gordon could do nothing but stammer about it, trying to understand it, never to blame her. Gone. Gone from the house he owned, had sheltered her in, and not a word.

Gordon faded like a flower; his spirits ebbed. He did not speak of her at all.

But all at once, he tells me he's seen her again!

The Metro mistake. Maybe he wanted to take the wrong train and only said it was a mistake. I wonder how often he sights her. Now, he tells me, the husband is back too. Jeff. I have a hard time remembering his name. Gordon has now seen them together. He is firm about it. He goes West on a business trip to a branch firm in Calgary. Alone in strange hotels, he will think of her, how she linked in step with that stern young man who looked me straight in the eye in a snow-crusted street that day that seems long ago now, but always to be remembered, a flash of light, a sighting from another world.

I need a new enthusiasm. I find one. Plants!

I am building a greenhouse. I discover new names. *Mimosa pudica, cryptanthus, maranta leuconeur*—their very sound excites me. Dieffenbachia, peperomia, and philodendron are abounding and easy, but Jerusalem cherry, Norfolk Island pine, and *passi-flora* (passionflower!) are ones you must hover over. I may even go on to orchids. I haunt the florist shops; I visit the botanical gardens.

Gordon complains he is getting hay fever at the wrong time of year. "You must get interested, too," I tell him. "It's better to share enthusiasms." This or something like it, I feel, must grow to fill the place for him of Mary Blaise.

What better thing is there to find when you get home from fighting with snow and ice, slipping and sliding, one side of your face stinging from the peppering of driven sleet, nose red and wet, feet numb from standing in slush trying to hail a taxi or wait for a bus—what better thing than the warm, close moisture of these exotically named creatures, alive, breathing out their secret life.

I have stopped going to the tarot reader because the last time there she told me, looking up from a strange card—the picture of a man wading out into a river and looking back toward the shore—*"Il n'est pas souvent qu'arrive l'amour."* Love doesn't happen often. Of course not. I recognized at once from the card what I was being told. It was Gordon out there, deep in the river of love. Those cards will get through to trouble me, every time.

5

The Halcyon Summer

The spring when Mary performed at the Passez-à-Droit Théatre on rue du Sénat opened the best period of their lives. She and Estes had choreographed the entire program and the six dancers they had practiced with brought new ideas in every day, as if they had been sent out to scavenge them. Were they gypsies, had they sprung up out of the ground when the final snows had melted? Only Estes, it seemed, knew where they had come from, or even who each one was, and each history. Two were from the United States, resisters like Jeff, and one, a black, had been in Chicago in '69 during the rampage attendant on the trials, and had often heard talk of Jeff Blaise. He had also, by coincidence (a visit home), been near the scene of the Martin Luther King assassination, and had seen something suspicious that he had thought of reporting, but he trusted no one these days. His elevation was higher than anyone's in the group, except at times Mary's; it was his feelings, he said, that sent him soaring so high. Two of the women were French and a third a Greek from Skýros. She was beautiful, with great almond eyes. They starred her in a routine they had worked up called "Arachne," where she became the center of circling dancers who were reeling and tumbling about her, at last fixing themselves in a web.

Mary scarcely bothered with their names. She had felt no interest in names since those days of meetings at Ethan's house, when all those anonymous, nonkin people, students of Ethan's, disciples, came trouping in out of the dark, to sit over wine and talk ideas, events, eat pizza and pretzels, dressed any which way. There were just faces, intense, bright, here today, gone tomorrow, endlessly replaceable. Some names were forever: Ethan, Jeff, Estes.

She sat up at night making costumes, practiced routines until she was too sore to climb stairs. Kathy was in nursery school. Jeff taught part-time in a high school—CEGEP, it was called—and had just found a second job in a school across the river, more advanced, reached by Metro.

Afternoons in weather still cool but sunny, as summer came slowly on, he would go by for Kathy at her school, then take her home to the little apartment below the studio where the dancers were practicing to a beat of taped music, off and on. "Once again. *Encore un autre fois.*"

Mary changed her name. She became Marie Carrée. Jeff was back with his old alias as Blaylock. Of course, he could be tracked, if anybody wanted to badly enough, but no need to advertise the name.

"Someday," he would say to Mary, when they were down to their last few dollars before some money came in, "we'll pay Fred Davis back." Sometimes she would join in, saying it with him. They would then collapse with laughter. Fred Davis had become as much a myth to them as Arachne. He seemed to have descended from another world at some unspecified prehistoric date and left an order for them to receive a monthly check.

Both the French and English papers in Montreal noted the performance of the group which called itself Les Huits. There were comparisons to Arthur Manning and Laura Lemming, calls to have more modern dance in Montreal, supplementing the steady brilliance of Les Grands Ballets Canadiens. Estes Drover gave interviews both in French and English. He had managed to work up enough French from having to do business in Montreal. He'd yet to take a lesson or study grammar from a book. Mary refused interviews. She would say, *"Il parle pour moi."*

Estes bought himself a green velvet jacket and wore a flowing black satin tie. The papers said he was enriching the city. *"Pourquoi 'Les Huits'?"* he rhetorically repeated. *"Il est un nombre parfait. L'octave s'est composée de huits sons divers, qui montent, vous savez, et qui descendent."*

He and Mary had devised a routine based on the figure eight, a moving mandala chain to the music of a Bach fugue. The group presented it as a first number, then returned to it briefly at the show's end. Estes was furiously accumulating reviews and applying for more grant money from Ottawa and Quebec.

Jeff made his dutiful calls to Ethan. Apologies for calling collect, a pay phone was necessary, Mary thought their line was bugged and might be right. "Think what a long way we've come." It was the job he meant, and Mary's dancing.

"Remember this," Ethan said. "All we did had to matter. No one could ever tell me differently. If not for us, all of us, crying out together, they would have had carte blanche. Each person was only a small link, but together we formed the human chain that turned them back." So he also wrote, in a hand weakened from the dire treatments they were throwing at him, often blundering into shapeless mistakes, wrenching to see on the page.

"I believe everything you are saying," Jeff told him. "I won't forget."

Ethan would die convinced the Movement had stopped the use of nuclear weapons in Vietnam.

Jeff called him from pay telephone booths, giving the number, waiting for Ethan to ring back. Lines were tapped, so the grapevine said. Canada playing patsy to the powerful bully to the south. Still, Jeff could describe his job as proof he'd landed on his feet. "The weather's not the greatest," he told Ethan. "But it's impossible not to be grateful. You might almost call it a free country."

"Apply to McGill for next year," Ethan advised. "I've got at least one strong connection."

"I can't blot it out that the thesis failed."

"Canada might take another view of it. Have you brought it with you?"

"I've got it somewhere. How are you?" Jeff kept asking. "Is it better?" A hundred times he'd vowed to come there, to get across the border some way. He'd done it before. He vowed to speak Cajun French and pretend to be from Guadeloupe.

"If you dare it," Ethan said, "I'll not draw a peaceful breath. Too much risk. Too many counts out against you. Promise. No, you must."

Jeff promised. Every word might be the last exchange. He went around with phrases ringing in his head. And all the words previously spoken as well, back through the years, winding back to the day he had first seen the gabled house, the afternoon he had sat before the Renoir in the Washington art gallery and said, "I want to go to France." *My master is dying; more than a father, he gave me a mind, a destiny.* He went around with stinging eyes, not from the wind.

Then he was standing near the stage door of the Passez-à-Droit Théatre, waiting for Mary and Les Huits to finish their closing performance. In a moment the door would fly open. Already there was the first of the final applause. He felt a presence behind him and turned to face Madeleine Spivak.

"It's Jeff, isn't it?" she said in the silence of his deliberately blank reserve. He was grizzled from a winter's growth of beard, not at all what he'd been before, but she could not forget his features.

"Yes, Madeleine. Are you well?"

She said yes, that she was well. He saw her then as timid, a sophisticate made timid by her feelings, so he bent and put a whiskered kiss on her cheek. "There's no way I can see you," he told her. Some days were fuller of feelings than seemed possible.

"Not even to talk a little?"

He shook his head. "There's no way."

She touched his hand and seemed, in her black coat, to melt backward from him into the nighttime side street beside the theater. He turned to welcome Mary, who was spent and glowing.

"Three curtain calls! The last one, they all stood up!" She ran under his outstretched arm.

I was recognized, Jeff thought, walking home with her, uneasy in the darkness. *Recognized.*

Summer weather, hot at last. They borrowed a car and drove into the mountains. They followed country roads and did not even wonder where they were leading to. Saint-Saveur, St. Jovite, Ste. Adèle, Ste. Agathe, Mont Tremblant. All these were known to skiers, as were country cottages, ski lodges, lakeside and roadside and mountainside were hidden among the leaves. They parked by lakes and swam, Jeff teaching Kathy to dog-paddle a little, and Mary, who swam like a duck, daring distant rocks, gaining solitary rafts, where she spread out flat in sunlight, or rose straight from her toes. She lifted her pale arms and stretched her dancer's back, flat as a board. She stood on one foot and pointed a toe at the sun. "I'm thinking of an Aztec dance," she called to Jeff. He didn't answer. He had been silent for a long time now.

Mary swam back to the pier. They had not asked themselves whose place this was, or why it was so deserted. They simply took what they found. She pulled up, dripping. "Come swim with me," she said to Kathy, who was sailing a toy boat.

"I don't want to," said Kathy.

"They do human sacrifice," said Jeff.

"Who?" Mary asked.

"The Aztecs," he answered.

"Can I be a yuman sacrifice?" Kathy inquired.

Mary said she couldn't.

Jeff brought a tape deck down and put on some rock music. They danced a little, barefoot on the pier. The sun held steady. "You'd be good if you practiced more," Mary told him.

"I'm good already," said Jeff.

"Oh," said Mary, sitting down, "I want my old Jeff back, just the way you were. You look older in that beard. And all that dark hair. I don't like it. Nobody cares if you're up here. I don't think they care."

"Oh, they'll keep caring, all right. But so do I. Care, I mean. That night we did the Job—for one thing it was dark, way darker than we'd counted on. I'd coached them what to do, but one guy hadn't showed and then I had to take part as well. I didn't tell you, did I, that somebody got shot. Just when we were clearing out. Still, the main generators did blow up. The plant itself, nothing it was doing was supposed to be known about. But after that people knew, the papers printed it. Not just our little paper, Ethan's; our readers knew all along. But the big ones. The San Francisco ones first, then others. I think it even made the New York ones. Ethan said so. Half of everybody got convicted. I should have been, too."

"You saved lives," she said. "Ruined some new torture they'd invented."

"Anti-personnel, they called it. Left you blind, deaf, and paralyzed. Friendly little things."

They were ready to go on. But walking toward the car, they saw a path leading away from the road to the pier, and at the end of it an A-frame cottage, white with bright red trim, like a gingerbread house, Mary thought, in a fairy tale. They all saw it at once and without discussion moved toward it. It was obviously empty. No car, as Jeff had remarked, had been on that road all summer. The weeds were high, the tracks grown over.

They walked to the door with Kathy between them, each holding one of her hands. Jeff tried the door but found it locked. Mary tried a window, which opened. They put Kathy through the window and she opened the door for them.

Within, the cottage was more spacious than it had seemed to be from the outside, with a large living room, set about with couches, dressed with Indian throw rugs and large cushions. The stone fireplace reached to the ceiling. A bronze fire set stood on the hearth. Jeff remembered Mrs. Bethany Burlingham and all but laughed out loud. They sat down together on the bright, ample, woven rug before the empty cavity.

The interior remembered winter. No one had come to tell it differently. They had never lived in a house before, not in five years of marriage, and never before that. Rooms, small apartments, a roof above them, cramped quarters, waiting till Kathy slept to make love. Jeff was sure she knew all about it anyway. "Nothing surprises that kid," was what he said. And he said, too, "I go around trying to live up to her."

In the cottage, above their heads, was a free stairway with a rope railing, like something on a ship, running up to a balconied level above. At either end, doors, probably leading to bedrooms, a real bathroom, maybe. Through windows toward the back, they could see a woodstack piled up neatly, the top logs just touching the panes.

"If only we could stay a while," said Jeff.

Mary had sprawled out on the rug. Kathy was sitting comfortably upon her.

"Let's," said Mary, and stretched like a cat.

"They must have a caretaker," she added. She felt at home.

"Not in evidence at present," he noted.

"Let's live here!" Kathy shouted.

They laughed, then fell silent.

Jeff stood up. "Okay," he said. "Let's."

They shopped for food in St. Jovite. Jeff brought his load of books in from the car. Ethan's latest reading list: long, detailed records of American moves in Mexico, Canal negotiations, Far Eastern strategies in diplomacy. Ethan's letter, the handwriting shaky, the words firm:

Look for the straight lines working beneath all the apparent backing and filing. They're there for us, more often than not. It's this sort of knowledge, banked up, that will turn you into the significant lecturer, maybe even writer, that was my vision. . . .

Fathers do not give up, Jeff recognized wryly. Mary made a late lunch. They brought in wood for a fire. They were as careful with what they found as jewel thieves.

At the grocery where they drove in to shop Mary found a drawing book and crayons for Kathy. "What color are bears?" asked Kathy.

"Brown," said Jeff.

"Black," said Mary, "and sometimes white, like polar bears."

"If you have three bears, are they brown and black and white?"

"That wouldn't work, not in the same family," her mother said.

"We're the three bears," said Jeff. "Goldilocks is coming with a shotgun, any minute."

But nothing happened. At the end of the week, with no grocery money left, Jeff gathered up enough firewood from the forest to replace what they had used. How carefully they swept out the fireplace and buried the ashes. How devotedly they washed and dried the sheets and pillowcases and cup towels and bath towels in the Laundromat in St. Jovite. How they cleaned and swept.

The night before, Kathy asleep for a contented final night in an upstairs room, Mary and Jeff had sat cross-legged before the fire and smoked the last of the small store of grass Jeff had brought from Montreal. The time went slowly, wordlessly, like a ritual, and slowly, too, they made love before the fire for the last time there. Firelight flickered over them, their strong young bodies moving in counterpoint with the flame's uncertain motions.

On the way back to Montreal, about to leave the little weed-grown roadway, Jeff stopped the car and turned to Mary. "I've never been so happy as I was there."

"I was happy, too."

"Me, too," Kathy echoed.

"I see why people put up monuments. But not for dead people. There ought to be monuments to great moments." He got out of the car and stood, raising his hand and finger, writing on the air: "Mary, Jeff, and Kathy . . . they were happy here." He stood for a time, looking back to where the road turned and up at the sky, toward dark clouds standing majestically up against the sun.

Reentering the car, he kissed Mary. "There's got to be something," he said. "Skywriting is better than nothing." He started the motor and drove on.

Along the auto route called Les Laurentides, a fierce thunderstorm overtook them, the rain so heavy they were forced to draw to the side of the road. Kathy was frightened and climbed over into her mother's lap. The thunder could be heard crashing, back along the lakes and forests they had left behind. They could see the flashes of lightning intensely repeated in the car mirror. "Jesus, it's sure catching it up there now," said Jeff. They saw the storm lift and pass.

Once they rejoined the highway, lanes multiplied and the tall city began to rise before them, the highway to swirl and melt into urban ramps and approaches. Shopping centers clipped past and row on row of high-rise apartment complexes. CENTRE DE VILLE, read the huge green sign. MCDONALD'S, cried a billboard. ST. LAURENT, boomed the signs, RUE DE LA GAUCHETIÈRE, LE POULET FRIT DE KAINTUCKY, RUE ST.-DENIS, L'UNIVERSITÉ DE MONTRÉAL, HOLI-DAY INN.

"We don't belong here," said Jeff.

"But we are here," said Mary.

"Polar bears are yellow," said Kathy. *"Ils sont jaunes."* She fell asleep on her mother's shoulder.

Mary was wondering if in the last routine she had worked out with Estes they were making their spirals reach too far toward the back of stage left. But if they moved to center stage . . .

6

The Main Line

Fred Davis stood before the green even spread of his lawn, so lately mowed and rolled by the same gardeners his father had dealt with before him. Like God on the Sunday of Creation Week, he saw that it was good. He circled, careful to step on flagstones. He checked the slates on the slope of roof above the library. He wandered to the end of the drive to ponder over a stone tool and storage outhouse, no longer in use. Convert it to some purpose? Tear it down? The fashioning was pure Pennsylvanian, native rock, rough surfaces, made to last. He let go of nothing. The lilacs, their blooms spent, had been nicely pruned.

Reluctantly, he turned his mind to treasures within. Kate, her blond hair turning gray with what went on inside her mind. They had just returned from a cruise. The Greek Isles, memories of Odysseus, the wine-dark deep, Penelope weaving as she waited out the years. Kate on deck, her eager talk throughout one afternoon, all facing off with a fellow researcher she had brought to light among the passengers. "We were all but there, I could see it just around the corner." A detailed account, featuring . . . changes in chromosomes . . . amino acids . . . variations in DNA . . . the researcher and his wife nodding in unison, the swish of evening waters, no island in sight. How, in this sea, freckled with islands, could there ever be a whole hour with no island in sight? Nearing Crete, they said. But no Crete so far.

"You certainly took an original approach," the researcher had agreed. "Too bad it got cancelled that way. No funding is the big cry in the whole business, the cutoff signal."

"When the tap runs dry . . ." his wife said.

"There ain't no water no more," he finished.

Kate burst in, "Oh, but you see there would have been. We had additional funding from a defense contract. It's just that my daughter—"

"I'm going down to dress," Fred told her, turning from the rail, hoping there was warning in his voice. *If she got started on Mary Kerr . . . But how did you ever stop her?*

Later, behind the researcher and his wife in the ship's corridor, Fred heard them exchange notes.

"That particular approach to the amino acids was checked out as early as '70."

"I thought so, but I didn't dare try to stop her."

That night Kate had fallen on the dance floor, though with a suddenly rough sea he managed to cover for her. Later she had been sick in the state room.

Alone on his impeccable lawn now, moving over his property, he knew that what he was doing was circling, avoiding the move of coming face-to-face with Kate. Confrontations led to decisions; decisions to action. Did he dare?

Inside, what did it matter what she was actually doing on this fair summer morning? It was her mind that made the climate he would have to enter. Mary Kerr and Kathy. Obsessively she dwelt on them. A drink would break the circuits. But the break itself was deadly.

This beautiful creature, found by chance, Fred told himself, was his to preserve, even to the point of killing for her.

Killing? He had just happened to stumble on the phrase. *Yet it might,* he concluded, *be what is now required.* Ethan Marbell, whom she lavishly blamed, was said to be dying. No reason to doubt that. But Jefferson Blaise was always healthily present among the dregs of her bitter cup. Her daughter's life, with that gruesome mate, would remain cursed as long as he lived.

Fred began to wonder how to pluck him loose so the poison could flow out, the streams clear. He thought he might travel a little. He would see what he could do.

7

Gerda's Journal

It is curious to report that the day I heard about the Satterfields' cottage burning down in the Laurentians, I was preparing to have a meeting of a writers' group in my house. Writing in my journal, to begin with, was what started me thinking I might take up writing seriously, and that connection was what led me once again to wonder about Mary Blaise. Perhaps I could write something—story or article—about her. Why not? A war resister's wife, known personally, might furnish an interesting subject. But how to find her? At the moment, finding her seemed of prime importance in the path ahead which I meant to travel. I would interview her. I wouldn't tell Gordon.

Searching through my memory, I came across the name of Leonard Abel, someone who had been inviting her to dinner and making noises of sympathy—Jewish, from someplace in Europe, now living out in the Notre Dame de Grâce section. I went straight in from the irises, took off my garden gloves, washed my hands, and searched the phone book. The Abels.

A woman answered. A baby was crying. She had to shout. She was calling for Leonard. I remembered he worked at the Jewish cultural center. Maybe they were closed till the fall. He must be out of school by now.

"Mary Blaise?" His voice hesitated. "Yes, we do still see her. I'm uncertain just where she lives. Perhaps I could look it up for you. May I ask who you are? I said, to whom do I speak?"

People who have learned English speak like that. I told him my name. Yes, he had heard of me. Mary had spoken of Gordon and me.

"Her husband's back," he said. "You didn't know that? She took the little girl and moved to east Montreal with him. We don't know where they live. Perhaps I can find out. Is it urgent? We've got our hands full now, you know. A baby boy." His voice shuddered with pride.

As I hung up, something else occurred to me. If I told Gordon my plan for writing about her, I could tell by his response what he felt. I would know if he was still in touch. It would be a clever, peaceful way.

No sooner had I put the phone down than it rang. Margery Satterfield was calling to say she and George were back from Madeira, a fine vacation, except for the bad news that in their absence their cottage in the Laurentians had burned. The roof and two walls were gone completely, the furnishings ruined beyond repair.

Now here is the unbelievable part, the reason I am writing in my journal once more, not doing any article or story, but just setting down this weird coincidence.

Gordon returned home that night upset about Mary Blaise. Not in the way I might have suspected, but about the Satterfield house! Mary had been seen up there by someone who had known her in her early days in Montreal. Someone who had lived, like her, in the house on Seymour Street.

I said, "What's that got to do with the Satterfield house?"

"She's suspected of having burned it down, that's all."

I thought I must be psychic. Mental telepathy must certainly be at work.

Gordon was not very interested in such theories. "No end to her misfortunes," was his comment. "Good deeds don't go unpunished. Now they're after me."

"After you? Why?"

"My name on her records. That suicide, paying bail. Her whereabouts are wanted, no recent updating of reports . . . thought to have left Montreal for the States. I said for all I knew she had."

"But you know better. You told me you sighted her, that day you took the wrong Metro."

He didn't answer.

It wasn't Leonard Abel who called the next day. It was Mary herself. A strained, rapid voice, begging to speak to Gordon. *So she doesn't stay in touch with him.*

"Can't you tell me what's wrong, dear?" I inquired, in a motherly tone.

"There's been an accident. Too complicated to explain. They think I set a house on fire. Also, they are looking for Jeff. He's here, but he doesn't go by Jeff anymore. They may find that out. If only Gordon will tell them I'm not into burning houses, had nothing to do with it, maybe they'll go away. We were up there, but then we cleaned up and left."

It was such a torrent spilling out that I couldn't think what to say, but when I didn't reply, she cried out, "I want to be believed! I want you to believe me!"

"We've always believed you, Mary. It's just that we haven't seen anything of you, or so far as I know you've not exactly been in touch. . . ."

"I know, I know. I don't like worrying people. I thought you all had done enough for us. With Jeff back, we shouldn't be begging or imposing."

She has this Southern accent, stronger at times than others. I thought she said "impoison." "What?" I asked.

"*Imposen,*" she shouted, and then I knew she was coming apart from whatever had happened.

Gordon was just entering the house, fresh from work. "Who's that?" He was hanging up his hat.

"It's Mary," I said, first putting my hand over the mouthpiece.

Astonishing. I was about to hand the phone to him. But he shook his head. "I'll call her," he said. I told her we would call her, took a number, and hung up.

Gordon sat down like a visitor, on a little chair in the entrance hall. He had not even taken off his mackintosh.

"She is going to want me to verify that boy as a blameless character, just somebody who can't agree with American policy."

"Well . . . isn't he?"

"No, he isn't."

He got up, removing his coat, and hung it up. He did not speak of it again until dinner. We had by then reviewed our social invitations for the weekend and decided whom to cancel from the guest list for our annual Canadian Thanksgiving Day cocktail party.

A silence fell over dinner, and Gordon said, "There have been some remarks at the office."

"About what?"

"The police. They sent someone by this time. I had to go out to talk with the officer and return. It came very close to having to go to the precinct station." He put aside his napkin. "I cannot, of course, support it."

"Is it so dangerous?" But I knew I shouldn't ask. Gordon has been with the Hudson Trust since we were first married—his minor position then has led always on to higher things. Now there is talk of promoting him to director of realties in greater Montreal, a position demanding the highest respect.

"It isn't widely known, but people here are getting blacklisted in the U.S. Not allowed to cross the border."

"You mean, like criminals?"

He sighed. "The authorities have to be careful. Precautions are necessary. I am risking that."

He was silent once more and (psychic again, if that is really my nature, as I firmly believe it to be) I knew that he was remembering her, the sweet and appealing nature that fate had cast before him, on his path through life.

But firmness with Gordon will always, finally, win. He would have to do the Right Thing. He would have to reveal what he knew to those who had the public trust to be in charge.

8

Gerda's Journal: Great Drama!

Great Drama!

Last evening we all went over there, over to east Montreal at their request, not only hers, Mary's, but her husband's, too. It was almost formal, like a formal engraved invitation, if you consider the dignified, commanding way it was put. First him on the phone, then her.

I thought we would be the only ones. However, a number of people were there, climbing up a stair in one of those rickety old three-story houses over near rue Rachel, one of those. We found ourselves greeted by Mary and Jeff, and Kathy, too, grown up enough to walk around and smile at everybody, wearing a little pinafore, blue, with a ruffle. Jeff—it was he, I now knew without a doubt, that I saw in that snow-plagued street, even with his beard grown out to hide his face; those eyes would give him away as fast as fingerprints— Jeff shook our hands and arranged some folding chairs for us to sit in, as long as they lasted; then he found some big cushions to put down on the floor. Mary gave the group of us a few glasses and odds and ends of cups, some cracked, to hold a little wine poured out from a large bottle of St. Emilion. We sat on chairs. Who were these people?

One by one, in a very polite manner, almost as if we were involved in some sort of ritual, we were introduced. There was Jeff's principal from the school he taught in, at Champlain, across the river. And a dancer Mary worked with, a tall haggard-looking man with sensitive eyes. The Abels, of course, and she with the baby in her arms, so proud she was all but suckling it in public. There were a couple from something called the Purple Window and a black man with them from somewhere in the South. Rags and tags of the human race. I know that people like this exist, but I am never thrown with them. I sat thinking I should have cancelled the writers' meeting, no time to get ready before tomorrow afternoon, tonight I was going to make up the sandwich spreads. What was this all about? We hardly dared to murmur at one another when in walked the Satterfields! They looked a little scared to be there at all, and infinitely glad to see Gordon and me.

As soon as they were introduced and seated with cracked cups of wine in hand, Jeff Blaise went to the end of the room and started to speak. We all looked toward him; we all grew quiet. I don't know how to speak of him as he was at that moment. Not tall, he still had the address, the presence, of an imposing person. He looked like the accumulation of all the things he'd seen and done and believed in. Superior. I watched Mary looking at him. He was being every bit what she thought of him. She sat with her legs tucked gracefully to one side, her arm around the little girl. A family.

"Well, I got everybody here so you'd know straight from me," said Jeff Blaise, "what happened in the Laurentians, up near St. Jovite. Mary and Kathy and I—well, you know us all, except for Mr. and Mrs. Satterfield—and maybe we're the same to you as I see us myself. We've been blown up here by a storm, waifs of the storm, as I see it. I myself was fighting the best I could, trying not just to wait it out but to do what I could to make it abate. I wanted to help, to restore some sense of the purpose and pride my own country ought to have—whether you agree with me or not isn't the point right now—the point is that I was sincere in what I did. I've risked my whole career—the one that from time to time was bright ahead of me—and for all I know now, I've lost any chance of that career. But I don't go around setting other people's houses on fire for no reason.

"My wife, Mary, here, and our little girl, Kathy—we went up there just for the day, to rest a little, because she and Estes Drover and some others had just put on quite a show with Les Huits—they were the leaders of that. She was tired and I was tired from teaching and keeping Kathy, so we went up there. Just when we were leaving we found the Satterfield house by accident and—well, we just quietly and with great respect did what we've been doing in your country for some years now: we refugeed in it. We took care of everything. We washed everything we used. We expected every day that a watchman would come—you ought to know this, Mr. and Mrs. Satter-field—if you've got a caretaker hired, you're wasting your money. He didn't show up for the whole week.

"I think I may have improved things a little. I repaired two sets of back shutters that were falling off, and mended the porch steps. They had gotten dangerous. We locked the front window when we left, along with the door. I thought we'd done so well, in fact, I even wished you'd been able to come back and see it and know we did it, but we didn't really want that to happen. What I saw us as was shadows that come and go—friendly spirits, Mary would say. She's better at things like that than I am.

"When we drove away, there was a heavy cloud coming on from the west, or rather northwest, behind us, and we had to stop by the side of the road when it overtook us, pelting down rain. It struck the heaviest back behind us, where we'd left. We could watch the flashes in our rearview mirror and see the rain curtain coming down. So in my opinion it was the storm that happened to the house. Lightning struck it. I think that if you get anybody to look closer, that will show up as the true explanation. I hear that a part of the wall with the fireplace was left and that some roaches—excuse me, evidence of marijuana—were found there. Well, you know, we just do that, most of us—your kids, too, I wouldn't doubt. It's a sort of harmless ritual, is the way we look at it, like two martinis in the living room before dinner. We put everything out cold before we left the next day.

"The reason I wanted you all here, though, was to say that we've put your country to the same use that Mary and I put your house to, and we just want to thank you. We just want to say we're grateful for your welcome, or at least for your lack of hostility. It must come from knowing that people can have differences with their country's viewpoint, not just trying to be difficult, or get out of combat, but about some serious matters, hard to discuss here now.

"Just bear in mind that all the different efforts you've heard about, when you hear us blamed and laughed at, for beards and lice in our hair, how we're always stoned on rock music or pot or worse, shooting up, might be just superficial signs of something desperate and serious underneath. There are killing devices stockpiled that it would make you shudder to think of ever using again. There are killers planning more. I don't know for sure, but some people think that except for us, they might have gotten loose. The ones that did are bad enough. Maybe we were able to jar the steering wheel enough to change the course of things, that little bit that makes the difference.

"I'm probably leaving here pretty soon. There's a shadow of some sort off in the woods. Swamp shadow, you'd say, down where I come from. I'm not positive about it yet. If it wasn't lightning hit the house, then whatever hit it was for me.

"If I leave, just go on, please, being kind to Mary here"—he couldn't look at her—"and Kathy, too." He gave us a little awkward bow and sat down.

I guess we all choked up, brimming with cold Canadian tears. I saw Gordon's face looking stricken, knowing he'd lost her for good, but I knew that wasn't really what mattered. No, I could modestly say, in that moment, I knew what did matter. I saw beyond.

Those beautiful children—the two of them, I mean—who could have been so great in their own country, talented, with something to give. I quit worrying over the writers' club meeting. I was just bowled over with the realization of how complicated everything was for these children. How bad a thing displacement is. How many people go through it. I thought of our own two boys, leaving home for whatever reason, but basically not political. They call sometimes, they seldom write. So back of politics something else is out there, some other presence must be shadowing everyone, in a way, causing things to happen, setting new courses.

What do we do to them? What do we really do to our children?

9

Mary's Tape—Parting

The reason Jeff called that curious meeting was that it had come to the surface right away—too quickly not to be suspicious, according to Jeff—that his name was not Geoffrey Blaylock and that he was wanted in the States for blowing up a munitions plant. It was all a plot, was what he thought, but then he'd seen a lot of plots, some that he'd thought up himself. "Extradition" was the word now, or so we thought, because the provincial police had gotten in conversation with the RCMP before you could draw your breath and say it. But outside of filling in a lot of forms, nothing whatever happened. They said he could get a lawyer. Jeff said he would think about it. We'd certainly no money for that. We waited, but nothing happened.

Except that Ethan died.

I came in from practice at the theater and found Jeff home early, sitting on the bed, holding the news about Ethan like an object. I knew then what he would do. But I waited for him to tell me.

"I can't live in exile," was what he finally said, two days later. "I won't do it."

The three of us walked near the river, out on Isle Ste.-Hélène. We went up to an old watchtower built of stone. There were little walkways over streams, and a lake where swans floated, thinking whatever swans think about.

When we went to the airport, I left Kathy with Estes. The ticket was for Chicago. Jeff was meeting an editor there to discuss ways of writing for *Ramparts*. It was clear they valued him. It was also clear that if he could cross this time, he could keep on crossing, daring fate. I didn't know if it would work. I just knew he had to.

Back at Estes's place, he had huddled with Kathy, telling her all sorts of secret things to remember, to promise, to hang on to. It was nice she and Jeff loved each other. I always thought Jeff might think she was a nuisance until she got big enough to march in a protest.

It was October, the most beautiful time there, and because of Canadian Thanksgiving, Jeff had a long weekend off from work. We sat in the airport. I never held anybody's hand so tight. I had gotten cold on the way and he had given me a jacket of his to wear. We looked out the window at the planes and then it was time. He went toward the passport check. It took them awhile over his, but then they stamped it.

"Jeff," I said at the last minute, and started after him. They caught my arm and held me back. He vanished around the corner. It was his jacket. I meant to give it back. But because I still had it on, it seemed it was me and not him going off toward the plane. The jacket had his smell and contour and it seemed to be on him still. It was a strange division, or rather a kind of swap: me going, he staying.

I hung around awhile until I could see the plane through the window, leaving the ground for a cloudless cold blue sky. *Someday,* I thought as I walked away, *I'll ask him, "Did you think you were me, waiting down below, and I rising up with the plane, leaving?"* I bet if I thought it, he thought it, too. We had gotten like that, since he came back this time.

They picked him up in Chicago, at the airport. Somebody from the Justice Department. But, as Jeff said, it might as well have been the Immigration people, or the State Department, or the CIA, or the FBI, or any number of other forces kept handy for the purpose of gathering up whoever did unlawful things.

They took him back to San Francisco where it all had happened, and I was without him again, in Montreal.

10

Mary's Tape:
The Courier

Soon after that Aunt Jane found us.

It was really odd how she came strolling along one of the leafy streets in east Montreal, side by side with Miss McIlwraith, the retired nurse who wouldn't let me kill myself. Miss McIlwraith is one of those nonpeople Jeff calls the messengers of the gods. This is their purpose.

Miss McIlwraith was bringing Aunt Jane along, and while I did notice them just as I was going out at twilight to the *dépanneur*, I didn't know at first who she was, only that she was somebody from what I used to call home, somebody out of the past, somebody looking for us.

It was a calm, warm twilight, peaceful under the rich autumn trees with the streetlights splashing light through the leaves like rain. Aunt Jane was wearing those beautiful slender shoes and those trim soft clothes people down there, the uppercrust people, the ones I was brought up with, pride themselves on. The hours and hours that go into it, just getting those clothes together. Then it's a habit: they'd sooner walk naked than be without them.

But she was actually there, not just something to imagine. What had she come all that way for except me? But why would she bother?

Jane would be knowing things she'd learned from Ethan. But who could guess, even knowing that she loved him, what she had in mind now? When Mother and Fred begged to come and take me home, I found ways of dodging it. What's kin? An accident of blood (except for Poppy). But then, I had to remember, there was Aunt Sally, who was now going blind and couldn't sew anymore. She'd sent me a crooked scrawl of a letter, written all over, it took half a day to read

it. She wanted me to go down to New York and see a ballet at
Lincoln Center. She had put in a check for the fare, the ticket, and
the hotel bill. The letter was like her—messy and full of heart.

I walked right up and stood in front of her. "Aunt Jane," I said.
"It's me, Mary Kerr. Are you looking for me?"

"Oh, Mary Kerr!" She just about cried with relief. That part of
town was already distressing her. She had been picking her way
around some dog shit.

She stood staring at me, almost like she was afraid she'd catch
something if she kissed me. I was just wearing a denim skirt, faded,
and a checkered shirt. Kathy was at home with Estes. I said hello to
Miss McIlwraith, who said she had to go back home and water the
plants. We went into a little coffee shop.

"How'd you find me?" I asked. "You found her, I know, but how
did you do even that?"

"I knew a nurse there was kind to you, so I kept looking for her.
When I talked to her, she listened. She tried to telephone you but
nobody answered."

"We were at the theater; we do some practice work there." I
smiled. "We do dancing. We're dancers."

"Mary Kerr, I don't want to ask you anything."

That meant, in terms of Kingsbury, North Carolina, that she
wanted to ask about everything. *Then what's on your mind?* I almost
said, but instead said nothing. I saw Aunt Jane out of place at the
cheap little table in the shop, her coffee in a thick white mug, sur-
rounded by signs about Coke ("*y de la joie!*") and *le bon pain français,*
none of which Aunt Jane could read. Her gray hair was shorter and
fluffier, and though her clothes looked expensive still, they didn't
seem to matter quite as much—that must be Ethan's influence. How
they'd had this romance going, and how she was proud of that now,
just knowing she'd had something like that in her life—maybe she'd
come all this way just to let it be known.

"Looks like you and Ethan would have gotten married." I did not
mean to say it aloud, but did anyway.

"It would have been foolish at our age," said Jane. "And besides,
he had a wife already. Also, there happened to be a point of chief
contention. We never resolved it. He was too radical for me. You
can't marry someone you believe to be basically wrong."

"What about his wife? Jeff knew her."

"Oh, Sybil. She lives in Mexico, almost the whole year around.

They had a son she lives with off and on. She came at the last, but only for a little while, a day or so; then she said it might be a long while yet that he had to live, though we all knew better, and went away up to Baltimore to some relatives. She came to the funeral."

I was silent.

"She wore jet black like a Mexican woman, with a black lace—what do they call them?—mantilla. She looked absurd to me. Lots of silver jewelry. I suppose she thought she was showing us how grieving ought to be done."

"But it was your grief."

"Child, of course it was. Ethan and I—as you have guessed, or he told you, perhaps. It started again—I mean our feelings began once more. We discovered them again that day you came back from Winston and your mother had gone off with Fred Davis. We often spoke of it." She looked at her nails and pressed her lips tightly together.

"I hope you spent time out on the lake and in the park. I hope you went off to Florida and Nassau and Hawaii. I hope you had fun."

"Nothing like that. Yet I did discover something. Ethan could have been accepted in Kingsbury all along. His ideas simply escaped most people. Many were shared. Trips, at any rate, were hardly necessary. We had some happy times. Mary Kerr, where is Jeff?"

"He's back in San Francisco. It was where he was wanted for something they thought he did. We had bad luck with a house that caught fire, so they found him. Somebody reported him, thought we were dangerous or something. I think Fred has found some way to cause this—all this trouble."

Aunt Jane did not seem to want to remark on this.

"Don't tell me she hasn't been back of your coming here," I pursued. I felt like accusing them all. "Maybe she got Fred to send you."

"Why wouldn't he send your mother?"

"They're smarter than that. When she tries seeing me, I say hello and go hide."

Aunt Jane finished her coffee and, scorning the paper napkin before her, extracted a small white handkerchief from her bag to wipe her mouth.

"I scarcely know Mr. Davis," she said.

"I'm scared of everybody," I told her.

The major question now arose. "What about Kathy? Is she here?"

So next, I thought, *we will cross the street and climb toward Estes, while the tenants stick heads out to wonder what this fine lady could possibly be doing there.*

"She's with this guy I dance with. We teach, direct a group. He's just a friend, though that's a lot. Come on, I'll take you."

The building smelled funny. I hadn't thought so much about it before. I'd not foreseen that Estes and Ahmed would be having an abusive name-calling up on the third floor, calling each other motherfucking assholes, among other things. I could not have predicted that Aunt Jane would go straight up the stairs anyway, not turning a hair or missing a step. Ahmed took one look at her and fled, leaving Estes standing in the doorway.

Aunt Jane said "How do you do?" without waiting for me to introduce her, then looked beyond him at once, or rather, it would seem, straight through him to where, over in the corner, Kathy was sitting at a little blue-painted table (Estes had rescued it from a junk heap and fixed a broken leg for her), doing some drawings for her preschool class. That she hadn't seemed to hear the argument meant, of course, what it was bound to mean—that she heard such things all the time. She had long straight hair, like mine, but blond, and her eyes, the shape of elm leaves, were wide-set, misty gray.

"This is Aunt Jane, Kathy," I said.

"Hello, Aunt Jane," said Kathy.

Aunt Jane went to sit by Kathy. She didn't try to say anything at first. "Which one is she?" Estes whispered.

"My father's sister." Poppy . . . well, of course she was. She had small shoulders like his and her hands were small and neat, the Harbison hands.

"What are you drawing?" Aunt Jane finally said.

"A house," said Kathy. She showed it, a barefaced structure, no porch.

"Why is it pink?" asked Aunt Jane.

"It just is," said Kathy.

Aunt Jane carefully transferred the large square sheet from Kathy's desk to her lap. She looked at it carefully. So carefully had Poppy also looked at drawings and messy sums extracted from the toils of Mary Kerr.

"Will you come and eat dinner with me?" Aunt Jane asked Kathy.

"If Mommy wants to," said Kathy.

The sound of Estes Drover's feet running down the stairs came clearly up to us.

Aunt Jane turned. "Do let's eat together. I've just so much to tell you."

I saw it then, out of the words so carefully determined to sound light and casual. The words were only the thinnest, most transparent veil over the vacant place within, the need to know, the need to love. It was need that was moving, travelling, reaching out, trying to touch.

"I guess," I said, and stood twisting a small, flat, gold ring on my ring finger. It was set with a blue stone and was something Jeff had wanted me to have before he left, his mother's. "I've nothing nice to wear," I said, and felt poor. Aunt Jane said that didn't matter a bit.

It was out of twisting the blue ring that I heard his voice again, and saw once more the lines corrugated on his forehead, getting to be permanent: "I can't keep on with this running, Mary. It's no way to live, or ask you to live. Maybe it was lightning struck the house. We know it could have been. But if the least little thing that happens shakes the whole world down around our heads, then that's opening the door to nonstop worry. Even if I get picked up, I may get a choice: Go to war or prison. They tell me the San Francisco courts are like that. They'll forgive anything up to machine gunning recruiting officers if you'll just go quietly out there and quit bothering them. I might just as well decide to go.

"Now, stop all this doomsday stuff. I'm coming back. I just got another offer for my columns. I'll call them "The Radar Screen" in memory of Ethan's paper.

"It's funny to have this crazy feeling of wanting to go, all the time knowing what a hell I'd be into. I just could never stand being sidelined.

"But maybe it'll just be a sentence. Or maybe the war might end before I get there."

"Do you hope it doesn't?" I asked him.

"In a way. Of course, I don't mean that, baby. You know I don't. . . ."

I told Aunt Jane, "He kept saying, 'If I could just see Ethan again.' Then it was too late."

"He telephoned," she said. "I was there when they talked."

11

The Ritz

So they came, mother and child, to the door of the famous hotel on Sherbrooke Street, the block that spoke of beauty and money. The revolving glass doors framed in black iron gave before them when they pushed and they stepped inside. Mary wore a simple, black, peasant dress from India, bought in an import shop on one of the streets to the east. Kathy's was similar. Their hair was clean and brushed silky, Mary's put up in the back (as Kate's had often been), Kathy's hanging straight, simple. They were enough to make people look up at them, yet they were quiet. They gave off an aspect of stillness, like the surface of a pool. Yet back of that stillness all the wretched turmoil of a decade might have been guessed at. To anyone with the perception to wonder about it, they could have been like a keyhole to look through, or a special lens.

From a corner of the lobby, Aunt Jane rose up from a straight chair with an elaborately carved back. She had been sitting on brocade. She wore a soft silk dress figured in green and beige. "There you are. We'll just go up to the room and eat. Is that all right?" They moved over deep carpets. The elevator purred upward. The man who ran it wore a fine uniform.

Aunt Jane had said she had a lot to tell, but once in the room she was in no hurry about it. It began to seem she had nothing at all in mind or had forgotten it.

But the room was grand. It had soft carpets and softer lights, a sitting area with chairs covered in flowered upholstery and a table with fresh flowers. Kathy picked up some fallen rose petals and held them in her palm. Out the window, down below, you could see a courtyard, enclosed by a high fence, with trees—a Lombardy poplar, a clump of birches, and bright flowers planted in oval beds, framing walks and a pool with a little house on an island in its center. There were ducks in the pool, so probably the house was for the ducks. All this absorbed Kathy, who also wanted to lie on the bed and take a bath in the long, gleaming bathtub in a room lined with pink tiles.

It was twilight outside. The sky was pink like the tiles. "We'll order dinner. They'll serve us here." Jane opened an enamelled menu. They picked out everything they wanted and it arrived on a special cart with covered dishes. A waiter served them.

They were almost to the dessert before Aunt Jane said, "I hear from your mother at times." There it was, the serpent under the rock.

"I hear from her, too," said Mary Kerr.

"Really? What does she write you?"

"She calls, too, sometimes. She and Fred are living an expensive life. She gave up her job, but she still wants to do something useful, something she was trained for. But he wants her to go places, take cruises, meet people she can enjoy. They went to Greece. Now they know all about Greece."

"So that's how she describes it to you."

"Maybe she leaves things out. I think she drinks too much."

"Only part of the picture, is how I understand it. She's getting psychiatric help, but how much good it does I don't know. She comes to Kingsbury sometimes. Her one fixed idea is how she lost everything because of you."

"Because of me she ran off with Fred?"

"Yes, in a way. Frightened. Wanting security."

"If he isn't enough—"

"Oh, he cares for her, is how she puts it. He cares for his house, too, and there is some vague talk of another woman, someone he won't give up. He goes to see his daughter at a ski lodge in California. He strained a ligament."

"I broke an arm," said Mary Kerr.

"I want some more ice cream," said Kathy. Aunt Jane telephoned to order another dish for her.

"What terrible times we live in," said Aunt Jane. "I remember Ethan saying that if we moved dangerously close to the center at any time, we would find something terrible. But I think now it is especially true. Don't you agree?"

"I managed to meet Jeff," said Mary Kerr, "and keep Kathy."

"But where is Jeff?" Aunt Jane persisted. "It seems such a long separation."

Mary was feeling panic. Wanting to turn corners, race over roof-tops like an escaping thief.

"You're here to get me back to Mother. I know you are! I won't go. You might as well know it. I won't. Not ever."

A well-bred, manicured, restraining hand. "Now, wait. She doesn't hope that, not for now. You might suspect that someday she will ask, beg—"

"Then she's after Kathy."

There were demons here. They had come out of corners to fly around them. They dove. Their wings brushed against her. Like bats, they tangled in her hair. She almost overturned the table.

"We're leaving now. It's her you're after."

Mary grabbed Kathy's arm and was heading out the door.

"No!" Jane ran ahead of her and got there first. "Mary Kerr, listen to me. Your father . . . he saw your mother clearly, but he never left her. Ethan . . . you'd never have known him but for Jefferson Blaise. The world is linked. It's bound together. Wander if you want to, if you must, but know the ties that bind are holding forever."

"I've got a right to say which ties I want and which I don't. I know already. My life is my own."

But Jane just stood before her, shorter than Kate, who had threat-ened from on high with deep frowns of righteousness. Couldn't Mary have pushed Jane aside? Yes, but Kathy had fled. She had rebounded halfway across the room and was standing there, quaking.

"Of course you've a right to say. But do you have that right for Kathy? I doubt even you think that."

The point scored. Mary puzzled over it, and lost the rhythm of her own thoughts.

"Let her know her grandmother, Mary Kerr. And through her, the rest of us, too. Let her at least try it. That's all. Think of it. No trouble to you. Kate's life, at present, is simply a dead end, a blank wall. Kathy is a little thing yet, but she can see, feel, judge."

"They'll take her," said Mary. "They've been aiming at that since her first breath."

"Not necessarily," said Jane.

Slowly Mary and Jane relaxed. It seemed almost time to smile, though nothing was decided.

"Mommy?" Kathy held out her arms, daring to approach, as if to prove what Jane was saying, that she could see, judge, and feel. They both put their arms out and picked her up. She came up willingly, so much lighter when lifted by two. She came up soaring, in fact. The waiter knocked, bringing the ice cream. They returned to the table. Kathy picked her spoon up, having evidently decided, out of such confusion, to think that nothing had happened.

"You named her after Kate," said Jane.

"Yes."

"Don't decide anything now. Let's go to one of the parks. We'll take a cab. They do look so pretty. Would you like to, Kathy?"

Kathy said that she would like to.

"I have so much to tell you," said Jane.

12

Fred's Mission

That same fateful summer, early on, had brought Fred Davis to sit in a corner booth of a downtown Philadelphia bar and talk things over.

"Why not hire somebody?" He thoughtfully repeated the question his woman friend had asked. She had been his mistress for years and he still liked to see her from time to time. "Once I thought the scheme out, I became very anxious to see it through. Certain matters have made me curious to examine them closely. How far do these people go, in their zeal? What crimes are they capable of excusing? It may not be so bad as it's painted. In that case, I might take steps to reestablish him. But on the other hand, if things seem to have gone completely to the bad, it would give me pleasure to root him out. And that way, don't you see, Kate would find the way open to getting both of them back into a normal, decent life."

"Mother and child," the woman friend mused. "One happy family."

"Now, don't mount your sarcasm. Stranger things have happened. People do come around."

She smiled. "A quest. You're setting off on horseback. Or trekking off into the jungle. Mind you don't tell your business to the wrong person. You might get shot."

"It's possible."

But flying out on a peaceful sunny day from the Philadelphia airport, he looked down from his first-class window seat past the great backward sweep of the silver wing that was bearing him steadily upward and saw the fair sight of city, river, and colorful countryside. He felt a great pulse of love and satisfaction. It was a beautiful country, no doubt about it.

On his various hops and stops he felt it again, in the three weeks that followed, each time the planes he sat in rose up to ride expertly in the cloud-fleeced skies. This surge of pride in what he was a part of. Not even during wars of the past had he ever felt for it so much. So the next step was easy: He himself became the roving patriot, on track of those who wished the country ill. Fred Davis was too complex actually to think this, but as plane after plane left with him aboard it, and as river and farm and city and mountains passed beneath his gaze, he felt it undiminished in his emotions, each time.

In addition, he enjoyed himself. He liked to stay in those old-fashioned elegant hotels his father had favored and at times had taken the whole family with him to enjoy. The click of heels in their marble foyers, the luggage racks pushed by willing bellboys. (He remembered his own childish voice: "Why are they always little men?" His mother: "Sssh, he'll hear you." His father: "Never thought of it before, but they are.") He liked the marble-lined men's room in the Washington Mayflower; the black man with the flashing white smile and his shoeshine chair, its metal feet waiting for the placement of supple leather, all in the accustomed place back of the newsstand in the Chicago Blackstone; the moan of New Orleans jazz from the bar of San Francisco's Mark Hopkins.

Wandering far, gathering facts. Washington: Someone had certainly been assigned to surveillance of Ethan Marbell. Fred was right. Connections to Jefferson Blaise. Jefferson Blaise lost track of after indictment in Chicago, reappearing in San Francisco where wanted for arrest in explosion of government installation erstwhile toy factory intended eventually for plastic anti-personnel weapons manufacture. . . . Whereabouts unknown. Speeches and public appearances broken off abruptly. Column continued to appear in subversive paper known as *The Radar Screen,* but might be written by others such as [a list of names]. . . . Paper once published in Evanston, Illinois, but now postmarked from some one of several substations in and around Passaic, New Jersey. Then a curious reference: someone thought to be Mary Blaise reported staying in a remote Ontario or Quebec community, north of Ottawa. Seemed to be a fugitive, as had no real reason for being there. Perhaps to meet husband or some conspirator. Only connection to anti-war movement, a telephone call from Ethan Marbell to the hunting camp where she was hiding.

Fred checked Chicago for a day or so, but as he imagined, no Jefferson Blaise had ever reported for trial. "Don't think it's so unusual," the precinct clerk told him. She scarcely looked up from her typing.

Two weak points were where he would press. San Francisco and Montreal. Wherever Mary had been, she was back in Montreal now. Wherever Jefferson Blaise was, he might show some sign of caring, at least for her and the child: he might be there, too.

Fred telephoned to Kate and learned that Ethan Marbell was still alive but probably not for long. Following leads to the possible publishing locale for Ethan's paper, he flew back to Washington and went by train to New Jersey. Wandering from point to point, he saw some close-up scenery scarcely as thrilling as that which passed below the plane wings. One afternoon he got mugged. A man came out of an alley and, shoving him against the wall, relieved him of his wallet. A group of passing workmen saved him injury; the man fled. It took an afternoon to cancel and replace credit cards. His arm was sore where he had been seized, his head sore from striking the wall. The next morning, right in Passaic, he found the press.

It was installed in the basement of an unused factory belonging to a New York company which manufactured fancy paper products, stationery, posters, and the like. Daggart and Lansdowne. His father, he thought he recollected, had had a friend named Daggart, could possibly be the same. The property, apparently awaiting resale, now stood empty. He pretended an interest in purchasing and finally unearthed an unwashed and unshaven tenant of a nearby rooming house, who unlocked the door and let him in.

He saw the idle press still sitting there, and copies of *The Radar Screen* scattered all over the table, some fallen to the floor. No one, apparently, had been about in some time, yet there was a bundle of blankets heaped in a corner, and a table piled with dishes near a sink bespoke of a hovel, used still perhaps for waiting or sheltering. Beyond the dishes a couple of needles rested in a plate. Marijuana roaches filled an ash tray.

The caretaker had not said a word. He had probably taken money to keep quiet, and all he wanted to do now was get away. He would say if asked he'd never noticed anything unusual going on.

But Fred Davis lingered, looking with curiosity at the press. What a small thing to have caused so much trouble. He thought of the resonating thunder of big city dailies reeling off the massive sheets of information, ads, social notes, sports finals, war news, accidents, controversy, alarms. This little gadget with its hand-turned wheel was scarcely more than a mimeograph machine. To think of it even trying to bring a government down was ludicrous. It could have been fitted in the trunk of one of those little German or Japanese cars now being peddled. He remarked the tin sheets of the final issue printed, tacked up in a neat line along the wall. He read a headline: THE TRUTH ABOUT CAMBODIA. . . . He did not pick up a copy to read, but stepped on several, going out.

Fred Davis went across the street to a cheap restaurant. It was twilight and he sat near the window to look out. He ordered a beer. He saw one person come, then a group of three, first trying the side door, then entering through the coal shoot. He had had enough, but still he sat awhile longer. The property was not theirs to use. *It was not theirs. What right did they have?* As he thought this, slow rage spread upward from the steady lifeblood throbbing in his chest, flushing his neck and prickling at the roots of his hair. The man who had been his father's friend—it was he these squatters were daring to defile. *I am doing what I can,* his thoughts ran, like a pledge addressed to a vanished face, which must have been a decent one, though he could not quite remember it.

In sumptuous cocktail lounges lined with leather or panelled in redwood, Fred sat cushioned before gleaming rails, sipping from crystal glasses. He made guarded conversation with whomever he sat beside. Sometimes he forgot what city he was in.

"They've made a mess of the whole country. It's a slime they trail around with them, ever see a snail?" This from one side.

"Weren't enough Kent States, ask me." This from the other.

In over their shoulders came the voice of a tall man with flushed drinker's cheeks, who said his home state was Miss'ippi. "You ever hear tell of kudzu? Well, when it grows you cain' hardly get rid of it because it puts down these little creepy roots. Strong! My job for the draft dodgers: put 'em to work in Junejulyaugust in the Miss'ippi sun, cutting kudzu off the roadsides, root by root by root. Wouldn't that give some of 'em second thoughts?"

En route to San Francisco, Fred's plane was forced down at Las Vegas because of engine trouble. He had not been afraid. He decided to pass the night there. He knew of an inn not far from the airport, but with a desert setting, and though the distance was short, he took a limo to reach it. The Hacienda: Spanish, low and verdant, glowing with soft lights. The desert night surrounded it; the moon rode high and brilliant. Entranced, he checked into his room, in a daze he went down to the bar, later he ate alone.

All he could think of was the beautiful country he had travelled through now for two weeks, stirring out records and memories of Jefferson Blaise. All Fred had scanted to do, and that deliberately, was look up the father. He wanted none of him, any more than he wanted actually to appear before Ethan Marbell, who was wasting out his last few days of life. Enough to have what was real, no emotions mixed in. But what he had really encountered was the land itself, the U.S.A.

He rang up Kate. "Darling, do you realize what it's like, this wonderful country?" He was apt to sound theatrical at times.

"What about it?" Kate asked, trying to keep her voice from slurring. He was in no mood for talk with her like that.

After dinner he walked out of the hotel, leaving the grounds behind, out into the dark, walked until only the lights around the heated outdoor pool were visible. The moon beat down. There was space and loneliness, there was beauty and a brooding spirit. From far off he heard a whimpering bark, from nearer a sound of two people laughing, though nothing moved. Sound here travelled far. He gulped down air so pure it might have just been created. Solemnly, he returned.

Light-headed in the bar, he talked with a woman who was travelling home by car, disliked Vegas for its gambling, could stand the Hacienda but not the Flamingo, all that glitter.

"Isn't this a beautiful country?" he asked her. He ordered them both another drink. Her questions nibbled around the edges of his business. "I'm searching for an eagle," he told her. She thought he was a conservationist after some rare species. She was around forty, he judged, a bit too tailored, likely divorced, alone but not unduly wary.

"What sort of eagle?"

"I often wonder myself," he said, with interesting mystery. "All I know is, it's not the American one."

"What will you do with it?"

"I mean to kill it," he said, and paid the bill. Back of his hexagonal glasses, as from an ambush, he had seen his attraction develop on her consciousness. He did not ask her to bed. For one thing, he had just thought of something. A messenger was what he needed. He had known it for a long time. Now it fell in place of itself, and he knew. *Of course,* he thought. *Of course.*

In the morning, he called Kate. "You know that sister-in-law of yours? What's her name?" Kate was foggy, this time with sleep. "Jane? Jane Harbison?"

"That's it. When this Marbell guy finally leaves us, she's going to want somewhere to go, won't she?"

"I don't doubt it," Kate answered. "But she can afford—"

"Affording is not what I mean. Wait till it happens, then invite her."

"Invite her to visit?" He could visualize Kate, mystified, stirring up on her pillows, wondering if she'd heard correctly. He had always made it plain he wasn't marrying a pack of Southern relatives. "You mean it? You want Jane to visit us?"

He said that he did. Then, with terms of endearment rendered to her, he hung up. She had no idea what he was about, in his present wanderings.

The engine trouble, the landing in Vegas—it had all been fortuitous. Providential, even. He saw what he had seldom thought about: the Hand of the Diety. The desert night under the blazing moon, the air of dizzying fineness, were still his to partake of in this clear but ordinary morning light. Again he wanted to say it, over and over, to say it: "Isn't it beautiful, this country?"

California lay before him. He was headed toward its conquest. He knew what he wanted from it. His contacts and possibilities were already firmly established in the East. There were doors to be unlocked in the land before him. But he knew, at least, which doors they were. Offices would be open already—the FBI, for instance, as he had made sure in Washington. A channel was already established to that other valuable set of initials—the RCMP. The plane was rising, the familiar silver wing was shimmering in sunlight. The state line would pass below without precise announcement. He turned to the little gray-headed man who was beside him, working a crossword puzzle. "Isn't this a great country?" he asked.

The man looked up, but only briefly. "Personally," he said, "I never liked it."

13

The Parks

Mary, Jane, and Kathy must have strolled through a dozen of them, up paths that wound mysteriously or ran formally straight between beds of verbena and salvia, or skirted little lakes, or broke into steps to climb past rock gardens that soared and tumbled, rich in clinging plants. So did the days pass.

Back in the east of the city, Ahmed and Estes Drover were latched into such an infernal quarrel that Mary let herself be persuaded into staying a night or two at the Ritz, where Kathy started trailing behind one of the waiters in the hallway (she even rode in his car while he slipped her petits-fours) and chatted in French with the maids. Ahmed's uncle was urging Ahmed to throw out the dancers and rent out the house himself, since the lessons Mary and Estes were offering were not well attended in the summer anyway and Estes was behind in mortgage payments. If the studio was out, the rents for the apartments could go up. Ahmed refused to stand up to his uncle because he was furious at Estes about something Mary did not care to hear about.

She walked in the parks with Jane Harbison.

After the gardens and the parks came the churches to admire, interspersed with the good city restaurants, each even better than the last. Kathy learned the names of strange things on menus, and Jane talked Mary into buying new dresses for herself and Kathy, too.

"I would love to see you dance again," said Jane.

"It isn't likely for a while. My partner, the one you met . . . is temporarily not working. We don't have a theater right now. Just the studio. But we will."

"I'm sure you will," said Jane. She wondered aloud if she really wanted *Rognons à la française.*

On a late afternoon, returning to the Ritz from a restaurant on a nearby street, Mary looked up and saw Estes Drover. He was across the street from the hotel and was waving at her.

"I have to see him," she said.

But he wouldn't cross to her. She dodged traffic, for Estes had a letter in his hand, and she knew it was from Jeff. She came up at his side, only to have him wordlessly thrust it in her hand, to see him turn back and hasten into an anonymous crowd.

14

Jeff's Message

She sat down to read it in the lobby of the Ritz, in one of the straight-backed chairs. Kathy squirmed in to sit beside her. She leaned her chin on Mary's arm.

Darling Mary:
Since we talked I've tried a dozen times to get you but it's only that Ahmed character who answers. He's promised to say I'm calling but every number I can give is temporary. I don't think he ever gave you any message. That's misery—but not like before, when I thought you'd split. Now I know you won't.
I told you I would have to give up and sign up, shed this whole trial mess. Hayden came here and we talked, a good visit. There was Paco, too, like old times, and Father Tomlinson. I felt they were launching me, like a ship. One phrase keeps running through my mind. We must have said it dozens of times: *We've helped,* we've done what we could, *We've helped,* we've slowed them. *We've helped,* maybe even stopped them. *We've helped.*

I think if this judge had been all, he would have let me off— he's about as anti-war, etc., as you could find. But my case has boiled up high on his docket and the best agreement he can get is to let me run away to the conflict. What a good joke it must be to somebody. We may never know who. Something's been at work.
Judge Madero is pretty unique. We've had some talks. He was in Korea, but since then, he says, the country's gotten wrong-headed, "A beautiful face broken out with smallpox. Go on out there and die." He was joking, but I got the drift.

My draft board was in Baton Rouge (still), so I had to call the old man to go down and get papers for me. We hadn't talked in what's maybe years. I've lost count. He's fine! Went AA along with his woman friend after the police had found them both passed out on the sidewalk down in a bad section of town. Some blacks had hauled them in off the street. He's getting married.

Maybe I should have stuck it out down there with him instead of plunging in with Ethan to try and turn things around. You've got to understand, though, that I'm not backing down. But to go to prison, what good would that be to you and Kathy? At least you'll get a monthly check. *Ramparts* showed up, when I didn't make the date in Chicago. They want news from another sort of front lines. A book will come out of it, and I'll tell you why. I'm going to be in on the last days. I'm certain of it. It's dying from the head down but the tail is still thrashing. How long? Don't know. I'll be in on the end. That's some consolation.

What I lie awake and wonder is, who got them to smoke me out as exploding a minor little munitions factory two years ago up north of Sausalito? Who? Does it connect to the fire at St. Jovite? My imagination sure gets active around three A.M., especially without you and Kathy around to touch and hold.

We had such a good few months in Montreal. Remember our little A-frame in the Laurentians? I'll rerun those like a private home movie all the rest of the time I'm away.

Another thing I keep wondering is how you must have felt that time you tried to write yourself off. You told me it was so you wouldn't be there for your mother to reject anymore. It would be a scene without you, and better. You thought. But, believe me, nothing could ever be better without you.

I keep thinking of the old man. When I get out of this, I want you to know him. I never said it before, never thought it before. He's come up out of it all, whatever held him down. That's something.

Let's say I'm going off the scene now, but just for a while. We'll strike up some new music once all this is over. They're bound to let us come back someday. There are some with big hearts still. Let's believe in them.

I think your Estes character cares enough not to let you down. I'll be back before you know it. I'll find you dancing.

Jeff.

When Mary finished the letter she walked over to Aunt Jane.

"Jeff's signed up for Vietnam. He's going out there, in spite of everything."

Aunt Jane then said a curious thing. "Then it will all be regular."

"Yes, regular," Mary agreed, seeing how the reasoning went. *If he gets killed, he gets killed regular. That would be better than doing anything that's irregular and staying alive at peace with what he thought was right.*

She was knotting her hands, standing there with Kathy just behind her (the child for one long singular moment utterly forgotten and knowing that she was). Mary felt the color draining from her, whitening out to nothing. *Only to be free of them, free of them all forever, their thinking so awful, so wrong, so nothing like Jeff. Get out now, at once, forever.* Suddenly she wheeled around, searching wildly until she found the door, then plunged for it, and would have made it through to wind up God alone knew where.

But what stopped her was something unexpected from Aunt Jane, who with the surprise athleticism of a girls' camp counselor, sprang up and ran in front of Mary and cried out, loud enough to be heard all the way to the mahogany registration desk.

"Mary Kerr, I wouldn't be here if I didn't love you! I wouldn't be here if I hadn't loved Ethan!"

Mary felt herself stopped, her body rejoining itself, her color coming back. Love. The manicured hands with their pale-colored nails and the rings, the white gold filigree and the star sapphire, pressed against her shoulders. She was stopped. Love.

Jeff had said it once: "When you stop, your strength goes. When you look back, you crystallize. When you hesitate, you're lost." She thought it was true.

She would always see that one moment when she didn't make it through the door of the Ritz, as the drop over a cliff's edge, the point of her own special strength's sudden decline.

Part V
Decisions

1

Mary

"I still can't get over it," said Estes Drover. "Why'd you do it, Mary?"

They were sitting on the steps of the rickety house. Mary was wearing one of the new skirts Aunt Jane had bought for her and getting it dirty on the steps. The place still smelled funny in that way she hadn't noticed before her long detour through the expensive world.

"Mother's feeling she was such a flop with me, and still wanting another chance. It's Mother they worry about, how she's facing a blank wall, drinking too much, no path in life. . . . I thought maybe it was even true."

"You thought— But you *know* it's not true, don't you? You always said so."

"What did I always say?"

"That it was all a power struggle. That your mother had to have power over you, had to get it any way she could, that she wore one mask after another to fool the world, to hope to fool you."

"Maybe I was wrong."

"Mary! They're both of them witches. Jane and Kate. You know that."

"She said she loved me. She said she loved Ethan. I thought or felt—it happened too fast to think—that if there really was some love in it, it came from Ethan and I couldn't doubt that. And that maybe he would want me to give in to her."

"Ethan's dead."

"Dying doesn't stop love."

"It doesn't stop her making use of love. Witches do that."

She was silent. It was only a faint thread she had followed, but better than none, she thought; in fact, it was all there was. Though maybe she would have been purer, better, to have done what Jeff said, exactly what he said, and stuck with Estes. Estes only.

"You'll never have her back," said Estes, dire and baleful.

Mary laughed. "She lapped up all that luxury like a stray kitten with a bowl of cream. Hors d'oeuvres, peach Melba, chocolate torte, a teeny little bit of wine, and all those fluffy little dresses. '*La jolie petite fille,*' said all the clerks in Holt Renfrew. She was bound to like it. Maybe I think she's due to know what it's like, not just luxury, but something more—splendor, maybe." She was thinking then of Aunt Sally, all but blind, and the money to go to Lincoln Center and sit in those velvet seats, watch the giant crystal chandeliers retract slowly into the sky of the lofty ceiling as the lights dimmed and the great curtains did majestically what they were meant to do.

I would like to take her there, she thought.

"That part's okay, I guess," said Estes, who would have liked Ralph Lauren slacks and velvet Cardin jackets. "It's just that, how you're getting it— They've started bribing. You'll be lured there. But you'll never really get her back."

Ahmed had talked his uncle into letting the studio go on for one more season. The old renters were squatting in their rooms, turning on their lights at this hour, slamming out the front door just below for something to eat at some little bistro or greasy spoon. Out to get a six-pack or some milk or cigarettes. Twilight. TV.

"While you've been funning around with your aunt, I've been seeing them down at Place des Arts. They may want to see some of our new routines. I hate to call our whole group out on spec. But maybe they'll want to."

"Get it in writing," Mary said, and giggled. It was something they always said.

"Passey-à-Droite is going in for plays next. The attendance we got encouraged them. We did it, they're making use of it."

"*C'est la vie.*"

"You damned right."

There was a long twilight pause.

Estes said, "God, I miss her."

"I miss her, too."

"We were like a family, Mary."

"I know."

They sat until it grew all the way dark.

"You went back to Ahmed just for us, for me," said Mary. "You made it up with that stupid bastard."

"Don't talk to me about Ahmed," said Estes, getting angry.

"Just that I know."

The late renters coming in the door couldn't see them. The dark had fuzzed over everything. They were still sitting on the stairs.

Mary thought of Kathy and Aunt Jane, probably just now getting into Philadelphia, catching a taxi. Kathy dutiful and alert and curious in her new little tailored coat, her real leather handbag, her thick, high, little-girl stockings. Never such splendor. She wore style like it didn't matter, the way you were meant to.

They'd be taking a taxi, giving an address, going out to the Main Line, where Fred Davis's house sat quiet on its manicured lawn. Aunt Jane, Mary suddenly realized, had probably wanted to know Fred Davis for some time. She would have to have an excuse to come there, a mission.

They would come to the door of heavy dark wood, set into an arch, curved at the top to match the stone frame, which rose in a Gothic point high above the child who waited before it. Fred Davis would open the door and step aside. There before them, at just the right distance, Kate McCanless Davis would be standing on an Oriental rug placed on the floor slabs of colored stone. Wearing what? Something lavender, maybe, or gray with touches of coral. Her hair softly up. "Jane," she would say. A quick embrace. Then kneeling. Arms out. "And here's—"

"No!"

Mary shouted suddenly, breaking the silence, startling the darkness.

"Did you have a nightmare?" Estes asked.

"Yes, a nightmare," said Mary.

Estes stirred. "This is no place to spend the night. Let's go out and eat."

"Just a minute. Just wait a minute more."

The awful vision was still pressing in, ringing and shuddering like a bright reflection in water struck by a stone. Onward they would bear her in triumph. In the triumph over Mary.

Jeff! She longed for him as she never had before. The three of them in the savage night, protected by love and firelight and a man's strength, now were scattered. The savages had won. The fire was out.

"Jeff!" She murmured it aloud.

No more visions, was what she hoped for.

It was time to go and eat. She reached up in the dark toward where earlier she had seen or been aware of Estes's long, bony hand hanging down toward her head.

She found it. It was there.

2

Jeff

He was in what was supposed to be a line of advance, though the line had gotten ragged crossing a river, sluggish with mud, the bottom slippery, the fallen logs and vines impeding, clutching as if with hands. Then it gained firm ground again and straightened, moved a few yards forward, fended around trees. Flashes, sound of firing, cries. Hitting the earth, feeling to see if any at first nonfeeling was spreading numb and chill, telegraphing that the tear of flesh or splintering of bone had come at last. Not yet. Hard earth had spattered against cheek, neck, and forehead. He raked it off. There was some guy down the line going, "*Yiiiii!* Jesus fucking got it! Quick, *yiii. . . .*"

Just the mines now. Line forming again, a few more yards of jungle, vines that bit, bugs that drank sweat, but thank God no snakes yet. Two more of the mines touched off, one missing everybody, one more and a foot just gone, medics panting back toward the stream.

"You telling me this is sneaking up on them? They'd have to be deaf as Aunt Mamie. . . ."

The vines tearing, the screen of desperately deep green.

Then it broke, broke off, ended in open space, silence.

Before them was a wide glade. *Glade? Where did that word come from?* He had never used the word, just seen it in books. But there it was before him: a glade. Wide, green, smooth, mellow, a glade in an old land, land lying the way land wanted to be. Peaceful as Sunday afternoon. Quiet.

He saw back then, telescoping back in time, the explosions that tore things up, the scarred finger ends, the truncheon smashing sideways into cheek and ear, blotting out the flaring sounds of Chicago streets in '68, back to that one quiet scene once more, like forever returning spring. He was walking again through those people Ethan Marbell had wanted to know more about, the ones starting an experimental colony. "Just go down there and look it over, get to know them, they'll probably be glad to talk to you." And there across the fence the unexpected girl was standing, quiet and curious, natural, like something grown up out of the woods back of her, looking, expecting nothing.

He was moving toward her.

The line was straightening. At the end on his far right, Lieutenant Bagley signalled them forward. Before them, on the other side of the glade, stood a wall of trees, opaque, as loaded with menace as the mind could make it.

They were walking steadily forward.

Mary, Jeff thought. *Be there.*

Lieutenant Bagley, in an explosion, turned into a scarlet cloud of blood and fire, marrow and shredded flesh streaking through.

Please be there.

3

Kathy

It was the faithful servant in the white jacket, he who had been with the family for years, from the time Fred Davis was a boy, who had returned to serve the meal that night. He had done it as a special favor, not usually being needed in the evening.

Kate sat at one end of the dark table with the high-backed chairs, made much lighter in appearance than was usual by the use of white embroidered linen place mats and matching napkins, and the addition of a large white Chinese bowl of larkspur in palest colors of green, pink, and white. All of them could see over it except Kathy, who had been placed on an enormous Webster's dictionary, but who still was a trifle low. Yet Kate, from the end of the table, could see her plainly, as could Fred from the head.

Her plate was served with lamb which the servant Phillip had cut up for her in bite-sized pieces, and asparagus, too, and duchess potatoes nicely browned. She had not touched her soup, and the bowls had been taken away. She did not touch her plate, either.

"She isn't eating," said Kate to Jane. "Do you want something else, darling?"

"No, thank you," said Kathy in a tiny voice.

Fred noticed that those great gray leaf-shaped eyes which had startled him earlier were fixed on the lovely woman he had married, whose happy look had just for a while returned. They had been fixed there for some time. Kate moved uncomfortably under their gaze. *Don't stare,* he thought of saying. Three times he had tried to distract the child, but regularly her steady gaze had returned to Kate. How precarious everything was, and how crucial. It came to him like a dark shadow, birdlike, flying across a window, that maybe all his efforts were for nothing. He summoned the weight of all he knew, had done, and was. He even thought, *I love her.* He meant Kate, but had seldom allowed his thoughts to say it. Now he freely, silently, let it come. They were bound to move ahead.

"So what do you want, sweetheart?" he asked Kathy, the tone demanding the gray leaf gaze to turn toward him. He watched as it slowly did so. *The captive princess,* he thought.

"I want to go home," said Kathy.

She turned back once more to fix on Kate.

4

Dilemma

Fred's problems at last caused him to be sitting waiting in a Sansom Street restaurant, a rathskeller, just out of and near the main business section of Philadelphia, down toward an area where secondhand jewelry shops flourished, one after the other, and little bent men squinted through eyepieces to judge the quality of gemstones. The restaurant had settled itself in this spot long ago, and set about successfully attracting businessmen who wanted a good lunch. But on Saturday few people were there, and no sounds of heavy traffic came down from the districts a few blocks away.

Fred was sitting where he could look out of the windows. He saw her coming. He could see her accustomed motion, exactly what he had come to expect of her, bending slightly forward along that side-walk empty of crowds, but by long habit adjusted to walking with and against crowds, acknowledging no one. A city woman. Dark. Neither short nor tall. Neither thin nor fat. He noted gray, unde-fended, in her hair. How could that be? It was.

She entered, found him, came to his table. He rose. They sat. Her suit was trim, her blouse crisp, her bag, of cavernous black leather, was worn and interesting. She put it on an empty chair. Stella Hon-deras. Estrella. Or sometimes, more intimate, a childhood name, Estrelita. No questions till they ordered lunch.

Then, "So what about the situation?" She knew what he was bound to have come for.

"It's not good," he admitted. "I must act." The day before, he had seen Kate do something he still could not believe. He would never reveal it; it had frightened him.

"Success on your trip, however. So you said."

"They broke all the rules, that bunch, and more than a few laws got smashed as well. The line Blaise stepped on was a little plant the government had bought up near San Francisco. There was news about its being a place for making some sort of war explosive. Not napalm, for a change, but some sort of handy little grenade-type gadget. Supposed to blind and paralyze wherever it hit. The crazy part is, they hadn't even started making the stuff. Just a night watchman out there. Nothing to stop them from hitting it. So . . ."

"So? What about it?"

"I got them to press charges. The FBI is more than interested, whenever they can get hold of something or somebody they can move against. You'll never guess all the places I've been—Texas, Michigan, New Jersey, Chicago. Discovering America. This really is a great country, you know. I fell for it, hook, line, and sinker."

"You got the boy locked up?"

"No, not that. Shipped out to Vietnam. I had hoped to get Kate's daughter and the little girl here, or at least into the country, near us, reinstated somehow. Not quite worked out yet. All I could get was the child."

"Living with you?"

"Yes."

"So the mother's bound to follow?"

"That's the hitch."

"She won't?"

"Won't. And furthermore, the kid—"

"The kid wants her mother."

"How'd you know?"

Stella laughed.

Their plates arrived. Sauerbraten. Red cabbage. Steins of beer. Stella took a sip and pushed hair from her neck comfortably.

"I really do not think," Fred Davis said, buttering his pumpernickel, "that Kate is a woman who should have children near her."

"You should have married me," said Stella. Her husband had abandoned her years before, leaving her to raise two little girls. She adored them.

"I know," Fred agreed. "You wouldn't now if you could."

"You fished up your Boston snob first. Look what happened to that. Then you picked your Southern magnolia. Now look."

"It's better not to marry," said Fred.

"Kate has told me for years," he continued, "she wanted more than life itself to have another chance at motherhood. She felt on the first round she'd had too much on her, responsibility, money worries. So I move heaven and earth. Well, wrong again."

"But what's wrong with it? Except the child is homesick."

"Kate expects too much, I think. Nothing short of being perfect. Little manners to observe, fine little dresses to wear just right. Her moods shift with the speed of light. Once she drove the child into a corner, screaming at her for something she'd done. I had to stop it. What happens when I'm not around? I've got that sister-in-law staying on, just to be there."

"It's a wonder you're still there," Stella remarked.

"Oh, not such a wonder, if you think of the basic satisfactions. No strain, and she's fine. Working with the city Commission for Historic Preservation. Now, that was a good start—before the child came. She's a wonder at it, interiors, restoration. The papers called for an interview."

Stella lit a cigarette. She was waiting.

"I have to conclude it this way: there's a mystery in her, a sort of gap. I can't see what it is. Perhaps it holds me."

Stella smoked and waited.

"I've gotten really fond of that child. She is bright, quick, observant. She must look like the father. My one real regret? I never met him."

"Why would you want to? I mean, such an outlaw? A fly in your ointment."

"I felt I'd gotten to know him, following his tracks. Once I thought I saw him, rounding a corner. It was impossible, but I ran anyway. No one was there. He became a fascination, like a quarry, something elusive, hunted. I see his face in hers."

He ordered rhubarb pie. She was content with coffee.

"I don't regret what I did, however. A total mess these people made of our country. No getting on with the war, no decent and reasonable finish to the whole commitment."

"He may be killed out there."

"More than likely."

"What 'decent and reasonable finish' did you want?"

"I'm no policy maker. The ones who are should have a free hand. We elect them. Let them govern."

She did not answer.

"Don't you agree?"

She was waiting for her task to appear. He had "helped" her for years, long after their affair had dwindled. She would not refuse whatever he asked.

5

Question without Answer

"So you did it," Kate said to him. "She's gone."

"Yes, I did it."

"I could feel it in the house the minute I woke up."

"I felt it was right. She left early to spare you pain."

Still in her satin robe, she sat down on the stairs, awkwardly, not her usual self, knees spread out peasant-fashion. She leaned her cheek into the wood. When he angled to glimpse her face, he saw it as weary, and for the first time, old. "Recovery by lunchtime," he recalled his jaunty prediction to Stella, but it did not seem possible now.

"And the boy?" She had to ask twice.

"The husband, you mean. You mean Jeff. Well, he took his choice, I'm told. War or prison. He chose war."

"Vietnam."

"It's the only one I know of."

Her voice when it came was strained and altered. "You as good as killed him." She buried her face entirely, sideways into her arm. She kept speaking, leaning her cheek into the banister, lips moving against the wood, so that he could barely make out words: "I never meant this . . . never meant it. I swear I—" She was not speaking to him: he knew that.

He would call the psychiatrist. He feared a heavy sea ahead. The psychiatrist had mentioned lithium, more than once.

In his upstairs office, surrounded by books his father had ranked on the shelves but seldom touched, he leaned back in his swivel chair and thought over words for so long that at last he whispered them, as though he spoke to someone. To whom? Stella, perhaps. Or even Jefferson Blaise.

Does every personality with a division in it have a missing center which has been given—or given up—to make life possible for someone else? Can wires once cut be rejoined?

He saw on the desk before him a leather-bound diary which, though beautiful, had never been written in. He should start keeping it, to note his progress with his wife. He opened it to the present day, and wrote.

I think she may feel that I took her authority away.

I wonder if she will leave.

He added, after some debate, one final line:

I miss the little girl.

Laying aside the pen, he closed the diary.
His next job was to get rid of Jane.

6

Waiting

Fall in Montreal and not a snowflake as yet. Winter holding off, holding in, thinking it over, like a snow leopard of the north, bracing to leap. But as yet, days of brittle sunlight, skies of hurting blue, clouds white as laundered sheets. River flowing steadily, ships going unhurried toward the sea.

Out on the islands, the fairgrounds were closing. Marie Carrée and Estes Drover had been taking their group for exhibition dancing once a week in the Community of Man pavilion. They had learned to dance Scottish reels and Indian war dances. The pay was good.

On this last day Mary and Estes were riding home by Metro, talking of the class enrollment for the next term. There was a fellow dancer from the old Manning group Estes hoped would come up and join them. He was really good, but had had some bad luck out in L.A. recently.

They came up the escalator from the Metro and started walking toward the studio.

They passed the *dépanneur*.

Before their building, looking up at its windows, a pleasant-looking dark woman was standing, holding a girl of about six or seven by the hand. The girl was pointing at the door, pulling forward as though to walk up to it, try the lock, perhaps for a second time. But for some reason she turned instead and looked down the street.

"Kathy!" Mary was running.

"Mother!" Kathy was running.

The two others were walking, happy observers, as who wouldn't be?

"Meetings should be like that," Mary told Estes. "I mean the ones life runs on, like wheels. They should be just like that, unexpected, but there they are. Forever."

"What do you base an idea like that on?" Estes asked.

They were out in the country east of Montreal, in a house lent to one of the dance group. Vlodya, her guests. She was Russian, by way of Prague. The house to her was a dacha. The snows had long since begun. It was after dinner, pitch dark outside. They were sitting by a fire.

Favorable articles, dressed out with photographs, had appeared in the French and English press. A DEADLY DUO LEAD DANCE GROUP TO SUCCESS, DEUX VEDETTES EXTRAORDINAIRES MENENT ENSEMBLE DE DANSE MODERNE. They had bought a dozen copies of each paper and tacked clippings to the walls on every side. Offers for other auditions were coming in from Ottawa, from Quebec City, a nibble of curiosity from Winnipeg.

"Base it on? Why, on what's happened to me, of course. What else?"

"Is there anybody else you met like that?" Estes inquired.

"First there was Jeff, then Kathy. I mean Kathy now coming back to me. In between there was you, just coming up to me in the Purple Window one night. Leonard Abel appearing at the library." *Poppy's coming that day was bad, not good; but still I always see him, how it was that day, coming to me.*

"It's what you don't, you can't, expect that matters," she went on. "Knowing what it is when you see it, that's the other half."

People appear, coming nearer. Jeff walks toward the fence where I'm standing. Voices call, dwindling but never quite extinguished, outside, from beyond the snows. Jeff will appear like that again; the voice must be Mother's, she the lost wanderer, calling; I the fixed point at home.

"Knowingness? Where do you get that from?" The young friend of Estes's was speaking. Young and agile, slight and tireless. His name was Jarvis Pike.

Mary sat thinking. Estes smiled, knowing her, how she thought of ideas like new costumes, trying this and that for the truest design. Being serious and not, all at once. He was working on that, too.

"Get it from?" she echoed. "You just have it. There's one thing more: foreverness."

Running through Estes's head still was their last program, a concoction they had themselves devised, served up with professional skill, and Mary (Marie Carrée), smoothly perfected, emerging from the group, moving with narrow control, back to side and again, fluttering down to the footlights.

Jeff will appear again. The bold corona she shone so brightly in, what was it made of but the ice of fear that she lived within but dared not touch?

"Foreverness," repeated Jarvis Pike, getting drowsy with wine.

"He's learning his lessons," said Estes.

In the firelight they were happy around her.

Mary cautioned Kathy, who behind them was swinging on the banister of the stairway, too high up, but sure she would never fall.

7

Foreverness

. . . There across the fence the unexpected girl was standing, quiet and curious, natural, like something grown up out of the woods back of her, looking, expecting nothing, but ready to know what was there.

He was moving toward her.

The line was breaking apart. At the head, Lieutenant DeSalvo had turned to signal them to either side of the path and down, go forward creeping, close to the ground. It was just beyond the turn of the path, DeSalvo knew or thought or saw whatever waited, what would be there for them.

Mary, Jeff thought, *if it would only be you.*
It's just from wanting that, only once again.

CPSIA information can be obtained at www.ICGtesting.com
Printed in the USA
LVOW06s1658180514

386287LV00005B/561/P